Schoolbook Nation

Schoolbook Nation

Conflicts over American History Textbooks
from the Civil War to the Present

Joseph Moreau

The University of Michigan Press
Ann Arbor

Copyright © by the University of Michigan 2003
All rights reserved
Published in the United States of America by
The University of Michigan Press
Manufactured in the United States of America
⊗ Printed on acid-free paper

2006   2005   2004   2003   4   3   2   1

A CIP catalog record for this book is available from the British Library.

Library of Congress Cataloging-in-Publication Data

Moreau, Joseph, 1967–
    Schoolbook nation : conflicts over American history textbooks from
the Civil War to the present / Joseph Moreau.
        p.   cm.
    Includes bibliographical references (p.   ) and index.
    ISBN 0-472-11342-9 (acid-free paper)
    1. United States—History—Textbooks. 2. United
States—History—Study and teaching—Political aspects.   3. United
States—Historiography—Political aspects.   4. Textbook bias—United
States—History.   5. Textbooks—Political aspects—United
States—History.   1. Title.
E175.85.M67   2003
973'.071'273—dc21   2003007212

For Julie

Acknowledgments

This book began as a dissertation I wrote while a student in the University of Michigan's Program in American Culture. I could not have completed that original work and then significantly broadened the scope of the investigation without the help of several generous individuals and institutions. Maris Vinovskis supported me throughout my research and writing, balancing his guidance with a willingness to let me pursue my own interests. Terrie Epstein first introduced me to a trove of literature on history teaching and has offered critical advice and encouragement since then. Andy Achenbaum understood the nature of my argument about the fallacy of a "golden age" of teaching before I did myself. David Scobey helped me to define the scope of my project, particularly in its early stages.

June Howard, George Sánchez, and Richard Cándida Smith secured the teaching appointments and other funding at Michigan that allowed me to pursue research, and Richard also offered helpful critiques of chapter 3. Jimmie Reeves, David Angus, and Richard Campbell were wonderful mentors.

I also benefited from the support of several other colleagues in Ann Arbor. Heidi Ardizzone read and commented on the first five chapters. Rebecca Poyourow and Paul Roberts gave advice in preliminary talks where I outlined my research goals. Eric Ivancich, Paul Ching, Amy Clark, and Joanna Broder edited and proofread. Michael Epstein, Mark Rogers, and David Westbrook aided me in other ways.

Transforming the dissertation into a book required far more work than I had initially anticipated. A postdoctoral fellowship funded by the Spencer Foundation and administered by the National Academy of Education gave me a priceless year of uninterrupted work. Kerith Gardner, Danielle Samalin, and Jessica Claire helped me put that time

Acknowledgments

to good use. Martin Wiener encouraged me to begin working before the funding was secure, and I cannot repay him for his faith in me and my research. LeAnn Fields of the University of Michigan Press took a risk by agreeing to publish before the manuscript had reached its final form. James Loewen and Gary Nash gave detailed critiques of an early version of the book, leading to a much stronger final text. John Hope Franklin allowed me to use material from his personal collection, and Dennis Hopper kindly gave permission to reproduce one of his photographs from the 1960s. Debi Hamlin and Jennifer Vinopal aided me in finding and preparing several illustrations.

I owe a debt of gratitude to librarians and archivists at the following institutions: Alabama Department of Archives and History, Montgomery; American Antiquarian Society, Worcester, Massachusetts; Syracuse University Library, Syracuse, New York; Bobst Library, New York University, New York; California State Archives, Sacramento; California State Library, Sacramento; Center for American History, University of Texas at Austin; Duke University Archives, Durham, North Carolina; Gutman Library, Harvard University, Cambridge, Massachusetts; Houghton Library, Harvard University; Library of Congress, Washington, D.C.; New York Public Library, New York; Louisiana State Archives, Baton Rouge; South Carolina Department of Archives and History, Columbia; Milbank Memorial Library, Teachers College, Columbia University, New York; Texas State Library, Austin; University Archives and Columbiana Library, Columbia University; University of Michigan Library, Ann Arbor; Wexler Library, Hunter College, New York.

Finally, I owe more thanks than I can express here to two people. Margaret Moreau encouraged me to pursue learning from an early age. Julie Wiener supported me emotionally and spiritually through years of research, teaching, and writing. She has also been a demanding and skillful editor. This book is, in many ways, hers as well as mine.

Chapter 2 from "Rise of the (Catholic) American Nation: United States History and Parochial Schools, 1876–1925," © Mid-America American Studies Association, 1997. Grateful acknowledgment is given to the editors of *American Studies* 38.3 (fall 1997): 67–90, for permission to reprint.

Correspondence of Edward Channing is reprinted by permission from Macmillan Company Records, Manuscripts and Archive Divi-

Acknowledgments

sion, The New York Public Library, Astor, Lenox, and Tilden Foundations. Excerpts and illustration from *Land of the Free,* by John W. Caughey, John Hope Franklin, and Ernest R. May (New York: Benziger Brothers, 1966), are reproduced by permission from Glencoe/ McGraw-Hill, a division of the McGraw-Hill Companies.

Excerpts from Harold Rugg's *America's March toward Democracy* and *The Conquest of America* (Boston: Ginn and Company, 1937) are reprinted by permission of Pearson Education, Inc.

Contents

Introduction   1

1. **From Virtuous Republic to Nation-State   26**

2. **Negotiating a National Past**
   Statewide Textbook Adoption and the Legacy
   of the Civil War   **52**

3. **Rise of the (Catholic) American Nation**
   United States History in Parochial Schools   **92**

4. **Race and the Limits of Community   137**

5. **Anglo-Saxonism and the Revolt against the Professors   175**

6. **Harold Rugg vs. Horatio Alger**
   Social Class and Economic Opportunity,
   1930–1960   **219**

7. **The Narrative "Unravels," 1961–1985**
   A Story in Three Parts   **264**

Conclusion   331

Notes   339

References   383

Index   391

Introduction

Our schools and colleges have a responsibility to teach history for its own sake—as part of the intellectual equipment of civilized persons—and not degrade history by allowing its contents to be dictated by pressure groups, whether political, economic, religious, or ethnic. . . .
Above all, history can give a sense of national identity.
—Arthur M. Schlesinger Jr., *The Disuniting of America*

Somewhere in the 1960s, American history lost its way.

Or at least the teaching of it did. That's been the popular theory for the last twenty years, disseminated by academics, teachers, journalists, and politicians. It goes something like this: Before 1960 American historiography was dominated by synthesizers, scholars like Richard Hofstadter and Charles Beard or, going further back in time, Frederick Jackson Turner and George Bancroft. They examined the grand sweep of America's past and explained it with a single, coherent story. Their narratives, after some simplification and trimming, were dutifully passed on to high schools and middle schools.

But then various groups wanted to have their own stories told. Historians began dismantling the old national narrative in their more esoteric professional work, but the trend soon appeared in books for younger students too. Well-meaning but misguided activists, so the story goes, soon demanded a more "inclusive" curriculum for their children. Schoolbooks ballooned to meet the demands, and the proliferation of new chapters, sidebars, and illustrations pushed the traditional high school history text toward or past the one-thousand-page mark. But the price of inclusion was fragmented incoherence. Unified accounts of the nation splintered into the African-American version, the women's version, the Latino version, the gay and lesbian version, and so on. American history had become, as a *New York Times* article put it, the "Humpty Dumpty of scholarship."[1]

That national breakup was already apparent by 1980, according to Frances FitzGerald, author of the groundbreaking textbook study *America Revised.* FitzGerald told readers about objections raised by the Council on Interracial Books for Children to a description of Squanto as a "friendly Indian" who helped the Pilgrims plant corn and survive on the edge of the wilderness. Council members found the book Eurocentric because it presented Squanto from the perspective of the colonizers. To Native Americans, they claimed, he was more like a collaborator with the invaders, while the real heroes were those who "fought to preserve and protect their people's freedom and land." To be fair, the council concluded, history should be taught from that vantage point as well.

"The implications of that objection are far reaching," noted FitzGerald. If "the texts were really to consider American history from the perspective of the American Indians, they would have to conclude that the continent had passed through almost five hundred years of unmitigated disaster." Despite the problems entailed in this sort of "multicultural" approach, however, she saw that writers and editors were trying to meet the critics halfway. The results were single books that often uneasily balanced contradictory views—those of Indians and Whites, Europeans and Africans, men and women—and a whole genre of once staid, nearly identical histories that now no longer exhibited a common orthodoxy. In charting this transformation, FitzGerald designated the 1960s as the turning point:

> Since the American Revolution, text writers . . . have always succeeded in painting a fairly simple picture of America. Even while the country was changing radically in shape, in population, even in looks, they had definite answers to the questions about who and what we were. These answers changed over time, but at any given moment they were remarkably uniform and remarkably simple. The shattering of this single image in current texts thus constitutes an important break with tradition.[2]

FitzGerald offered a compelling story. It dovetailed neatly with a popular perception of the 1960s as, for better or worse, a cultural and educational watershed. It also gave advocates and opponents of this

Introduction

new history a basis for their competing claims, which they would advance passionately for years to come. The problem was that FitzGerald's argument was, in many respects, simply wrong. It exaggerated a bygone serenity in the textbook-writing business, ignoring evidence that the alleged rupture in the national story had at least two precedents. More importantly, it tended to reduce potentially substantive debates about educational reform into an endless inquest into the 1960s and the novel social activism and scholarship the decade was said to have produced. The influence and limitations of FitzGerald's thesis were never more apparent than during the controversy over national history standards in the mid-1990s.

The idea for standards, codified baselines of knowledge and skills in different subjects, sprang from a bipartisan effort to improve American education. Inspired by withering critiques of the current system, particularly in the 1983 report *A Nation at Risk,* and spurred on by President George H. W. Bush and the nation's governors, Congress created a council to oversee the standards project in 1991. The responsibility for history went to a task force headed by Lynne Cheney, chair of the National Endowment for the Humanities (NEH) and wife of then Secretary of Defense Dick Cheney. The actual work of devising the standards was then passed to the National Center for History in the Schools (NCHS), headed by Gary B. Nash and Charlotte Crabtree, at the University of California at Los Angeles.[3]

The release of the standards in the fall of 1994 promised to be a relatively sober affair, about what one might expect at the conclusion of an official, apparently consensus-oriented undertaking. A Gallup poll had shown that four out of five Americans supported the general concept of standards.[4] And after over three years of work, educational professionals from across the political spectrum had enjoyed plenty of time to shape the final document, or so it seemed. But enthusiasm for reform masked profound and bitter differences about how to improve history teaching, and this diversity of opinion would soon make headlines. The players fell into three camps: cultural nationalists, conservatives, and a more heterogeneous group that defied a simple label but was defined mostly by its opposition to the first two camps.

The cultural nationalists had dominated the debate over reform during the 1980s. Their most effective spokesperson was E. D. Hirsch Jr., a professor of English at the University of Virginia. In 1983 he wrote an article for the *American Scholar* called "Cultural Literacy," which he soon lengthened into a book of the same name. Hirsch argued that schools were no longer providing students with the common cultural vocabulary that allows Americans to communicate effectively with one another. To make his point, he cited a personal example from his father, who had worked in a commodity business where the timing of sales and purchases was critical. When he wanted his colleagues to take immediate action, the elder Hirsch would often employ the phrase "There is a tide," without further explanation. The allusion was to Shakespeare's *Julius Caesar:*

There is a tide in the affairs of men
Which taken at the flood leads on to fortune;
Omitted, all the voyage of their life
Is bound in shallows and in miseries
On such a full sea are we now afloat,
And we must make the current when it serves,
Or lose our ventures.

Because most of his associates had been schooled in a traditional curriculum grounded in the English and American literary canon, they instantly understood the point. The reference to Shakespeare's "tide" not only telegraphed the basic message of "act now" but also provided a rich context that allowed listeners to understand why they should act and the consequences they might expect if they did not. Because today's schools did not teach enough Shakespeare, claimed Hirsch, his father would now have to explain in detail what he meant, a tedious and inefficient alternative to uttering the pithy phrase. Or worse, he could use it unadorned and have some people walk away baffled.[5] The problem extended well beyond Shakespeare, claimed Hirsch; there had been a breakdown in fundamental knowledge in geography, science, economics, religion, and history, too, particularly American history.

Hirsch blamed this decline in cultural literacy on what he saw as the reigning educational philosophy of formalism. Introduced to American schools through John Dewey, formalism was a reaction against the lockstep rote learning that had characterized instruction in the nineteenth century. Formalists who had campaigned for progressive education, wrote Hirsch, wanted to build learning around a child's interests and preexisting knowledge. The specific content of the curriculum did not matter that much, because they assumed students would develop the same analytical and other skills no matter what they studied. This strategy of formalism, valid to a point, had been carried too far, according to Hirsch. Educators had to acknowledge that students must master certain essential facts and ideas. He claimed that workers in a national economy need this common cultural language to function effectively—his father's allusion to *Julius Caesar* writ large. Other leading industrial powers, like France and Japan, directed schools to ground students in their own cultures, thus giving them an advantage over the United States, which apparently had lost the will to do so. Situating his argument in a discourse of national competitiveness, which had been the theme of *A Nation at Risk,* helped to make *Cultural Literacy* a best-seller, but it gave Hirsch a mostly undeserved reputation for economic and political conservatism. In fact, he argued that the *real* losers in the drift to cultural illiteracy were not American corporations, but children from disadvantaged backgrounds who attended schools using formalist pedagogy and then found themselves unable to compete in the labor market. As *Cultural Literacy* pointed out, many elite private schools had never embraced content-free formalism to the degree public schools had, and their generally more affluent students graduated with distinct advantages. Hirsch wanted to democratize education by breaking a cycle that blocked the upward mobility of many poor and minority students by denying them access to elite knowledge and training. To the charge of conservatism, Hirsch asserted that while the contents of his cultural literacy were traditional, they were not tied to any particular agenda or ideology. To prove the point, he quoted articles from a Black Panther newspaper of the early 1970s that, while deeply subversive, still employed references to the Book of Exodus, the Declaration of Independence, and the speeches of Abraham Lincoln, all part of the Western canon.[6]

Two prominent historians, Diane Ravitch and Arthur Schlesinger Jr., allied themselves with Hirsch. Ravitch was also seeing a breakdown of cultural literacy, and she blamed the same misguided pedagogy for the collapse of history, geography, and civics into what she saw as the unfocused pseudo-discipline of social studies. In 1987 she cowrote *What Do Our 17-Year-Olds Know?* Her answer: Not enough, especially when it came to American history. Only 32 percent of them could correctly identify the half-century in which Americans fought the Civil War.[7]

Schlesinger was an elder statesman in the profession, best known for his award-winning *Age of Jackson* and his more personal account of the Kennedy Administration, *A Thousand Days.* In 1991 he published *The Disuniting of America: Reflections on a Multicultural Society.* He repeated some earlier arguments by Hirsch and Ravitch, but his concern lay less with the stifling of individual mobility or the intellectual decay of precollegiate education and more with the peril of national disintegration. Since the 1960s, said Schlesinger (and here FitzGerald's older thesis came into view), the history taught in primary and secondary schools had become a pawn of pressure groups organized along racial and ethnic lines. The American history once taught in schools, with its melting-pot theme and dedication to the political ideals of the Founders, had helped to mold a single people from a diverse citizenry. Schlesinger saw that in the move to multiculturalism, with its multiple perspectives and frequent diversions from a unifying, national story, history teaching was veering from two of its basic goals: providing fundamental knowledge of key figures and events and inculcating in students a respect for the common cultural heritage that undergirds the nation-state.

Like *Cultural Literacy,* Schlesinger's book gained national popularity. But *The Disuniting of America* was more fiercely polemical than the earlier book. Where Hirsch's opponent had been an abstract theory, formalism, Schlesinger's enemies were flesh and blood. He offered an especially unflattering portrait of Afrocentrists, who were trying to introduce more African-based history and culture into the curriculum of the public schools. He questioned their scholarship, including the claim that the ancient Greeks had stolen their mathematics and philosophy from Black Egyptians. He also mocked what he saw as a pathetic effort among a minority of American Blacks (he disdained the recently coined "African-American") to recover long-severed ties to Africa, pointing to scholar Arthur Smith's decision to Africanize his name to Molefi Kete Asante as an example of the trend.

Schlesinger was especially troubled by claims from some Afrocentrists that young Blacks learned differently from Whites and might benefit from a specially designed curriculum, heavy on what he considered a questionable history of racial uplift, provided in schools that were racially segregated either by default, through failure of integration, or by design. Pilot programs on this model had already begun in Chicago, Washington, D.C., and other cities. Employing history to build racial pride would ultimately prove self-defeating, according to Schlesinger, because it would corrode faith in professional objectivity. "The use of history as therapy means the corruption of history as history," he warned. While it would fail to promote minority children's self-esteem, the history teaching demanded by Afrocentrists and other multiculturalists might lead America down the road to a Yugoslavia-like national crumbling:

Introduction

Instead of a transformative nation with an identity all its own, America in this new light is seen as a preservation of diverse alien identities. Instead of a nation composed of individuals making their own unhampered choices, America increasingly sees itself as composed of groups more or less ineradicable in their ethnic character. The multiethnic dogma abandons historic purposes, replacing assimilation by fragmentation, integration by separatism. It belittles unum and glorifies pluribus.[8]

To the right of cultural nationalists like Schlesinger, Ravitch, and Hirsch lay the conservatives. They embraced early proposals for national standards in history and other subjects because they believed schools had to return to a traditional curriculum and a more disciplined approach in the classroom. Hirsch was something of a cultural relativist. He championed the culture and history of the West simply because Americans needed *some* common cultural language; if we had not, by chance, inherited that tradition, then some other one would do. The Japanese seemed to be getting along fine with theirs. The conservatives went further. They argued not only that the heritage of the West formed the core of American identity but that it was superior to its rivals abroad and to the intellectual mélange offered by multiculturalists, deconstructionists, feminists, and others of that ilk at home. Their vision of the nation's past, and of the way it had been taught until the 1960s, was warmly sentimental. As one historian put it, these conservatives tended to counterpose a "chaotic present and a disastrous future" against a "nostalgic vision of an intact and uncontested intellectual world" that we were losing or that we had already lost.[9]

Allan Bloom's *The Closing of the American Mind* epitomized the conservative outlook among scholars. However, it was Newt Gingrich, the House speaker trained as a historian, who best described their vision of America's past in his less weighty tome *To Renew America,* published shortly before the standards themselves:

From the arrival of English-speaking colonists in 1607 until 1965, there was one continuous civilization built around a set of commonly accepted legal and cultural principles. From the Jamestown colony and the Pilgrims, through de Toqueville's *Democracy in America,* up to the Norman Rockwell paintings of the 1940s and 1950s, there was a clear sense of what it meant to be an American.

Schoolbook Nation

That "common understanding we share about who we are and how we came to be," claimed Gingrich, was now under siege by cultural elites, particularly multiculturalists, who were replacing traditional history with "the notion that every group is entitled to its own version of the past."[10]

This argument took claims in *The Disuniting of America* to the point of caricature. Gingrich was both more sweeping than Schlesinger in his diagnosis of the country's ills and, curiously, more chronologically exact, leaving his readers with little more to speculate on than what month of 1965 America began to implode. Of course, the cutoff date was hardly arbitrary. It called to mind specific historical events—the radicalization of the left wing of the civil rights movement after passage of the Voting Rights Act; the Watts riot; the expansion of Lyndon Johnson's Great Society programs. More importantly, 1965 served simply as the middle year in a decade that for Gingrich symbolized promiscuous sex, casual drug use, declining respect for authority, and the collapse of academic rigor in schools and colleges. The country was still suffering from the moral hangover of that troublesome decade, Republicans charged, and Democrats like Bill Clinton were to blame. Thus even before the standards appeared, history teaching was becoming a proxy in a broader cultural and political war.

The final participants in the debate over educational reform might be called "progressives" or "radical multiculturalists," but neither name really captures them because they lacked the ideological coherence of the nationalists and conservatives. What united them was their lack of nostalgia, their distrust of Hirsch and what they saw as the prescriptive and trivia-oriented nature of his cultural literacy, and their more open hostility to conservatives like Gingrich. This group included teachers and other professional educators still committed to the social studies approach and frustrated with dismissals of it by scholars like Ravitch. Others were historians who since the 1960s had engaged in research that had broadened the field of historical inquiry away from the nation-state and toward local or non-elite groups— women, racial and ethnic minorities, the working class, gays and lesbians, and others. Gary Nash, codirector of the standards project at the NCHS and author of books like *Red, White, and Black: The Peoples of Early America,* fell into this category. In their conflicts with conservatives, some of these scholars engaged in a sort of counter-nostalgia, exaggerating the narrowness of historiography before 1960 and the blossoming of research afterward. FitzGerald's thesis sometimes served their interests as well.[11]

Introduction

The last members of this diverse lot were so-called pressure groups who advocated a more culturally inclusive history curriculum and were usually organized by race or ethnicity. They worked most effectively at the state and local level (Latinos in Texas, for instance, or Iroquois in New York State) by lobbying for adoption of certain books, persuading legislators to draft bills mandating multicultural reforms, and introducing curricular materials directly into public and private schools. Because many of these activists worked outside the historical and educational establishments, it was easy for some cultural nationalists and conservatives to brand them and their ideas as unprofessional and ill informed. Militant Afrocentrists like Leonard Jeffries, chair of Black studies at City University in New York and consultant to the state on curriculum reform, made that job easy. With a devotion to biological determinism that would have made nineteenth-century phrenologists blush, Jeffries claimed that the skin pigment melanin accounted for cultural differences between races. An abundance of melanin made Africans a generous, humanistic, and communal-oriented "Sun People." A lack of it made Europeans a coldly individualistic, greedy, and warlike "Ice People."

Extremists aside, Afrocentrists and other advocates of multicultural history raised troubling questions about the effects on generations of minority children of a school history that, when it addressed people of color at all, often treated them as passive figures acted upon by others. "In most classrooms, whatever the subject, Whites are located in the center perspective position," wrote Molefi Kete Asante of Temple University. "How alien the African American child must feel, how like an outsider! The little African American child who sits in a classroom and is taught to accept as heroes and heroines individuals who defamed African people is being actively de-centered, dislocated, and made into a non-person."[12] Schlesinger and conservatives to his right thought curriculum reform in the name of racial justice had gone too far by the 1980s. Asante claimed it had not gone far enough.

Relationships among all these groups had been less than cordial during the 1980s and early 1990s, but they had not done much public sparring over the standards while the NCHS was drafting them. Settled in their respective corners, they seemed to be waiting for the signal to come out fighting. Lynne Cheney, the former NEH chairperson who had initially shepherded the project, rang the bell and started the bout.

In early October 1994 Cheney got an advanced look at the report. At over six hundred pages, it included thirty-one content standards, which outlined the general historical information students should know and

9

the skills they should demonstrate, along with hundreds of pages of related questions and activities. The thirty-one standards were fairly traditional, but the activities bore the imprint of recent scholarship and multicultural influences. On October 20, a few days before its release, Cheney denounced the whole standards document on the op-ed page of the *Wall Street Journal*. Leftists had hijacked the standards, she claimed, and their biases could be gleaned by a brief glance at the number of times certain historical figures appeared in the report. Harriet Tubman, an African-American who spirited escaping slaves out of the South, popped up six times. But Ulysses S. Grant, who led the troops who finally crushed the Confederacy, appeared only once. Paul Revere was nowhere to be found. While the document breezed by the Constitution, complained Cheney, it dwelt on a trifling bit of African history, asking students to "analyze the achievements and grandeur of Mansa Musa's court, and the social customs and wealth of the kingdom of Mali." The authors "tend to save their unqualified admiration for people, places and events that are politically correct," she observed.

Revisionist historians with a "great hatred for traditional history" had taken control of the project, and various "political groups, such as African-American organizations and Native American groups," had complained about alleged omissions and distortions in early drafts of the standards. Nobody dared to "cut the inclusive part," leaving the final document disjointed, prejudiced, and incomplete.[13]

Cheney's allies, many of whom had clearly not even read the document, responded to her call to prevent its official adoption. Conservative commentator Phyllis Schlafly said the standards were brimming with multicultural items with "little or no importance to American history." Former Republican presidential contender Patrick Buchanan pronounced the standards "horrendous." The headline in an opinion piece in *U.S. News and World Report* labeled them "bunk." Radio host Rush Limbaugh called for them to be "flushed down the toilet."[14]

Many of those involved in composing the standards leaped to defend them. In a lengthy follow-up letter to the *Journal,* Nash and Crabtree disputed Cheney on several points. They argued that the standards did not neglect the Constitution, as she had implied; five of the thirty-one content standards were devoted to its creation, ratification, and achievements. Furthermore, the vast majority of the one thousand individuals named in the document were men traditionally emphasized in American history, among them George Washington, Thomas Jefferson, John Hancock, and Alexander Hamilton. Multiculturalism, they affirmed, had not run amok: "The emphasis

Introduction

in these standards is upon the great issues, debates and developments that shaped the course of history, and upon all those—men and women, named and unnamed, from all walks of life and all ethnic, racial, religious, and national backgrounds—whose contributions have been part of the very warp and woof of the American experience."[15]

Initially, the cultural nationalists leaned toward the conservative position. In an essay in *Education Week,* Diane Ravitch praised what she saw as the document's genuine accomplishments. It was intellectually engaging, and it incorporated African-Americans, Native Americans, women, and others. But in honoring the nation's diversities it ignored commonalities, according to Ravitch. It failed to balance national ideals and accomplishments with national failures, leading to a gloomy view of the American past where the Ku Klux Klan and Joseph McCarthy loomed too large. "It aims to enhance the self-esteem of racial minorities and women," continued Ravitch, "but those who seek a common identity might well conclude that the founding, settling, and growth of our nation were shameful events." The divisive sort of history prophesied by FitzGerald with the anecdote about Squanto as a "friendly Indian" in *America Revised* seemed to be shaping up as the new orthodoxy. Especially troubling for Ravitch, and later Schlesinger, was the writers' use of the term "American peoples" instead of the singular "people."[16]

The standards split the scholarly community. Some sided with Ravitch. Walter MacDougall, a professor at the University of Pennsylvania, thought the standards incorrectly made "minority and female struggle versus white male resistance" a centerpiece of American history while treating the idealism of leaders like Woodrow Wilson as foolish or hypocritical. Panels of historians set up by the Council for Basic Education found that many of the teaching activities presented a "disproportionately pessimistic and misrepresentative picture" of the American past. Disputing them, Columbia University historian Alan Brinkley, author of a popular textbook, thought the standards reflected "a very centrist view of history." His Columbia colleague Carol Gluck, who had helped to write the document, argued that if it had been "hijacked," then it was "hijacked by America, through an admirable process of open debate that could probably only happen in the United States."[17]

Unlike many a row in academe, the conflict over the standards made compelling news. Key issues in the debate, like race and the alleged excesses of political correctness, blended neatly into the 1994 Congressional campaigns.[18] Cheney and Nash became lively antagonists on

11

Schoolbook Nation

PBS's *McNeill/Lehrer News Hour*, ABC's *World News Tonight*, and NBC's *Today Show*.[19] Commentary on the standards from the right, left, and center continually reinforced FitzGerald's earlier thesis: Historical revisionism now making its way into schools was a product of the unique upheaval of the 1960s; before that, curriculum developers and textbook writers did not have to grapple with the question of national identity and its ties to race, class, and gender. Today, observed a *Newsweek* writer in a fairly typical comment, there "is no longer an agreement on which history to teach, nor how best to teach it." For conservatives like Gingrich, the alleged uniformity of history written before 1965 reflected a consensus about American values. For less sanguine observers like FitzGerald, the history once taught in schools reflected the dominance of certain groups both inside and outside the educational establishment. "What is noteworthy is that until the 1960s the voices were pretty much alike; after that, they became much more varied, and the public debate over texts altered dramatically," she had written in *America Revised*.[20] Discordant voices of, say, political leftists or Blacks in the South had once been effectively muffled, FitzGerald implied. Now they were heard.

Fixation on the 1960s sometimes became farcical. History was now being written by "oppression-minded people who trashed the dean's office" back then or at least "wished they had," according to John Leo in a column from *U.S. News and World Report*. How did he know? In a question on critical figures in America's struggle for independence, the standards writers mentioned Ebenezer McIntosh. After calling several historians who had never heard of McIntosh, Leo learned that he had been "a brawling street lout of the 1760s who whipped up anti-British mobs and sacked the homes of various colonial officials." That background "helps explain why McIntosh managed to overcome natural handicaps (great obscurity, whiteness, maleness) and get himself mentioned in a modern text as somebody children ought to know." Leo pegged him as "a sort of early Abbie Hoffman or Jerry Rubin."[21]

A few commentators recognized how such arguments confused the issues. Making claims about a bygone placidity in how Americans used to remember the past, noted Nash and Crabtree in their account of the standards imbroglio, "requires a convenient forgetting of the long story of historical controversy in this nation." They knew part of the misunderstanding lay with the need to simplify the complex story of the standards for diffusion through the mass media.[22]

The problem went deeper than they acknowledged, however. Even

Introduction

in measured analysis by respected historians, those same distorted views about history teaching in grammar and high schools kept reappearing. It was not that these men and women agreed with the facile claims of Gingrich in *To Renew America* (one quipped that the Speaker was a great storyteller—"it's just the history that trips him up").[23] They knew historians had long disagreed on critical issues, such as the failures of Reconstruction and the wisdom of United States entry into World War I. Teachers of survey courses for undergraduates regularly designed their syllabi around those opposing viewpoints. In that sense, the myth of past consensus was absurd. That racial and religious politics helped to determine what sort of history gets written also seemed fairly clear to historians, particularly after Peter Novick's comprehensive study of the profession, *That Noble Dream,* appeared in 1988. Shuffling through the correspondence of nominally "objective" Protestant males who dominated the American Historical Association (AHA) for the first half of the twentieth century, Novick unearthed numerous jabs at Catholics and Jews deemed unable to write detached, well-rounded accounts of the past. Furthermore, the AHA had recently witnessed a raucous debate about the fragmenting of historiography that foreshadowed the uproar over the standards.[24]

No, the problem for historians, teachers, and others who tried to engage in thoughtful exchanges about the initial draft of the standards did not lie with their analytical skills or breadth of reading in contemporary scholarship. The problem was that few had bothered to look at how schools had actually taught American history to precollegiate students. The simplest way to begin that task was to examine textbooks. That undertaking was daunting, however. Hundreds of textbooks had been written between the 1820s, when the first focusing on United States history appeared, and 1990; the most popular among them had gone through more than a dozen editions. Most libraries, even those at major universities, had only a scattershot collection of such books. And, according to near universal agreement, the texts were achingly dull. So historians, like other commentators, tended to rely on secondary accounts, particularly FitzGerald's. She had said that until the end of the 1950s the books had been ideologically monochromatic and resistant to change, and scholars took her at her word, in part because her argument seemed to jibe with their own hazy recollections of learning history in high school. The real world of history writing for schools before 1960 was something of a terra incognita. Conservatives praised it for its unified outlook; advocates of multiculturalism denounced it for its exclusions. But few had actually explored it.

Schoolbook Nation

As the controversy over the standards progressed, new and old misconceptions about textbooks and teaching began to pile up. Take the strange case of Crispus Attucks. Attucks was a sailor of mixed blood, part African and likely part Indian, who died at the hands of British soldiers in the Boston Massacre of 1770. For conservatives who spotted him in recent textbooks, he was a prime example of history by quota, an inconsequential figure belatedly appended to the nation's story to please Black activists.[25] In fact, Attucks had appeared prominently in what was probably the most widely used textbook of the 1870s and 1880s, Thomas Wentworth Higginson's *Young Folks' History of the United States*. True, the decades of Jim Crow had not been kind to Attucks. But his memory was kept alive in supplementary histories used by significant numbers of African-Americans in the South. He also appeared intermittently in mainstream histories. The 1950 edition of a popular text entitled *The Story of American Democracy* included a picture of him alongside Jefferson, Patrick Henry, and Paul Revere.[26]

And what of Revere, the midnight rider whom Cheney could not find in the standards and whom other critics thought was being forgotten for Attucks? His alleged removal from texts had been a favorite complaint of critics on the right since the 1920s, when groups like the Sons of the American Revolution and the American Legion mourned his passing, along with that of other Revolutionary heroes like Nathan Hale. Revisionists, it seems, have always had it in for Revere, while patriots have always saved a hallowed place for him.

A few months before the release of the standards, the self-identified Irish-Italian John Leo had written another attack on historical revisionism, this one based on his reading of a new edition of a popular American history textbook. In a magazine column titled "Affirmative Action History," Leo noted that the book sported only two illustrations of Irish-Americans. One was a ward boss, and the other was Jack Kennedy. Yet the same book was bursting with "75 to 80 illustrations of Indians and Indian culture."[27] Leo's implication was clear—the squeaky wheel gets the grease. Politically active Native Americans were better represented than the quiescent Irish. Perhaps so. But early in the twentieth century, Leo's Irish-American kin had been just as noisy as today's activists (perhaps more so), and German-Americans had been equally adept at putting the squeeze on publishers and school boards. Their persistence is one reason why elderly Americans once committed to memory the Revolutionary exploits of naval commander John Barry and drill instructor Friedrich von Steuben.

One could string together numerous, isolated examples such as these, but it is more important to correct the larger errors they point to. First, the efforts of pressure groups to influence the history curriculum are not new; they are nearly as old as the mustiest textbook. When William Bennett and other conservatives decry the "growing" and "alarming" politicization of history, they suffer from a puzzling amnesia. Second, those activists and the textbooks they have tried to shape have generally not been unified in outlook. Thomas Higginson, the White author of the nineteenth-century text that mentioned Crispus Attucks, had commanded a regiment of Black soldiers during the Civil War. One of his competitors was Alexander H. Stephens, who also happened to have been the vice president of the Confederacy. As one might expect, their textbooks' views of the war and the rest of American history differed considerably.

The split between Higginson and Stephens mirrored larger divisions. In the late nineteenth century, White Southerners like Stephens and large numbers of Catholics assailed the bias (pro-Northern in the first case, pro-Protestant in the second) they believed permeated popular histories of the day. Their separate protests gave rise to texts prepared specifically for parochial schools, mostly in the urban North, and for racially segregated public schools in the South. The influence of just the Catholic schools at that time would dwarf the power of today's Afrocentric-oriented academies and public schools, the ones that have so troubled Schlesinger.

Interestingly, the threat that Catholic and neo-Confederate histories posed to the dominant historical narratives of the day, written almost entirely by Protestant New Englanders, stirred a backlash with a strangely modern ring. Massachusetts minister Edwin Mead assailed what he saw as willful historical distortions and a lack of academic rigor in Catholic texts. Mead's fellow minister and popular writer Daniel Dorchester feared that these volumes would stymie native-born Protestants' efforts to assimilate Catholic immigrants. Others were concerned that books like the *Southern School History of the United States* would impede that region's reintegration into the national community. Their specific complaints included the seemingly recent issue of history by quota, which, in fact, White Southerners had pioneered at the end of the nineteenth century. Confederate veterans and others in Dixie would count text lines to make sure writers had carefully balanced Southern and Northern "patriots" in coverage of the Revolutionary War and the "War Between the States." Whites in the South fretted that without proper role models their children would grow up without respect for their ancestors or themselves.

Schoolbook Nation

The point here is not that history is merely repeating itself. The political and cultural contexts for educational debates today are considerably different than they were in the 1880s or 1920s. However, we return to many of the same questions as the decades pass. What sort of national identity should schools foster? Can the stories of minority groups, however defined, be integrated into classrooms and textbooks without upsetting the "main story" of American history?[28] Do competing versions of our past, sometimes taught in socially segregated schools, threaten our national unity?

History does not repeat itself, but, as Mark Twain reminds us, it rhymes. The meter of our arguments over national character, the steady rising and falling of public interest in questions of race, class, religion, and other markers of identity, continually echo through the hallways of our schools. This national soul-searching has always played out through textbooks, especially those purporting to explain the country's past. Thus the historiographic cacophony that FitzGerald attributed to the breakup of the national narrative in the 1960s is not really new, and recent claims about the "end of history" or the "disuniting of America" are alarmist, misguided, and ahistorical. Yet these claims are reassuringly familiar. For those who would influence textbooks and teaching—Protestant elites in the 1870s, Irish-Americans in the 1920s, and conservative politicians today—the sky has always been falling.

In the chapters that follow, I have tried to do two things simultaneously: explore some of the conflicts that have swirled around history teaching *and* show how these battles have shaped the texts themselves. I hope I have been fair to their authors and to all parties involved in the textbook wars, but one can never be entirely unbiased. We may search for the Promised Land of objectivity, but nobody, in the end, can enter it. Writing history is always political. It always reflects the relations of power in the society. Whose records do we deem worthy of precious shelf space in archives and libraries? Who has access to these sources, or to education in general? Which articles will be published, and whose books reviewed? These sorts of caveats and warnings are commonplace today, but they bear repeating because so many participants in the debate over history teaching find it easy to forget them when they become inconvenient.

Our "values are not matters of whim and circumstance," declared Schlesinger in *The Disuniting of America.* "History has given them to us." Elsewhere, he noted that it may be unfortunate that dead White

Introduction

European males have played such a large part in shaping American culture, but "that's the way it is. One cannot erase history."[29]

Schlesinger makes an important point: The story of the past cannot be reworked willy-nilly and still command respect. But his statements are curious. History is both the mover ("History has given") and the moved. In a rush to discredit multicultural revisionism, Schlesinger has bypassed the role that humans play in assembling a story from an unwieldy tangle of sources. Despite his guarantee, history also surely *can* be erased. In the nineteenth century, for instance, histories of the United States devoted considerable space to Native Americans, often providing detailed maps showing the dispersal of tribes and languages. While racist assumptions marred the books' discussions of Indian history, it nevertheless was an important part of the American story. When professional historians early in the twentieth century decided to frame America's story around the growth of long-term political and economic institutions, however, they deemed Indians essentially irrelevant, and the pages devoted to them dwindled. A more recent effort to explain the country's early history as the meeting and blending of peoples from Europe, Africa, and America has brought Indians back. The recent change reflects new historical evidence, the continuing search for truth, and, undeniably, the power of nonwhites who have entered the profession in recent decades.

Hirsch was more circumspect and conflicted than Schlesinger on the question of whether bodies of knowledge might be divorced from the politics that, in part, produced them. His cultural literacy was deeply traditional, he admitted, but no "matter how value-laden or partisan some of these common elements were in their origins long ago, they now exist as common materials of communication." Later he retreated somewhat and suggested, like Schlesinger, that "history had decided what those common elements are."[30] Genuinely committed to using cultural literacy to empower the poor and the nonwhite, Hirsch was uncomfortable confronting the fact that the tools of cultural literacy structured that noble task, that his strategy came with a cost.

That cost became clear in the debates over the standards. Conservatives repeatedly employed variations of Hirsch's argument about cultural literacy to belittle figures like Crispus Attucks and the "Boston street lout" Ebenezer McIntosh as politically correct add-ons who would only distract students from more weighty matters. Hirsch's focus on critical individuals and events also obscures the past in a systematic, not random, way. It recognizes primarily those with wealth or official position, who in America have tended to be White males. Even they can fare poorly, however, as the case of McIntosh shows. Individually, he may not be that important. However, he can usefully represent the thousands of laborers in Boston and other cities who helped make the American Revolution in as fundamental a way as Patrick Henry or Thomas Jefferson, a point Nash and Crabtree made in defending their inclusion of him.[31] Hirsch argued that his cultural literacy has an "inherently classless character." But Henry and Jefferson made it into his *Dictionary of Cultural Literacy;* McIntosh and the working-class Sons of Liberty did not. The traditional content of a canon like Hirsch's can actually undermine his egalitarian goals, telling certain students that the history of people like them is not important and thereby reinforcing social hierarchies.

Schlesinger argues that militant multiculturalists use history as a weapon. But the corollary is that for him history is a fortress, one that guards the valuables previous generations have acquired, however heroically or shamefully. Claims that history has only recently become politicized make sense only when we present bodies of knowledge as objective or self-evident and erase records of the struggles that put them in classrooms and textbooks in the first place. This book grows out of a cultural studies tradition that attempts to make forgotten conflicts visible again.[32]

Examining textbooks through the lens of the "nation" is an effective way to unmask these conflicts. Nationalism has been a potent intellectual and emotional force since the late eighteenth century, one for which millions have willingly killed or died. Yet the meaning of the nation has never been fixed, and articulating one idea of the nation has generally meant subordinating or rejecting another. During the Civil War, Abraham Lincoln called on Americans to "bind up the nation's wounds" and to rededicate themselves to the cause of liberty. The Republicans he led had repudiated a nationalism that could embrace slavery, the doctrine of state sovereignty, or, for the party's radical wing, even racism. Sixty years later Congress heeded calls to "keep America American" by passing legislation that restricted immigration from eastern and southern Europe and even more tightly blocked the entry of Asians. In doing so, legislators endorsed a nation conceived in racial and linguistic terms over a competing one rooted in cultural pluralism. Written history always reflects these differences, privileging one idea of the nation over another.

When public schooling began to spread outward from New England in the early nineteenth century, it became clear to many observers that

Introduction

mass education might be a powerful force in determining what kind of nationalism predominated. Industrialization weakened ties within extended families, and schools, in turn, became critical institutions for transmitting both useful knowledge and social values across generations. The cultural authority that Protestant, New England–based textbook writers might wield was already troubling some White Southerners by the 1840s. They called for boycotts, complaining that textbooks showed insufficient respect for the Southern way of life and misrepresented its central economic institution, slavery. These critics understood the links among textbooks, cultural homogeneity, and the political nationalism emanating from the North in calls for a perpetual, indivisible union of the states. The ideal of national unity that many textbooks and teachers in the public schools espoused in the antebellum era did not emerge spontaneously from the American people as a whole. It embodied several regional biases—support for industrial growth, preference for free over slave labor, and suspicion of minority groups that exercised significant cultural autonomy. The last of these sentiments often found expression through anti-Catholicism, in both textbooks and the public utterances of leaders of the common-school movement, many of them Protestant ministers.

After the Confederate States of America were defeated, fewer and fewer people questioned the proposition that the history curriculum and textbooks should reflect and promote national cohesion—a view so ingrained today that Schlesinger can equate it with historical objectivity itself, as he does in the quotation that begins this book. They did fight over what national unity signified, however. Alexander Stephens, the Confederacy's former vice president, argued that a simple devotion to what he described as the political principles handed down by the drafters of the Constitution should bind Americans together. In his *Compendium of the History of the United States,* a textbook that appeared only seven years after the war had ended, he called passionately for sectional reconciliation. But he demanded a central government whose powers were carefully circumscribed, as, he argued, the Founders had intended.

Frederick Douglass, former abolitionist and then the most prominent African-American leader in the Republican Party, saw how neo-Confederate understandings of American history would undermine the Fourteenth and Fifteenth Amendments and their original purpose of securing a single, national citizenship for all men in the country, regardless of race. In the 1870s Douglass condemned textbooks written from Stephens's point of view. Similarly, many Catholic clergy and lay leaders criticized Protestant control of the public schools and the history curriculum. They particularly resented textbooks that too closely linked Protestantism to American nationalism or ignored the role of Catholics in the country's past. However, when Catholics and White Southerners began writing and using their own schoolbooks, they never justified their actions on the grounds of separatism. Instead, they argued simply that *they* best understood what made Americans a single, unified people.

More groups, from Civil War veterans and populists to professional historians and German immigrants, entered the textbook debates as the nineteenth century drew to a close. Each of them based the validity of their claims on their stance as national patriots. All wanted to graft their particular views onto the universally appealing concept of the nation.

It was hardly coincidental that schoolbooks became a locus of conflict in disputes over American identity. Parents or, in an increasing number of states, taxpayers had to buy them. They were ubiquitous. Millions of students depended on textbooks for at least part of their understanding of the American past. Though no writer, teacher, or parent could control how students would interpret a book, it still held enormous symbolic value. It provided a context for popular understandings of the past, what the British scholar Stuart Hall calls the "horizon of the taken for granted."[33] If popular histories rarely discussed African-Americans following emancipation, for instance, it was easy for White students to imagine Blacks' irrelevance to the national community. Implications for public policy were obvious.

Edward Austin Johnson, a Black teacher and school principal in North Carolina, saw just that problem with the histories of the 1890s. In 1892 he penned the *School History of the Negro Race in America,* a supplementary text for children of color in the South who, in a traditional history, would rarely see African-Americans outside of racially stereotyped roles. The book placed Americans of African descent squarely within the pageant of national history, starting with their arrival in Virginia in 1619. Johnson specifically included events like the Virginia slave rebellion led by Nat Turner in 1832 and the exploits of Black soldiers and sailors in the Civil War. He hoped to undermine the ideological foundations of Jim Crow by offering students historical models to contest their growing exclusion from political power and public memory. Johnson's concern about racist accounts of the past alienating children of color parallels the fears of Afrocentrists today.

Introduction

The theory that Western knowledge owes a debt to Africa, and particularly Egypt, is hardly new, either. On the first pages of his book Johnson declared that all "*the science and learning* of ancient Greece and Rome was, probably, once in the hands of the foreparents of American slaves."[34] Though only a few individuals or groups ended up writing textbooks, as Johnson did, most found ways to influence their content. Laws passed late in the nineteenth century gave them that opportunity. Where individual teachers and schools generally had chosen which textbooks to use, the power of adoption steadily passed to local, county, and, in the South, state officials. Reformers had initially set up adoption committees to combat corruption, especially publisher kickbacks to poorly paid school officials and teachers. But, once established, review boards and the public hearings they held also provided an arena for different social groups to spar over what sort of books children should read. Activists lobbied board members, who took their recommendations under advisement when selecting books. Frequently, boards or state legislatures also set up official criteria specifying what sort of books would be acceptable for schools.

The country's largest publishers began seeking writers or manuscripts that they expected would meet the standards of the largest number of districts. When they realized that no single history could satisfy all competing demands, publishers resorted to niche marketing. In the case of Catholics and White Southerners, small regional and religious presses laid the groundwork for these submarkets. Once they had proved such books could be profitable, larger firms followed suit.

The path from history writer to the ultimate textbook consumer, the grammar school or academy student, was relatively short and direct in 1820. Eighty years later it had become considerably more complex, expensive, and overtly political. Writers and editors developed different languages to communicate with adoption committees and textbook activists. Edward Channing expected the blue cover of his *Students' History of the United States* to signal his sympathy for members of the Grand Army of the Republic (GAR) in their historical disputes with their gray-clad former adversaries in the United Confederate Veterans (UCV). A sketch of Lincoln on the frontispiece, instead of the more typical portrait of Washington, sent the same signal.[35] Throughout the South, in contrast, publisher representatives sought UCV endorsement of their books. For Irish-Americans, influential in cities like Boston and New York, mention of Revolutionary heroes like John Sullivan became de rigueur for adoption. Over time, publishers grew more adept at meeting expectations of various activists and balancing conflicting historical claims. The adoption process gave all citizens a venue for influencing the content of books. However, control was never democratic. Publishers who tended carefully to the concerns of Union veterans or women in the Daughters of the Confederacy showed considerably less interest in the sensitivities of African-Americans, who had little official political power in the South after 1900. Labor leaders who pressed for books sympathetic to the cause of workers also learned that the selection process often muted their voice. Following the rise of an ethos of educational professionalism and "expert" control of schools, representatives of the working class rarely sat on adoption boards. Middle-class political appointees, not surprisingly, tended to approve histories that praised industrial capitalism and portrayed labor activism as a threat to national unity.[36] There were few groups whose interests the text writers and editors could afford to ignore entirely, however. Adoption battles, waged where state regulation and market forces intersected, became mirrors of wider conflicts over class, race, and other issues. The most successful texts featured historical narratives that marshaled widespread support, or at least acquiescence, among various parties.[37]

Given the publishers' financial incentive to publish single textbooks that would sell in every region, combined with a prevalent feeling that all schools should be teaching essentially one version of the country's past, one would expect these narratives to move slowly toward consensus. For much of the time, they have done just that. Religious, political, and racial disputes gave rise to competing sets of histories for Catholics and White Southerners in the late nineteenth century, but these separate texts slowly merged over the next fifty years. By the 1950s books exhibited a relatively stable, consensus-oriented vision of the American past. What leftist critic Michael Apple calls the "romanticized common curriculum" of the right is not entirely a myth; FitzGerald *did* see a certain homogeneity in textbooks of the postwar era.

What is important to remember, however, is that on occasion, social conflicts become so intense that the natural drift toward consensus slows, stops, or breaks up altogether. These counter-trends occurred in the 1890s, 1920s, and, as participants in the standards debate understood, the 1960s. Yet textbooks and history teaching in the intervening eras were hardly free from politics. Writers and editors had simply fashioned narratives that aroused the least controversy, in part by capitulating to the very sort of pressure groups that Schlesinger con-

Introduction

demns today. Like any intellectual patchwork, this history ended up riddled with ideological inconsistencies, leaving it vulnerable to the next wave of attacks. In the early 1960s, for example, African-American critics blasted textbooks that combined a bland affirmation of human rights and democratic principles with racist accounts of Reconstruction that seemed to endorse Jim Crow.

The following seven chapters explore shifts in understandings of our nation and its history as the "official knowledge" in textbooks responded to market forces, political pressures, and intellectual movements among historians and educators.[38] The first chapter examines how histories in the nineteenth century imagined a modern American nation-state. The next two chapters look at the rise and fall of separate histories for Catholics and Whites in the South. Chapter 4 investigates how textbooks early in the twentieth century discussed race, and chapter 5 shows how "Anglo-Saxonism"—one manifestation of the volumes' linking of race and ethnicity to national identity—collapsed amid a wave of protests in the 1920s. Harold Rugg and his social studies textbooks, which looked frankly at America's divisions along class lines, are the subject of chapter 6. The final chapter examines how the consensus narrative of the 1950s fell apart and how text writers and editors have, with only partial success, tried to assemble another one in its place.

This study relies on analysis of more than one hundred textbooks published between 1824 and the present day.[39] Making broad assertions about typical content requires knowing something about how widely each textbook was used. David Saville Muzzey's histories, mainstays of high school courses for much of the twentieth century, deserve more attention, for example, than an obscure volume. Gauging popularity is not always easy, however, because publishers, wary of offering too much information to their competitors, have only rarely released sales figures. I have generally determined the extent of textbook use through three factors: records of adoption, when available; number of editions published; and frequency of mention in educational and other literature of any given period.

Even when carefully chosen, the textbooks, along with records of debate over their adoption, can reveal only so much. Too often, commentators on history in the schools have forgotten a basic tenet of cultural studies. No artifact, from a storybook to a television program, can determine how people will interpret it. Many writers have assumed that history texts simply reflect the worldview of an amorphous American public or that their content is absorbed fairly directly into the minds of young readers. In *America Revised*, FitzGerald claimed that children growing up in the 1950s "believed in the permanency of our American-history textbooks. To us as children, those texts were the truth of things: they were American history." One might immediately ask who the "we" is here. Did all young people approach the books from the same perspective and invest them with the same authority? The answer seems to be "no," but only recently have scholars begun to examine how students actually interpret the history they learn in school and how their understanding is affected by a range of personal factors, along with the influence of other sources of historical knowledge, like parents, television, and the Internet.[40]

My work focuses primarily on the production end of the textbook story. Thus I have avoided the arduous task of determining how students actually construct historical outlines and maps in their own minds. However, only when we combine research into curriculum development with examination of how subject matter is actually assimilated and remembered will we gain a more complete picture of the historical consciousness of Americans, past and present.

While this book serves a narrower goal, I cannot claim to have finished a definitive study of even these textbooks—they are simply too rich a source. Repeatedly, I had to pass by intriguing historical topics or textual passages to keep my analysis from growing unwieldy or the number of chapters from spiraling upward. I have not, for instance, explored the complex relationship between ideas of gender and nation, though there were plenty of tantalizing leads to follow. I have not treated women's history, or the campaigns to include more of it in the history curriculum, in detail. The book's lengthiest chapter examines the trend toward multiracial history by comparing shifting treatment of African-Americans from the 1950s to 1980s. But the focus on that most contentious aspect of textbook "integration" meant passing quickly by changing depictions of Latinos, Native Americans, and Asian-Americans. The story in this book is an important one, I hope, but it is far from complete.

Will a richer understanding of the way history has been taught and learned change the tenor of our debates over the curriculum? Probably. It might well have made for a more thoughtful, less partisan discussion of the standards. The prevalence of the 1960s-as-pivot theory clearly played to conservatives, who used it to brand the document as one more misbegotten scheme of left-wing educators and politicians. The United States Senate, mindful of the public's shift to the right during the 1994 election year, officially condemned the standards by a vote of ninety-nine to one, with the lone dissenter arguing that the censure was not harsh enough. Whatever the faults of the document, the lopsided nature of the vote suggested that meaningful deliberation had come to an end. The standards for national history survived, but only in truncated form. While the thirty-one individual standards remained, the approximately four hundred pages of teaching examples, source of much of the controversy, disappeared. The original reference to American "peoples" became "people," pleasing cultural nationalists Schlesinger and Ravitch, who endorsed the revised document enthusiastically.[41] Cheney, whose initial article in the *Wall Street Journal* had started the conflict, ignored their calls to back the new version.

As the furor died down, attention turned to new editions of textbooks and state-level history standards, with educators looking to see what influence, if any, the national standards might have had. Many participants in the ongoing debates returned to their old positions, arguing the same points with little new insight. We seem caught in a variation of George Santayana's dictum: Those who do not learn from the history debates of the past are condemned to repeat them.

1. From Virtuous Republic to Nation-State

Scholars looking at popular textbooks from the nineteenth century have tended to notice their conservatism. One found them "remarkably resistant to change," while another, who had combed through dozens of trade and school histories, wrote with exasperation about their "mind-boggling persistence of orthodoxy." But one aspect of these books—the way they imagined what the nation is—changed profoundly between the 1830s and 1890s. One gets a sense of this rupture in continuity by even a quick glance at two popular texts, the 1843 edition of Emma Willard's *Abridged History of the United States; or, Republic of America* and Edward Channing's *A Students' History of the United States,* published fifty years afterward.

Willard opens her book by defining the nature of its subject matter:

What constitutes a nation? First, there must be a country, with natural divisions of land and water; second, there must be men, women, and children to inhabit that country; and third, those inhabitants must be bound together in one, by living under a common government, which extends its protection over all, and which all are bound to obey.

To every nation there belongs a *history:* for whenever the inhabitants of any large portion of the earth are united under one government, *important public events* must have taken place. *The record* of *these events* constitutes the history of that country.[1]

Several things are worth noting in this passage. Willard envisions the nation as the coming together of a fixed body of territory and a group of people whose unity is defined essentially by political bonds descending from the state. By this definition, other nations of the era might include France, the Ottoman Empire, and certain tribes of American Indians. National history for Willard is a chronicle of important but discrete events. By using the term "public," she suggests these events occur in the realm of the state, primarily in war and politics. Glancing ahead in the book, we would find that history is a play in which heroic soldiers and statesmen take almost every role: the plucky but resolute John Smith saves the first English colony at Jamestown, George Washington crosses the Delaware, and the Founding Fathers assemble in Philadelphia to write the Constitution. These critical individuals quickly come to embody a nation that Willard first presents in a fairly abstract and legalistic manner.

Compare that idea of the nation and its past to one suggested by a note to teachers in Channing's book:

> Emphasis upon the whole trend of history should be accompanied by a recognition of its organic nature, permitting manifold points of view: its various aspects, as constitutional, economic, social, ethical, religious, artistic, should be set forth, and the temperament of each student allowed to place its own accent. Students should be encouraged to centralize their private work upon congenial aspects, and their various results should be gathered together as so many elements of the one complex truth.[2]

By Channing's time, history has grown more complicated. A detached, scientific prose replaces Willard's measured cadences, so reminiscent of the King James Bible, the one book she knew most of her students would have read regularly. A history of trends that can be examined from multiple perspectives supplants a fairly unproblematic history of public events. Development occurs in a number of realms beyond the political and military, which are not even mentioned directly in this passage, and the nation, as the subject of the narrative, can be best understood by studying these "various aspects."

What happened? How had a nation characterized by political union and symbolized through heroic individuals been reimagined as an organic unity of the American people expressed not only by great men but also through more impersonal social institutions? The answers are complex, and they offer a glimpse into how a political and intellectual upheaval in the middle and late nineteenth century shifted Americans' sense of their identity more than at any other period in their history.

This story must begin, as Willard's does, with definitions. As I will use the term here, a "nation" is a body of people who think of them-

ABRIDGED HISTORY

OF THE

UNITED STATES,

LIBERTY PEACE AND SAFETY

WITHIN

THE CHAIN OF UNION WITHOUT VIOLENCE AND FRAUD

OR

REPUBLIC OF AMERICA

NEW AND ENLARGED EDITION.

BY EMMA WILLARD.

NEW YORK:

PUBLISHED BY A. S. BARNES & CO.,

51 & 53 JOHN STREET.

SOLD BY BOOKSELLERS, GENERALLY, THROUGHOUT THE UNITED STATES.

1858.

The frontispiece of the 1858 edition of Emma Willard's *Abridged History of the United States*. The protective eagles and banner surrounding the feminine spirits of liberty, peace, and safety suggest both the strength and the fragility of a republic based on individual virtue.

selves as united by some combination of factors, including language, ethnicity or race, religion, political ideas, and various aspects of culture. "Nationalism" is the belief that a national people should have a homeland in which only members of that nation may exercise political power—that they should have a "nation-state." A "republic" is a state in which sovereignty rests in a body of citizens who are able to elect their own representatives to government. Republics bear no necessary relation to nations or nation-states. Nationalism can be fulfilled through various kinds of states, from the constitutional monarchy of Britain to the one-party dictatorship of Nazi Germany. Republics can unite several national communities, as they do the French, Italian, and German speakers of Switzerland or the even more diverse populations of India. They can also bring together only a portion of some larger nation. Nations, of course, can exist for hundreds or thousands of years without a state of any sort, the lot of the Kurds in the Middle East today. But since the rise of nationalism in the late eighteenth century, more and more people have come to believe that the nation-state should be the primary political unit across the globe.[3]

Statesmen writing in the first decades after the founding of the American republic, roughly the time Willard composed the first edition of her history, generally believed that the United States lacked a distinct national identity, though many wished it might develop one. The word "nation" never appears in the Constitution. "Union," which does, was a more malleable term that could paper over different understandings of precisely what the United States was or, more importantly, what it might become. For some of the practical-minded Founders, the union was a device to secure certain results, a way to simplify commerce among the states, better organize for defense, coordinate policy with Indian tribes (which they *did* call nations), and "secure the blessings of liberty." Others used "union" in a way that suggested "nation."

The differences went well beyond semantics. Thomas Jefferson and like-minded members of the Republican Party did not see the new government as a sacrosanct expression of a collective American people; it was a political agreement, or compact among the states. Jefferson claimed that when the government overstepped its bounds to challenge the sovereignty of the states or the liberties of the people, its laws could and should be ignored. Extremists argued that an individual state might legitimately decide to opt out of the compact altogether. Federalists like Alexander Hamilton, more concerned with economic expansion that depended on a strong central government than with state sovereignty or individual rights, endorsed a union in which the central power reigned supreme. Hamilton knew that a sturdier sense of American nationhood would better support that government, but in his guarded moments he wondered if national feelings could be generated and sustained over a vast territory.[4] By the start of the nineteenth century, then, Republicans and Federalists had set out the terms of the dispute between understandings of the United States as a compact or an absolute union. Its final resolution in Hamilton's favor came only with the end of the Civil War.[5]

Conflict over the meaning of "union" contributed to a more general unease about the fragility of the American republic. Well versed in classics on ancient Greece and Rome, the Founders feared the United States might follow their trajectories of republican decay and collapse. Several possibilities seemed threatening. Instability in a system that placed political authority with the states and the central government might rip the republic apart. Centralization might smother democracy. If commerce expanded, the delicate social bonds that made the republic possible might fray as individuals pursued wealth and power at the expense of their fellow citizens. Beneath confident rhetoric about America's destiny lay what one historian has termed a "subsoil of terror."[6]

Prominent thinkers of the era hoped that schools might be able to cultivate the virtues young people would need to safeguard the social and political system they would inherit. Benjamin Rush, a signer of the Declaration of Independence, thought schools should operate as "republican seminaries" teaching humility, self-denial, and brotherly kindness. Noah Webster, best known for composing the first dictionary of American English, argued that schools should place greater emphasis on imparting virtue than on developing specific skills, or that "the heart should be cultivated with more assiduity than the head." Significantly, these thinkers believed virtue developed best through direct transmission of unambiguous moral lessons. They deplored activities like novel reading, which, they feared, failed to provide such lessons and, worse, offered the sort of frivolous diversion likely to lead to moral corruption. Both Rush and Webster also saw schools as nationalizing institutions that would "render the mass of people more homogeneous and thereby fit them more easily for uniform and peaceable government." Americans might not yet be a unique people, but the right kind of teaching, particularly in history, could help to produce a national consciousness. Identification with the nation might then reinforce the republic's political foundation. Every "child in America should be acquainted with his own country," wrote Webster. "As soon as he opens his lips, he should rehearse the history of his own country; he should lisp the praise of liberty and of those illustrious heroes and statesmen who have wrought a revolution in her favor."[7]

Authors of the first widely used history texts attempted to create the kind of usable past Webster desired. To use the words of Charles A. Goodrich, from the preface of his *History of the United States of America*, such a narrative would set before us "striking instances of virtue, enterprise, courage, generosity; and, by a natural principle of emulation," incite "us to copy such noble examples." At the same time, it would illustrate the "blessings of political union and the miseries of faction."[8] While Goodrich did not address the issue directly, history written for young people also had to finesse controversial issues, like the question of whether the union was absolute and indestructible or merely a compact among the states. It also had to tread lightly on slavery, which from 1820 onward seemed to be forcing the competing theories to a showdown. To meet all these goals, writers had to create a body of national myths and symbols that transcended real divisions in the country.

Accounts of righteous warriors and statesmen met these demands almost perfectly, at least for a time. The pioneer in this endeavor was Mason Locke, or "Parson," Weems. He scoured the historical record, and, more often, his own fertile imagination, to fill a biography of Washington first published in 1806. It included the now familiar story of the future president chopping down a cherry tree and then confessing the misdeed to his father, who could not bring himself to punish a boy who "could not tell a lie." The cherry-tree myth did not appear in many conventional histories. But the same sentiments, with what are, to modern readers, utterly transparent efforts to manipulate the past to impart simple moral lessons, popped up again and again in discussions of Washington. Here is Willard's account of the general-in-the-making:

> When in school he was pains-taking, and exact in the performance of his exercises; and at the same time, so true in his words, so righteous in his actions, and so just in his judgments, that his school-mates were wont to bring their differences before him for decision. Superior also in bodily health and vigor, he excelled in athletic sports, and adventurous exploits. He loved the military; and tradition reports, that his first battles, in which he commanded, were mimic engagements, which he taught to his school-fellows.[9]

Goodrich saw similarly noble traits at the end of Washington's life and made a point of contrasting the two-term president's self-imposed retirement to the bloody or ignoble ends of other world leaders. "There is no parallel in history to this," he informed his young charges. "By the side of Washington, Alexander is degraded to a selfish destroyer of his race, Caesar becomes the dazzled votary of power; and Bonaparte, a baffled aspirant to universal dominion."[10]

Few passages better link the representation of the nation through individuals and history's role as a moral instructor. The allusions to war also suggest a prevalent theme in the texts. Political and military affairs consumed about three-quarters of text space in antebellum histories, sometimes more. Battles alone accounted for more than half of a schoolbook Willard wrote in the aftermath of the Mexican War.[11] By providing outside enemies—Mexicans, British, Indians—war better defined Americans as a distinct people. It put White Americans, North and South, on the seaboard and in the interior, into a common narrative framework.[12] War also allowed presentation of numerous examples of the steadfastness and self-denial worthy of imitation. In one history a royal governor offered Joseph Reed, a congressman and general, ten thousand pounds to desert the Revolutionary cause: "'I am not worth purchasing,' replied the incorruptible patriot; 'but such as I am, the king of Great Britain is not rich enough to buy me.'"[13]

Accounts of Benedict Arnold, a debt-ridden and profligate soldier who *did* turn traitor for British gold and ended up loathed by his countrymen, inverted the narrative to teach the same lesson. Aaron Burr, who schemed to set up his own kingdom in the West, also served as a "warning to those who, in a free country . . . listen to the suggestions of criminal ambition."[14] These villains spurned the modest rewards of virtue and pursued power, wealth, and personal aggrandizement in ways that threatened the survival of the republic. The lack of moral ambiguity in such parables often allowed writers to avoid subtler issues of historical causation. The British treatment of the colonies was unfair because King George III was tyrannical. The Americans' position was just because of the rectitude of Washington. The Loyalists were unworthy because of the treachery of Arnold.

The textbook writers' attempts to fashion a national mythology paralleled a broader movement among the country's novelists, poets, painters, and critics to define and express a unique national identity. Influenced by the romantic movement in Europe, many Americans sought out the "representative man" at one with his people. In popular literature, for instance, mythical versions of Davy Crockett and Daniel

From Virtuous Republic to Nation-State

Boone came to symbolize the rough-hewn frontier spirit even before the real men died. Gentlemen historians like George Bancroft chose more sedate models than Crockett or Boone, but the underlying process of linking man and nation remained much the same. One historian has spoken of American identity early in the antebellum era as a "roof without walls," with the roof representing the political structure established by the Constitution and the absence of walls representing the lack of a fully developed intellectual and popular culture.[15] These cultural nationalists tried to put brick and mortar into the walls to ensure that the roof would not come tumbling down.

Men and women throughout the United States participated eagerly in this nation-building enterprise, out of patriotism, hunger for the accolades of their fellow citizens, and sometimes profit. In 1820, for instance, an organization offered a gold medal and four hundred dollars to the man or woman who could compose a school history that would provide students "a correct knowledge of their own country, and a patriotic attachment to it." A writer named Salma Hale, whose account of Aaron Burr is quoted above, walked away with the prize. For nationalists, the focus on textbooks made perfect sense, because printed media are crucial in establishing a national consciousness. That fact was valid elsewhere as well. At the same time residents of the United States were wrestling with their identity, the reach of individual newspapers was partly determining the boundaries of nation-states in South America.[16] For this country, textbooks may have been even more important. By the end of the 1820s, before the rise of wire services, nationally distributed newspapers, and mass-subscription magazines, children throughout the republic began to share the same spellers, arithmetics, geographies, and histories. Textbook writers and publishers could wield tremendous cultural authority, a fact Noah Webster had understood when he began producing his own highly successful texts in grammar, spelling, and related subjects.

As the slavery issue increasingly split North from South, however, the history writer's search for common symbols and representative men with equal appeal across the sections became more difficult. Despite the best efforts of nationalists, the peculiar institution was making the republic more heterogeneous or, more accurately, splitting it into two nations. While a few abolitionists crafted readers and spellers that condemned the traffic in human beings, history writers who hoped for wider sales approached the topic warily. They did not advocate slavery. Almost all of them had been born and raised in New England, and their provincialism showed in favorable treatment of the

Puritans and their descendants. Some authors voiced suspicions about the idleness and aristocratic pretensions of Southern landowners, qualities they saw as natural by-products of slavery and the scattered plantation system. A few openly denounced the Atlantic slave trade, but their critiques stopped short of an outright condemnation of the practice of slavery *within* the United States. Writers also avoided any discussion of the actual conditions the slaves endured. They valued the blessings of union over any benefits that might be gained from pressing Southerners on the issue.

What the sectionally divided country most needed, these books suggested, was tolerance. Like generosity and selflessness, this was the sort of republican "virtue" writers developed extensively in their narratives. Religious intolerance in the Old World, they intoned, had driven America's founders to the New. Unwillingness to live with Quakers or other dissenters was the one blot on the otherwise upright record of the Puritans. Acceptance of diverse religious beliefs made model colonies of Rhode Island and Pennsylvania and heroes of their founders, Roger Williams and William Penn. The writers' religious tolerance was not all encompassing, however. Most books had little or nothing to say about Jews. Several writers, including Emma Willard, offered only grudging acceptance of more numerous Catholics. When the topic of Mormonism arose near the close of the histories, Joseph Smith often appeared as a rabble-rouser and charlatan, and authors sometimes depicted the Latter-day Saints' errand into the wilderness of Utah as just-deserved punishment for their queer views. Textbooks promoted religious, political, and social tolerance when it assured fidelity to commonly held values and where it made a federal union out of a diverse citizenry possible. While chattel slavery had clearly dropped from that list of common values by the 1850s, both school and trade histories suggested that readers could tolerate both the views of those Southerners who wanted to open the Western territories to slavery and those of the free-soilers who wanted to close them off to the institution.

The last chapter of an 1858 edition of Willard's history showed how slavery and the implicit conflict between the compact theory (then generally favored by slave owners because it limited the central government's interference in their "property" rights) and the absolute theory of union had undermined a usable past built around virtue-fostering stories of individual heroism. In Willard's book the problem grew most apparent when she was forced to address the 1850 Compromise. Congress had approved the compromise, which was actually a patchwork of bills, to mollify supporters and opponents of slavery and allow California to become a state. In fact, it only exacerbated sectional discord. One measure, the Fugitive Slave Act, radicalized many Northern Whites. Watching bounty hunters round up and repatriate escaped slaves living in nominally free states forced "moderates" to confront their own complicity in the system. Not surprisingly, Willard did not dwell on such unpleasant facts but tried to strike a reassuring note:

> The compromise measures proved the quieting of the fearful storm. Those who passed them, did, like the framers of the constitution [*sic*], agree to apprehended evils to prevent disunion, and thus preserve the country at its vital point. Some condemned, but the nation at large approved; and no rallying cry so touched the heart of the people, as "The Union, the whole Union!" "Our Country, one and entire!" . . . The restoration of confidence between the good and patriotic citizens of the north and south will be full of happiness and prosperity to both. The colored race, as they are the first to suffer by the loss of such confidence, so they will be the first to benefit by its return. Already we hear more and more of efforts at the south to improve them, as intellectual, moral, and religious beings.[17]

Willard's discussion mixes contradictory and ultimately incompatible ideas. Most startling is her allusion to an "apprehended evil" that must be slavery and the willingness of the Founders to recognize it when they devised the republic's central document in the 1780s. How could morally unassailable men like Washington, models of virtue, compromise with evil? And what would such compromise say about the worth of the nation these individuals so directly personified? Her narrative recalls, no doubt unintentionally, the argument of abolitionist and fellow New Englander William Lloyd Garrison. He had damned the Constitution as a "covenant with death and an agreement with hell" for its recognition of slavery. Yet Willard also offers a defense of the institution that echoes South Carolinian and former vice president John Calhoun's claim that it was not an evil at all but a "positive good" for slaves themselves, who benefited from the moral instruction it offered. Willard strains to find a middle ground. And, despite her deference to the "good and patriotic" citizens across the United States, her wording implies a clear distinction between the peoples and interests of the "north and south." The call to "Union" rings hollow. Is it an absolute union with social and legal recognition of slavery either everywhere (the apparent stand of the Supreme Court in the

Dred Scott case, decided a year before) or nowhere at all? Or is it a union of compact, which does not depend on such "national" homogeneity and would allow the development and eventual secession of its distinct societies? Willard cannot say.

By 1865 the Union Army and passage of the Thirteenth Amendment, forever ending slavery, had answered the question for her. What is surprising is that much of the noncommittal, artificially balanced history that Willard, Goodrich, and their peers developed before the war lingered in popular textbooks for more than two decades, despite its omissions and unresolved contradictions. Publishers continued to reissue old histories, adding hastily appended chapters on the Civil War and its immediate aftermath but generally leaving the narrative framework intact. Even texts whose first editions appeared after 1865 suggested only dimly the changes the war had wrought in popular and intellectual conceptions of the American nation and its past.[18]

An 1879 edition of William M. Swinton's *Condensed School History of the United States,* one of the most popular texts of the postwar era, still blamed the conflict on zealots from both sides. "There can be no doubt that at the time of Mr. Lincoln's election the great majority of the American people, North and South, sincerely loved the Union, and would have preferred to see it maintained at any sacrifice," wrote Swinton. What, then, drove Americans to the battlefield?

> It is true that there were extreme men on both sides. At the North there were Abolitionists, who were bent on the destruction of slavery, even if the Constitution and the country were destroyed with it. But they were small in number and took little part in the election. At the South, there was another inconsiderable party of extreme men, who were anxious for nothing but to see the South separated from the North.[19]

In an 1868 edition of his history, George Payn Quackenbos lavished praise on Henry Clay, the "greatest of modern orators," who tried to mediate between such extremists in Congress and drafted the Compromise of 1850, his "last and greatest triumph." In Quackenbos's narrative, peacemakers like Clay joined a pantheon of individuals led by Washington who embodied their nation's ideals. Quackenbos, a Republican who surely cast his vote for Lincoln in 1860, still found kind words for John Calhoun, the South's most staunch defender of slavery and state sovereignty. Another textbook first published in 1874 gave a comparatively detailed account of the causes of the war but still

FALL OF CAPTAIN LAWRENCE,—" DON'T GIVE UP THE SHIP."

This reverse was followed by another in August. The
sloop Argus, after carrying the American minister to France,
had cruised in the British Channel, committing great havoc
among the enemy's shipping. Several vessels started in pursuit, one of which discovered her by the light of a ship that
she had taken and fired. A well-contested action followed,
which resulted in the capture of the Argus and the destruction of a great part of her crew.

Commodore Porter, in the Essex, had selected the Pacific
for his sphere of action. In a five months' cruise, extending
over the summer of 1813, he captured twelve armed wha-
lers, of which he fitted up several as tenders, and dispatched
others to the United States with valuable cargoes of oil.—
On the 5th of September, Lieut. Burrows, in the Enterprise,
a few days' sail from Portland, fell in with the English vessel

on each side ? What became of Capt. Lawrence ? What reverse followed in August ?
Recount Commodore Porter's achievements. Describe the conflict between the En-

**Captain James Lawrence's dying exclamation to his crew, from the
Illustrated School History of the United States (1868) by George Payn
Quackenbos. Nineteenth-century textbooks relied on stories of heroic
individuals engaged in acts of selfless patriotism.**

listed the "evil influence of demagogues" prominently among them. "In order to gain power, many unprincipled men in the South were anxious to destroy the Union," wrote the author, "while others in the North were willing to abuse the Union for the same purpose." The problem with these arguments was that they made the great sacrifices of the war not only regrettable but perhaps even preventable, if only more compromisers had taken the place of Clay and Daniel Webster or if the Virginia-led effort to broker a peace after Lincoln's election had succeeded. An understanding of the war as a critical, and necessary, turning point in the development of the nation, one that we take for granted today, was largely absent.[20]

Writers' reluctance to address slavery and their disjointed treatment of the Civil War often left the narrative confused and incoherent. The pedagogical style that structured the books made that problem worse. Educators throughout much of the nineteenth century believed that learning history meant acquiring facts. Memorization served as both an end—knowing facts was useful for children—and a means. The mental discipline required to commit facts to memory was yet another way to build virtue. That pedagogy largely determined the content of books. Tomes by William Swinton and John J. Anderson, another best-selling textbook author of the postwar years, were literally catalogs of facts. Dates "are inserted with great frequency," boasted Anderson in the preface to his book, with years for battles and the achievement of statehood being his special favorites.[21] Publishers numbered every paragraph and often placed key words to be memorized in bold face, all the better to serve students in their classroom "recitations," when they repeated those facts aloud (often verbatim from the text) to prove they had mastered the material.

Chapters devoted to individual colonies dominated the pre-Revolutionary narrative, and most of those chapters covering the years after 1789 appeared chronologically according to presidential administration. These divisions fragmented the narrative subject, the United States, across space and time. Facts on a common subject, such as slavery, usually appeared at widely separated points in the text, from the arrival of the first shipment of Africans in Virginia in 1619 to the Emancipation Proclamation 250 years later. Often writers made little effort to trace continuity of thought or action across succeeding eras. Thus military or social conflicts, from land disputes with the Indians to the Civil War itself, continually "arose" somewhat mysteriously. Narrative focus on the heroic individual and the dramatic event also made it difficult for readers to follow ongoing historical trends.

From Virtuous Republic to Nation-State

Why did these postwar histories remain so similar to their antebellum predecessors when the United States had endured such wrenching changes, from unprecedented war casualties and breakneck industrial expansion to emancipation itself? There are several possible reasons. Publishers approached the market conservatively. Demand for texts did leap dramatically after the war, a result of the expansion of public schools combined with the efforts of politicians and educators to give American history a more central place in the curriculum.[22] But overproduction and cutthroat competition made sales and profits difficult to predict, particularly in the 1870s and 1880s. Publishers liked to keep a proven title, author, or historical style as long as it would sell. The last edition of Emma Willard's history appeared in 1873, three years after the author had died. Works by Charles Goodrich lasted even longer. School districts also tended to adopt a book for several years, generally about five, and even when the term was up, many preferred to stay with an old author. Parents, who still bought textbooks directly, could save money by using an old edition, at least until the last chapter, when "new" history arrived. Publishers often accommodated this approach, altering only the last pages of reissues. That way, new and old editions often had page-for-page correspondence. Finally, during Reconstruction and through its early aftermath, Americans fought bitterly over what meaning and historical significance to assign to the Civil War. Publishers, fearful of alienating committees and teachers who chose texts, likely believed a fact-based, conceptually vague approach was the safest way to move their product.

Whatever the cause of this narrative stagnation, by the late 1880s history textbooks had clearly drifted behind new currents in American thought, particularly in regard to ideas of nation. Before the war, suspicions about the social and moral costs of becoming a true nation could be found alongside enthusiastic efforts to cultivate a unique national culture. Southerners, in particular, expressed misgivings about the social homogeneity and political centralization that nationalizing entailed. On the eve of war, one Georgian declared that the "seductive dream of *national unities*" promoted by monarchical governments in Europe undermined republican liberties there and might destroy them on this side of the Atlantic.[23]

Transcendentalists centered in New England, with their reverence for the individual and dread of any social system that might encourage lockstep conformity, harbored similar fears. One argued that "nationalities are stains upon the globe when they purchase their soulless corporation life with the human happiness they should foster." Qualms about expanding the power of the central government extended to abolitionist and slaveholder alike. After Congress passed the Fugitive Slave Act, Ralph Waldo Emerson argued that the ideal of union could never justify the hunting of escaped slaves through the streets of Northern cities. As the Civil War began, the poet James Russell Lowell still wondered whether a "conscious nationality and a timely concentration of the popular will for its maintenance can be possible in a democracy."[24] The question as Lowell and others saw it was twofold. Would Americans willingly make the sacrifices needed for national self-preservation? And, echoing the fears of the Founders' generation, would such an effort lead to a more despotic form of government and society?

After the war most Americans outside the South answered "no" to the second question. Concern that nationalism and republican ideals might prove incompatible virtually disappeared. The joyful declaration that the United States had at last matured into a nation became a trope in sermons, editorials, and speeches throughout the North. "We believe that God Almighty is shaping a free and exalted civilized nation out of this republic," wrote one minister in 1864, welcoming the change. Three years later, when Massachusetts senator Charles Sumner asked a New York audience, "Are We a Nation?," the question was fast becoming rhetorical. As a former slave with an acute understanding of these issues, Frederick Douglass claimed that by advancing the "cause of human freedom," the war had indeed guaranteed the "final unity of the American nation."[25] The change even registered at the level of common speech. The country's name evolved from the plural (the United States *are*) to the singular (the United States *is*).

This transformation intensified belief in the sanctity of the nation. Americans desperately sought meaning in the deaths of more than half a million soldiers in the war. For the newly freed slaves and the former "free colored" population, such meaning was not hard to find, but for many Whites the problem seemed more complex. Amid social convulsions during and after the conflict, they struggled to establish a sense of continuity with the country's antebellum and colonial pasts. The claim that the war represented a triumph of the nation and the national ideal resonated deeply. As one political theorist has written, nationalism, like religious faith, is especially well suited to offer an "imaginative response" to human suffering, transforming "fatality into continuity, contingency into meaning"—a power that can glimpsed today in highly emotional responses to tombs of the unknown soldier constructed by many nation-states.[26]

From Virtuous Republic to Nation-State

President Lincoln understood this power. In his most powerful wartime speeches, the Gettysburg and Second Inaugural Addresses, he evoked ideas of *nation,* not union. The dead in battle gave their lives as part of the "unfinished work" of building the American nation, claimed the president. Their sacrifice lay inexorably in the path set by the Founding Fathers, who had merely created a new nation *conceived in liberty.* By making equality and liberty dependent on the political form of the nation-state, and by making American history the story of development toward that ideal form, Lincoln's rhetoric began to embrace the tenets of an influential philosophy that came to be called organic nationalism.

Elisha Mulford, a Connecticut-born Episcopal clergyman, best articulated organic nationalist thought in his 1870 book *The Nation: The Foundations of Civil Order and Political Life in the United States.* "I have sought, however imperfectly," he wrote in the preface, "to give expression to the thought of the people in the late war, and that conception of the nation, which they who were so worthy, held worth living and dying for." He began by explaining what the nation was *not* and specifically attacked Southern doctrines of state sovereignty. The nation did not result from a political agreement among the states, and thus secession, which was based on the compact doctrine, was indefensible. The nation was not a device secured to achieve certain ends, political or material, he claimed. It preceded the Constitution, springing organically from the people in their entirety. The American nation, not the citizens of the separate states, had fought and won the Revolutionary War, according to Mulford. As a "moral organism," the nation exercised a sovereignty whose supreme right was self-preservation. Statesmen who argued otherwise engaged in legal sophistry:

[The nation] is not a confused collection of separate atoms, as grains of sand in a heap. . . . It has the unity of an organism, not the aggregation of a mass; it is indivisible; its germ lies beyond analysis, and in it is enfolded its whole future. This unity is the postulate of the existence of a people as a nation, and the condition of its independence. An identity of structure also pervades the whole. Thus the defect of a part injures the whole; and if a part be severed it ceases to exist, as the limb which is cut from the body, or the branch from the tree.[27]

Mulford's idea of nation resembled the antebellum belief in absolute union, advanced by statesmen like Daniel Webster. Differences between them lay mostly in emphasis. Initial construction of a central state was a less important element of nationalism to Mulford than to Webster, and so Mulford did not dwell on the Constitution or the men who devised it. He argued that the development of the nation over time was also more critical than its origins, which lay "beyond analysis." Mulford, who had studied in Germany, framed his argument within the context of leading works by nineteenth-century European intellectuals. For example, his reliance on gradualism harked back to Charles Lyell, an English geologist whose studies of fossils led him to argue that the planet developed slowly over time according to scientific laws. The organic metaphors showed intellectual debts to Charles Darwin, who developed Lyell's theories further when he published his critical work on biological evolution, *On the Origin of Species,* in 1859.

Mulford also placed American history explicitly within the context of nationalist trends across the globe. America's past, like that of many European countries, had been characterized by progress upward toward the ideal form of nation, according to Mulford. The United States had certainly *not* declined from an ideal republic of the late eighteenth century, as many Founders and, later, textbooks authors like Willard had feared it might.

Two aspects of Mulford's thought proved especially relevant to the way history would now be written for schools. First, he saw the nation encompassing the whole "conscious life of the people," including "its literature and arts, its manners and laws," and its industry, religious faith, and education. Politics might be one manifestation of national life, but the nation arose from an entire culture. This claim called to mind those antebellum nationalizers who self-consciously tried to create and define a national culture but often looked mostly to political figures for inspiration. One had actually written an epic-style poem about Washington, because, well, full-fledged nations were *supposed* to have epic heroes. Mulford clearly had a broader definition of culture than some of these predecessors.

Second, because the nation evolved like a biological organism, its history was not merely a "succession of separate events and actions," which was the way Willard and her contemporaries had understood it. Human societies progressed from family to tribe on up to nation, or they faced extinction. According to Mulford, several forces retarded the advancement to full nationhood, and two of the most important were state sovereignty and slavery. Slipping into a hypothetical tone that might have seemed odd to some of his American readers, Mulford wrote of slavery that it "may be for the nation gradually to overcome it by ameliorating laws and institutions, or in some moment to meet it in direct conflict."[28] Either way, the natural antagonism between it and the nation would not cease. Thus the North had been doubly bound to defend the nation against those twin pillars of Confederate ideology.

Mulford offered a theoretically sophisticated but relatively straightforward interpretation of world history and, more particularly, the American experience. Once people understood that the nation was the goal of history, they would see that all of America's past, despite apparent randomness, had been tending toward the Civil War's final, conclusive battle at Appomattox.

When a new generation of historians examined history in the public schools through the lens of organic nationalism, they found it sadly wanting.[29] Francis Newton Thorpe, who taught political science at the University of Pennsylvania, attacked existing trade and school histories vehemently in his 1886 manifesto *In Justice to the Nation: American History in American Schools, Colleges, and Universities.* In language heavy with organicism, Thorpe argued that Americans had been awakened into national self-consciousness since 1865, when "our history assumed a character of its own." But a true account of America's past "had yet to be written." Existing studies were filled with "disconnected" facts, a "mere brief of elections, administrations, wars and victories." The problem lay in historians' neglect of American institutions, wrote Thorpe. To understand historical change, teachers and students had to look at long-term economic, legal, social, artistic, and educational organizations and patterns. These were the threads on which facts had to be strung to produce any useful sense of narrative order, according to Thorpe. Development, not the isolated battle or act of statecraft, constituted real history:

Our history is not in Congress alone; that is, indeed, a very small part of it. Our discoveries, our agrarian interests, our settlements westward, our educational affairs, the work of the church, the organization of charities, the growth of corporations, the conflict of races and for races, at times in our history, are all sources for research.[30]

Thorpe argued that the nation must be the "great theme" of American history. Antebellum nationalists, including textbook writers, had generally tried to depict the nation by either creating or manipulating existing cultural symbols, a man like Washington or an event like the battle with the British at Lexington, whose entry into the cultural lexicon and the memories of generations of children owes much to Emerson's 1836 poem ("And fired the shot heard round the world"). But where antebellum schoolbook authors found the essence of the nation in relatively static narrative elements—the valiant individual, the heroic deed—Thorpe's new writers would seek it in stable but ever-progressing institutions. These new historians would have an easier time than chroniclers before the Civil War. By 1890 permanent institutions had had significantly more time to develop, so there was more to study. And the most divisive institution, slavery, had finally been swept away. With it went much of the need to maintain the delicate narrative balance between elements of Southern life (slavery, states' rights, and agrarianism) and those of the North (free soil, free labor, industrialism, and the central state). Emma Willard's futile attempts to straddle the line between free-soiler and apologist for slavery could be abandoned. When historians at the end of the nineteenth century discussed the common beliefs and practices that made Americans a distinct people or nation, that culture was mostly Northern in character.

Eleven years after Thorpe penned *In Justice to the Nation,* a historian at Syracuse University explained how this new institution-based approach could revitalize history teaching. In *Method in History for Teachers and Students,* William H. Mace explained that America's past could be divided into three great phases of nation-building. In the first, which extended from the colonial era to the end of the Revolutionary War, Americans made initial progress toward their own nationality. But the national sentiment that arose after the Constitutional Convention of 1787, which began the second phase, had a fundamental flaw, according to Mace. Early nationalists followed the lead of Alexander Hamilton, who championed economic and political centralization through a national bank and federal assumption of the states' war debts. For them, a central government existed to promote business growth, not to carry out the will of the great mass of people, whom Hamilton and others in the Federalist Party mistrusted. In Mace's formulation, many early nationalists had opposed real democracy. Supporters of the common man, like Jefferson, had sought to restrain federal power.

As this second phase in American history progressed, however, principles of nationalism and democracy steadily coalesced. When suffrage expanded to all White males regardless of wealth, both the mass of voters and leaders of the parties discovered that a strong central government did not threaten individual liberties but, in fact, strengthened them. The movement climaxed around 1830 when a man of the people and ardent nationalist, Andrew Jackson, won the presidency. Liberty and union now operated in harmony. The "central principle" of history, argued Mace, is the growth of institutional life, and in these two stages of American history that growth shifted from the local to the national. The great exception to the rule, particularly after 1832, was the South. It resisted central power, popular rule, and free labor as the engine of economic progress. Slavery was antithetical to the national spirit, according to Mace, and could never enter into a dialectical relationship with it as "democracy" had done. Friends of the "peculiar institution" pushed gag bills in Congress, showing they cared little for free speech when it threatened their interests. Conflict over slavery had even "de-nationalized" churches into Northern and Southern branches. The next great phase in American history had to end with either the destruction of slavery or the disintegration of the nation, argued Mace. Union victory, of course, saved the nation and guaranteed the continuity of its political, economic, and social institutions.

Mace did not so much create this new narrative as distill it from recent historical work.[31] Herbert Baxter Adams, a professor at Johns Hopkins University, had begun the move to institution-based history in his graduate seminars in the late 1870s. Responding to the postwar spirit of nationalism, many in the first generation of professional historians (those with a university appointment and/or a doctorate in history) chose to study and teach American history. By the mid-1890s many of the narrative elements of American history that Mace promoted had already appeared in school histories by the professionals, who now supplemented their teaching salaries by writing for younger audiences. Their ranks included Alexander Johnston, John Fiske, Edward Channing, and John Bach McMaster, who worked closely with Thorpe at the University of Pennsylvania. Mace finished his own textbook in 1901.

Their new approach to American history offered several advantages. In an earlier textbook by Willard or Goodrich, what narrative climax there was came with victory in the Revolution or adoption of the Constitution. After 1789 there wasn't much historical progress to cover. That was part of the reason why later chapters sometimes ended up as a tally of elections and a year-by-year outline of events. But the newer history moved the culminating act of national creation from 1776 or 1789 to 1865. It now took three-quarters of a century to bring the ideals of the Founders to fruition.

In the new narrative, the roles of those Founders and other virtuous heroes like Christopher Columbus and William Penn also changed. As institutions moved toward the forefront of American history, individuals receded. The United States and its republican principles had withstood the test of Civil War. Individual virtue, while still important, was no longer the linchpin of national survival. The "subsoil of terror" that underlay historical discourse before 1861 was gone. Within limits, children might even be introduced to "objective" or scientific history that offered a more honest look at important historical figures. A question in John Fiske's *History of the United States,* from 1894, signaled the change:

> Is the George Washington of our thought to-day like the real Washington of the Revolution? What things do we leave out of our Washington that belonged to the real one? Is the Benedict Arnold of our thought to-day like the real Arnold? If not, what is the difference? . . . May not events as well as men become different in popular thought from what they really were? If so, give illustrations.[32]

This invitation to disentangle pleasing fiction from historical fact was heady stuff for Americans raised on the story of the cherry tree. And in time it would produce a backlash against historians and a call for a return to orthodoxy. But the Civil War had made a more critical look at national heroes necessary. Recall Emma Willard's discomfort in explaining how the Founders tolerated the "evil" of slavery. Once the nation had condemned human bondage unequivocally by law, that former tolerance of the institution had to be addressed. Mace fretted that a student would "find it difficult to reconcile Washington's love of liberty, and his sacrifices for it, with his owning slaves."[33] The same held true for Jefferson, Jackson, Patrick Henry—the slave owner who declared, "Give me liberty or give me death"—along with a host of other figures. Even New Englander and nationalist Daniel Webster had condemned abolitionism for threatening the ideal of union in his famous "Seventh of March" speech in support of the Compromise of 1850. A student had to be warned against projecting current moral standards onto the past, said Mace, and "trying men in the light of his own times." But moral contradictions could not be ignored, at least for older children. The great alleged value of history, which had remained more or less constant since the days of Noah Webster and Benjamin Rush, was that it stimulated love of country. Students' recognition of hypocrisy would lead to disillusionment, undermining patriotism. Better to have teachers and textbooks emphasize the flawless nature of these men's ideals and let students develop some understanding of their more imperfect characters. Jefferson really *did* believe all men were created equal, students should conclude, even though he kept slaves.

This new scientific approach to history, which stressed the desirability of individual interpretation and judgment based on historical evidence, received the guarded endorsement of professional educators. When a panel of historians that included future president Woodrow Wilson drafted an influential curriculum plan for the National Education Association in 1892, they heartily approved of the trend toward critical thinking in the precollegiate classroom. But the authors of the so-called Committee of Ten Report also thought history should still serve as a moral instructor, as it had in the days of Goodrich and Willard. Historian Lucy M. Salmon, who served on a similar committee a few years later, declared that the "ultimate object of history, as of all sciences, is the search for truth, and . . . that search entails the responsibility of abiding by the results when found." Yet she added that when discussing national heroes with young people, one had to avoid presenting "blemishes the world has gladly forgiven and forgotten for the sake of a great work accomplished and a noble life lived."[34]

Despite the misgivings it inspired, the plan to give young people at least some indication of the faults of earlier Americans did allow history writers to underscore the theme of progress that underlay the narrative of national development. The United States had progressed politically and morally by expanding the right to vote and then abolishing slavery. It had extended the benefits of knowledge by introducing the New England system of common schools (a much discussed "institution") in the South and West. Americans had reformed formerly "dreadful" prisons and abandoned outmoded practices like imprisoning debtors and branding criminals. The early years of the republic had been a golden age in the eyes of text writers like Emma Willard. But during that same era, countered John McMaster in his *School History of the United States,* the "humane spirit of our times was largely wanting."[35]

In this new history, increased wealth and rising standards of living for all Americans joined moral and social advances, particularly now that the country had unshackled itself from the inefficient system of slave labor. Comparisons between the relatively backward conditions of 1790 and those at the time of writing became a cliché in texts. In McMaster's book, a faintly comic Washington wandered through the late nineteenth century like Rip Van Winkle. The account of Washington's journey, prefaced with descriptions of Northeastern cities in the early years after the Revolution, reads almost like poetry:

> And how different these cities were from those of our day! What a strange world Washington would find himself in if he could come back and walk along the streets of the great city which now stands on the banks of the Potomac and bears his name! He never in his life saw a flagstone sidewalk, nor an asphalted street, nor a pane of glass six feet square. He never heard a factory whistle; he never saw a building ten stories high, nor an elevator, nor a gas jet, nor an electric light; he never saw a hot-air furnace, nor entered a room warmed by steam.
>
> In the windows of shop after shop would be articles familiar to us, but so unknown to him that he could not even name them. . . . Fancy him trying to understand the advertisements that would meet his eye as he took his seat [on a streetcar]! Fancy him staring from the window at a fence bright with theatrical posters, or at a man rushing by on a bicycle![36]

In these new histories, technology was not just something to marvel at or an end for its own sake. Rather, it helped to bind up the nation's wounds in the aftermath of the Civil War and Reconstruction. John Fiske declared that the inventor of the railroad "ought to be ranked among the chief builders" of the United States. "How snug and compact they make this country, and how much easier to govern!" The speed of trains settled the qualms of earlier Americans who had wondered if a republic could be sustained over continental distances. What's more, railroads tended to rub off local prejudices and "enlarge people's minds" through the frequent and easy contact they afforded.[37] It was the breakdown in that sort of communication that had contributed to the outbreak of the Civil War, text writers had maintained since 1865 (partly to avoid the deeper issue of slavery). The professional historians agreed. And feats of technology like the steam locomotive, they claimed, then knit the sections back together. Other nineteenth-century inventions, from the screw propeller to the telegraph and telephone, also helped to make a more perfect union.

Industrial products and the factories that manufactured them became critical new elements of national myth, a means of speaking of Americans as a single, unique people, as the passage from McMaster suggests. Stories of the "New South" that emerged from Reconstruction, for instance, always noted the region's economic expansion and its growing similarity to the industrial North. When educators at the end of the century spoke about the need for history to embrace the "whole life of the people," they often conceived of American citizens as industrial consumers. Historians discussed American literature, education, religion, and other social topics more completely than their antebellum predecessors had. But the theme of breathless progress that began to dominate their texts fit best with institutions like the factory system, scientific agriculture, and central banking. Along with the political heritage of the Founders, these institutions became the sinews of the nation.[38]

The tone of the this new history was considerably less personal than that found in earlier books. Channing advised readers of his *Students' History of the United States* that they "must learn to view history as the resultant of countless forces, which finds its completeness only in so far as the manifoldness of these forces is recognized." In his dense prose, a patina of scientific rationalism often obscured the importance of the individual and moral choice in advancing history. In a world where "forces" directed institutional change, there was little need for the stories and parables that formed the core of many antebellum textbooks. When Channing proposed this history to his publisher, he wrote that he "had in mind . . . giving 'real history' and not Indian fights and folklore." In the preface to the finished work, he wrote that the "elucidation" of the more important problems of institutional change had "made it necessary to omit much interesting historical material," including "details of military history, descriptions of colonial life," and "anecdotes of the heroes of colonial days."[39] Take these elements from Willard's books, and there would be little left.

This fresh look at the national past had both a forward-looking, modernist surface appearance and a socially conservative undercurrent. Emphasis on relating the story of a people as a whole allowed educators to begin moving beyond history as the account of great men. Writers at the close of the nineteenth century also encouraged students to think critically, at least to a point. These textbooks cultivated more individual interpretation and less memorization of facts and precepts than earlier tomes had. But the heavy-handed moralism of the old textbooks had nevertheless revealed their authors' belief that students would grow up to become critical historical actors. "Nothing but virtue and the continued blessing of heaven can save us, as a people, from the corruption and ruin which have been the unhappy termination of former republics," intoned one author in the 1830s. Another writing almost fifty years later still warned her readers in the same spirit: "Children of the common schools! In thirty years the great republic will be in your hands to wreck or to save and carry forward to a greatness and glory beyond what even your fathers planned." For these earlier amateurs, individual virtue counted because it determined America's destiny. But the nation-state of professional historians was more solid than the republic, and its institutional foundations reached deep into the past. Individuals were not irrelevant, but larger forces and movements often dwarfed them. Children of the working class who attended grammar schools and even some high schools in increasing numbers at century's end had to understand their proper place in the scheme of things.[40]

The problem with colorful stories of past heroes, argued Alexander Johnston of Princeton, was that the "mass of pupils" had little chance to emulate a John Smith or Pilgrim Father in contemporary, industrial America. They needed "to learn from history the simple and homely duties of good citizenship."[41] Good citizenship now increasingly meant not only loyalty to the elected government but allegiance to the various economic and social institutions that had grown up alongside it. In the hands of many of these writers, history had led rather inevitably to the wonderful world of the present, so radical tampering with current political or economic relations seemed unnecessary and perhaps unwise. Not coincidentally, the new history tended to buttress the social position of historians themselves. White, middle-class, and Protestant men dominated the profession, and they legitimated their authority by joining national organizations like the American Historical Association, founded in 1884, and by distributing doctoral degrees through a network of elite colleges and universities.

One could easily exaggerate the extent of change in textbook renderings of the national story between the 1830s and the early 1900s. Not all professional historians had Johnston's patronizing attitude regarding the "mass of pupils" then attending public schools. Charles and Mary Beard, for instance, were political progressives who championed the cause of the poor and the working class in their professional writing and, to an extent, in their textbooks, which were popular for much of the first half of the twentieth century. Amateur historians also continued to write some widely used books for classroom use. Colorful and "unscientific" anecdotes still found a place in many histories, particularly those designed for students in elementary schools. The conviction that stories of revered historical figures could provide ethical training for young people weakened somewhat but never disappeared. Nonetheless, the change was still dramatic. A student who had pored over a textbook in the 1840s would have been startled with the histories her grandchildren brought home in 1910. The books would be physically larger, their extra heft due in part to a need to explain the passage of another sixty years. Inside, the very subject of the text would be transformed. The United States would no longer appear as an agrarian republic. The share of space devoted to national heroes, war, and isolated acts of selfless patriotism would be considerably smaller. The need to create such a body of myth to confront fears of republican decline and the threat of national disintegration over the issue of slavery had passed, a fact this elderly woman reading over her grandchild's shoulder would grasp intuitively. The new nation would find its embodiment less in individuals and more in impersonal, and particularly economic, institutions. Writers would express newfound confidence in national cohesion borne of civil war. The new nation would exhibit continuity across space, as the South was returned to the fold on Northern terms, and across time, as historians replaced weakly connected facts and stories with discussions of historical cause and effect and long-term development. National history would be the story of a solid community advancing steadily through the passing decades.[42]

A precarious union of semi-sovereign republics would be reimagined as a modern nation-state.

2. Negotiating a National Past

Statewide Textbook Adoption and the Legacy of the Civil War

It would be difficult to find two schoolbook authors more unlike each other than Alexander H. Stephens and Thomas Wentworth Higginson. Stephens was born near Crawfordsville, Georgia, in 1812. Despite frail health that would trouble him throughout life, he worked his way through college and into Congress, where he fought vigorously for the interests of Southern slaveholders. He was generally a moderate on sectional issues. Nevertheless, he once suggested reopening the Atlantic slave trade to help ensure that forced instead of free labor would dominate much of the new territory in the West, thereby shoring up the waning influence of supporters of that peculiar institution in Washington. In 1861 he overcame his misgivings about secession and assumed the office of vice president of the Confederate States of America (C.S.A). While others in the new government attempted to justify the breakaway from the North with talk of states' rights and the resurrection of the Founders' ideals, Stephens bluntly outlined the C.S.A.'s raison d'être in his "cornerstone" speech in March. The Confederacy, he told his Georgia audience, had repudiated those statesmen of the Revolutionary era who had believed that slavery violated the laws of nature and must eventually be eliminated. Those old ideas

were fundamentally wrong. They rested on the assumption of equality of races. This was an error. . . . Our new government is founded upon exactly the opposite idea; its foundations are laid, its cornerstone rests upon the great truth, that the negro is not equal to the white man; that slavery—subordination to the superior race—is his natural and normal condition.[1]

52

Negotiating a National Past

A few months after the Confederate vice president's address, a young White colonel in Massachusetts took command of the Union's first African-American regiment. Thomas Wentworth Higginson was a Yankee of the Yankees, descendant of the first minister in the Massachusetts Bay Colony, graduate of Harvard, and ardent abolitionist. Where Stephens was physically small, usually weighing under one hundred pounds, and plagued by arthritis, colitis, and other ailments, Higginson was tall and robust. He had once helped to batter down a courthouse door in a successful effort to free a fugitive slave, receiving a severe cut on the chin from local police during the mêlée. Initially a disunionist eager to end Northern complicity with slavery, Higginson embraced the nationalism sparked by the war, particularly as it began to align the Union's cause with abolition.[2]

Both men survived the four-year conflict. Stephens endured a brief imprisonment for his role in the Confederate government, while Higginson spent much of 1864 and 1865 recuperating from a battle wound and aftereffects of a bout with malaria he had contracted on maneuvers in Florida. In the early 1870s each man decided to write a history of the United States for schools. They sought to show a generation with few, if any, personal recollections of the Civil War how that great clash fit into the larger sweep of American history. Not surprisingly, their visions differed.

Stephens saw the War Between the States—a phrase implying the clash of sovereign political entities and not of a politically divided but essentially single people—as tragic and probably avoidable. The North, increasingly under the sway of a small but vocal minority of abolitionist "agitators," had abandoned its obligations under the Constitution and federal law. In Stephens's version of events, South Carolina had rightly feared the centralizing despotism of the North when it exercised its legal right to secede after Abraham Lincoln's election. The rest of the Lower South and much of the Upper South properly followed that state's lead. But then agitators were able to use the fall of Fort Sumter to "inflame the minds of the people of the Northern States," which led to the "most lamentable as well as the greatest of modern wars." Perhaps forgetting the sentiments in his own speech of 1861, Stephens characterized the Confederates as the true heirs of the Founders, with a constitution "based upon all the essential principles of the Federal Compact of 1787." Lincoln, in contrast, had trampled over the law by raising federal troops without authority and imprisoning suspected Confederate sympathizers without charge, according to Stephens's textbook. About the slaves,

J. W. Higginson

Col, 1ˢᵗ S. C. Vols.

Alexander H. Stephens, vice president of the Confederate States of America, and Thomas Wentworth Higginson, commander of the first Union regiment of "colored troops," in images dating from the Civil War. Within a decade after the conflict ended, both men would publish textbooks in U.S. history. *Alexander Stephens portrait courtesy of the Library of Congress. Thomas Wentworth Higginson portrait reproduced from Thomas Wentworth Higginson,* Army Life in a Black Regiment *(Boston: Houghton, Mifflin and Company, 1900).*

whose cause lay somewhere near the heart of the war, the author had almost nothing to say.[3]

Virtually all his peers in the history-writing trade ended their books with a salutary assessment of present-day America and hopeful predictions for the future, but the former vice president closed his with a note of grim foreboding. The ongoing plan of Republican Reconstruction and the enfranchisement of the ex-slaves, he wrote, had inaugurated a new war upon the Constitution. President Ulysses S. Grant was falling into the trap of his party's program of tyranny, with its consolidation of power in the capital and the "destruction of the reserved rights of local self government." Using the Roman Empire as a precedent, Stephens warned darkly that unless voters reversed current trends the "entire overthrow of the Federal system, and the subversion of all the free institutions attempted to be secured on the American Continent," would follow.[4]

Higginson drew just the opposite lesson from the Civil War. Robert E. Lee's surrender at Appomattox Courthouse had established that the United States was at last a worthy, indivisible nation, not a mere alliance of states. Repentant White Southerners might be forgiven for espousing the doctrine of states' rights, Higginson told his young readers, but equal honor could never be paid to "mistaken men." As far as their object was to retain possession of their slaves, no excuse could be made for them. The villains in Stephens's book were the heroes of the *Young Folks' History of the United States.* John Brown, whom the author knew personally (he had been privy to plans for the raid on Harpers Ferry), received praise for his "courage, fortitude, and simple ingenuousness." Instead of being mere objects of history, as they were with Stephens, slaves and free people of color played active roles in Higginson's textbook. Crispus Attucks, a free man of mixed race, was the first American to die for the Revolutionary cause in the Boston Massacre of 1770. A century later "colored troops" fought bravely for the freedom of their compatriots in the South. More than almost any other author of school histories in the nineteenth century, Higginson envisioned the nation created by the Civil War not merely as one based on the supremacy of the central government over the states but as one embracing African-Americans as integral parts of the national community.[5]

Publication and widespread use of textbooks whose content diverged as starkly as Stephens's and Higginson's did not bode well for educational nationalists who since the late eighteenth century had dreamed of schools that would "render the mass of people more homogeneous" and expected history instruction to play a central role in creating a unified patriotism.[6] Neo-Confederate textbooks like Stephens's also complicated the simple truism that victors write history for the vanquished. By war's end, prominent thinkers in both the North and South recognized that the long-term meaning of the Civil War might lie as much in the history books as on the battlefields. Groups of Southern Whites led by the United Confederate Veterans soon began an effort to control presentation of the past to young people by taking their case directly to textbook publishers and teachers. The organization of Union veterans, the Grand Army of the Republic, undertook a similar campaign in the North.

At the heart of this dispute lay the question of what sort of nation the Civil War had created. At one extreme were "unreconstructed" White Southerners like Stephens, who saw the war as a historical aberration and longed for a return to the status quo *ante bellum,* the abolition of slavery excepted. To them the nation was a sacred trust handed down by the Founders. Nostalgia governed their historical vision, and they advocated a quick reconciliation of North and South. At the other extreme were "radical" Republicans who maintained that the war had marked the end of an unworkable balance of power between the Washington government and the states and had initiated the era of an activist central state committed to extending liberty to all the nation's citizens.[7] Frederick Douglass, one of the greatest advocates of equal rights for his fellow African-Americans, challenged the country to remember the Civil War with awe. He hoped that the Union's cause, emancipation, and the postwar Constitutional amendments guaranteeing citizenship to the freedmen would be bound inextricably together in a collective memory of the war as *the* critical moment of American regeneration. He feared a sentimental union of Whites across the sections and a "generous forgetfulness" that would celebrate martial heroism on both sides but gloss over the distinction between "those who fought for liberty and those who fought for slavery; between those who fought to save the Republic and those who fought to destroy it." By 1871 Douglass was already condemning Southern history textbooks that he saw washing away that meaning for future generations of Americans.[8]

The new battle for memory had been joined, and it would grow in intensity, reaching a peak in the 1890s and subsiding slowly over the next two decades. It would bring together (and drive apart) historians and publishers with varied political leanings, veterans seeking respect for their wartime sacrifice, educational reformers who sought to put textbook selection in the hands of "experts," and Southern politicians and opinion leaders who saw in history a way to justify the erection of Jim Crow. Eventually the antagonistic narratives best embodied in the works of Alexander Stephens and Thomas Wentworth Higginson would largely converge. And the search for maximum profit, as much as political passion or the waning of sectional antagonisms, would determine the content of that consensus narrative.

Calls in the South for education loyal to regional institutions and ideas predate the Civil War. In the first decades of the nineteenth century, for example, Thomas Jefferson expressed anxieties about large numbers of Southern youth who received their education at Northern colleges and universities. But a significant movement to produce textbooks specifically for the South did not emerge until the 1840s as disputes over the extension of slavery in the territories crystallized political and cultural differences between Northern and Southern states. Writers for the influential *DeBow's Review,* most prominently its editor, James DeBow, called for a "war against Abolition teachers and Anti-Slavery Text Books," claiming that the South had been deluged with both. They argued that the content of popular textbooks exhibited a peculiar bias against the region, one that over time might threaten social peace. Histories, DeBow said, were "filled with praise and glorification of the first settlers of New-England and Northern States generally," along with their abolition-minded progeny. Textbooks depicted individuals who settled in the South as "a race of immoral reprobates, who have handed down all their vices and evil habits to their descendants of this day." He singled out a school history by Marcius Willson on this second count and censured a widely popular text by Samuel G. Goodrich (under the pseudonym Peter Parley), the *Pictorial History of the United States,* for its attack on the morality of slavery.[9]

DeBow blamed three groups for this state of affairs. First were the abolitionists, the source of hatred for slavery and the Southern way of life that depended upon it. Second were educators and parents in the South who were only too willing to use "incendiary" textbooks, despite the danger their propaganda presented to the plastic minds of children. Earning DeBow's harshest criticism were the Northern publishers who printed whatever they thought would sell. "The brains of boys and girls are regarded as a California placer," he wrote soon after the 1849 Gold Rush began, "to be dug, washed out, and sifted, for the benefit of *pri-*

vate interest, and no more labor is given to a book than will carry it out into common use, by the means of the usages of trade."[10]

DeBow, who had considerable experience in the publishing industry, knew that antislavery zealots actually had little control over textbook content. Most authors wrote schoolbooks to offend the least number of book buyers possible. So while a few writers might condemn the horrors of seventeenth-century slave ships, they were usually silent or circumspect on the practice of slavery in the United States. In the 1858 edition of her best-selling American history, New Englander Emma Willard, as we have seen, even offered a meek defense of the institution as beneficial for slaves. Publishers hardly dismissed the importance of the South in calculating potential sales. They put Southern imprints on their books to curry favor in the region, a practice DeBow criticized. And on the same pages of the *Review* where DeBow savaged the industry, a leading New York publisher, A. S. Barnes, advertised its "School Books by Southern Authors." Below these titles readers would have seen listed Barnes's National Series of Standard School Books, which included readers, spellers, geographies, grammars, math books, and Willard's history. The latter texts, read the advertising copy, were "prepared by the most thorough educators, and with special reference to their adaptation to the youth of the land, in all parts of the Union."[11] The company thus shrewdly played both to sectional patriotism and to the desire among Southerners to read the same books and magazines as their Northern peers.

DeBow's rhetoric about textbooks waving the "black piratical ensign of Abolitionism" and corrupting the minds of White children in the South was mostly that—rhetoric. In a bid to galvanize his readers, he took quotes out of context and grossly exaggerated the frequency of attacks on slavery. His real fear was the long-term influence of books produced for a mass audience that was shifting demographically northward throughout the first half of the nineteenth century. The power of these books and the de facto national curriculum they represented, he surmised, might undermine the unique quality of life in the South and maybe, eventually, even threaten its system of labor. Therefore, DeBow argued that state governments and owners of capital in the South should encourage the development of a sectional textbook industry.

Others joined the chorus for schoolbooks true to the region, including the *Southern Quarterly Review* and the *Southern Literary Messenger*. Southern Methodists called for adapting school materials to the "circumstances of the South." Business leaders meeting at the 1856 Southern Commercial Convention set up a committee to look into the issue and requested that the Louisiana legislature appropriate one thousand dollars to encourage the publication of suitable texts. A relative of South Carolina senator John Calhoun even founded the Southern Literary Company to print such books and "render the South independent of Northern fanatics."[12]

The crusade had some successes. Publishers did revise books. Two Southern-oriented student histories appeared: John Bonner's *A Child's History of the United States* in 1855 and B. R. Carroll's *Catechism of United States History* in 1856. But for the most part the quest to produce textbooks in the South failed during the antebellum era. The movement encountered numerous obstacles. There were almost no preexisting publishers in the region that could begin a line of schoolbooks. Even DeBow had to get his *Review* printed in New York. Capital was tied up in land and slaves, and investors with money to spend found little financial incentive to place it in risky publishing ventures. Even if a firm were able to produce books of suitable quality to rival Northern competitors, the South had limited means to transport them. Extensive rail lines centered in Northern cities made New York, Boston, and Philadelphia ideal distribution centers, and only Baltimore could begin to compete with them. But the problems did not stop there. With the possible exception of North Carolina, states south of the Mason-Dixon Line had extremely limited public education systems. Elite planter families who sent their children to private academies were often comfortable using Northern textbooks or patronizing Northern schools and colleges. Without broad-based schooling and a significant level of sectional consciousness across class lines, the drive for Southern books could not gain much momentum.

Ironically, it was Reconstruction, which Southern texts would later depict as the grimmest chapter in American history, that helped to make their widespread use possible. Republican-led state governments firmly established public schools and the principle of direct taxation to support them, despite opposition from landowners and others who claimed such schools were luxuries and tools of Northern invaders. Even as political power passed to Democratic governments, no Southern state seriously considered dismantling its school system. Between 1871 and 1890 the percentage of the Southern population enrolled in public schools nearly doubled, with the greatest gains in the earlier, Republican years.[13] Growing numbers of students began to make it more feasible for publishers to target books to a specifically Southern audience.

At the same time Republicans were establishing schools, Reconstruction also introduced a political ideology that conservative Whites found alien and threatening. In the North, the Civil War had inspired a new nationalism based on universal membership, political equality, and the supremacy of the federal government. For influential political theorists like Elisha Mulford, healthy societies progressed naturally toward the ideal form of a consolidated nation-state. In *The Nation: The Foundations of Civil Order and Political Life in the United States,* Mulford claimed that because the nation exists as an organic being, it justly regards "all division as a sundering of life." One divisive force that had threatened the nation, secession, was now dead. With it, in this formulation, perished the argument that the states could serve as a bulwark of individual rights against a potentially despotic central government, a Southern creed since Jefferson's time.[14]

Mulford believed, however, that one of the great dangers to the nation that had survived the Civil War was racial division. A true nation exists, he wrote, as a fraternity of equals in which there is "no difference of wealth, or race, or physical condition, that can be made the ground of inclusion or exclusion from it." Slavery made a mockery of that ideal and had been justly destroyed. But a society free of slavery that could embrace certain races only as inferiors was not a nation at all. Mulford did not quite repudiate the dominant racialism of his time—some racial groups, he acknowledged, might well exhibit certain properties distinct from others—but members of all of them shared the duties and rights of citizens. Wrote Mulford:

> It [a nation] has no longer a moral foundation, nor a universal end when it asserts as its grounds the rights of a race, and not the rights of man; and the government which no longer recognizes justice as necessary, nor subsists in the sovereignty of the people in a moral organism, but is in identity with a race, is the sign of an extirpating civilization.[15]

Republicans, who dominated Congress in the 1860s and 1870s, struggled to capitalize on postwar patriotism and translate this inclusive theory into law, most notably in the Fourteenth and Fifteenth Amendments, making male ex-slaves citizens of the United States and securing their right to vote. They tied the liberty of the freedmen to the cause of national union for which so many Northerners had died. In his 1867 address to New York Republicans entitled "Are We a Nation?" Charles Sumner attacked the "preposterous pretension" that skin or hair color should determine eligibility to vote. "And now that the Rebellion has been crushed, it re-appears in still another form, by insisting that each State at its own will may disregard the universal rights of the citizen," intoned the Massachusetts senator. "Here again do State Rights, in their anarchical egotism, interfere with National Unity." Sumner and other Republicans went further. They argued that the ideal of national unity, and implicitly political equality without regard to race, had been the ideal of most of the Founders, even slaveholders like Washington.[16] Thus, they said, the nationalism of the 1860s and 1870s was not really new or radical at all.

Whether motivated by genuine dedication to human rights or a more self-serving desire to bolster party strength, the commitment of most Republicans to racial inclusiveness was real. They were willing to use force to make that vision a reality, by sending federal troops to quell Ku Klux Klan uprisings, for instance. But they also looked to less coercive measures, including public education. House member and later senator George Boutwell argued that the theory of human equality, the new basis of the national government and chief safeguard of republican institutions, could be best inculcated in schools. In 1867 Congress established the Federal Bureau of Education, a politically weak agency but one that showed that politicians were beginning to think of schooling in national terms. President Ulysses S. Grant called for a constitutional amendment requiring states to maintain free schools, and during the 1870s the House passed several measures to establish a national education system.[17]

Most alarming to Southern conservatives were proposals to promote these ideals through racially integrated education. Republicans attached provisions for mixed schools in amnesty bills for ex-Confederates, and Charles Sumner pushed hard for an antisegregation clause in the Civil Rights Act of 1875. Similar measures appeared in proposals for federal funding of education through the 1880s. Leading Southern politicians claimed that efforts to integrate races in the classroom would lead to the horror of miscegenation, but some, including ex-Confederate general P. G. T. Beauregard, supported them.[18]

The revolutionary potential of this new nationalism, and especially its manifestation in Southern public schools, set the context for a renewed call for conservative textbooks true to the South. Slavery was gone forever. The hope that schools might shore up the peculiar instiution, which Debow and others had expressed before 1861, had died. But if historians could construct a usable past that absolved the South of guilt in the war and showed the wisdom of Confederate policies, they might yet gain the ideological upper hand over Republican radicals in the North and their allies in the South. In 1869 ex-Confederates established the Southern Historical Society to explain to the rest of the nation, as one former C.S.A. senator put it, "the great principles for which we struggled."[19]

That goal also guided several writers who produced textbooks for the South during the years of Congressional Reconstruction from 1867 to 1877. They included elder statesman Alexander Stephens, as well as two Southern school principals, John S. Blackburn and William N. McDonald, coauthors in 1869 of *A Southern School History of the United States*. Joseph T. Derry, a Georgia teacher who wrote a catechism-style American history six years later, also hoped to use history to undermine Republican influence in the region. Looking over more than a dozen textbooks popular in the North during this period, one Southern editor claimed that their "grand moral" was "that the people of the North alone are fit to rule, while the people of the South deserve only to be ruled by them."[20] The Southern authors of these new histories tried to show that the South, by which they meant the White South, knew best how to manage its own affairs.

A few key characteristics set these books apart from their counterparts in the North. First, they departed from the narrative centered closely on New England that most writers had adopted from popular trade histories by George Bancroft and others earlier in the century. Southern authors featured more Southern colonial and antebellum history and tried to counter disparaging comments about the region that appeared in a few of the Northern histories. Virginia, in particular, boasted a large share of Revolutionary heroes in these new volumes, and the Old Dominion served as the true birthplace of America's free institutions and a "worthy Mother of States and Statesmen."[21] The Puritans of New England, in contrast, were criticized for religious intolerance, cruelty, and narrow-mindedness. Likewise, the Puritans' nineteenth-century descendants came under fire for hypocrisy, as they condemned the institution by which their slave-trading forefathers had nicely profited. These Southern writers thus tried to undermine claims of Northern moral and cultural superiority they found in popular texts.

Stephens and his peers seemed to recognize, however, that direct attacks on people in the North, with the exception of abolitionists, looked petty. Instead, they based most of their critique of Reconstruction on a historical defense of state sovereignty and secession. Stephens established that position by devoting more space to the Constitutional Convention than any other school history of the period. Rebutting contemporary arguments by Sumner and other nationalists, Stephens claimed that the Founders had considered and then soundly rejected the idea of establishing a consolidated, or "national," government striking the very word from the final document. "All held it to be a limited Government clothed only with specific powers conferred by delegation by the States," wrote Stephens.[22] When that government overstepped its bounds, the states were free to ignore or resist its laws. That was the rationale behind the Virginia and Kentucky resolutions, drafted by Thomas Jefferson and James Madison in response to the Alien and Sedition Laws passed under the administration of President John Adams. Stephens gave these nonbinding resolutions, which had been rendered moot by the Civil War, a hallowed place next to the Constitution in the appendix to his history.

Stephens and like-minded Southern politicians in the first years after the war argued that the United States was the creation of a legal compact, not, as theorists like Elisha Mulford claimed, a nation that transcended its legal framework. The Constitution, as written and understood in the 1780s, was sacrosanct to Stephens. Its division of power between the states and the central government

> presented the most perfect model of a "Confederated Republic," as Washington styled it, ever before established by the wisdom of men. Its new features and striking peculiarities were without example or a parallel in the annals of History. Its wonderful and matchless framework . . . has attracted the attention and excited the admiration of men of the greatest learning and highest statesmanship throughout the civilized world.[23]

And that "most perfect" Constitution recognized slavery as an institution under the jurisdiction of the states, claimed Stephens and the other Southern textbook writers. Abolitionists, not slaveholders, threatened domestic tranquility, according to this narrative. In Derry's history, for instance, Benjamin Franklin's petition urging Congress to take steps to abolish slavery "excited the alarm of all true friends of the federal system."[24] In arguing that the federal government's survival at the end of the eighteenth century depended on the general acceptance of the institution, these Southern books were more intellectually honest than many Northern textbooks, which tried to dodge the issue. But the

Southern texts grew less accurate as they charted or, more accurately, ignored the country's shifting attitudes toward the practice. Southern writers often seemed perplexed that so "settled" an issue as slavery could have repeatedly threatened the country. Abolitionists remained a tiny, fanatical minority in their books, while statesmen and sectional compromisers like Henry Clay, "laboring always for the good of the entire country," received overwhelming support from all the states.[25] This confusion arose in part because of the books' relatively narrow focus on politics. Blackburn and McDonald made some effort to see slavery as a moral and social question that could divide the country, but Stephens and Derry treated it as a straightforward legal issue. Stephens referred to escaped slaves euphemistically as "fugitives from service." He never mentioned Nat Turner and the slave revolt he led that had terrified White Southerners in 1831 or discussed Harriet Beecher Stowe, whose emotional appeals to readers of *Uncle Tom's Cabin* invigorated the antislavery cause twenty years later.

These Southern writers failed to consider how a majority of Northerners who did not become abolitionists nevertheless found slavery increasingly incompatible with Christian morality and the republican destiny of the country and so sympathized with the cause of their more radical peers. Readers of Stephens's book and the other histories simply saw repeated instances of lawlessness on the part of a small, criminally inclined group of New Englanders who were, inexplicably, opposed to the Southern way of life. These agitators introduced illegal bills for abolition into Congress; refused to abide by the Compromise of 1850, with its "efficient mode for the reclamation and rendition" of fugitive slaves; and aided John Brown's attack at Harpers Ferry.[26] Within the narrow perspective afforded by these books, the decision of the Southern states to secede, a legal option they said the Founders recognized and that many contemporary thinkers in the North supported, made perfect sense.

Just as reasonable was the desire of Southerners after 1865 to return to the peaceful state of affairs preceding the war, especially now that they had made the enormous concession of ending slavery. The postwar amendments had been "carried through by force and usurpation," Derry told his readers. "It is sincerely to be hoped that the people of the North and the South will ere long forget the strife and bitterness of the past, and that they will vie with each other in re-establishing . . . a reverence for the Constitution, and for the rights of the States thereunder." Race and the struggle for civil rights still hovered in the background of this evidently even-tempered call for reconciliation, because all the talk about state sovereignty really cloaked the writers' hopes that African-Americans in the South could be safely relegated to positions of second- or third-class citizenship. In Derry's history, the least sophisticated of the three books, that subtext occasionally became explicit, and all of Stephens's lawyerly subtlety was lost. For example, Derry expected his young readers to memorize the answer to a question he posed about economic recovery in Virginia, Tennessee, Georgia, Texas, and North Carolina: "Q: To what do they owe their prosperity? A: To the fact that the white population is largely in excess of the negro population, and hence their state governments are entirely in the hands of whites, *the only race that ought ever to bear rule in this country.*"[27]

In the first twenty years after the war ended, however, public schools in the South did not especially favor these mostly legalistic apologias for the Confederacy. Instead, the most popular American history in the region was a textbook first published in 1870 by George Frederick Holmes, a professor of history at the University of Virginia.[28]

Though he and his publisher designed the work for Southern audiences, Holmes proudly noted that "no charge of partiality or prejudice, of sectional or political discoloration" had been brought against it. A product of the Old South, Holmes refused to idealize it, particularly in editions of his work that appeared in the early 1880s. After offering a positive note on the "rustic industry" of Northern farms, he wrote that in "the South were large plantations cultivated by slaves, whose rich owners lived in ease and luxurious indulgence." The plantation owners "were easily tempted into extravagance" and, more ominously, "dissipation," a term that suggested sexual relations between the races. Holmes addressed other taboo topics as well. In his book, the original settlers of Jamestown came off as careless, ill-disciplined adventurers in search of quick wealth. Later, he mentioned an attempt by firebrands leading the secession movement to revive the much despised Atlantic slave trade in 1860, a point that complicated arguments by Stephens that the Civil War had been waged essentially over the principle of states' rights. The Constitution, so hallowed by Stephens, was for Holmes an "assemblage of compromises, unsatisfactory in diverse particulars to the men who devised it, and containing many germs of future discords."[29] Sectional conflict ran deep in Holmes's narrative. The Civil War was inevitable, not the creation of fanatical abolitionists or ambitious Northerners seeking to exploit the slavery issue for political gain.

One would expect historical claims like these to have infuriated members of the Southern Historical Society and other conservatives in the region, especially since a *Northern* firm, the University Publishing Company of New York, published Holmes's book. Yet *Debow's Review* and numerous educators in the South endorsed the text.[30] That support can be explained in part by Holmes's regional reputation as a scholar and his impeccable credentials as a Southerner; he had liberties that a textbook writer born outside the South lacked. The popularity of his work also reflected the politically unsettled nature of the region at the time. Democrats regained control of the last pockets of Republicanism in Louisiana and South Carolina when Reconstruction ended in 1877, but reactionaries met defeats on various fronts, including in their effort to dismantle public school systems. Black men faced frequent intimidation but were still able to vote across much of the South. Neither Jim Crow nor a dominant popular understanding of the war and its aftermath had yet emerged.[31]

Holmes's book spoke to the indeterminacy of the times. Believing that during the "late sad years, passions have been too violent and wounds too fresh for the preparation or reception of a dispassionate account" of the war or the events leading to it, Holmes deliberately adopted a spare prose. He mostly recited facts while avoiding commentary, the reference to the "dissipation" of some slaveholders being one of the few exceptions to that policy. He called his book a "serviceable manual for schools" but understood that a more complete and accurate textbook would have to wait for a future writer.[32]

What came to be called the telegraphic style dominated the school histories of the day. It was characterized by extensive presentation of discrete bits of information, but little treatment of historical cause and effect. Authors employing this style included William M. Swinton, John J. Anderson, George Payn Quackenbos, Joel Dorman Steele, and Mary Elsie Thalheimer. Except for the imprimatur of the University of Virginia, which marked it as Southern, Holmes's textbook was virtually indistinguishable from those written by Northerners. By avoiding the divisive, emotionally charged issues wrought by the war and emancipation, these books offered a loose consensus on the national past. Publishers preferred it that way, because they had learned from DeBow and other Southerners that controversy only threatened sales. But that tenuous consensus could not last. By the middle of the 1880s, several factors had begun to undermine it.

First, the potential for profits in the textbook market had been rising steadily. If the genteel myth of nineteenth-century publishers as disseminators and guardians of high culture is true to some extent, humble schoolbooks made it possible. By 1850 they constituted 44 percent of book sales in the United States. D. Appleton and Company produced American editions of Charles Darwin's *Origin of Species* and Lewis Carroll's Alice books, but when asked in 1880 for his all-time biggest seller, publisher William H. Appleton answered without hesitation: Noah Webster's *Speller*. His firm sold a million copies of that title a year, more than any other book in the world except the Bible. For publishing executives like Appleton, the school market provided stability in an industry vulnerable to booms and busts in the economy. Textbooks were easy to produce, particularly with recent improvements in technology, and with minor revisions they had remarkably long shelf lives.[33] Schoolbooks also had an audience that was increasing in size as more children entered public schools and stayed for longer terms.

As the pie got bigger, however, more publishers tried to grab a slice. Aggressive marketing, initially stimulated by a short-term dip in demand during the Civil War, soon cut deeply into profits. By the 1870s competition among the leading textbook producers had become cutthroat. Agents scoured the country, often securing sales through payoffs to teachers and local adoption boards. An honest school board member, one agent is reputed to have said, is one that once bought, stays bought. Colorful stories of corruption abounded. One had a publisher stacking a school meeting by diverting voters to a local saloon for free beer, whiskey, and cigars. For publishers, the biggest problem was "even exchange." Agents would agree to take all of a school's copies of a competitor's book and replace them, at no charge, with new ones from their own firm. They hoped the new text would find a more permanent home in the school, allowing the publisher to recoup losses through later sales. But over the short term, of course, even exchange always racked up debts for the more aggressive firms.[34]

Agents became the bane of the industry. Local bookstore owners despised the agent system because direct sales from publishers eliminated their role as middlemen. Parents, who usually had to buy the books, felt that corruption burdened them with extra costs.[35] Publishers acknowledged problems with their business practices but noted, sadly, that until competitors could agree to a reasonable system of rules, Hobbesian market conditions would reign. Three efforts to secure gentlemen's agreements about fair practices failed. Finally, in 1890, the five leading textbook publishers—A. S. Barnes; Ivison, Blakeman, Taylor and Company; D. Appleton; Van Antwerp, Bragg and Co.; and Harper and Brothers—merged their textbook operations to form the American Book Company (ABC). Capitalized with five million dollars and incorporated in New Jersey (for its liberal antitrust laws), ABC instantly dominated the textbook market and soon swallowed up two dozen smaller companies. Corruption, the appearance (if not always the reality) of immense profits, and now the "Book Trust" intensified public disgust with the industry.[36] G. A. Gates, president of Iowa College, called ABC's monopoly more complete than Standard Oil's. And it was all the more insidious because the publisher might gain de facto control of school curricula and, with them, the minds of future citizens. "It ought to be deemed less dishonorable to sell the body of a child into slavery than to give away a child's soul into the possession of a power whose only interest in it is measured in the money that can be made out of it," intoned Gates. "Its dishonor strikes at the very heart of the nation, and the coming years are sure to reveal moral and social and political disaster traceable to the domination of this school book monopoly."[37] It was a reprise of DeBow's argument from the 1850s, but now, curiously, with slavery as a metaphor for evil, not a system to be defended.

In the South, ABC became a symbol of Northern commercial exploitation and Republican political domination, and attacks on the company united people across class lines. Conservatives in the tradition of DeBow who decried Northern publishers' control of Southern education, often to little effect, suddenly found themselves aligned with populists. The Farmers' Alliance censured ABC for encouraging fraud, raising prices, and filling its books with praise for the virtues of American industry and the corporations that the Alliance opposed.[38] A different agenda than the neo-Confederates, perhaps, but a common enemy. Expressing popular sentiment, North Carolina's superintendent of public instruction declared that syndicates were using money "to control the judgment and action" of school boards and teachers. "If our Southern people are wise," he wrote in 1890, "they will look carefully after the books that are put into the hands of their children."[39]

Texan Ben C. Jones thought he had an answer to the problem. His state was paying over two million dollars to "northern monopolies" each year for texts for its students. "We can print these books for them for half this sum and keep the money at home for citizens of Texas," Jones declared. "The monopolies may suffer if we should do so, but the citizens of Texas will be the beneficiaries."[40] A few states, most notably California, went the route of state publication. But Texas and most of the South chose a less drastic alternative: state regulation of book adoption. Proponents saw state adoption, by the state board of education or a body appointed by the governor, as a solution to several problems. It would staunch the flow of dirty money to teachers and local school officials. It would allow a single board to negotiate the lowest price for books and guarantee that rate for every district, eliminating the possibility that agents would take advantage of less savvy local officials. State adoption would also make it cheaper for families who had moved from one town to another and who might otherwise have to buy a new set of schoolbooks for their children. Finally, it would allow educational "experts" and other representatives of the middle class to choose the best books. State adoption appealed especially to those who dismissed local instructors as incompetent and searched for ways to teacher-proof the system.[41]

Despite these supposed advantages, state adoption was not an easy sell in the South. Publishers fought hard against it. The American Book Company faced charges in Texas of funneling cash to legislative candidates in its attempts to kill adoption bills during the 1880s and 1890s, and in Alabama the company was accused of "inciting" local school boards not to abide by adoptions once such a bill had become law. Where they could not stop state adoption, publishers sought and often were able to win exemptions for certain school districts, usually cities with some minimum population level. In Texas, which began adoption in 1897, legislators set this level at ten thousand. Such exemptions were justified on the grounds that urban districts had different needs than rural ones. Roughly translated, that meant that city children were academically ahead of their rural peers and that urban teachers and superintendents were better educated and thus capable of choosing textbooks on their own. Other groups joined publishers in the fight against state adoption. The Texas State Teachers Association resisted the plan, and one opponent labeled it a paternalistic, undemocratic approach that would "completely stifle opinion or choice on the part of teachers and intelligent school officers in the counties." That claim was not far-fetched. South Carolina, an early and enthusiastic supporter of state adoption, even passed a regulation denying paychecks to teachers who persisted in using books of their own choosing.[42]

Many officials saw creeping loss of home rule in adoption proposals, a charge that had special resonance in the South during Reconstruction and its aftermath. "When once you begin to centralize power over the schools in the State capitol, there is no telling where the centralizing tendency will end," declared Georgia's state school commissioner in 1902.[43] Virginia's state superintendent, W. H. Ruffner, took an even stronger stand, arguing that adoption would lead to despotism, intellectual death, and perhaps worse:

> I know of individuals, but of no party which openly declares for
> a National System of education, with its national school law,
> national school officers, national series of textbooks to be pre-
> scribed [for] every school in the land, and national uniformity
> enforced by a National Board of Education in Washington. I
> am sure no such party . . . can ever exist among educators, for
> *educational reasons of the most overwhelming character.* But it is
> undeniable, that the political tendencies of the last fourteen
> years, in the direction of centralization, have affected the educa-
> tional departments of the Several States.

The coded language of "overwhelming character" referred to racially mixed schools, which many White conservatives saw as the gravest educational threat of the era. Elsewhere in his report, for instance, Ruffner more explicitly addressed the danger to White schoolgirls presented by Black males "whose notorious laxity in their sexual relations need not be dwelt upon."[44] But, the superintendent implied, there was a more immediate problem with centralizing adoption in Richmond. It might not ameliorate corruption at all, but simply elevate it to a grander scale. State officials might prove no more immune to temptation than local ones.

These fears notwithstanding, the majority of Southern states embraced some type of uniformity by the turn of the century. Plans changed over time as states experimented. Texas adopted single books. Virginia opted for multiple adoptions, which allowed local districts to choose from among a short list of acceptable titles. Some states mandated books for grammar grades but not for high school. But while state adoption began, for the most part, for financial reasons, to hold down costs and trim corruption, it had another, largely unintended effect. The existence of a single board nominally accountable to the people gave a few well-organized constituencies, concerned mostly with the ideological content of textbooks, a powerful lever with which to influence adoptions. Oddly, it was successful protests over textbooks in the North that inspired groups in the South to use that lever.

Beginning in the 1880s, the association of Union veterans, the Grand Army of the Republic, turned its attention to problems of history instruction in the schools. They focused on presentation of the causes, conduct, and outcome of the Civil War, claiming that children should learn that the conflict, at its heart, was one of right versus wrong. They condemned neo-Confederate textbooks like those written by Alexander Stephens and Joseph Derry on these grounds, of course. But they also directed much of their ire at fact-based compilation histories, which in their often bland, telegraphic style avoided taking clear moral or political stands on the issues of slavery, state sovereignty, and the legitimacy of secession. These were the books most schoolchildren in the North and South were reading, and their authors' attempts to render history without sectional bias had gone "beyond the bounds of reason," according to the Wisconsin department of the GAR.[45] "There must be some things that will not be pleasant to many of those who took part in the effort to destroy the Union," declared the chairman of the GAR's textbook committee. The problem lay with publishers' efforts to compile histories "for the purpose of a national system of education," claimed this official, referring to books designed to be acceptable across the country.[46]

Had he been reading the *Southern Historical Society Papers,* this ex-soldier would have come across the same argument. A Confederate veteran reviewing Mary Thalheimer's *Eclectic History of the United States* complained that books like it were "manufactured like oleomargarine" and "all gotten up with the aim of pleasing everybody and offending no one." Publishers would continue printing these "worthless school histories," the reviewer concluded, as long as they could make money by doing so.[47]

The GAR, and later the United Confederate Veterans, which organized its own history committee in 1892, made the publishers' goal of securing profits ever more challenging. In 1895 the *Grand Army Record* launched an attack on David Montgomery's *Leading Facts of American History* and *Beginner's American History,* published by Ginn and Company of Boston. The Union veterans listed numerous problems with the books, from statements that respectable men had believed in the right of a state to secede, to restrained treatment of the horrors of Southern military prisons, to an anecdote about a naive Northern recruit accepting an umbrella from his mother as he marched off to war. The *Record* then printed a "roll of dishonor," listing Massachusetts towns using Montgomery's texts. Ginn officials speculated that a rival publisher had orchestrated the campaign but reluctantly made about fifty changes to the books, enough to endanger sales in the South.

Leading professional historians fared no better than the amateur

Montgomery. The American Book Company garnered more unwanted publicity when newspapers revealed that the star author they had recently recruited for a school history, John Bach McMaster, had been meeting with the GAR's history committee. McMaster apparently hoped for some sort endorsement for the book (it never came), but he denied doing "history made to order." Houghton Mifflin found itself in the unenviable position of defending John Fiske and his American history from assaults by Confederate *and* Union veterans. "To write a history of this country, without giving offense to anyone," lamented Fiske, "one should stop at 1492."[48]

What sort of history did ex-soldiers in the South advocate in the 1890s? In some ways, it paralleled what the GAR recommended. Members of the United Confederate Veterans were sensitive on questions of Southern manhood and honor. Any suggestion, however implicit, that Southern soldiers had not fought bravely could doom a history book. Veterans from a particular state or county would carefully scrutinize depictions of battles in which they had fought—proof that all politics is, at some level, local. Discussions of inhumane conditions at Andersonville and other Confederate prisoner-of-war camps, which the GAR demanded, had to be approached cautiously or, better yet, excluded. The UCV also objected to histories that appeared to glorify Union soldiers at Southerners' expense. John William Jones, a veteran who would shortly write his own book, condemned one history for including twenty-six sketches of Union officers, but only eleven of Confederates. That problem afflicted more than just histories. Veterans in Texas, for instance, condemned a math book that allegedly insulted the South by asking students to determine General Ulysses S. Grant's age, in days, when he captured Vicksburg, Mississippi.[49]

Objections went well beyond battlefield coverage, however. Any critique of Southern society before, during, or after the war could be held to impugn the integrity of the Confederate soldier. Authors had to tread lightly around slavery. The UCV grew outraged at the slightest intimation that the South had fought for the perpetuation of the institution. Confederate soldiers, the UCV maintained, had met their adversaries over the honorable principle of state sovereignty as laid out by the Founders of the republic. Under pressure from veterans, Texas mandated that any approved history must make this Confederate motivation explicit. Because Southern veterans saw the conflict as a noble war for liberty, much as they viewed the Revolutionary War, a phrase like the "War of the Rebellion"—much less the "Pro-Slavery Rebellion," which some GAR members demanded—was unacceptable. So was the term "Civil War." It implied that by 1860 the United States had reached a critical level of national unity and that secession attacked the legitimate national authority of Congress and the Lincoln Administration. The "War Between the States" was more appropriate because it located sovereignty at the state level and did not so clearly suggest such treason.

How the South lost the war also became critical for veterans. The reasonable conclusion that internal dissension contributed materially to defeat, which Southerners Blackburn and McDonald had suggested in their 1869 textbook, was disappearing in a rose-tinted view of Confederate unity that only the passing of three decades could allow. Nor did the South lose because of battle tactics or the handicaps imposed by slavery, according to the veterans. It had simply been overwhelmed by superior numbers.[50] And even after military defeat, Southerners were still defending the principle of "home rule" amid tyranny imposed by a vengeful regime in Washington. To some extent, argued Confederate veterans and other revisionists, the South's defense of Constitutional liberty proved successful, as the last federal troops departed the region in 1877. Thus both the Union and the Confederacy could be said to have defended vital principles in the war. That Reconstruction-era Republicans might actually have been the ones defending Constitutional ideals by fighting *for* Black suffrage was, of course, unthinkable to these conservatives.[51]

As the incompatible demands of veterans in the North and South made the old nationwide sales strategy less tenable, publishers that had been catering specifically to the Southern market experienced a small boom. In addition to those firms that had produced the earlier histories by Holmes, Stephens, Derry, Blackburn, and McDonald, whose books enjoyed some resurgence of popularity in the 1890s, these companies included F. F. Hansell of New Orleans, publisher of three histories by Henry E. Chambers; B. F. Johnson of Richmond, Virginia, responsible for successful U.S. histories by Susan Pendleton Lee; and the R. H. Woodward Company of Baltimore, which released the first edition of John William Jones's *School History of the United States* in 1896. The quality of paper, binding, and illustration in books printed at Southern firms lagged behind Northern ones, but their freedom from charges of corruption and partisanship, faced by texts put out by Northern "monopolies," partially offset these disadvantages.[52]

Jones and Lee best articulated the Confederate veterans' view of American history. Jones was the proverbial "unreconstructed rebel" and the South's leading proponent of the Lost Cause myth. Born in

Virginia in 1836, he became a Baptist minister and served in Lee's army. He led a revival among soldiers in 1862 and 1863, earning the sobriquet "the fighting parson." After the war he became secretary of the Southern Historical Society and later served as chaplain to the UCV for nineteen years. Lee was born in Lexington, Virginia, in 1832, into a family of eminent soldiers and statesmen. Her father, an Episcopal priest, served as a brigadier general in the Civil War. After finishing a hagiographic volume on the elder Pendleton, she wrote her first American history, which was published in 1895.[53]

Both writers sought, as Jones phrased it, to relate "the exact truth on all disputed points" but, like so many other critics, condemned historians whose efforts at neutrality had led them to be "colorless on great questions that have divided the sections." Lee apologized for the length of her *Advanced School History of the United States* (over six hundred pages) but said she wanted to present more than a "dry compendium of facts" and to thereby avoid repeating the mistake of other writers.[54] Jones and Lee built upon the foundations laid by earlier neo-Confederate textbooks by portraying the Puritan settlers of New England in a harsh light, giving more space to events in the colonial and antebellum South, and, most importantly, explaining the wisdom of state sovereignty and the propriety of secession in 1861.

Unlike their predecessors, however, they examined slavery in some detail. Jones and Lee argued that while slaves were a peculiar burden to the South, White Southerners were not responsible for the institution. They blamed, alternately, Dutch traders, the British, and especially New Englanders for the curse of human bondage. The "first honest opposition to slavery came from the Southern colonies of South Carolina and Virginia," Lee told her readers. Both colonies passed bills restricting the importation of slaves only to see Parliament promptly declare the legislation null and void. During the Constitutional Convention, Southern states led by Virginia, Delaware, and Maryland fought for an immediate end to shipments of Africans to the United States but were thwarted by New England:

> It will thus be seen that New England favored the perpetuation
> of the slave trade, because her slavers found it very profitable,
> while these other states were in favor of abolishing it, although it
> was greatly to their interest to purchase negroes from African
> slavers than from the Northern States, who now began to find
> slave labor unprofitable, and were selling their negroes to the
> South, instead of setting them free. New England's history on

this question is one of sordid self-interest and meddlesome interference, instead of philanthropy.[55]

As this passage suggests, advocates of the Lost Cause myth did not believe moral concerns motivated Northern opponents of slavery. Both Lee and Jones, whose narratives stressed the importance of Christian virtue, emphasized that point. Residents of Massachusetts had engaged in slavery from the beginning, they argued, by selling their Indian war captives in the seventeenth century. In the nineteenth century, cotton manufacturers in New England shared in the wealth created by slave labor. Slavery died out in the region not because forced labor pricked the New England conscience, according to Lee and Jones, but because the African proved racially ill adapted to Northern climes, where "he dwindled and was comparatively useless when exposed to the long, cold northern winters." The gentler weather in the South, far more than the profit motive of planters (on which these authors were carefully silent), drew the slave to that region. There he found the raising of tobacco, rice, and cotton "occupation[s] suited to his health and capacities."[56]

Bypassing for a moment that morally convenient bit of racial determinism, there are kernels of truth in this narrative of events. The whole country, including New England, had been complicit in slavery before 1861. But the suggestion that Northerners imposed the peculiar institution on the South and struggled to keep up the slave trade against the best efforts of White Southerners was fanciful at best.

Reading these two books, it might have been difficult for young students to see why Whites in the South would have had any misgivings about slave trading in the first place. Lee, like her peers writing for the Southern market, painted a romantic picture of slavery and race relations in the South. Under the influence of the institution, White Southerners

saw hundreds of thousands of African savages civilized and Christianized; and many of them thought it the greatest missionary agent the world had ever known. The kindest and most affectionate relationships existed between the slaves and their owners. A cruel or neglectful master or mistress was rarely found. . . . The sense of responsibility pressed heavily on the slave-owners, and the rule among them was to do the best possible for the physical and religious welfare of their people. They did not consider the bondage in which the negroes were held a hardship or wrong to them, as they were fed, clothed, lodged, and cared for, better than any other menial class on the globe.[57]

Lee hedged on the question of whether it was moral to have one human being own another, in body if not in soul. She noted that the Bible sanctioned slavery but admitted that, like any institution, it might be subject to abuse. At one point she compared slavery's relationships to those in a family. A man may abuse his wife and children in isolated cases, but, she reasoned, such abuse does not justify abandoning the idea of the family itself.

The metaphor was apt, because people of color in her book occupied the position of children, generally dependent on and devoted to White benefactors but irresponsible and dangerous when freed from White control. That childlike yet reckless nature of the African race had been the danger in abolitionists' plans for sudden emancipation before the war. Most White Southerners had been committed to the goal of ending slavery, according to Lee, but they did not know how to go about it without creating social chaos. The French, she noted, had made an "experiment" of abolition on their Caribbean islands, and the slaves "had proved so degraded and idle and vicious that the Southern states naturally shrank from having such a population in their midst."[58]

Such was the lesson Lee applied to Reconstruction. Republicans had experimented with the defeated South by freeing the slaves and later granting Black men the right to vote. Southern Whites, courageous in accepting defeat, nevertheless understood the "character of the negroes," according to Lee, and saw the need to apply legal control over them through anti-vagrancy laws, generally known as the Black Codes. Republicans, led by Charles Sumner and Thaddeus Stevens, opposed the codes not out of true sympathy with the ex-slaves or the belief that they were worthy of complete freedom and citizenship but due to vindictiveness against former Confederate enemies.[59]

Lee argued that carpetbaggers backed by the Radical Congress proved to be the "best tools to harry and insult the hated white southerners." They encouraged ex-slaves to address imagined social injustices by requesting the intercession of officials in the Freedmen's Bureau. "One of the exhibitions of independence in which the colored people most delighted," wrote Lee, "was to take possession of the whole sidewalks in the towns and force the whites into the gutters or the mud. To avoid unpleasant collisions, white women and children, and the more peaceable among the men stepped aside into the mud or dust, and quietly passed by." In a muted suggestion of sexual attacks on White women, she added that sometimes freedmen committed "outrages too horrible to be described." The better class in the South, she complained, had to face not only these haughty ex-slaves but also the so-called scalawags, poor Whites who collaborated with the Republican regimes and were "often below the negroes in moral point of view."[60]

Lee, Jones, and other writers of Southern histories employed scalawags and former slaves as foils for the aristocratic heroes of the Confederacy. Robert E. Lee, Stonewall Jackson, Jefferson Davis, Nathan Bedford Forrest, Jeb Stuart, and others appeared in their histories as socially conservative models of Christian virtue. Jones closed a four-page tribute to Davis with his assessment of the ex-president as "a great soldier, an able and incorruptible statesman, a gifted orator, a true patriot, seeking only the good of the land he loved, and a stainless Christian gentleman." Davis was "worthy of the study and imitation of the youth of America." Jones praised Jackson for his humility and Christian asceticism, and Stuart for his "unsullied character and temperate habits, never using tobacco or even drinking a glass of wine." Robert E. Lee earned the most accolades of all for his devotion to duty, efforts to end sectional enmity after the war, and refusal to cash in on his fame by lending his name to interested advertisers.[61] These two authors thus repeated the practice of history writers earlier in the century who had held up heroes of the Revolutionary War as moral exemplars for children. But to many veterans in the North, of course, the Confederacy's latter-day models of virtue were still the same traitors who had tried to destroy the republic.

Southern veterans fought hard to get books by Lee and Jones into the public schools. In 1900 they successfully pressed South Carolina to use Lee's primary and advanced texts exclusively. They scored their greatest victory in Virginia. Because the state had a multiple adoption system whereby local officials could choose among several acceptable books, veterans targeted one county after another in their campaign, eventually eliminating Jones's and Lee's competitors in almost every district.[62] Yet it would be easy to dismiss their efforts, and those of the United Daughters of the Confederacy, whose influence waxed as UCV members aged and died, as a final echo of decades-old animosity. In the 1936 book *The Road to Reunion,* historian Paul S. Buck suggested that by the turn of the century the "irreconcilables" had been rendered insignificant. The "only outlets for their venom were the relatively harmless activities of insulting the heroes of the other section, founding historical societies on narrow bases, and vexing the writers of history textbooks."[63]

But when Southerners, led by veterans and the more middle-class Daughters of the Confederacy, sought to rewrite the history taught to children, they wanted more than final exoneration for the soldiers, statesmen, and loyal women of the Confederacy. They wanted to use the past to legitimate the new social order they were creating. The detailed discussion of state sovereignty they mandated for American histories, the extended praise for slaveholders like Davis, and the sunny depictions of slavery itself could not lend much moral authority to a collapsed social order. But they could buttress an official system of racial inequality built on its ashes. By influencing how history would be taught, advocates of the Lost Cause could attack the radicalism latent in the memory of the Civil War and Reconstruction. The nationalism of racial inclusiveness and political egalitarianism that surfaced in the late 1860s and 1870s, which embraced people of color as national citizens, could be dismissed as a delusion, sentimental at best and malevolent at worst.[64]

It was hardly coincidental that Southern textbook activism peaked in the 1890s and in the first years of the new century. In 1890 Southern senators defeated Henry Cabot Lodge's Force Bill, which would have mandated federal supervision of elections in the South to guarantee African-American voting rights. In the ensuing eighteen years conservatives in every Southern state waged a successful program for disfranchisement through poll taxes, literacy tests, and other means. The history that Southern children read in school offered ideological justification for the effort by state legislators to enact Jim Crow into law.

Sometimes liberal nationalism could simply be written out of the past. In his history's copy of the Constitution, Jones omitted the Thirteenth, Fourteenth, and Fifteenth Amendments, as if the end of slavery and the rise of African-Americans to full citizenship had no more substance than a past night's dew dissolved by the morning sun. Usually the rewrites that veterans and others in the South demanded were more subtle. A telling example is a revision to a school history written in the late 1890s by three Texans named Oscar H. Cooper, Henry F. Estill, and Leonard Lemmon. The authors had envisioned their *History of Our Country* as a textbook for Southern students, and their publisher, Ginn and Company, reeling from attacks on another of its histories, marketed it that way.[65] But the book still troubled veterans in Virginia for not hewing closely enough to Confederate orthodoxy. Texas, which eventually adopted the book, demanded revisions. Ginn and the authors promptly complied. A new edition placed blame for the Civil War more squarely on the abolitionists; absolved Southern "extremists" who had helped to precipitate the war in the earlier version; proclaimed that the "masses" of people in the South supported secession as the only means to preserve their sacred rights; offered detailed legal justification for the states' breakaway; and heaped more praise on Lee and other Confederates. The authors also continued to remind readers that "the South was not responsible for the existence of African slavery in the United States" and concluded, a bit remarkably, that Southern Whites "suffered more from its existence than anybody else."[66]

Cooper, Estill, and Lemmon also made some important cuts. In the first edition a section entitled "Negro Troops" explained how prisoner exchanges during the war broke down:

> The Union authorities now [in 1864] began to enlist negroes in the service. This movement aroused prejudice at the North, and caused great indignation in the South. The South had not recognized the slaves as free, and consequently when the negro troops were taken as prisoners, they refused to exchange them as prisoners of war. A general stoppage of exchange was the result.[67]

The authors missed a few facts: Black soldiers had first entered the army in 1862 (serving under Cooper, Estill, and Lemmon's fellow textbook author Thomas Wentworth Higginson), not 1864. In addition, the Confederates had vowed not only to abstain from trading these soldiers as prisoners but to execute them.[68] Nevertheless, readers could still have understood one reason why exchanges broke down and gotten some idea of the importance of "colored soldiers" in the war. In the new edition, however, the section on "Negro Troops" disappeared. In its place students read that in 1862 a "general system" of prisoner exchange was agreed upon:

> But it was not long before *obstacles were presented.* A Confederate soldier was found to be worth more to the South than a Union soldier to the North. Each Southern soldier captured lessened by one the fighting force of the Confederacy, because the South early enlisted all her able-bodied men and had no source from which to recruit her depleted armies, while the greater population and wealth of the North readily supplied the places of captured Union soldiers. In 1864 the Federal authorities again resorted to the policy of refusing to exchange prisoners.[69]

Negotiating a National Past

In place of a relatively clear explanation of why exchanges initially broke down, we get a cryptic reference to "obstacles." Why did the African-American soldiers vanish from the book? No credible historian doubted their importance. They had provided critical manpower as the North began to waver in its commitment to the war on the eve of the 1864 elections; by early 1865 there were more African-Americans who had served, or were still serving, with Union forces than there were White soldiers who were still fighting in all the Confederate armies. In the first two decades after the war, popular histories, and not just Higginson's book, discussed their contributions. A widely used text of the 1880s, for example, noted that in the 1863 Union assault on Fort Wagner in Charleston Harbor, Black enlistees "showed so much bravery that the prejudice against negro soldiers disappeared, and great numbers were enrolled."[70] Even Southerners Blackburn and McDonald mentioned them, although disparagingly, in a school history they wrote when memories of the war were still fresh. But Cooper, Estill, and Lemmon understood that the history conservative Whites advocated left little room for African-Americans as historical actors bringing about their own liberation and advancement. Such roles conferred political legitimacy, which proponents of Jim Crow were loath to recognize in the reactionary climate of the 1890s.

Men and women in that era were not the first to make such a connection. Lincoln had understood the implications of enlisting Negro troops at the start of the war. By serving in the army and navy they would not only help to crush slavery but perhaps critically undermine the foundation of White supremacist thinking that denied Blacks equal rights as citizens. In 1864, for instance, Lincoln was already encouraging the governor of Louisiana, a state under Union control, to extend the franchise to African-American soldiers who had "fought gallantly in our ranks." It was uneasiness over just this sort of threat to the racial caste system that had killed Confederate proposals, supported by Davis and Lee, to enlist slaves in the Confederate armies in the final months of the war.[71] As firsthand recollections of the conflict faded in the following decades, however, the history of Black soldiers could be at least partially effaced from collective memory, particularly when all-White Democratic boards controlled textbook adoption.

Blacks still appeared in Southern histories. But they were generally consigned to stereotyped roles as buffoons or "faithful darkies," popular in the imagination of the Lost Cause.[72] A typical history published in Virginia told readers of "ridiculous scenes" of Black legislators in Reconstruction-era Florida. They sat at their desks, smoking cigars,

A regimental flag employs both words ("One Cause, One Country") and images (note the bust of Washington) to underscore national unity across racial lines. Neo-Confederate devotion to the myth of the "faithful darky," combined with the indifference of many Whites in the North, stripped textbooks of the story of African-American soldiers and sailors in the Civil War. *Courtesy of the Library of Congress.*

horribly mispronouncing legal terms, pretending to read journals they often inadvertently held upside down, all the while spending White citizens into abject poverty. The same books repeatedly praised the loyal slave who neither understood nor aspired to freedom, let alone coveted a role in the state and national governments. Several quoted extensively from a book by Henry W. Grady, a prominent journalist in the South:

> History has no parallel to the faith kept by the negro in the South during the war. Often five hundred negroes to a single white man, and yet through these dusky throngs the women and children walked in safety. . . . Unmarshalled, the black battalions moved patiently to the fields in the morning to feed the armies their idleness would have starved, and at night gathered anxiously at the big house to "hear the news from marster."

The "Black battalions" fighting for the Union, who shouldered rifles instead of hoes, got only a passing mention in the same grammar school history. As federal troops advanced southward, "some" liberated slaves entered the service, but most "remained quietly on the farms, laboring without complaint, content to be at the old home in the old way."[73]

African-American soldiers did not disappear completely from textbooks used in the South, but the trend toward invisibility was unmistakable. Their erasure, along with that of prominent and successful Black leaders like Frederick Douglass, contributed to the general impression the books left that freedom and citizenship were unearned gifts bestowed by a foolish government upon the "negro." They were gifts, according to this narrative, that he had proven entirely unprepared to handle during the folly of Reconstruction, Even if the authors did not explicitly endorse disfranchisement in their final chapters (several did), they manipulated the past to make Jim Crow seem both desirable and inevitable.

The various elements of the Lost Cause myth—fanatical abolitionists, chivalrous Southern officers, courageous White women back on the plantation, loyal slaves, vindictive Republicans—held a central place in histories used in the South at the turn of the century. Northern publishers whose agents saw their books assailed before Southern boards for not hewing closely enough to this mythology had three options. They could ignore the complaints of veterans who had a virtual lock on book selection, figuring sales in the North could carry their titles. They could publish separate histories for Northern and Southern markets, a potentially expensive and labor-intensive business strategy. Or they could revise existing books and hire new authors who could create histories that might be able to sell nationwide, replicating the success of the compilation-style histories that dominated sales from the late 1860s to the 1880s. Different publishers chose different routes.

Macmillan and Company of New York, publishers of Edward Channing's high school level *Students' History of the United States,* initially opted to ignore the South. Channing represented the new generation of professional historians dedicated to the ideal, if not always the practice, of objectivity. He did not at first wish to "truckle" to the UCV and other White conservatives in the region, and his publisher backed him up. They chose to include illustrations of abolitionists John Brown and Wendell Phillips and of prominent Republican Charles Sumner in their history but to exclude those of Jefferson Davis or any Confederate generals. They fully understood that this decision would doom sales south of the Mason-Dixon Line. But financial acumen also tempered Channing's historical judgment. In letters to MacMillan he stressed that in his manuscript he would "say nothing to stir up the GAR." And as time passed he grew more willing to alter content to fit requests of adoption boards, though mostly for states in the West. When he wrote his final schoolbook, the elementary-level *Elements of United States History,* Channing had grown downright cynical. In a letter to the firm, he described *Elements* as a "Book of Lies" written with no missionary enterprise, "but [as] an attempt to do something towards lining the pockets of the Macmillan and Company, especially its President and incidentally of yours truly."[74] That viewpoint notwithstanding, Channing and Macmillan essentially wrote off the Southern market for all his books, often not even bothering to present them before adoption committees. As Macmillan executives expanded their line of schoolbooks in later years, however, they did more carefully address concerns of Whites in the South.

Several of the major schoolbook firms, including Ginn and Company, D. C. Heath, and the American Book Company, immediately chose to publish separate histories for the South. They found Southern-born authors whose books would sell in Dixie, hired Southern agents to market them, and established branch offices in the region. With the deep pockets only it had, ABC also quietly acquired controlling interests in at least two publishers that had already successfully catered to Southern schools, a move that would help trigger an antitrust suit in Texas.[75] Executives at ABC made their first direct overture to the South with the 1893 publication of *The History of the American People,* by Josiah H. Shinn of Arkansas. They also acquired the rights to a popular grammar school history by Lida A. Field from a publisher in Georgia. Ginn and Company, as previously mentioned, published the school history by Cooper, Estill, and Lemmon. About a decade later they also released a high school history by Nathaniel Wright Stephenson, a historian from South Carolina. In 1904 D. C. Heath entered the market with the first of two histories by Southerner Waddy Thompson.

To further counter their image as rapacious, corrupt Northern monopolies indifferent to concerns in the South, the publishers sent advance copies of their books directly to local branches of the United Confederate Veterans. The aging ex-soldiers appreciated the attention. In 1903 Virginia veterans happily acknowledged receipt of a new ABC text and declared that while it might have been more forceful in defending secession, the book was nevertheless "well gotten up" by the publisher.[76]

Efforts to please turned farcical by the early 1910s as publishers tried to out-Southern the competition. No longer were the enemies of true history just Northern historians, but Southern writers who failed tests of orthodoxy. D. C. Heath sent missives running into dozens of pages to the Alabama textbook committee in 1912. One, likely written by their star author, Waddy Thompson, listed 160 alleged "errors and omissions" in a competitor's book. The criticism sounded familiar. The rival book failed to show the full "aggressiveness" of the abolitionists, spoke inappropriately about the "shame" of slavery, neglected to mention the extent to which the Freedman's Bureau had caused "trouble" among Blacks, and was too soft on Republicans who had "forced negro domination on the South." Mere Southern birth, this reviewer lectured committee members, could not guarantee that a writer would produce a book free from Northern bias. The critic attacked *Our Republic,* by Franklin L. Riley, J. A. C. Chandler, and J. G. de Roulhac Hamilton, with special vehemence. They had done a disservice to the South by dwelling on Confederate valor and battlefield victories *too* extensively, making the hardships of soldiers and their eventual loss difficult for young readers to understand.[77]

Lead writer Riley was not to be outdone in this competition, however. He dispatched his son to the adoption board in Arkansas, where the junior Riley condemned a rival text for devoting more pages to Lincoln than Davis, among other sins. "What will the little children think about the South after reading this book?" he asked.[78] White children bereft of proper role models, Riley implied, might not develop true appreciation of the golden era of the Confederacy along with its most important legacy—racial pride.

The lengths to which publishers and authors went to fan sectional animosity suggested that real disputes over content, like the old soldiers who led them, had begun to fade away. That change again left open the alluring possibility of nationwide sales. As early as 1895 the UCV's history committee had declared that "the South wants no history in her schools that cannot be taught to children in any state of the Union." That was more an ideal than a practical goal, considering that the two veterans' organizations could not at the time even reach agreement on a name for the Civil War. Tensions eased, however, in a wave of sentimental patriotism following the Spanish-American War in 1898. The former Confederates sent "fraternal greetings" to the GAR. Reunions welcoming the former enemies followed, along with the return of captured battle flags to home states and the reinterment of numbers of ex-Confederates at Arlington National Cemetery. "I have lived long enough and wide enough to be out of sympathy with the idea that a history should be Southern," wrote one Tennessee veteran, endorsing what he believed was a truly nonpartisan history in 1912. He concluded that "if it is not good for the whole country, it is not good for the South."[79]

Most surviving veterans and other textbook activists in the South were thus abandoning James DeBow's old dream of separate textbooks for the region. Debow had feared creeping nationalism from the North and had hoped such books would help to preserve a unique regional culture based on slavery. After slavery collapsed, the preservationist ideal had remained. It gave rise to a successful series of texts produced under the auspices of the University of Virginia during Reconstruction, along with volumes in history by Alexander Stephens and other neo-Confederates. Twenty-five years later, as conservatives struggled to implement legal segregation and Black disfranchisement on the South, that same spirit led to a renaissance in Southern-oriented textbooks. But by the time Southerner and historian Woodrow Wilson entered the White House in 1913, the movement for sectional histories had largely played itself out.

The logic of the market dictated how this happened. Recall that most Southern states at the turn of the century had begun to adopt textbooks on a statewide basis while most states in the North still left those choices entirely in the hands of local officials (states and territories in the less populous West split more evenly on the issue). Publishers had more incentive to meet the specific demands of a large, single purchasing unit like Texas than those of a multitude of smaller ones in Illinois and Massachusetts, each with different expectations and preferences regarding content. Groups like the UCV that could send representatives to Austin had a powerful say in what books Texas would adopt; Texas and other states of the South, in turn, exercised a disproportionate influence over what kind of history students in the rest of the country would read. Authors and editors seeking to maximize profits by selling books nationwide ignored the concerns of disfranchised African-Americans in the South, of course, because they lacked the political power to sway adoptions.

Publishers had been "made to understand that unfair school history could not be bought or used," as one satisfied White activist in the South put it. Perhaps thinking of the heyday of Dixie's attacks on the "book trust," the chairman of the UCV's history committee declared confidently in 1910, "We do not fear the bookmaker now."[80] That spirit of conciliation grew out of publishers' increasing skill in pleasing veterans and members of the United Daughters of the Confederacy. When ABC's home office was considering adding a new high school history to its titles in the early 1910s to replace its rapidly aging tomes for Southern schools, it queried a sales agent in Mississippi for advice. "There would be no advantage in a Southern author," answered the agent. "In fact, I think a man of National reputation, whether he be Northern or Southern, is what we want." He suggested two authors who could write an "ideal" history after—and the addition is important—"you and your assistants had carefully edited it."[81] As books became longer and more expensive to produce, few historical details could be left to chance or the whims of an individual author. Whites in the South no longer demanded their own textbooks, but they still pressed for their own unique version of events in any volume they adopted, and they would continue to do so successfully for decades to come.

Though publishers grew adept at anticipating problems with manuscripts, they could still make mistakes. Macmillan and Company, which had at first not been especially sensitive to book protests in the South, found itself mired in controversy over a text by Henry William Elson used in 1911 for the introductory American history course at Roanoke College in Virginia. Elson's depiction of the war as a rebellion led by slaveholders, combined with his straightforward note that masters and female slaves sometimes engaged in sexual relations, reignited Southern passions over the history issue. The book's alleged "attack" on the "sacred family relations of our people" brought torrents of angry letters to the *Roanoke Times,* later reprinted in the journal *Confederate Veteran,* and a call for book burnings at the campus. Professors at the college mounted a defense of the book on grounds of academic freedom. Elson, however, promised to revise later editions of the history in deference to White Southern opinion.[82]

In calling for the removal of Elson's book, one writer in the *Confederate Veteran* declared that "in no wise can I understand how national loyalty is to be promoted by vilifying any section of our common country."[83] That she and other Southerners could take such a stand as "nationalists" speaks to the success they had had in defining the terms in the debate over national reconciliation. Theirs was not the nationalism of Thomas Wentworth Higginson, Frederick Douglass, Charles Sumner, or Elisha Mulford. For the latter group, nationalism meant the political equality of all citizens and the supremacy of a central government that would guarantee these rights against attacks by the states. For the ex-Confederates, their descendants, and large numbers of Northerners as well, national reconciliation meant the emotional reunion of Whites across sectional lines. Membership in the national community was explicitly racialized, in the South by Jim Crow and in the country at large in 1898 through the acquisition of island territories whose dark-skinned inhabitants were denied citizenship. Whites in the South could even embrace the supremacy and grandeur of the government in Washington once it was clear that it would not tamper with segregation and disfranchisement, a point made most dramatically by the Supreme Court in *Plessy v. Ferguson* in 1896.

School histories that once again sold nationwide in the 1920s reflected the prevailing racist and imperialist outlook, what one scholar at the time termed "integral nationalism."[84] The new history reflected some concessions by advocates of the Confederate tradition as well. While romantic depictions of slavery remained to some extent, most books more explicitly condemned the institution. Even a Southerner writing essentially for a sectional market explained how slavery had held back population growth and economic expansion and even called the Emancipation Proclamation "one of the great strokes of the Lincoln Administration."[85] But discussion of the social evils of slavery, from its physical brutality to issues like slave breeding in the border states, was limited or usually nonexistent. In these newer schoolbooks the White South became a tragic figure, forced to defend a destructive system it had inherited through the misfortune of mild climate and the greed of colonial-era slave traders. Trapped by circumstance in an ultimately doomed cause, people from Robert E. Lee to anonymous women on the home front struggling against war-imposed shortages appeared as heroes and heroines. Andrew C. McLaughlin's explanation for Confederate defeat in his 1919 edition of *History of the American Nation* seemed specifically targeted to Southern White sensitivities in its appeal to race-based patriotism:

> It was not lack of bravery, skill, or determination that defeated the South. It was slavery. While the lumber, iron, and coal of the North were put to service by an intelligent people, whose very industrial success prompted to new energy, the South was laboring under a destructive system which had been abandoned by every other part of the Teutonic race; and the fearful penalty of slavery was civil war and disastrous, overwhelming defeat.[86]

These textbooks portrayed the Civil War as the crucible of the American nation-state, which was sanctified through Anglo-Saxon blood shed on both sides. Reunion, for Whites, meant setting aside past differences and embarking on a common destiny. In this national narrative, the crushing of slavery and the passage of the postwar amendments played peripheral roles, and African-American soldiers perhaps no role at all. As an attempt to overturn the racial hierarchy in the South, Reconstruction became a terrible blunder. In the 1870s and 1880s, Thomas Higginson had extolled the advances of the postwar South, particularly what he then saw as the general acceptance of Black men's right to vote. But a little over two decades later, David Saville Muzzey, the most popular history-textbook author of the first half of the twentieth century, condemned the Republican programs without hesitation. "To reverse the relative position of the races in the South, to stand the social pyramid on its apex, to set the ignorant, gullible slave in power over his former master, was no way to insure either the protection of the negro's rights or the stability and peace of the Southern governments," wrote Muzzey. Republicans like Charles Sumner were misguided humanitarians who "let their sympathy for the oppressed slave confuse their judgment of the negro's intellectual capacity."[87]

As books like these by Muzzey and McLaughlin gained popularity, the fears of Frederick Douglass and other postwar Republicans were at least partially realized. A "generous forgetfulness" partially obliterated the distinction between Southerners who fought to create an exclusively slaveholding nation and Northerners who struggled, hesitantly at first, for freedom.

Schoolbook Nation

Many forces helped to fashion these schoolbook narratives, which African-American scholar W. E. B. Du Bois would cite as leading examples of the "Propaganda of History" when he published his revisionist work *Black Reconstruction* in 1935. Professional historians, who repeatedly criticized efforts by veterans and other groups to control the curriculum, nevertheless chose to downplay divisive sectional issues in their academic work. They sought to make the virtually all-White and all-Protestant American Historical Association a "national" organization, and that meant not unduly offending Southern members. Veneration of objectivity made it easier to study slavery dispassionately as an economic institution and to ignore its sexual, physical, and emotional abuses. Racism throughout the country also made it easier for Whites in the North to accept romantic images of slavery and horrific accounts of Reconstruction dominated by vengeful Republicans, bumbling freedmen, and righteous ex-Confederates.[88] No Southern adoption board mandated purchases of Thomas Dixon's novels, which extolled the virtues of the Ku Klux Klan and the dangers of race mixing. Nor did any textbook committee force Americans to purchase tickets for D. W. Griffith's *Birth of a Nation,* the landmark film adapted from Dixon's work and released to theaters in 1916.

Yet the power of statewide adoption in the South to determine what sort of history Americans read in the classroom should not be underestimated. The "truths" of history proved remarkably malleable when subjected to a process that was nominally controlled by educational experts but in practice remarkably responsive to well-organized lobbyists. Authors and publishers repeatedly altered their initial versions of America's past to appease critics in the South. Sometimes the changes seemed small. In a book by John Fiske, John Brown's "religious zeal" became "fanatical zeal," an adjustment that blurred the line between abolitionist ideals and mental illness.[89] At other times they were more significant. In the 1870s, for example, Higginson had soberly informed readers of the *Young Folks' History of the United States* about the Confederate massacre of Black prisoners of war at Fort Pillow, Tennessee, in April 1864. But by the turn of the century, Confederate veterans were loudly objecting to coverage of the massacre and other events that contradicted the mythology of the valiant White South and the Lost Cause more generally. Heeding their requests, subsequent writers avoided the episode.[90] Many went even further in that direction, excising the entire history of Black soldiers in the Civil War, as Cooper, Estill, and Lemmon did when they revised their *History of Our Country.*

Negotiating a National Past

Added together, all these changes amounted a profound revising of America's story. If the content of these textbooks can be said to reflect general historical memory, then Southern reactionaries achieved significant victories in the struggle to control that memory. And a method originally devised to eliminate corruption rampant in the textbook industry at the end of the nineteenth century helped them to do it.

3. Rise of the (Catholic) American Nation
United States History in Parochial Schools

Soon after the Confederacy's former vice president, Alexander Stephens, drafted his textbook, two Catholic presses released histories for the growing numbers of students in parochial schools. Challenges to textbooks written by Protestant New Englanders had now appeared from two quarters.

The timing was not coincidental. Catholics, like White Southerners, were struggling to control the meaning of a nation that many Americans believed had been created or radically transformed by the Civil War. Both groups feared the triumphant nationalism proclaimed by leaders in the Republican Party, with its emphasis on cultural homogeneity, political centralization, and social perfectionism, which had been realized most profoundly in the recent destruction of slavery. At an 1884 Republican rally, a New York minister christened Democrats the party of "Rum, Romanism, and Rebellion." No phrase better captured how popular rhetoric linked moral degeneracy, Catholicism, and secession as enemies of national unity.[1]

In their bid for voters in the late nineteenth century, Republicans made the public school their most potent symbol of the nation. The free school, free state, and free church formed the "triple armor of American nationality," according to one commentator.[2] And the greatest threat to public schools, Republicans charged, lay with the Catholic Church. "Romanists" not only refused to support common schools, according to this argument, but were establishing their own schools at a quickening pace. Such institutions instructed young Catholics, many of them recent immigrants with little understanding of American ways, in anti-republican doctrines and loyalty to a "foreign potentate," the pope. Critics claimed priests and sisters taught their young flock to think of themselves as Catholics first and Americans second. Republican leader and Methodist minister Daniel Dorchester warned that the so-called school question revealed two peoples "struggling within the womb of the nation." Celebrated cartoonist Thomas Nast captured the alleged Catholic threat visually for *Harper's Weekly.* One of his sketches showed Catholic bishops, their bisected miters transformed into the jaws of voracious alligators, preparing to devour innocent schoolchildren (see fig. on p. 94).[3]

Catholics saw issues quite differently. They pointed out that many early advocates of public education envisioned the state-financed common school as a Protestant institution that would lead to mass conversions of Irish Catholics. The perceived need to preserve the faith from such influences stimulated the development of separate schools in the 1840s and their massive growth soon after the Civil War ended. By 1884 approximately twenty-five hundred Catholic institutions served over half a million children.[4] The textbooks used in these schools became powerful vehicles for countering prejudices against the church, though Catholic children were naturally almost the only ones to read them.

Histories of the United States, in particular, began refuting stereotypes of the faith and its adherents as intolerant, superstitious, and subversive. Where nativists charged that the swelling Catholic population was a recent and unwelcome addition to the American scene, these textbooks traced the church presence in the Americas back to 1492. Where critics of the church portrayed it as antiquated and backward-looking, these books presented clerics and Catholic laypeople as scientifically and socially progressive. Most importantly, where Republicans cast Catholics as a divisive force in an essentially Protestant nation, these texts showed how Catholics had played decisive roles in formulating American ideals, particularly religious tolerance.[5] In highlighting Catholics and their contributions, the texts partially overturned the prevailing view of American history as the triumph of mostly Anglo-Saxon Protestants in the New World.

Catholics' efforts to create their own version of the country's history and then present it to a captive audience of schoolchildren infuriated many Protestants, who were, of course, trying to do the same thing. A writer for the Congregational publication *Independent* denounced the "Roman Catholic manipulation" he found in readers, geographies, histories, and other texts. He cited John Rose Greene Hassard's *Abridged History of the United States,* first published in 1887, as a typical offender. Hassard's book did not commit any "violent perversion of facts," said this writer, but its more subtle reimagining of American history accomplished the same end: "Catholic agencies are magnified . . .

THE AMERICAN RIVER GANGES.

Rapacious bishops menace the public schools in this Thomas Nast cartoon, which appeared in *Harper's Weekly* in 1871.

matters of greater importance are passed over in silence, the edge and nobleness of Protestant history are blunted, and the point is pretty effectively made to stand out everywhere that what the country needs for the perfection of citizenship is Roman Catholicism, and that the best that is in it has come from this source." Another critic concluded that the child who "learns history from such books learns no history."[6]

Hostility to Catholic schools and their curricula persisted for decades. It culminated in 1924, when Oregon passed a measure designed to close all such schools at the primary and secondary levels. For significant numbers of non-Catholics throughout the nineteenth and early twentieth centuries, the church and its schools seemed implacably opposed to national values and true American patriotism. Those sentiments, and the insularity they helped to engender among Catholics, only increased demand for Catholic histories. Church leaders took quite seriously the charge that their faith and America's political and religious liberties made a poor fit, and they wanted their schools to offer a firm response to the allegations.[7] Catholic educators sought a "usable past" that integrated their church and its followers seamlessly into a narrative of American social and material progress. Done correctly, such a history would encourage devotion to both the United States and the Christian faith, making Catholicism and patriotism mutually reinforcing principles, not opposing ones. That effort is perhaps best illustrated by the embossed cover of Sister Mary Celeste's *American History* of 1926. It shows an exultant Columbus raising a cross on San Salvador. Behind him waits the *Santa Maria*. Further in the distance, factories send plumes of smoke into the air beside the towering skyline of a modern city. Above the panorama hangs the Great Seal of the United States and the words "For God, For Country."

The balance between what was appropriately Catholic and what was appropriately American proved difficult to maintain, however. On one level writers championed the cause of religious and cultural pluralism through stories celebrating Catholics as a righteous though historically persecuted minority within the United States. Thus parochial schools and the histories used in them rested in part on recognition of Catholic differences from the nation's Protestant majority. At the same time, however, these writers sought to rebut charges that Catholicism was an anti-national force by showing how very *American* it was—how neatly it fit into the dominant culture and established institutions. The impulse to erase marks of Catholic difference grew over time, resulting in books that sometimes downplayed the long history of bigotry against Catholics and even capitulated to the more xenophobic strain of early twentieth-century nationalism. This narrative evolution began to make Catholic histories obsolete. If they closely resembled their common-school counterparts, some Catholics asked, why publish them in the first place?

Large publishers, who were eager to avoid the expense of creating separate books for parochial schools, confronted the same question. They began to make mainstream books more acceptable to Catholic educators, initially by dropping offensive content and then by featuring Catholics more prominently. The result was a slow merging of these two sets of histories, much like that between Northern and Southern texts. This chapter takes the story of Catholic books from their inception in the 1870s to the late 1920s, when that convergence was well under way.

A recurring pattern of hostility toward Catholics in the British colonies, and the later American states, encouraged Catholic separatism and ultimately the decision to create independent schools in the middle of the nineteenth century. Puritan Massachusetts barred the emigration of priests. New Hampshire kept Catholics from voting. Several other colonies taxed Catholics for the support of a state church, always Protestant. When political calculations did not mandate greater discretion, Benjamin Franklin and other leaders of the Revolution were wont to rail against the "idolatrous papists."[8] Conditions for Catholics improved considerably after the Revolution. But by the 1840s, waves of immigration from Ireland and Germany had transformed what had been a tiny minority into a powerful religious and political force. Class tensions combined with religious ones to produce a nativist backlash. Pamphleteers circulated lurid tales of priestly debauchery, infanticide, and the imprisonment of helpless girls behind convent walls. The most famous and profitable of the captivity narratives was *Maria Monk's Awful Disclosures of the Hotel Dieu Nunnery of Montreal,* first published in 1836. Though soon revealed as a fraud, the work contributed to a climate in which rioters felt justified in raiding convents, sacking churches, attacking Catholic immigrants in the streets, and burning Irish homes. Capitalizing on anti-Catholic sentiment, the Know-Nothing Party won control of several statehouses in the 1850s, achieving its greatest success in Massachusetts. Former president Millard Fillmore, who had been a Whig, led the party's national ticket in 1856. The Know-Nothings quickly disintegrated after a poor showing in that election, victims of political realignment over the slavery issue, but the anti-Catholicism that led to their rise continued.[9]

The most contentious political issue dividing Catholics and Protestants during the antebellum era revolved around school funding. Before 1800 most schools in the United States were private and sectarian. In the first few decades of the nineteenth century, however, school reformers advocated a greater role for the state in education. Their arguments rested on claims by statesmen like Benjamin Rush and Noah Webster that government had a vested interest in supporting schools because they could encourage republican virtue and a degree of cultural conformity. Public schools, the reformers said, could bring children together for the nonsectarian portion of their education. Older denominational institutions could continue as Sunday schools. Most churches acquiesced in the so-called Protestant Compromise, but conflict with Catholics was inevitable. Catholics argued, with considerable justification, that the nonsectarian approach amounted to Protestantism of the lowest common denominator. Teachers often demanded daily readings from the King James Bible (KJV), to which Catholics objected. In Oswego, New York, one instructor whipped a Catholic boy for refusing to use the KJV. The town backed the teacher's approach, an indication of public passion over an issue that spawned riots in other cities.[10]

The conflict over Bible reading revealed deeper divisions over schooling. Many of the most vocal supporters of common schools were openly hostile to Catholics. In his 1835 book *A Plea for the West,* minister Lyman Beecher claimed that Catholics were plotting a takeover of the republic and that public schools represented the best way to repel the coming assault. The visions of nineteenth-century evangelicals, who dominated the drive for public schools, had little place for devout Catholics. Even educational pioneer Horace Mann questioned the wisdom of allowing them to teach in the public schools.[11]

For men like Beecher, state-financed schools were the solution to the social and cultural problem posed by Catholics. For many Catholics, the real problem was the public school itself; they had to pay taxes for an institution that seemed designed to turn their children into apostates. Their solution to that problem was simple. Allow the Catholic Church, and any other denomination that wished to do so, to maintain separate schools. Then take that portion of revenues raised from Catholics for the public schools and transfer it to parochial ones. After all, that had been an accepted pattern of funding before the common-school movement began. It satisfied the needs of the state for an educated citizenry and allowed parents more freedom in choosing schools. In a few districts, compromise worked. In most, Protestants balked. Conflict first flared in New York City in 1840 and then spread throughout the Northeast and Midwest.[12]

Catholics' demands for what they saw as their share of public funds further convinced many Protestants that a single school for all citizens was the true guarantor of the republic. Lack of wholehearted support for the common school, they charged, smacked of disloyalty. Transfer of any tax revenues to parochial schools now became unthinkable. "They demand of Republicans," declared one newspaper in 1841, "to give them funds to train up their children to worship a ghostly monarchy of vicars, bishops, archbishops, cardinals and Popes! They demand of us to take away our children's funds and bestow them on the subjects of Rome, the creatures of a foreign hierarchy." Beecher and others charged that Catholic clergy failed to back public schools because "popery" could ensnare only the ignorant and illiterate. Pronouncements from reckless members of the Catholic hierarchy only stoked Protestant suspicions. Peter LeFevere, a bishop in Detroit during the 1850s, called public schools "infidel" institutions. Borrowing the arguments of nativists, one priest claimed that the public schools of Boston bred prostitutes.[13]

As the debate lost even the veneer of civility, many Catholic parishes began building and privately supporting their own schools. That approach continued after the Civil War, becoming an official policy for all Catholic communities in 1884. But poverty, limited availability of parochial schools, and the preferences of some parents for public schools kept the share of eligible Catholic children enrolled in denominational institutions at about 40 percent nationwide. In some cities and among certain ethnic groups, however, that number was much higher.[14]

While partial segregation of Catholic and non-Catholic students cut down on the number of violent encounters over schools, it did not resolve underlying tensions. Opposition to parochial schools and alleged Catholic influence over public ones became a rallying cry for Republicans in the 1870s, particularly as attacks on ex-Confederates in the Democratic Party began to lose appeal. In 1875 President Ulysses S. Grant, accompanied by half a dozen generals he knew from the war, addressed the issue before a gathering of Union veterans. If "we are to have another contest in the near future for our national existence, the dividing-line will not be the Mason and Dixon's, but between patriotism and intelligence on one side and superstition, ambition, and ignorance on the other," intoned Grant, using unmistakable code words for the Catholic Church. That same year presidential hopeful James G. Blaine proposed amending the Constitution to forbid the transfer of public funds to parochial schools. Republicans placed the measure in their platform in 1876. The party also endorsed classroom use of the King James Bible, still an explosive issue.[15]

Not all Protestants backed the Republican position on the school question. Lutherans, for instance, generally favored the Catholic approach to funding. But continuing efforts by Catholics to secure public money for parochial schools, combined with ongoing construction of them, convinced members of other denominations to close ranks behind the evangelicals—mostly Baptists, Methodists, Presbyterians, and Congregationalists—who tended to split more firmly from Catholics. As early as 1856 a writer for the *Episcopal Church Review* claimed that only public schools could create a "true American nationality of character." That argument grew in intensity and sophistication among Protestants in the two decades after the Civil War. Methodist Daniel Dorchester developed it extensively in his 1884 book *Romanism versus the Public School System*. The "Roman Catholic theory of parochial schools," he declared, "separates the children into two nationalities, and almost into hostile camps."[16]

The emphasis on nationalism marked a subtle shift in anti-Catholic rhetoric. Before the war, charges against Catholics centered on dangers they posed to the republic. Recent immigrants from Catholic countries, it was said, lacked the requisite education, self-control, and freedom from foreign (read papal) influences to vote intelligently. Such republican virtues had to be acquired over several years in a Protestant environment. Once they were, Catholics' threat to the state diminished. That reasoning partly explains why Irish immigrants vexed the Know-Nothings far more than assimilated Catholics with English ancestry did. After the war, however, foes of Catholics began to stress that Rome and its followers imperiled not only the smooth functioning of republican government but the very cultural and social bonds that made Americans a single people, or nation. Republicans capitalized on this newer fear when they directly linked the dangers of the defeated Confederacy and the still-growing church. In a cartoon alluding to the attack on Fort Sumter that began the Civil War, Thomas Nast showed Irish clerics preparing to open fire on the public schools with an "ecclesiastical canon."

The new strategy, and the broader prejudices it played into, were not lost on Catholics. A writer for the *Catholic World* condemned a church opponent for flaunting "what I may call the Bloody Shirt before the eyes of his readers." That same phrase had generally referred to an effort to rouse voters by calling up memories of the Union dead in the Civil War.[17]

Again, Elisha Mulford's *The Nation: The Foundations of Civil Order and Political Life in the United States* opens a window into nationalist thinking of the period. In this influential book, which went through sixteen editions between 1870 and 1898, Mulford maintained that all societies developed naturally toward the ideal form of the nation, which would be both politically and, to a great extent, culturally homogeneous. Ancient Israel provided the first example of such a national community, and Mulford, like others from the Puritans onward, imagined Americans as the latter-day heirs of God's covenant with His chosen people. Several forces might thwart the natural development of nations, according to Mulford, including tendencies toward confederacy and empire. In the ancient world, a tepid system of alliances had left Greek city-states quarrelsome, divided, and prone to invasion. In the modern world, confederate organizations had nearly sundered the United States.

While confederacies divided nations from within, empires smothered them from without. An empire, Mulford argued, is an "accumulation of peoples, and is formed not in organic relation, but is held by a formal and external bond, which is the imperial decree." The Roman Empire that crushed Israel served as the ancient illustration; the Roman Church that adopted many of its organizational principles, the modern. To safeguard its own temporal power, the Catholic Church had repeatedly blocked national aspirations, according to Mulford. Only the collapse of its spiritual monopoly in western and central Europe had made the modern growth of nation-states possible. The preaching of Martin Luther, Mulford claimed, brought "the awakening of the national spirit." The church, however, struggled to regain its political and religious dominance after the Reformation:

> The nations have been involved in a conflict with Rome for their integral unity and being. The struggle has been for their existence, their order, their freedom. There is none as it has sought to realize its freedom, that has been exempt from the secret or open assault of Rome. Its attack has taken on every form, and there is no weapon however cruel, and no device however false, which it has not used, and no ally however evil, which it has not engaged. It has appeared on every field as the foe of the life and liberties of nations.[18]

Mulford detailed that record of attack with examples of church-state conflict in England, France, Germany, the Low Countries, and Italy. Everywhere he raised the specter of ecclesiastical despotism weakening and dividing peoples. With "some eminent individual exceptions," he noted, church officials had favored the Confederacy and saw no glory in the nation's deliverance from slavery. Though it was not certain if the church would attack the United States directly, the threat would continue, according to Mulford. America's "unity and *education* and freedom will meet in Roman catholicism [*sic*], it may be guarded and often concealed, but an unceasing antagonist."[19]

Mulford's analysis was a long way from the fevered imaginings of *Maria Monk's Awful Disclosures.* He based his conclusions on close reading of classical and modern philosophers, to whom he had been exposed during extended study in Europe. His claim that Protestantism was critical for the development of nationalism in Europe was hard to refute and, in fact, remains widely accepted among scholars today.[20] His argument that church officials had tried to subvert nationalist movements had firm historical grounding as well. During the nineteenth century, popes and bishops repeatedly advised Catholics to keep their national impulses subordinate to their faith. The Vatican also condemned separation of church and state, a doctrine that many Americans believed underlay their own national unity and civil peace. To many an opponent of parochial schools, even their pedagogy looked like a threat to America. Many evangelicals believed that public schools cultivated moral reason in children. They expected that a personal understanding of good and evil, and with it a dedication to Christian righteousness, would lead to national regeneration. They argued that Catholic schools, in contrast, taught children to follow the dictates of popes, bishops, and priests blindly. Catholics thus never developed their own sense of moral direction or an ability to seek truth on its own terms. The fear that young people might learn to think for themselves, argued opponents of Catholic education, was the *real* reason for the clergy's opposition to Bible reading in public schools.[21]

Josiah Strong, a leading social reformer and evangelical leader, developed this argument in *Our Country: Its Possible Future and Present Crisis,* a popular book that sold nearly two hundred thousand copies in the three decades after its first publication in 1886. "Everyone born a Roman Catholic is suckled on authority," wrote Strong, arguing that the contrast between a Catholic spirit of submission and a Protestant one of manly independence could be seen most clearly in the contest over education. "The public school seeks to give both knowledge and discipline, not only truth but the power to find truth. The parochial school aims to lead, rather than to train the mind," he wrote. "The one system is calculated to arouse, the other to suppress, the spirit of inquiry. The one aims at self-control, the other at control by superiors." The effects of the Catholic approach to learning could be seen across the globe, according to this line of reasoning. While "Protestant nations are marching with such giant strides to the conquest of the world," remarked Dorchester in *Romanism versus the Public School System,* "why is it that papal nations remain stationary or settle into decadence?"[22] For Dorchester and Strong, the United States was undeniably a Protestant country, one fated for unparalleled greatness. But it was their underlying fear that America's destiny might yet be snatched away by a growing enemy within, by foreign agents sapping at the nation's vitals, that lent such emotional power to the school question.

Protestants who feared the influence of parochial schools sought greater regulation of them, particularly at the state level. They demanded the teaching of English, often its exclusive use, and instruction in patriotism and American history. But history, like many academic subjects, presented a problem for devout Catholics. For much of the nineteenth century, anti-Catholic sentiments riddled many widely available textbooks, a problem that had led to the hierarchy's official call for more appropriate volumes as far back as the 1830s.[23]

Readers, geographies, histories, and other schoolbooks portrayed the church as a haven of ignorance, superstition, greed, and lust. A tongue-twisting sentence from an 1850s spelling book combined a vocabulary lesson with a study of clerical dissipation: "The controversy at the monastery with regard to the profligacy of the clergy encouraged proselytism." Histories were subtler, but bias was unmistakable. In her *History of the United States; or, Republic of America,* one of the most popular texts of the century, Emma Willard termed Catholicism "popery." Marcius Willson referred to "Popish priests" in his schoolbook and was even less politic in his trade histories. Until Luther, he told his readers, Christians had been "supinely acquiescing in the numerous absurdities inculcated by the 'head of the Church.'" He added that one sixteenth-century pontiff was "exceedingly profligate, and is known to have been a disbeliever in Christianity itself, which he called '*A very profitable fable for him and his predecessors.*'" Willson even lent some support to the hoary claim that the pope was the Antichrist.[24]

Direct schoolbook attacks on the church became less frequent as the century drew to a close and publishers became sensitive to the concerns of Catholics who sent children to public schools. But overt bias did not disappear entirely. An 1870s American history still classed Catholics as papists and lamented the lack of "pure religion" before the Reformation. A textbook on the recommended reading list for Virginia teachers condemned the "idolatrous and dangerous doctrines" of the church.[25]

It was easy enough for writers or publishers to remove an offensive term or even entire passage from their books. A more intractable problem was the way Catholicism had been embedded in larger narrative frameworks. From the 1820s onward, belief in American exceptionalism dominated both trade and school histories. Writers contrasted the unique political freedoms, economic opportunity, and religious tolerance of the United States to the monarchies, class strife, and bigotry of the Old World. The Reformation assumed a central place in the story of America's rise. As Willson explained in the trade history mentioned earlier, it led to "the advance of civilization, true religion, and republican principles, throughout all subsequent history." Willson suggested that the seed of the American nation had been planted by Luther in Germany and then transplanted to America by the Puritans. Willard sketched a similar picture, though she was somewhat kinder to Catholics. The church's absolutism in moral and political realms, she wrote, was necessary to restore order in the aftermath of the Roman Empire's fall, and its monks and priests saved remnants of ancient learning for a thousand years afterward. Subsequently, however, "light broke in on the darkness of the ages" with the discovery of America, the spread of printing, and the Reformation.[26] After that, Catholicism became a reactionary force best quarantined in the Old World.

Contrasts between the progressive-minded settlers of the New World (coded Protestant) and the backward-looking peoples of Europe (coded Catholic) appeared frequently in these histories. Ministers earned praise for their thrift, devotion, and republican simplicity. "In the United States," noted a history from the 1830s, "there are indeed no 'rich and splendid situations in the church.'" The author made the explicit comparison to Anglican prelates, but applying it to Catholic officials in Europe required no leap of imagination. Unlike open attacks on "popery," such comparisons remained common in textbooks for decades, even into the twentieth century. A popular title from the 1880s imagined the English gazing enviously upon their cousins in America during the seventeenth century: "They saw colonies there governing themselves, and churches prospering without bishop or priest. They saw New England people making laws much simpler and juster than those of England, and they asked why all this could not be done at home." Democratically inclined Americans, such passages suggested, found little use for ecclesiastical hierarchies of the Catholic or Anglican kind.[27]

These histories made the Puritan of New England the central character of the American story. That bias was only natural. Most authors were from the region, and they had access to a large collection of colonial records from Massachusetts, which established the first state historical society in 1794. Writers of school histories also cribbed heavily from adult-oriented, multivolume works by scholars like George Bancroft. Bancroft, the Massachusetts-born "father" of American historiography, had written the first national history by making the story of the United States, in part, the story of New England writ large.[28] In both trade books and schoolbooks, Puritans appeared as the proverbial Americans—liberty-loving, hard-working, practical, scholarly, and devout.

Schoolbook Nation

John Clark Ridpath, who wrote trade histories and schoolbooks, offered a typically glowing portrait in a text for young readers:

> The gaze of the Puritan was turned ever to posterity. He believed in the future. For his children he toiled and sacrificed. The system of free-schools is a monument to his love. The printing-press is his memorial. Almshouses and asylums are the tokens of his care for the unfortunate. With him the outcast found sympathy, and the wanderer a home. He was the earliest champion of civil rights, and the builder of THE UNION.

Ridpath admitted that in "matters of religion the fathers of New England were sometimes intolerant and superstitious" and that their form of worship could be "cold and severe." But he concluded his chapter on colonial New England by declaring that "Puritanism contained within itself the power to correct its own abuses. The evil of the system may well be forgotten in the glory of its achievements. Without the Puritans, America would have been a delusion, and liberty only a name."[29] Thus while writers acknowledged the Puritans' chief flaw of intolerance, they also used it to highlight their virtues more plainly. Detailing a few of the prejudices of initial settlers had another advantage for writers, as Ridpath suggests here. They could then better render American history as a tale of moral and social progress led by the Puritan spirit.

Schoolbooks often borrowed another narrative element from heftier tomes by trade historians, particularly Francis Parkman. Parkman, another New Englander, penned the nine-volume series *France and England in North America.* His books portrayed the continent as an epic battleground in which forces of Protestantism, led by the progressive, democratic English, were pitted against those of Catholicism, backed by the corrupt monarchies of France and Spain. The ritual, dogma, and ancient history of the Catholic Church both repelled and fascinated Parkman. He admired the fierce determination and spiritual conviction of French missionaries in Canada but believed that British settlers had to triumph over them and their faith in order to set the stage for the American republic. Willard, writing at roughly the same time as Parkman, shared those views. In a chapter offering grudging respect to the Jesuits, she nevertheless compared their zeal unfavorably with the devotion of the Puritans. Catholic missionaries, she pointed out, "unfortunately mingled worldly policy with religious enthusiasm;

Rise of the (Catholic) American Nation

and sought not only to win souls to Christ, but subjects to the King of France, and the papal dominion."[30]

Parkman and Willard's explicit coupling of Catholicism with political despotism began to disappear from books destined for the school market by the 1870s, a casualty of Catholic complaints. But the underlying narrative often remained unchanged. Ridpath declared a bit euphemistically that British victory in the French and Indian War meant that "the decaying institutions of the Middle Ages should not prevail in America," discreetly avoiding mention of what one such institution might be. Professionally trained historians, who began to dominate textbook authorship in the 1890s, also saw American history partly as a religious rivalry between Catholics and Protestants. In David Saville Muzzey's *American History,* for instance, that story played out in Texas in the 1830s. Mexican officials "subjected" the province, with its "predominating Protestant religion, its traditions of free government, and its freedom of speech and press, to the Roman Catholic Spanish officials of the smaller province of Coahuila," Muzzey told his readers. Elsewhere in his books Muzzey strongly condemned slavery, but not here. As his morality tale cast Catholics as oppressors, Muzzey sidestepped the fact that Mexican officials also opposed the liberty-loving Protestants' introduction of that institution to the territory.[31]

Like the amateurs who preceded them, most professional historians still saw the British triumph in the French and Indian War as the turning point in the battle for Protestant ideals. William H. Mace, a professor at Syracuse University, dealt somewhat obliquely with the issue in his *School History of the United States.* French loss meant merely that America would have no "state religion" and that it would inherit a tradition of political liberty. Mace was considerably more blunt in a guide for teaching history that was exempt from the political trials of adoption. There he told instructors why 1763 was a red-letter date in American history:

This struggle decided that North America should become a new home for English Protestantism, and that French Catholicism must return to European soil. This result lifted a great load from the minds and hearts of the English colonists. Yet, even if victory had belonged to France, the religious effect would have been just as great, and the principle of historical growth would have been as fully illustrated. Again, this war brought into personal contact the Puritan, the Baptist, the Dutchman, and the Cavalier; they messed together, marched together, and fought together; they shared each other's joys and sorrows, victories and defeats. Seven years of this and other forms of mutual intercourse did much to tone down religious exclusiveness and prejudice. A series of military events thus produced profound religious effects. This war also decided that free instead of parochial schools should bless America.[32]

Mace's passage shows how cultural battles between Catholics and Protestants were played out through written history. Forgetting some of his more dubious conclusions (when had Québec and Mexico, both predominantly Catholic, both in North America, become homes for English Protestantism?), note how he used Catholicism as a foil for the development of a religious tolerance that embraces a melting pot of Protestant creeds—Puritan, Baptist, Anglican. The "Catholic" of Maryland, a colony originally founded for persecuted members of the faith, is conspicuously absent. Mace then took the dispute over schooling, which did not emerge until the 1830s, and projected it almost seventy years further back in history—and declared victory for the common schools! Like Beecher, Strong, and Dorchester, Mace exuded confidence that providence had made America a Protestant nation and at the same time barely camouflaged his fear that it might not remain so much longer. As large numbers of immigrant Catholics were developing a siege mentality in the nineteenth century, so were many of their Protestant antagonists.

Thus, essentially two factors led Catholics to create their own history textbooks. First was a general climate of prejudice in the United States. Second was the narrower question of schooling itself. Struggles over the meaning of American nationalism, and how it would accommodate the pluralist challenge Catholics posed, erupted continually around the issue of education. The teaching of history became particularly contentious. Robert Ellis Thompson, a writer on educational policy influenced by Elisha Mulford, argued that well-written history should make "a student feel that his calling, as a member of a nation, is a lofty and solemn thing." For Thompson, a supporter of classroom reading of the King James Bible, and for many like-minded advocates of public school expansion, America's national consciousness was bound inextricably with its Protestant heritage. That bias pervaded popular school histories for much of the nineteenth century, sometimes in overt attacks on Catholics but more often through exclusion of them from an American story of progress. Naturally, Catholic educators found such books unacceptable. And once enough parochial schools had been opened to support their own niche market for textbooks, Catholics gained the opportunity to launch a curricular counteroffensive.

In new texts designed specifically for their own schools, Catholic writers depicted a nation that included Catholics more fully as equal, even favored, citizens. Their books rebutted claims that Catholicism was an intolerant, anti-progressive force, what Josiah Strong called a "fossil faith," which Protestant America had left behind in Europe.[33] Writers of these texts now gave Catholics important roles in the story of national creation and development. Disputing a popular theme in public school texts, they sought to demonstrate to students that Catholics were not simply a group to be tolerated, in tribute to Protestant magnanimity, but one to be celebrated for their part in the pageant of American history. They started, appropriately, with Columbus.

Stories about the explorer had been a staple in school histories since the mid–nineteenth century. Most authors adopted the worshipful tone of Washington Irving, who began publishing a three-volume biography of the Italian navigator in 1828 and soon raised him to the status of national hero. In the hands of Catholic writers, however, he took on additional meaning. They took the daring and industrious adventurer who sailed west seeking the riches of the spice trade and combined him with the devout Catholic. This Columbus's motives for undertaking his voyage also included converting the natives of East Asia and gathering capital for a military campaign to recapture Jerusalem from the Turks. Writers thus linked the discovery of the Americas to the Crusades and the early efforts of Franciscan missionaries in China, both of which were covered in many of these texts. "Columbus was deeply religious," one author informed his readers. "While he had made earnest studies in the sciences, the leading motive of his life was the hope of seeing the Catholic religion believed by all the peoples of the world." This depiction of Columbus contrasted sharply with that offered by authors writing for public schools. Many of them downplayed his Catholicism, while others, including Emma Willard, tied early explorations of the New World to the Renaissance, the Reformation, and a general reawakening of a Europe that had slumbered under the influence of the church.[34]

Unlike their peers in public schools, parochial school students also learned that Columbus's eventual success in persuading King Ferdinand and Queen Isabella to bankroll his venture was due to the intercession of his friend Juan Pérez. This influential prior of a monastery in the Spanish port city of Palos almost always merited an illustration in these books (see fig. on p. 109). He believed, noted one text published in 1914, in the "globular theory of the form of the earth" that had been "preserved during the Middle Ages partly by Arab philosophers, but chiefly by the great monastic and secular scholars of the Catholic Church." The "worthy priest" also helped to secure a crew for Columbus by convincing the people of Palos "of the feasibility of the voyage and the unreality of imaginary ocean terrors." Now properly fitted out, Columbus set sail "relying firmly on God and his own scientific theory."[35]

The authors' emphasized science and knowledge in their version of this story quite intentionally. Charges that the church resisted intellectual progress had stung American Catholics for decades. In a typical attack on the "educational pretensions of Rome," Dorchester asked, "How has she treated the profound original investigators, like Galileo, who have pushed their inquiries beyond the old dusty beaten paths into new realms of thought and discovery?" Catholic journals and newspapers shot back. A writer for the *Catholic World* claimed that mankind owed to Catholics most of the leading inventions of the past, from the printing press and compass to clocks and telescopes.[36]

Accounts of Columbus and Pérez in these histories allowed Catholics another means to contest this negative stereotype of the church. When mainstream publishers began targeting the parochial school market, they showed special sensitivity to the relation of scientific advancement, a critical element of the narrative of progress in public school histories, to the church. In 1921 editors and readers at the American Book Company suspected that the manuscript for a grammar school history might not be ready for publication. One critic asked, "Would a biography of [John] Holland, the (Irish Catholic) inventor of the submarine be out of place? I think not, provided equal space be given, in the same chapter, to the Wright Brothers, inventors of the airplane."[37]

Authors of books for parochial schools developed positive themes of Catholic discoveries and contributions to knowledge most extensively in early chapters on the exploration of the Americas, however, as the example of Columbus suggests. Beginning with his landing at San Salvador and the chanting of the Te Deum, a prayer of thanksgiving, Catholic ritual played a central role in these accounts. Where it was almost always absent in illustrations from common-school texts, in

FATHER PEREZ PLEADING WITH ISABELLA.

9. Father Juan Perez.—About the year 1484, while on a short journey, Columbus accidentally stopped for refreshment at the monastery of Santa Maria de la Rabida, about half a league from Palos.[21] Here he found a warm friend and powerful advocate, in the person of the prior Juan Perez. This good Franciscan, struck by the noble appearance of the stranger, entered into conversation with him, soon appreciated his genius, and beholding in Columbus the marks of a providential election, devoted himself to his interest, with an ardor which ceased only with life.

10. When, in 1491, Columbus was about to leave Spain

Catholic textbooks, unlike their public school counterparts, emphasized how the timely intercession of a Franciscan prior made the "discovery" of America possible. They also argued that Catholic missionaries "consecrated America with blood shed for Christ" long before the arrival of Protestants. And in one book, the Catholic "Pilgrims" of Maryland upstaged the earlier settlers from the *Mayflower*. All illustrations are from *Sadlier's Excelsior Studies in the History of the United States* (1879).

MARTYRS IN THE NEW WORLD.

Potomac, and cast anchor near an island which they called
St. Clements. On board, were about three hundred colonists,
including four Jesuits (Fathers Altham and White, with two
lay brothers). Having landed on the Festival of the Annun-

LANDING OF THE MARYLAND PILGRIMS.

ciation, Mass was celebrated for the first time in that wild
region. A large cross was also erected as a symbol of
Christianity, which had now taken possession of those shores.
Two days later, the town of St. Mary's was founded, nearer

Catholic volumes a prominent cross invariably appeared alongside Europeans as they made their way through tropical jungle or northern forest. The cross, noted one history, "always accompanied, and sometimes even preceded the banner of earthly conquest." As a testament to the religious devotion of conquistador and voyageur, America became a "veritable geographic litany of saints." In some cases, such as the St. Lawrence and St. John's Rivers, the Catholic names stuck; in others, they did not. Hernando DeSoto's River of the Holy Ghost became Father Jacques Marquette's River of the Immaculate Conception, only to revert to its original Indian name, the Mississippi.[38] Unlike mainstream texts, Catholic histories usually included these lost appellations.

Even more important than Catholics' roles as explorers, the books argued, was the willingness of Jesuits and Franciscans to give their lives for their faith. The work of martyrs filled the pages of these textbooks, and often the "sublime death of missionaries" was not for the squeamish. In a school history published in the late 1870s we read of the end of Jean de Brébeuf and Gabriel Lalement:

> Amid the din rose the voice of the old Huron missionary
> [Bréboeuf] consoling his converts, denouncing God's judgements on the unbeliever, till his executioners crushed his mouth
> with a stone, cut off his nose and lips, and thrust a brand into
> his mouth, so that his throat and tongue, burnt and swollen,
> refused their office.
> They tore off his scalp, and thrice, in derision of his baptism,
> poured water over his head. . . . Hacking off his feet, they clove
> open his chest, took out his noble heart and devoured it.[39]

The author borrowed this graphic account from John Gilmary Shea, the first widely read and respected Catholic American historian and a key source for textbook writers. The opposite page featured a woodcut illustration of the missionary seconds before he is to be burned at the stake. He stares skyward as the crown of martyrdom descends on a shaft of light (see fig. on p. 110).

On one level the author seemed to have chosen this incident to impart to students a sense of the drama of America's past. Many contemporary texts, often called "compilations," provided little more than a collection of facts and dates students were expected to memorize. As the author of this book noted in his preface, the "'dryness' of American history is, at present, proverbial with teacher and student." But the meaning of such stories went deeper. The cruel mock baptism endured by Brébeuf suggested a more profound one experienced by the continent itself. Such suffering showed, as another text stated, that missionaries had "consecrated America with blood shed for Christ, and made our country a holy country before it was ever a republic."[40] Authors often placed these acts of martyrdom at sites they designated as future homes of American states, including Kansas, New Mexico, Michigan, and Maine. Catholicism thus gained spiritual claim to the land well in advance of Protestant settlers.

These books advanced the theme of "prior claim" even when priests did not die at the hands of Indians. Catholic students first saw California not through the eyes of victorious soldiers in the Mexican War or gold prospectors who trekked to the territory in 1849 but from the perspective of Junipo Serra and other leaders of Indian missions who arrived more than one hundred years before the Americans. "For many years the Jesuits conducted flourishing missions in Lower California, and besides converting the natives taught them the arts of civilization," reported a typical Catholic history published in 1892. Charles H. McCarthy, a professor at Catholic University in Washington, D.C., told students that the missions marked "the beginning of California." What Serra did for California, the Belgian Jesuit Peter DeSmet repeated among the Flathead Indians in Oregon Country. McCarthy argued that his textbook, unlike those made for public schools, showed the important part Catholics had played in the "winning of the West." A geography volume meant to accompany one publisher's history text featured study questions that included the following: "Where, in many of the States, were the first settlements formed?" Answer: "Around the humble cross that marked the site of a Catholic mission."[41]

Texts by Catholic authors did more than fit Catholics into a preexisting narrative of discovery and settlement. They also challenged several myths common in mainstream books: that Indians were irreconcilably hostile to "civilization"; that westward expansion was an essentially Anglo-Saxon triumph; and that White, mostly nuclear families first productively tilled the soil, transforming wilderness into economically productive national space. The claim that celibate priests had undertaken many of the earliest acts of nation building, and that these included conversion of the Indians to Catholicism, deeply troubled critics of these histories. The geography text with the question about the "humble cross" of the missions infuriated one Protestant reviewer, who addressed the subject in a book published in 1888:

And this is a good sample of the proportion assigned to Jesuit missionaries all through these books. . . . The descendant of the New England Puritans, or of other worthies whom some of us have been in the habit of thinking as standing for something in this American enterprise, is moved to ask the Jesuit, when he reads of all his accomplishments in these books, "Did any body help you found the American republic?"[42]

Nativist rhetoric in the late nineteenth and early twentieth centuries was premised on the understanding that Catholics, at least significant numbers of them, had arrived in America only recently. By stressing a narrative of "firsts"—first Europeans to see the New World, first to introduce Christianity and civilization to Indians, first to found a city in the United States (St. Augustine in Florida)—these histories partially reversed that model. Their authors argued that Catholic legitimacy in America, whether through the efforts of lay explorers, missionaries, or colonists, was centuries old and could be traced at least as far back as Columbus and Juan Pérez. Perhaps even further, to Norse and Irish Catholics who, they noted, appeared to have arrived on the continent before 1492. "The discovery of America was pre-eminently a Catholic enterprise. In fact, Protestantism did not yet exist," claimed the author of *Sadlier's History*. In this Catholic version of events, Columbus and his immediate contemporaries departed from a united Europe that still recognized the pope as successor to St. Peter and arrived in a world where millions of "souls might be harvested for heaven."[43] The authors thus placed America's discovery in an era of spiritual harmony. Martin Luther smashed that unity in the Old World, seriously disrupting continued exploration of the New, according to one history. However, the America these writers depicted held the promise of eventually restoring sectarian peace. But to achieve that end Catholics would first have to endure hardship among the Protestant majority.

While Catholic schoolbooks treated the history of the French and Spanish in North America more thoroughly than their common-school counterparts, all authors devoted the largest share of their pre-Revolutionary narrative to the British colonies. Catholic writers, however, often subjected the early settlers of Massachusetts to a level of criticism uncommon among other authors, except those who penned texts for the Southern market. While they acknowledged Puritan contributions to American culture, they made Maryland their most truly American colony. Established by the Catholic Lord Baltimore, it served as a model for religious tolerance, home rule, and amicable relations with the Indians.

In *Sadlier's History,* the 1634 arrival of three hundred English colonists on the Festival of the Annunciation clearly vied with the landing of the *Mayflower* as America's founding myth. The "pilgrims" (the term was used for the Marylanders and not for the settlers at Plymouth; see fig. 9) arrived in the *Ark* and the *Dove* after fleeing religious persecution in England. "Mass was celebrated for the first time in that wild region," wrote the author. "A large cross was also erected as a symbol of Christianity, which had now taken possession of these shores." Another text pointed out that these pilgrims planted their original settlement, St. Mary's, "near the sites of the future Mount Vernon, and the future political center of the nation, the capital city of Washington"—a geography lesson clearly meant to tie this city's founding to the nation's future destiny. The Marylanders were "imbued with the true colonizing spirit." The contrast was not to the Puritans, for even these books grudgingly noted their industriousness, but to the original Protestant settlers at Jamestown. "In six months," noted one writer, John Hassard, in what would become a stock refrain in these books, "St. Mary's made more progress than Virginia had in six years."[44]

While the first Lord Baltimore and his sons Cecil and Leonard Calvert set up the colony as a refuge for English Catholics, they welcomed all Christians. It was a liberal gesture, which the books stressed, but also a practical one, because religious exclusion would have antagonized the British king and other colonists. The policy became official with the Toleration Act of 1649. "There was never any departure from this rule as long as Maryland remained Catholic, and it was a rule that prevailed nowhere else," wrote Hassard. The colony also sought peace with the region's native inhabitants. "Maryland, unlike most of the other colonies, never had any serious Indian troubles," according to one author. The settlers paid for the land, the Jesuit fathers learned the Indian languages and worked to convert the natives, and the "red men responded well to their zeal." Protestants outside Maryland, however, *were* always menacing this idyllic community, claimed the texts. Anglican Virginia "was jealous from the beginning," but others were even more hostile. Baltimore had welcomed members of Virginia's Puritan minority, but later, in league with the Commonwealth Parliament in London, those same Puritans disfranchised the Catholics and "sent Father Andrew White, the Apostle of Maryland, in chains to England."[45]

Schoolbook Nation

The misguided zeal of the Puritans better illustrated the true Christian devotion of martyrs and missionaries like White, who stood trial and later gained his freedom. In many Catholic histories, particularly those published before 1900, Massachusetts was the tale of a colony gone wrong. While the authors were generally sympathetic with the Plymouth Pilgrims, they were much less so with the Puritan settlers of the Great Migration of 1630. "Although they had left England on account of religious persecution, they had no idea of granting to others the liberty of worship which they claimed for themselves," noted Hassard. All the Catholic authors discussed the persecution of Quakers and the expulsion of two religious dissidents, Anne Hutchinson and Roger Williams, topics covered with less indignation by Protestants like John Ridpath. Catholics also noted that Massachusetts banned the entry of Jesuits, a fact other histories generally ignored. Hassard castigated Bostonians for burning an effigy of the pope each year, a practice continued until the Revolutionary War, when no less a figure than George Washington rebuked them for the "ridiculous and childish custom." Several writers dwelt upon Puritans' exacting morality, from the prohibition of mince pie on Christmas Day to the sundry restrictions in the Blue Laws of Connecticut. "Amusements were prohibited, and gayety was deemed sinful," read one book's section on Puritan "Manners." The words wrapped around an illustration of two sad-looking men, their wrists and ankles clapped in the stocks, being punished for some unknown but apparently petty transgression.[46]

The authors' emphasis on this aspect of Puritan life reflected social conflicts at the time they wrote, as did much of the history in these books. In the late nineteenth century, conservative, native-born Protestants regularly condemned Catholic immigrants for public drinking and for failing to observe the Sabbath with appropriate decorum. Here, in an indirect way, Catholics tried to shift the argument by suggesting the real problem lay in Protestant self-righteousness.

The witchcraft delusion of 1692 provided Catholic writers with their strongest corroboration for charges against the Puritans. In Hassard's book, an Irish Catholic woman unable to recite the Lord's Prayer in any language but Latin was the first victim. The trials and executions were an "extraordinary episode" that, according to another writer, "astonished the civilized world." Later Catholic histories noted that belief in witches was common in contemporary Europe, but none mentioned similar episodes under the Inquisition. The Salem trials, concluded a nineteenth-century text, shocked even Indians in the region. They "could not but contrast a religion which permitted such cruel fanaticism, and whose ministers had acted so prominent a part in the fearful tragedy, with that of the mild, devoted, and self sacrificing Jesuit missionaries of Maine." Books for public schools also covered the Salem trials but, as one might expect, never used them to show the greater virtues of Catholics. Many Protestant authors considered the affair an unfortunate historical anomaly; others tried to qualify the guilt of the perpetrators. "The Puritans were very much ashamed for what they had done, though they had acted with entire honesty," explained Edward Taylor, author of a history issued in several editions from the 1870s through the 1890s. "One old judge used to keep a day of fasting and prayer every year to atone for the sins he had committed."[47]

Catholic texts also showed considerable sympathy for another group that endured even greater wrath from Protestant settlers in New England—the Indians. While Indians had first welcomed the colonists, according to these histories, they soon discovered that the Puritan policy toward them was generally one of extermination. Frequent wars ensued. Often the books linked Puritan violence against Indians with that against Catholics. Almost all included an account of the death of Father Sebastien Rasles, a Jesuit missionary among the Indians along the Kennebec River in Maine. In 1724 a party of English colonists attacked the village where he ministered. Seeing he was the target of the assault, a text explained, Rasles came out to meet them: "Pierced by several bullets, he fell at the foot of the mission cross. Seven chiefs, who had gathered about him, shared his fate, and the settlement was annihilated." After "hacking his body to pieces," the attackers "rifled the altar, profaned the Host and the sacred vessels, and burned the church." Several books pictured the Jesuit. In one, he lies dead, his arm wrapped about the cross; in another, he shelters an Indian woman and her child as he struggles to stay the hand of a marauding soldier.[48]

Disagreement over Rasles's true part in the long series of conflicts among English settlers, Indians, and the French divided Catholic and Protestant writers. Several books intended for public schools described events far differently. Emma Willard claimed that Rasles had collaborated with the governor of Québec to encourage Indian attacks on English settlements, most notably the town of Brunswick. Another writer speculated that the Jesuit "abetted their cruelties with his own hands."[49]

Catholic texts argued that attitudes toward Indians, Catholics, and their fellow colonists showed that "the Puritans practiced in the New World the same intolerance from which they suffered in the Old."[50] In short, they betrayed the promise of America by introducing here the same sectarian strife that Luther and Calvin had begun in Europe. Maryland began its history by opening its doors to Catholic and Protestant alike; Massachusetts began hers by expelling to Rhode Island, Connecticut, or New Hampshire those colonists who failed to toe the line on narrow Puritan doctrines.

That historical vision sometimes clashed sharply with its Protestant counterpart, as the case of Father Rasles shows. In the seventeenth century, the settlers of New England first advanced the claim that they had built a "City on a Hill," a shining model of how decadent Christianity, riddled with the empty ritual and superstition of the Old World (i.e., in its Anglican and especially Catholic forms), might be purified in America. Their nineteenth-century Protestant descendants partially secularized that narrative, making the republic a political as well as spiritual example for the world. A sense of Protestant destiny remained, however. In one of his less charitable moments, George Bancroft condemned Maryland's founder, Lord Baltimore, for bringing "antiquated and rotten" social forms to America. Catholic historians, in contrast, made Marylanders and Catholics elsewhere in the Americas truer inhabitants of the "City on a Hill." Bancroft's Catholic colleague John Gilmary Shea thought responsibility for bringing "rotten" ideas to America did not belong with Catholics, and he had no patience for Protestant scholars who held their ancestors in such high esteem. For "writers to claim for the Fathers of New England the high honor of establishing liberty of conscience . . . is a farce too contemptible for consideration," Shea declared in a Catholic journal, saving that distinction, again, for the colonists in Maryland. Puritans were better understood as "tyrannical," "intolerant," "cruel and unmerciful," "grasping and avaricious," and—flinging an anti-Catholic charge back at its source—"full of superstition." Shea had to pull some of his punches when writing textbooks. In one, a brief reference to the Massachusetts settlers rehabilitated them into "industrious, earnest men, who suffered much, but gradually prospered."[51]

Shea's peers who targeted the school market were often similarly circumspect, but the worldview of Catholic scholars and trade historians still clearly shaped their schoolbooks. While they did not completely abandon the popular narrative of American promise in which Puritans acted a decisive part, they did question many assumptions that underlay it.

The Puritans, identified as such, usually made their final appearance in these books when the authors discussed British actions on the eve of the Revolution. In 1774 Parliament passed the Québec Act, which extended that province's boundary southward to the Ohio River and guaranteed freedom of worship for French-Canadian Catholics. The move galvanized anti-British and anti-Catholic sentiment in the English colonies, fueling anger that led to the war's first battles the following year. New Englanders in particular felt that Britain planned to use the legislation to hem them in by ringing their settlements with spiritually if not militarily hostile forces. Opposition to the Québec Act united the colonists, but their fury over the alleged Catholic threat it represented chilled relations with the Québecois and undermined subsequent efforts to form an alliance with Canada.

Textbooks for the common schools treated this episode with remarkable brevity. They often lumped the Québec Act with the four "Intolerable Acts"—including those authorizing the quartering of British troops and the closing of the Port of Boston—without mentioning its provisions. Where authors did discuss the Québec measure, they emphasized the boundary issue, not the religious one. Their reticence is not hard to understand. Suggestions that hostility to Catholics united the thirteen colonies, even in a small way, fit poorly with stories that stressed the growth of religious tolerance in early America. Catholic texts, however, approached the episode differently. One author, Thomas Bonaventure Lawler, actually praised the British for this "act of justice" to the French-Canadians. But many writers had Irish ancestry, as did their readers, so tributes to English liberality remained quite limited. The act was, according to one book, a transparent attempt by the "same power that cruelly persecuted Catholics in Ireland" to dissuade Québec from joining the increasingly restive colonies to the south. But the parochial school texts also criticized the Americans. "It was hard for the Puritans to learn the lesson of toleration," declared one history. "It was Puritan intolerance and bitterness, rather than the action of England, which prevented the Canadians from sympathizing with the Revolutionary cause. For the Continental Congress to permit an address in which the Catholic religion was said to inculcate 'persecution, murder, and rebellion,' was, to say the least, not tactful."[52]

These textbooks went to great lengths to show American Catholics' wholehearted support for the War of Independence, the prejudices of their compatriots notwithstanding. Catholics constituted about 1 percent of the population of the United States in 1790, but their exploits filled far more than that proportion of pages devoted to the Revolution. Each history included a retinue of Catholic heroes, many of whom went unmentioned in common-school texts. There was Maryland's Charles Carroll, the "richest man in the colonies," who risked his fortune by signing the Declaration of Independence. There was John Barry, the head of the American navy, who captured five British ships on the Delaware River without losing a man. In the Old Northwest Father Pierre Gibault came to the aid of George Rogers Clark, blessed French settlers who joined the conflict against Britain, and enlisted "Christian Indians in favor of the Americans." The "heroic march of Clark and the friendly offices of Father Gibault" secured this territory for the young nation, one writer reminded his readers. Several lesser figures also usually merited mention, including the Catholic Indian chief Orono, who assisted Washington's army. And there were Catholics among the noble foreigners who "played a glorious part in the winning" of independence. They included the Poles Thaddeus Kosciusko and Casimir Pulaski; the German Baron De Kalb; a little-known Italian named François Vigo; and, of course, the Marquis de Lafayette, the Frenchman who also served as a hero in books designed for public schools. Inclusion of figures like De Kalb, Pulaski, and Vigo especially pleased communities of German, Polish, and Italian immigrants. They identified with these figures on ethnic as well as religious grounds, though these books usually stressed the latter. Books for parochial schools, unlike their Protestant counterparts, also emphasized that two of America's critical allies in the war, France and Spain, were *Catholic* countries.[53]

Suggestions of Protestant mistreatment of Catholics, relatively common in coverage of colonial history, generally disappeared while authors explained the course of the war itself. Unlike stories of discovery and exploration, accounts of the Revolution did not stress Catholic primacy. Instead, the authors emphasized inclusion. Catholic heroes did not replace what had already become a national pantheon; they supplemented it. John Hancock always joined Charles Carroll. John Paul Jones appeared alongside John Barry. Clark accompanied Gibault. This pattern recurred throughout the books. Writers linked well-known national heroes with the church, individual Catholics, or Catholic causes. At the close of the war in 1781, for instance, parishioners chanted a solemn Te Deum at St. Joseph's Church in Philadelphia. "Members of the United States Congress, Washington, Lafayette, and many of the distinguished generals and citizens attended," explained one of several histories that covered this event, which seemed to celebrate national unity under Catholic auspices.[54]

A subtle merging of political and ecclesiastical history became even more pronounced in discussion of the appointment of America's first ishop, a cousin of Charles Carroll. "It is interesting for Catholics to ote the fact that, simultaneously with the election of President Washigton as the civil executive of the young nation, Divine Providence rovided the infant American church with a spiritual executive in the erson of the illustrious Right Reverend John Carroll," noted one ook. Lest readers suspect the church might vie with the elected govrnment for authority, a charge nativists repeatedly lodged against 'atholics in the nineteenth and early twentieth centuries, one book dded that the pope had "inquired of Congress in what manner the rrangement" for Carroll's appointment could be made "without intering with the laws of the nation." Congress "assured him that the Jnited States had no jurisdiction over matters purely spiritual." In the 909 edition of his *History of the United States for Schools,* John P.)'Hara informed readers that Bishop Carroll became "a warm friend of Vashington and Franklin and other American leaders." O'Hara made ttle effort to square that amity with what he characterized as an apparntly rampant "fear of Catholicism" in the colonies as late as 1774.[55]

When discussing revered national heroes, it was usually best to ccentuate their positive relations with Catholics. When Washington vas elected for his first term, Carroll had sent a letter congratulating im on behalf of America's Catholic clergy. The new president replied vith a statement thanking Catholics for their efforts in the war. No nainstream texts ever mentioned Washington's note, but nearly all 'atholic ones quoted from it.

Like O'Hara, other writers did a poor job of explaining how prejudice had largely disappeared by the end of the war. They simply laimed that, after the military victory itself, the greatest triumph for his persecuted minority lay in the gratitude and respect they had arned from their countrymen. "In the day of trial the Catholic faith ad proven the grandeur of its principles," concluded one text, without larifying what the principles were, beyond the willingness of individual Catholics to fight. With the faithful's unflinching loyalty to the ause, and the softening of Protestant hearts, there "dawned a new era)f Catholicity in America."[56]

Catholics, along with many other Americans in the nineteenth and arly twentieth centuries, envisioned martial duty as a test of worthiess for citizenship and inclusion in the national community. These vriters thus repeatedly noted the heroism of Catholic soldiers and ailors. They were not alone in this strategy. White Southerners like 'ohn William Jones and Susan Pendleton Lee, who also wrote textooks during this period, stressed the importance of military sacrifice

too, giving extended coverage to regional heroes and Revolutionar
battles that took place in the South.

The same emphasis on wartime devotion returned in the Catholi
texts' coverage of later conflicts. In the Civil War, Philip Sheridan an
William Rosencrans led the roster of Catholic patriots. Writers tie
another national leader, this time Lincoln instead of Washington, t
the service of Catholics. Sister Mary Celeste's *American Histor*
quoted Lincoln praising the charity and benevolence shown by th
"Nuns of the Battlefield" (a photograph of a monument dedicated t
them appeared in the text). Once more, young readers saw the "hero
ism, devotion, and self-sacrifice shown" by Catholic soldiers, and b
the priests and sisters who ministered to them, "lessening the ignoran
prejudice felt against the Church." One thing had changed in this wa
however. While individual Catholics joined the Union or Confederat
armies, "Catholicity took no sides."[57]

In this narrative of events, one can again see Catholic author
responding to attacks made on the church at or near the time the
wrote. For Protestant intellectuals like Elisha Mulford and politician
like Daniel Dorchester, the failure of the church to repudiate slavery o
side with the Union was proof of its indifference, even hostility, to th
cause of national unity. These writers reached the opposite conclusion
The church had not equivocated on sacred moral issues. Instead it ha
shown that it is "always a peacemaker, never a partisan." Wherea
Methodists, Baptists, and other denominations had split into Norther
and Southern wings before the war, the Catholic Church "still stoo
undiminished in strength and unbroken in unity—the pride of her chil
dren and the admiration of thousands who, before the war, had looke
upon her progress with pride and jealous concern."[58]

On one level, this "impartiality" was critical to what writers saw a
the Catholic mission in contemporary America and the culmination o
the narrative trajectory in their histories. The country had first bee
discovered and explored by Catholics; Catholics championed the caus
of religious toleration, which created friction with other, less charitabl
settlers, especially the Puritans; Catholics and Protestants then unite
in the cause of independence; and now Catholicism had finally rise
above the political and religious fray.

These history writers portrayed Catholicism as a potentially bindin
force in American society using one of two techniques. The first relie
on negative example. In their books, nationally divisive forces ofte
arose outside of and in opposition to the church. Hassard informed hi

Rise of the (Catholic) American Nation

readers that Charles Guiteau, who assassinated President Garfield in 1881, had "at one time played the role of an anti-Catholic lecturer." Thomas Lawler noted that anti-Catholic agitators had the audacity to smash a block of stone that the pope had sent for the Washington Monument. Another book's treatment of anti-Catholic riots in Philadelphia linked attacks on Catholics with those on the nation itself. One church that the rioters destroyed, the author pointed out, was "memorable for having first rung out a peal on the Declaration of Independence."[59]

The second technique for displaying the power of Catholicism to bring Americans together was more direct. Writers argued that while the church and its members served as targets of bigotry, they sought reconciliation and offered solutions to a nation divided along lines of religion, class, region, and race. There can be "no true, permanent union except where the spirit and the faith are dominating forces," argued the authors of one text.[60]

In the preface to a text from the 1870s, Bishop John Spalding argued that if religion is the surest guide to patriotism, a point most critics of the church would surely have conceded, then perhaps the very diversity of America's Protestant creeds might prove America's undoing. Scientific rationalism, materialism, and atheism had led to the "breaking down of religious beliefs in various nations" during the nineteenth century, Spalding argued. In such environments, local questions take precedence over national ones, partisan strife replaces the "passion of patriotism," and the state may be driven to protect itself through force. That, Spalding implied, had happened before and during the Civil War. Protestant churches had been unable keep themselves, let alone the nation, in one piece. What force could prevent a recurrence of this danger? Spalding then turned nativist fears that the Catholic Church would fracture the American community on their head. Nothing could prevent such an outcome but a "great moral power" that could create respect and encourage obedience:

> The Catholic Church is that power, and the mission which she is destined to fulfil in behalf of American society is as yet hardly suspected, though an observant mind cannot but fail to perceive its vast importance. No other religion in the United States has unity of doctrine and discipline, or the consciousness of definite purposes, or a great and venerable history, and a confidence born of a thousand triumphs and victories wrung from defeat.

. . . Outside the Church there are shifting views, opinion, and theories; but there is not organic growth and progressive development of faith and discipline.[61]

Here is an argument that, on first examination, seems to support nativist theories that the church was plotting some sort of takeover of the republic—hardly the sentiment one would expect for a textbook on U.S. history. Spalding imagines an America where Catholics will assume theological, if not demographic, preeminence. In several ways his Catholic nation is the mirror image of the Protestant one advanced by Josiah Strong and Daniel Dorchester. He even employs the kind of organic metaphors favored by nationalists like Mulford. But now, instead of a Protestant majority assimilating the papist immigrant, Catholics and their church will assimilate the Protestants. Like Strong's polemics in *Our Country,* this argument appears to rest on the premise that profound differences separated Catholics and Protestants in America and that resolution had to come with the victory of one over the other.

There is a paradox at work here, however. Bishop Spalding was not a defiant ideologue eager to spar publicly with opponents like Strong. He could imagine a *Catholic* America because he thought there were few fundamental differences—religious, political, cultural—between the country's Catholic minority and its Protestant majority. America was already quietly advancing toward Catholic ideals, in Spalding's mind, as Catholics were advancing toward American ones. People "hardly suspected" the destiny of Catholicism in America because these changes were so gradual and natural. With this short passage, Spalding suggested where he stood in the greatest dispute within the American church.

Two related questions had divided Catholics since the middle of the nineteenth century. How far should the church accommodate itself to the political and cultural environment of the United States? And how much autonomy should ethnic or "national" communities—Italians, Poles, Mexicans, Germans, and others—exercise within that church? Clear lines had been drawn over these issues by the early 1860s.[62] Orestes Brownson, a New England Congregationalist who had converted to Catholicism and who was also a prominent writer and editor, took an early, strong stand in favor of ethnic and ecclesiastical assimilation. Many recent immigrants, by which Brownson meant the Irish, had failed to live up to either Catholic or American expectations:

Rise of the (Catholic) American Nation

The civilization they actually bring with them, and which without intending it they seek to continue, is, we being judges, of a lower order than ours. It may be national prejudice and our ignorance of other nations, but it is nevertheless our firm conviction, from which we cannot easily be driven, that, regarded in relation to its type, the American civilization is the most advanced civilization the world has yet seen, and comes nearer to the Catholic Ideal than any which has been heretofore developed and actualized.[63]

He thus argued that the American church should slough off the foreign cultural trappings of Catholic immigrants and more openly embrace the American tradition. For Brownson, who often appeared uncomfortable with his Irish coreligionists, that tradition was distinctly Anglo-American.

Brownson found his most vocal opponent in the Irish-born archbishop John Hughes. Hughes did not equate middle-class, Anglo-American culture with what was either appropriately Catholic or American, as Brownson did, and he feared the consequences of conflating devotion to church with loyalty to nation. He encouraged the development of a Catholic identity that embraced various national traditions and the increasingly working-class culture of American Catholics. As one historian has argued, Hughes had abiding faith that America's republican tradition embraced pluralism. He accepted Catholics' outsider status as a critical component of their American identity.[64]

What came to be called the Americanist controversy reached a climax in the 1880s and 1890s. Church "liberals," who included John Spalding, were the heirs to Brownson. They tried to assume roles as mediators between Catholics and the country's native-born Protestant majority. They tried to finesse real differences between official church positions and the values of Protestants, such as the separation of church and state (the Vatican opposed it) or whether the responsibility for educating children lay with parents (the stance of most church leaders) or with the state (the position of many opponents of Catholic schools).[65] The liberals sought compromise on funding and other aspects of the school question and deplored provocative statements from both camps. In 1890 Bishop John Ireland even addressed a meeting of the National Education Association (NEA), a stronghold of Protestants often hostile to Catholics. Where Catholic conservatives welcomed acrimonious debates on education and other issues, liberals denied that differences of opinion were actually that broad and tried hard to bridge them amicably.

The success with which church leaders had centralized power in Rome over the course of the nineteenth century troubled many liberals, who had difficulty explaining to Protestants why the process was not deeply antidemocratic and antithetical to American values. Most liberals had opposed the doctrine of papal infallibility when it came before the church in 1871, seeing that it would only bolster Protestant suspicions that Catholics would never become freethinking, trusted citizens. After the doctrine passed, liberals tried to downplay its importance. While respectful toward immigrant communities in the church, liberals also championed assimilation, including the use of English in parochial schools. Liberals reasoned that separatism unnecessarily forced immigrant Catholics to prove loyalty on two fronts, religious and ethnic. They also saw that isolation from the society at large impeded Catholics' economic advance. Finally, liberals saw that some independent-minded ethnic parishes threatened ecclesiastical authority, making some measure of assimilation critical for order in the church itself. A splinter group of Polish-Americans underscored that danger when they formed the Polish National Catholic Church in the 1890s.[66]

On educational policy the liberals essentially accepted the argument that all schools should cultivate a single national character, provided that teachers and textbooks noted the contributions of various communities and creeds to that character.[67] Public schools could do that best for non-Catholics, they said. But for immigrant Catholics and their children, parochial schools could bridge the gap between a foreign national identity and a developing American one. Significant numbers of Catholics, however, questioned this need for linguistic and cultural assimilation. German-Americans, for instance, frequently called for autonomy in their parishes, parochial schools, and communities. Editors at the Buffalo, New York, *Volksfreund* even declared that America is "no nation, no race, no people like France, Italy or Germany. We have citizens of a republic, but no nation and, therefore no national language outside the languages the immigrated races speak in their families."[68] This kind of stance made liberals uneasy, and it would be especially problematic for church leaders once war broke out in Europe in 1914 and "Americanization" campaigns heated up at home.

Liberals' embrace of church-state separation and their endorsement of some aspects of modernist thought finally triggered Vatican intervention into what mostly had been a conflict within the American

Rise of the (Catholic) American Nation

church. Pope Leo XIII condemned the "Americanist heresy" in his *Testem Benevolentiae* of 1899. Leo checked the liberals' advance, but a simple pronouncement could hardly resolve so complex a conflict. It simmered on, playing out in the Catholic press and parochial schools.

Conservative and liberal discourses competed uneasily with each other in schoolbooks. The first acknowledged Catholic difference from the nation's Protestant majority in religious and, to a lesser extent, ethnic terms. The conservative narrative also tended to emphasize prejudice against American Catholics and their resilience in the face of persecution. But these writers were also using their textbooks to refute charges from various groups that Catholicism and its adherents represented a challenge to dominant beliefs and institutions. In doing so, they tilted toward the liberals, effacing marks of Catholic difference and underscoring for their readers the importance of conforming to prevailing cultural norms. Contradictions between pluralist and assimilationist impulses filled these histories. That is why Catholics in them were both the most familiar Americans, here since 1492, and a people set apart. They earned the admiration of their fellow citizens in the Revolution and the Civil War and seemed to merge into the larger, Protestant-dominated society. But each time they overcame the ill will of the past, prejudice against them inexplicably returned.

One hears the voice of the conservatives most distinctly in depictions of the Know-Nothings and the nativist riots of the 1830s, 1840s, and 1850s. Almost every Catholic textbook covered the assault on the Ursuline convent near Boston in the summer of 1834. "Vile books, sermons, and lectures against the Catholic religion" fed popular excitement, according to one text. Then a mob drove "out the defenseless nuns and children, and burned their home to the ground. St. Mary's Church was also plundered and given to the flames." In the Bible Riots of 1844—so called because of disputes over use of the King James Bible in public schools—an "army of ruffians, hounded by pulpit harangues of fanatical ministers," destroyed churches, homes, and a library. The "most violent outbreak" of anti-Catholicism, wrote another author, occurred on "'Bloody Monday,' August 5, 1855, in Louisville, Kentucky," where "nearly one hundred Irish were killed and twenty houses burned, while the city authorities, dominated by the Know-nothings, calmly looked on." The claim that civil authorities remained indifferent to Catholics' suffering appeared repeatedly. At the Massachusetts convent, they "made no attempt to protect the institution." The leaders of the mob, according to another text, "were subjected to only a farcical trial, which resulted in their acquittal." In New York City in

1844, the bishop and individual Catholics fought back. They "publicly declared that if the laws of the state would not protect their lives and property, they would know how to defend themselves."[69]

The tone in these accounts mixed bitterness, defiance, and rage. Textbooks for public schools rarely offered the sobering lesson that popular prejudices could threaten the rights and well-being of an oppressed minority and that local and state governments could become complicit in bigotry and lawlessness (except in horridly distorted accounts of Reconstruction where ex-Confederates were the hapless victims). Nor did they suggest that groups denied official justice should take up arms to protect themselves. Not surprisingly, mainstream texts approached these historical events much differently than Catholic ones. Discussions of the riots and other attacks were generally brief and offered few specifics. A few books for public schools even managed to discuss the Know-Nothings without addressing their hostility to Catholics, a narrative sleight of hand akin to presenting abolitionism while completely ignoring slavery.

Presentation of Catholics as outsiders, however righteous, did not always sit well with Catholic educators. Their discomfort grew over time, as did that of publishers, who were eager to avoid material that would arouse religious controversy. Translated into historical narrative, that meant focusing attention on America's ecumenical harmony since 1789, particularly that between Protestant and Catholic. This goal clearly motivated editors, sales agents, and manuscript readers at the American Book Company as they pored over drafts of Charles McCarthy's histories during the 1910s. The publisher had first considered financing a "Catholic United States History" in 1912 to compete with Lawler's *Essentials of American History,* a text by rival Ginn and Company that dominated sales to parochial schools. Publisher William Livengood knew Catholic educators had been stung by critiques of their first school histories as too sectarian in spirit, and he wanted a book "to which objection could not be raised by the impartial student of history." McCarthy made an ideal choice as author. His Ph.D. and university appointment gave him scholarly credentials. In addition, he had studied under John Bach McMaster, a highly respected figure among the first generation of professional historians and also a successful textbook writer in his own right. While Livengood gave McCarthy considerable freedom in writing his grammar and high school textbooks, he also began the project with a clear idea of what "impartiality" would look like. "There are those who would want mention made of every petty quarrel between Catholics and non-

Catholics in the early days of our history," he wrote to a sales agent. "On the other hand, there are those, and it is they we should follow, who keep in mind the function and scope of a textbook and who agree that a great many of the above subjects must necessarily be omitted."[70]

McCarthy's discretion on such matters received repeated praise from those who read his early manuscripts, along with calls to take it further. A priest from a Chicago boys' school noted that the author "avoids doctrinal controversy, is severe only against bigotry and injustice, and is generally careful not to furnish material for nourishing hatred and religious animosity." Many teachers, this reviewer added, "appreciate the force of conservative understatement as opposed to overstatement and exaggeration in partisan claims and charges." Another reader recommended that McCarthy condense his treatment of anti-Catholic demonstrations in Massachusetts in 1834 and completely omit the burning of the Ursuline convent: "Such events have had but little if any permanent influence upon the history of our country; and their mention in schoolbooks can have no other effect than to perpetuate animosities which ought to be forgotten."[71]

After the United States entered the war in Europe in April 1917, pressure to downplay historical resentments increased. Publishers and church officials felt the need to distance themselves from groups like the German-American Alliance, an association of immigrants and their descendants that included large numbers of Catholics. The group had long championed the cause of parochial schools, fighting proposed laws against them in Nebraska and other states. But they also had advocated classroom use of the German language, a policy many Americans now saw as little short of treason. In December 1917 Louis Cadieux, a sales agent in Boston, recommended dropping the phrase "for Catholic Schools" from one of McCarthy's histories:

> A reference to Catholic schools on the title page and cover will not help sales and it may antagonize further certain representative Catholic educators and leaders who, in the case of a book of this particular kind, resent a too highly colored "Catholic label" on the ground that it might lead to the inference that Catholics insist on having a special brand of "truth" taught to their children and one that a non-Catholic seeker after truth could not consistently accept.[72]

The phrase did eventually appear below the title, but the wish of some church members to delete such references spoke to a growing desire. Many Catholics, especially those entering the middle class, wanted integration into a national community with nominally equal places for Catholic, Protestant, and Jew. Still devoted to their faith and their schools, they nevertheless hoped to abandon what historian Jay P. Dolan has called the "fortress mentality" that had sustained ethnic communities amid widespread prejudice in the late nineteenth century.[73] Catholic texts reflected their hope and at the same time underscored their lingering sense of being outsiders. During the war and the years that immediately followed it, conformity to prevailing American ideals and prejudices came to be a mark of true membership in the nation. These histories captured the sense of dual consciousness that such chauvinism could provoke in Catholics.

Consider McCarthy's discussion of Catholic immigrants of the mid–nineteenth century, who inspired the rise of the Know-Nothings:

> The Irish of that era, oppressed by greedy landlords and a tyrannical government, naturally had a standard of living that differed from that which prevailed in the United States. Moreover, they were for the most part Catholics. The difference of race, customs, and religion would beget antipathy against the newcomers. The Germans, of whom some were Catholics, spoke a tongue unknown to the great majority of Americans. Besides they brought with them many strange customs.[74]

McCarthy contrasted immigrants to the native-born along lines of class, culture, language, ethnicity, and religion. Elsewhere in his history readers saw that the first three differences could be altered by the American environment. The newcomers and their children would keep their faith, however, even if it consigned them to continued minority status. McCarthy and other Catholic writers praised that continued devotion. They coded the American-ness of these citizens through their Catholicism, championing a pluralistic vision of America that embraced religious differences.[75] The value of maintaining a culturally distinct ethnic identity was less clear for McCarthy, however. While he sympathized with the "Irish of that era," he assumed a somewhat detached perspective, seeing their arrival through their eyes *and* through the eyes of native-born Americans. By the end of the passage, he had completely abandoned the outsider position. German customs were not strange "to the Americans." They were simply "strange."

Occasionally, Catholic texts advocated assimilation so fervently that their sentiments bordered on xenophobia. A history published in

Rise of the (Catholic) American Nation

1914 admitted that some nineteenth-century immigrants had been too vocal in maintaining "Old World" ways, another slight at German-Americans and an echo of Brownson's disdain for the Irish. The book also declared that newcomers from northern Europe, who dominated immigration before 1880, made "intelligent" and "enterprising citizens." More recent arrivals from southern Europe and eastern Asia formed a "less desirable element" in the population. That was a remarkable concession, considering that many of the undesirables were Italian Catholics.[76] In a cultural climate that sanctioned such views, the very existence of Catholic histories sometimes appeared to undermine the message that church liberals wanted them to deliver: that Catholics were just like "other Americans" and that their contributions fit into a fully integrated narrative of national development.

Writers and editors who wanted parochial schools to buy their books had to balance Catholic boosterism with a more frank discussion of ethnic and religious differences separating Catholics and the country's Protestant majority. Over time, they leaned toward relatively innocuous celebration of Catholics' accomplishments—Columbus setting sail with Father Pérez's blessing or John Holland perfecting the submarine for use by the U.S. Navy. No book mentioned the divisive doctrine of papal infallibility, though it played an important part in the history of the American church, mostly by animating anti-Catholic groups like the American Protective Association at the end of the nineteenth century. No book addressed the genuine differences between official Catholic doctrine and American beliefs about the separation of church and state. Instead, like Sister Mary Celeste's history from the 1920s, they informed readers that American "ideals of toleration, of liberty and democracy, have had their origins in Catholic sources or have been upheld by Catholic exponents." Sometimes books avoided the rancor over the school question, which had led to the publication of these volumes in the first place. Sister Mary Celeste's book made public and parochial schools nearly indistinguishable in design and practice. "Catholic boys and girls want to attend school for just the same reasons that actuate other American boys and girls; that is, they want to find that place in life in which they will do their best work; they want to know how best to use their leisure time; and they want to become good citizens," she informed her students, blandly reaffirming the educational philosophy the NEA established for public schools with the influential 1918 report *Cardinal Principles of Secondary Education.*[77]

Eager to show that fellow Americans almost fully accepted Catholics as members of the nation, these writers began to place anti-Catholicism far into the past. Or they tried to make it the provenance of cranks and extremists, like Garfield's mentally unbalanced assassin Guiteau. After discussing the appearance of *Maria Monk's Awful Disclosures* in the 1830s and anti-Catholic riots in the following years, McCarthy reminded his young audience that the "great men of America have never encouraged intolerance." He wisely avoided claiming that Ulysses Grant had snubbed Catholics in official appointment as late as the 1870s, as the writer of an earlier text had done. Grant, war hero and president, simply did not fit the profile of a bigot or of a leader who would countenance anti-Catholic views among his subordinates.[78]

Writers' efforts to explain widespread prejudice and to absolve "great men" and the vast majority of other Americans of responsibility sometimes ran into contradictions. They appeared most starkly in books designed for younger students. Near the end of her history, Sister Mary Celeste told readers about the 1924 appointment of two new American cardinals, George Mundelein of Chicago and Patrick Hayes of New York. "Not only the Catholics of America, but all Americans united in expressing their gratification at the honor bestowed" on the two citizens, Sister Mary Celeste assured students. Two paragraphs later she noted that Cardinal James Gibbons was known at home and abroad as the American Cardinal: "He was so called because of his interest in and participation in every movement distinctly American, democratic, and popular. He was highly esteemed by 'popes, presidents, and workingmen.'" Yet on almost the same page she discussed the nationwide revival of attacks on the church also taking place in the 1920s, just as she was finishing the manuscript.[79] Young students would have been hard put to resolve that incongruity. They would have been aware, however, of the depth of anti-Catholic sentiment in the country. In 1928 Republicans exploited it to obliterate Al Smith's hopes of winning the White House, reducing the Catholic ex-governor of New York to an increasingly bitter player on the sidelines of national politics.

Two fateful decisions by the nation's lawmakers and its highest court during the 1920s, however, aided the assimilation of Catholics and, ultimately, their separate history. Congress severely restricted further immigration, reducing past waves of Catholic newcomers to a trickle. And in 1925 the Supreme Court set an important precedent in *Pierce v. Sisters of the Holy Name*. Capitalizing on the anti-immigrant backlash, a coalition of organizations that included the Ku Klux Klan had sponsored a referendum in Oregon mandating that all children between eight and sixteen attend public schools. Similar proposals had appeared in other states for decades. But this time Oregon voters passed this proposed amendment to their state constitution. Had it gone into effect, it would have destroyed the still relatively small network of parochial schools in Oregon and threatened larger ones elsewhere. The court ruled the law unconstitutional, finally dashing hopes among militant anti-Catholics that the struggle to close parochial schools could succeed anywhere in America.[80]

As Catholics slowly began to feel more secure about their schools and their place in the country, many came to doubt the necessity of a "Catholic" version of the nation's past. "I don't see any particular reason for the existence of books for parochial schools unless they are really worthwhile," wrote a sister at the St. Thomas the Apostle School in Chicago while reviewing McCarthy's *Elementary History of the United States*.[81] What was worthwhile? Essentially, a history written to the same academic standards and with the same content as one used in public schools, only with the addition of a few famous Catholic Americans and a brief history of the church in the United States. The need for a usable past that forcefully integrated Catholics, one inspired by the strength of church opponents like Lyman Beecher or Josiah Strong in the nineteenth century, was disappearing.

Publishers accelerated the merging of Catholic and mainstream narratives. They took careful note in 1888 when a Boston school board dominated by Catholics dismissed a teacher and dropped a textbook, both for offensive statements regarding the sale of indulgences prior to the Reformation.[82] By the 1870s publishers had eliminated almost all overtly anti-Catholic material from their histories. But after the 1888 incident, which garnered national attention, they addressed the concerns of Catholics even more seriously. Macmillan and Ginn and Company entered the Catholic history market in 1902 and 1909 respectively, partially displacing texts by the Catholic firms Benziger Brothers and W. H. Sadlier. Authors of books intended primarily for public schools also took church members into consideration. Updating an edition of his *Short History of the United States* in 1901, Edward Channing asked his publisher to pass on word of any objection to the book from "good Catholics" so that he might "address the grievance."[83]

Channing had learned the importance of adjusting history when writing his longer *Students' History of the United States* four years earlier. The first draft had contained a passage on "the Spanish Armada, 1588." In it, he had originally written that "Spain was intensely Catholic; England the most formidable Protestant power." As their navies clashed, "the fate of the Spanish monarchy on the one side, of Protestantism and English freedom on the other, hung in the balance."

The text had already reached the galley stage in printing, making changes cumbersome. But Channing's editors deleted the first line and dropped the critical "of Protestantism" from the second. The defeat of the armada, a critical prelude to English colonization of North America, was thus changed from a climactic duel between Protestantism and Catholicism to one merely between rival European states. All that remained from the first draft was a vague reference to the "religious differences" between England and Spain contributing to the conflict. The link between Catholicism and political tyranny, one essential to earlier writers like Francis Parkman and Emma Willard, had been severed. Apparently, Channing did not object.[84] The change likely saved sales, about which he was acutely concerned.

As textbook makers grew savvier, complaints from Catholics diminished. During the 1920s, communities in New York, Chicago, and other cities demanded that history textbooks for public schools include heroes of their own ethnic backgrounds (see chap. 5). Publishers responded favorably. Once Irish-, German-, and Polish-American figures appeared more frequently in mainstream texts, another feature that distinguished books made for parochial schools began to disappear. Demand for Catholic histories lessened. Catholics had become so comfortable with leading texts on the market, one editor bragged in the 1930s, that he needed only to mention the Revolutionary War hero John Barry in a footnote to pass muster with them.[85] He exaggerated. Though the market for specifically Catholic histories shrank, it lingered through the 1960s at the elementary and middle school levels.

Catholic histories for high schools were all but gone by the 1950s, however. A teacher looking for one in 1962, one year after an Irish-American entered the White House by convincing voters that his Catholic identity did not conflict with his American one, would have been disappointed. There was only the "John Carroll Edition" of Lewis Paul Todd and Merle Curti's *Rise of the American Nation.* Editors had tactfully avoided the label "for Catholic Schools," preferring the more neutral reference to Carroll, America's first Catholic bishop.[86] There was little to differentiate the Catholic version of this best-selling history from its public school counterpart, except for the addition of several sidebars on prominent Catholics. A consensus history melding the perspectives of America's Protestants and its White, ethnic Catholics had been forged.

For an educational nationalist like Arthur Schlesinger Jr., the slow withering-away of Catholic histories might look like a victory for the melting-pot ideal. It was, but it came with costs. Two of them were conceptual clarity and historical accuracy. When editors lopped off passages from Channing's manuscript, the final book did not become more broadminded and tolerant. It simply made less sense. Religious competition *did* play a critical part in European colonization of North America. Papering over genuine conflicts of ideas between Catholics and Protestants, and often between the Holy See and American members of the church, did not make Catholic books any less sectarian or parochial (in both senses of the word), either. A string of nineteenth-century popes had little use for American ideas of liberty of conscience and worship. In 1864 Pius IX proclaimed that it was an "error" to believe the pontiff "ought to reconcile himself to, and agree with, progress, liberalism, and contemporary civilization." Catholic histories, generally narrated by ideological opponents of men like Pius, simply ignored such troublesome facts. So did mainstream texts, once their authors tried more diligently to woo Catholics. In doing so, they lost a chance to dispel dangerous myths about Catholicism—that it is monolithic in thought and that American congregants are always ready to follow the dictates of Rome.[87]

There was another, more dispiriting cost involved in the fusion of Catholic and more conventional histories. Their record was not perfect, but Catholic writers often tried to discourage the ethnocentrism and arrogance that appeared in other textbooks. Sister Mary Celeste told her readers that "because they are members of a universal church, which belongs not to one nation but to all, they ought to look with respect on governments and customs not their own." Another book observed that "Mother Church folds her arms about all her children and questions not their color or their race."[88]

As long as Catholic writers conceived of themselves and their readers as members of an aggrieved minority, they were often willing to consider the plight of those in similar straits. Sometimes the nature of the history they told made such an alignment natural. As Sister Mary Celeste pointed out, the Klan of the 1920s directed its ire at three principal groups—"Catholics, Jews, and Negroes." In the early twentieth century, Catholic schools were private, largely urban, and located principally in the North and West. Thus Thomas Lawler did not have to worry about placating White racists on state adoption boards in the South when he wrote his *Essentials of American History*. He treated Crispus Attucks as a hero of the Revolution and even praised Toussaint L'Ouverture, who led the revolution that toppled French rule in Haiti. Another book devoted a paragraph to the accomplishments of abolitionist and civil rights leader Frederick Douglass, a persona non grata in almost every history for public schools. The authors also noted the role of "colored troops" in the "Civil War," pointedly rejecting the "War between the States," the term favored by White Southerners.[89]

A healthy skepticism about the benevolence of the state and its actions, apparent in stories of nativist violence, surfaced elsewhere in these histories as well. Catholic texts sometimes favored Indians in their conflicts with settlers. Sadlier's *History* blamed official policy for the decimation of native populations, quoting a government document admitting that treatment of the Indians had been "UNJUST AND INIQUITOUS BEYOND THE POWER OF WORDS TO EXPRESS." The "course of our government has always been fatal to the red man," concluded the author, who wrote while fighting in the West still raged.[90]

Catholic books were hardly free of racist stereotypes and the historical distortions they give rise to. One offered a rather bucolic view of slavery in colonial Maryland, complete with "black babies gamboling in the sunshine." Another encouraged students to identify with missionaries who toiled in "miserable Indian wigwams among those who were treacherous, ungrateful, and at very best slow of comprehension."[91] Nevertheless, for as long as they lasted, these books represented dissident history. However incomplete, their racial inclusiveness provided a welcome contrast to many texts of the late nineteenth and early twentieth centuries.

4. Race and the Limits of Community

In the past thirty years, writing American history has often revolved around the search for commonalities. Authors of textbooks, in particular, have sought narrative themes that rise above divisions of geography, faith, social class, and race. This pattern goes back to the nineteenth century, but the ways writers have depicted the past to allow them to speak of Americans with pronouns like "we" and "us" have changed considerably over the last century. Consider Andrew C. McLaughlin's description of the colonial South in the 1919 edition of his *History of the American Nation:*

> In Virginia and South Carolina were two strongly contrasted
> societies—on the tide-water rivers a race of planters dressing
> richly, owning large estates, riding in coaches, and living in a
> sort of baronial style; in the farther upland, hardy settlers clear-
> ing the land, building log houses, planting corn or little patches
> of tobacco in the wilderness; and, still farther on, the bold fron-
> tiersmen, the vanguard, the leader of the slow but steady move-
> ment toward the setting sun. There is little resemblance in life
> and habits between the wealthy planter and the man of the back
> country. The planter is waited upon by slaves; the frontiersman
> must defend himself and earn his own hard livelihood. Yet both
> are Americans and both are devoted to liberty.[1]

On one level, McLaughlin argues that dedication to republican ideals unites these people into a national community. The rich planter, the poor but proud settler, and the bold frontiersman are all dedicated to liberty and thus are true Americans. By evoking the national theme of westward expansion, the "steady movement toward the setting sun,"

McLaughlin shows that this story of freedom applies to the whole country, not just the South.

One point McLaughlin did not have to make, because virtually all his readers, even children, would have understood it, is that these men are White. His vision of cross-class solidarity depends on removing African-American slaves as subjects of the story. Conditioned as we are today to expect racism in textbooks and teaching of the past, McLaughlin's bias is both obvious and predictable. What is more interesting about this excerpt is how the barely visible *presence* of nonwhites—the slaves who wait on the planter and, implicitly, the Indians who threaten the frontiersman—are essential to McLaughlin's vision of a White nation. The story of race in textbooks published at the end of the nineteenth and start of the twentieth centuries is not just about exclusion of people of color. Commonly held ideas about race, about the essential qualities of a range of different racial groups, also gave order and meaning to the narrative that writers like McLaughlin presented.

Textbooks on American history had linked concepts of race and nation since their mass publication began in the 1820s. But events and trends between 1880 and 1925 focused greater attention on this issue. In the South, state governments controlled by the Democratic Party stripped African-American men of their right to vote (women, of course, had never had the right) and forced them into what was, at best, second-class citizenship. In the North, immigrants from southern and eastern Europe began to outnumber those who hailed from western Europe, the British Isles, and Scandinavia. That shift provoked fears that these newcomers would jeopardize America's supposed racial and cultural homogeneity. In the West, new legislation promised to end the "Indian Question" by breaking up remaining tribes and integrating their members into the surrounding settlements. At the same time, restriction on immigration from Asia reflected hopes among Whites that the Chinese and Japanese could be kept out of the country. These social and demographic changes forced all Americans to grapple with the question of what racial boundaries, if any, marked the national community.

The first generation of professionally accredited historians had compelled themselves to answer that question, either directly or indirectly. They had chosen to redefine history, embodying it less in the acts of statesmen and soldiers and more in the whole life of the people. And that new emphasis on social history required explaining precisely who the American people were. In writing about day-to-day life in the 1790s, for instance, writers had to decide whether to include slaves and

Race and the Limits of Community

free Blacks in their narratives. Similarly, could they choose to ignore Mexican-Americans in the far West of the 1880s? And what of Indians now confined to reservations? As they answered these questions, writers of the most popular books began to wrap race into their larger story of American progress. They associated Whiteness with civic order and commercial expansion. When nonwhites and, in some authors' scheme of things, less than fully White European newcomers appeared in the books, they served a number of roles. African-Americans, for instance, sometimes became foils for industrious Whites. Many immigrants from eastern Europe shuffled voicelessly across the page, grateful if often uncomprehending recipients of racial and social uplift. Even more frequently, authors depicted nonwhites as hindrances, even threats, to the nation's social and economic advance.

Understanding the relationship between race and nation in these histories requires knowing how writers used the concept of race. It was a remarkably flexible term for them, with meaning heavily dependent on context. At its broadest, "the race" denoted the whole human race. The term "race" also designated what were believed to be the four or five primary, biologically determined classes of humans. As one textbook author explained, all people were either copper-colored like Indians, "white like Europeans, . . . black like the Africans, or yellow like the Malays and the Chinese." Below this primary level, race became more fluid, and the criteria determining it harder to trace. References like those to the Latin, Teutonic, or Aryan races blurred distinctions of culture, linguistic origin, religion, and supposed biological inheritances like skin color. Such designations lacked clear definitions in popular discourse. Some people included all the French among the Latins, for instance; others did not. Authors also used "race" in a way that modern readers would see as synonymous with "nation" or "tribe." Histories contained references to the Irish race, the race of Serbians, and the Iroquois race. Finally, authors used "race" to designate a group defined by class, place of habitation, occupation, or other factors. In the earlier passage, McLaughlin referred to a "race of planters" in the South, while another writer discussed the "race of hardy fishermen" in New England.[2] This final, narrow sense of race is not relevant here. Nor is the first, very broad understanding of the human race.

The other, intermediate, and more ambiguous uses of "race" were critical in textbooks, however. Here "race" pivoted between grounding in biology and in cultural environment, between nature and nurture. Consider Henry William Elson's condemnation of slave breeding in the antebellum South in a history published in 1906: "It is no doubt true that the negro, especially while in bondage, did not experience in the same degree those intense family ties which are characteristic of our own race. But that the black race was not devoid of these finer feelings was shown by many heartrending scenes at the auction block."[3] According to Elson, men and women of African descent are innately less capable than Whites of intense devotion to family, though such affections can be developed to a limited extent outside the brutal institution of slavery. For this author, mental and spiritual qualities were bred into the bone of the four or five primary races.

Compare Elson's assertion to another writer's discussion of White attempts to block Black suffrage after the Civil War:

> [The] freedmen . . . were densely ignorant and utterly unfit to make an intelligent use of the ballot. The Southern whites often refused to let the negro cast his ballot, and in many cases refused to count it when it had been cast. But such a state of affairs is not likely to continue. As the negro becomes intelligent he will doubtless be allowed to cast his vote as he pleases. Since he has the constitutional right to vote, the Northern and Southern people alike see the great necessity of educating him so that he may be qualified to exercise that right.[4]

This writer suggested that the freedman's ignorance resulted from the degrading conditions of slavery. Education and greater familiarity with the demands of freedom would make him a useful citizen. Maybe people of African descent were naturally less capable than Whites. Maybe not. But the writer provided only environmental evidence at this point.

Rarely did textbooks of this era come down unequivocally on the side of nature or nurture in explaining alleged racial traits. All of the writers, like most of their fellow Americans, were racialists. They believed that racial origin determined at least some traits beyond merely superficial distinctions of color. Many, perhaps most, were racists, believing that such distinctions made one race superior to another. They differed on questions of the extent to which various races might be raised to "American" standards of civilization and integrated into the nation. Those authors like Elson who saw racial traits as relatively fixed set clear racial boundaries to the national community. His direct address to readers of his "own race" in a book purportedly covering national history established that bias. Writers who saw fewer inherent differences between races wrote more inclusive books, as one would expect.[5]

Relative to school histories published at the turn of the twentieth century, those popular from the 1820s to the 1870s placed minor emphasis on race as a subject or determinant of the American story. Instead, republican ideals of human equality and universal rights, a legacy of the Enlightenment and the Revolutionary War, still continued to inspire writers. While dedication to those ideals waned in texts at midcentury, it revived briefly but intensely during and immediately after the Civil War. To these writers the United States was a beacon of liberty to the world, a partially secularized version of the Puritans' "City on a Hill." America welcomed immigrants who aspired to the democratic life and exported its political philosophy to the emerging republics in the New World and to the decaying aristocracies in the Old. Bound by a faith in democracy, the country as these authors imagined it did not have, nor did it need, a fixed demographic composition. In principle, it welcomed all people regardless of race.

When Charles A. Goodrich concluded his history in the 1820s, he betrayed little anxiety over racial and ethnic diversity in the young republic:

> Two centuries have elapsed since the first settlements were commenced in the United States by Europeans, yet the people have not acquired that uniform character, which belongs to ancient nations, upon whom time and the stability of institutions have imprinted a particular and individual character. Although partial changes have occurred, which have been noticed in the progress of this work, yet, so far down as the present time, the essential variations which have taken place are few.
>
> The general physiognomy is nearly as varied as the origin of the population is different.[6]

Goodrich linked institutional growth, cultural homogeneity, and the development of unique physical characteristics ("general physiognomy") of a national race. He expected citizens of the United States to develop their own identity based on these factors, like the "ancient nations," but did not see the heterogeneous population of his own time as an impediment to American progress. His sentiments paralleled those of J. Hector St. Jean de Crèvecoeur in his *Letters from an American Farmer,* written in the 1780s. Crèvecoeur, who believed the intermixing was already well under way, proudly called Americans a "promiscuous breed" mixing English, Scotch, Irish, French, Dutch, German, and Swedish elements. Both Goodrich and Crèvecoeur took for granted that these "new" Americans were descendants of Europeans. Both ignored Africans and Indians as contributors to this people, even though well over a quarter of the population within the bounds of the United States in the early nineteenth century traced their origin to these two groups.[7]

Textbook writers, along with many other Whites, never imagined nonwhites as real or potential Americans, and so the racially inclusive sentiment of their writing was often more apparent than real. Some antebellum authors, for instance, took the romantic image of the Indian slipping quietly toward a "melancholy doom" quite literally. The "early inhabitants" of North America, declared one school history first published in 1855, "as a people have long since passed away, although a remnant yet lingers in some of the States." The author concluded that the "people whose history we would learn are the European colonists, who in the providence of God, have been permitted to spread themselves over this broad land, and to make it the prosperous country in which it is our privilege to live."[8]

Americans of African origin, even more than Indians, had clearly not begun to "pass away" as the antebellum era advanced. But textbooks depicted them as largely irrelevant to the American story. When mentioned at all, Blacks served as objects of action directed by White slave traders, plantation owners, and abolitionists. That well into the nineteenth century Whites could imagine millions of African-Americans as somehow safely outside the national community seems incredible today, but the belief was quite common, even among opponents of slavery. As late as 1862 President Lincoln seriously contemplated a mass resettlement of Blacks in Central or South America once the Confederacy had been defeated.[9]

Antebellum textbooks presented numerous racial and national stereotypes—the docile African, bloodthirsty Indian, liberty-loving Englishman, and acquisitive Jew.[10] But deep animosity did not influence most caricatures of nonwhites because authors did not perceive them as significant threats to the White, western European character of the nation. Writers also lacked a well-developed, widely known "science" of race to employ in any discussion of the topic. By 1865 both of these conditions had changed.

In his *Notes on Virginia,* Thomas Jefferson hypothesized that the White race of Europe and its offshoot in America were innately superior in mental and physical capacity to Africans. But he admitted that, as a scientist, he could offer no conclusive proof for the claim. The scientific racism of the nineteenth century grew out of the desire of Europeans and Americans to find such proof by measuring the innate racial differences Jefferson presumed to exist. Frenchman Paul Broca attempted to show that Whites had larger cranial volumes than Africans, Asians, or American Indians, and thus bigger brains and greater intelligence. Other scientists tried to quantify differences in skin color and facial angles (the more vertical the line from forehead to chin, the more advanced the race).

Efforts to quantify alleged racial distinctions mostly failed. Limited data, imprecise measurements, and a priori conclusions marred supposedly objective experiments. Where the science was weak, the spirit, apparently, was willing. For example, the American scientist George Morton, who amassed a collection of over one thousand skulls from individuals around the world, first measured their volumes with mustard seed. Records show that when handling skulls of Whites, he packed the seed tightly into the cranium, exaggerating its apparent size. With other skulls, he did not. Morton also became the leading proponent of polygenesis, which held that the primary races were actually separately created species. An ally of his, Josiah Nott, claimed that his own experience as a physician in Mobile, Alabama, lent credence to the theory. Crosses between Black and White parents produced children who were less prolific than those of the pure races, Nott said, much like breeding a horse and a donkey produces a sterile mule. Despite such dubious evidence, or the lack of it in Nott's case, polygenesis had considerable respect in the scientific community. Harvard professor and naturalist Louis Agassiz supported it, and the theory also circulated widely among nonscientists. Beginning in the 1850s, textbook writers like George Payn Quackenbos felt obliged to refute polygenesis in their school histories. The contention that some races are innately superior to others did not present a problem for Quackenbos; that separate creation could not be reconciled with a literal reading of the Book of Genesis did.[11]

Closely related to these quantitative approaches to race were anthropological studies of how each race produced primitive or advanced cultures. English philosopher and scientist Herbert Spencer argued that the state of civilization, or lack of it, marked a race's position on an ascending ladder of development that all races must climb, at least as far as their natural abilities allowed. Europeans held the highest position on the ladder, according to Spencer, while Africans and native Australians lagged furthest behind. Superior races might be able to help inferior ones along to some degree, but each race had to find its own way; environment and training could not remedy biological deficiencies. Thus Spencer thought it a mistake to take individuals of an inferior race and attempt to integrate them into a more advanced society. Miscegenation was equally ill advised.[12]

Once scientists and lay writers combined Spencer's vision of race progress with Charles Darwin's ideas of competition among different species, the chilling implications of scientific racism became clear. Nonwhite races, as throwbacks and evolutionary dead ends, might well face an extinction that, eventually, would benefit humanity. John Fiske, an American historian and popularizer of Spencer's work, made claims along that line. They were central to "Manifest Destiny," one of Fiske's best-received lectures, which in 1885 appeared as an article in *Harper's Magazine.* Following a pattern of social evolution, Fiske said, men were becoming "less brutal and more humane" as civilization stretched outward from centers in Europe and North America. People who were English in language, religion, political habits, traditions, "and to a predominant extent in the blood" would continue to spread across the globe. By 1985, Fiske concluded, the "English race" would outnumber the Chinese. Faced with superior competitors for their land, some races, particularly indigenous Australians—"a race of irredeemable savages hardly above the level of brutes"—and Africans, at least those outside the benevolent care provided by Whites, would dwindle and disappear.[13]

At the end of the century, doctrines of scientific racism reached mass audiences in America through magazines, museums, fairs and expositions, public speakers, schoolbooks, and other media.[14] Fiske, for instance, wrote one of the most popular textbooks in American history, which went through thirteen editions between 1894 and 1923. But racist frameworks of American history never completely dominated textbooks, not even Fiske's. Inclusive visions of America as a refuge for all those seeking liberty and economic opportunity, an inheritance from the early republican era, remained. Sometimes authors explicitly challenged racism. The 1889 edition of one racially progressive text, for instance, discussed prejudice against Chinese and Japanese immigrants and then applauded the presidential veto of an act to bar their further entry into the country. "The veto," declared the writer, "was in accordance with the well-established theory that this country should welcome industrious and law-abiding immigrants from any quarter of the globe."[15]

Scientific racism held enormous appeal for White Americans, however. Amid the social turmoil begotten by industrial expansion, mass immigration, and the unsettled legal status of Blacks and Indians, the science of race provided a comforting explanation for past national progress and a reason why that progress might be threatened by the loss of White dominance. In schoolbooks, it also assuaged guilt. It helped authors explain to young readers the inevitability of wars against, or political subjugation of, certain races. "With the advance of the white man the red race is rapidly passing away," intoned one author popular in the South, "in accordance with a well-established law of nature, that causes an inferior race to yield to a superior when one comes in contact with the other."[16] Scientific laws neatly removed moral culpability.

Europe's Descendants: The American "Race"

Increasing race consciousness in textbooks published after 1880 was evident in growing praise for early American settlers of northern and western European origin, forerunners of what people at the time called "native stock" or "native Americans." At its most benign, this form of White nationalism amounted to expression of ancestral pride, either *by* the author or *for* communities expected to purchase the books. Textbook committees in towns and cities in the Midwest with large Scandinavian populations, for instance, preferred histories that dealt at least briefly with the "discovery" of America by daring Norse seafarers. Publishers often obliged them with the heroic tale of Leif Erickson.[17]

A few quotations from popular books suggest the general tenor of thought on these groups of Europeans. The English settlers were invariably a "sober minded" and "self reliant people." Early inhabitants of New Amsterdam could claim "sturdy Dutch stock," while Germans showed "unusual energy and intelligence." Huguenots, the Protestant refugees from Catholic France, proved themselves a "most desirable acquisition" by their "severe morality, marked charity, elegant manners [and] thrifty habits." No "better emigration ever came to America," claimed one book. The Huguenots' descendants "rivaled the sons and daughters of Englishmen, Scotchmen, and Germans in nobility of character and enduring worth." The Scotch-Irish earned accolades as a "manly, sturdy race," who were also frugal, "deeply religious," and the "greatest Indian fighters and marksmen." Textbook writers lauded Irish and German Catholics, who streamed into the United States in their largest numbers during the middle of the nineteenth century, with considerably less enthusiasm, except in books for parochial schools. But if they wrote nothing else positive, writers at least noted that German and Irish immigrants aided the Union's cause in the Civil War.[18]

These various northern and western European stocks constituted what several turn-of-the-century authors referred to as the American "race." Some groups in this race remained culturally distinct, but all could safely intermarry, making a uniquely American people possible. Writers found different ways of naming this partially amalgamated race. Two Midwestern historians claimed that the "Englishman and his kinsfolk from northern Europe" founded America. Another author called the new people "not English though predominantly Anglo-Saxon." A best-selling intermediate-level history labeled Americans "our own English-speaking race," a popular term that emphasized English origins yet still blurred ethnic boundaries. Echoing Crèvecoeur, many authors claimed that the mixing of nationalities made Americans a "greater and stronger people." The "great population," said Henry Elson, resulted from the mixing of "numerous European peoples." Coauthors of one book argued that "one of the fundamental facts of American history is the mingling of different stocks." The grafting of "foreign elements" onto the English population "broadened their vision and compelled the enlargement of their ideas." Another historian suggested that by the dawn of the twentieth century it had become difficult to trace the original nationality of Americans, so mixed had the constituent groups become.[19]

Edward Channing, who in the 1890s became one of the first professional historians to enter the schoolbook market, developed this concept of an American race most completely. The English were the "most important" contributors to the "American people," according to Channing. They provided America's language, laws, and culture and predominated in the critical region of New England. But south of Massachusetts other stocks diversified the racial base of the nation:

New York City, originally settled by the Dutch, was a cosmopolitan city even at the outbreak of the Revolutionary War. . . . In Pennsylvania and Maryland were people of many races and innumerable religious creeds, and in the extreme south were large numbers of Germans, French, Scots, and Scotch-Irish. These various races were all drawn from the two great branches of Aryan stock,—the Germanic and Keltic,—which have always shown the greatest power of amalgamation. They lived happily together on American soil, and, by a process of assimilation,

laid the foundation of a strong aggressive race, the American
people, which came into existence in the epoch between the
inaugurations of Thomas Jefferson and the accession of Andrew
Jackson.[20]

Channing's history exhibited virtually all of the distinguishing characteristics of the racial melting-pot theory common in textbooks of the
era. There was the beneficial mixing of racial stocks. Elsewhere, Channing linked that intermingling to the "expansion of intellect" and the
"fertility of invention" early in the nineteenth century. He included in
this race all Americans who might trace their ancestry to northern or
western Europe. Channing's "Aryan" race, considered biologically or
linguistically, lacked clear boundaries, however. Racial discourse, then
as now, was characterized by a helpful imprecision that allowed a
speaker to address numerous groups, each of which could interpret the
same message slightly differently.[21]

By arguing that the American people had been formed definitively
between 1800 and 1830, for instance, Channing appealed to nativist
sentiments of the "old stock," particularly New Englanders likely to
buy his high school text. Yet by using the term "Keltic" he seemed to
add Irish Catholics to the pot (a shrewd move for book sales), though
they did not arrive in the United States in great numbers until the
1840s. Channing did draw some clear lines. Millions of Africans and
their descendants who were in the United States in 1800 were clearly
not part of this race. Channing also avoided mentioning southern and
eastern Europeans, the so-called New Immigrants coming to the
United States at the time he wrote.

Italians, Poles, Russians, Hungarians, Croatians, Greeks, Jews of
various national origins, and other New Immigrants held an anomalous position relative to what Channing and other writers saw as the
national race. Theories popular early in the twentieth century held
these immigrants to be distinctly inferior to native stock in the United
States. Theodore Roosevelt openly fretted about the prospect of "race
suicide" as newer immigrants outbred increasingly middle-class, old-
stock couples who chose to have fewer children. What came to be
called "Nordicism" reached fullest development in two widely read
works, Madison Grant's *The Passing of the Great Race,* first published
in 1916, and Lothrop Stoddard's *The Rising Tide of Color,* released four
years later. Grant and Stoddard believed different races had certain
unchanging moral, intellectual, and spiritual traits, and they sought to
refute claims by those scientists who thought environment played a

more important role than race in determining character. For these two writers, race was destiny.

Grant, in particular, thought racial divisions *among* Europeans were critical. He separated Europeans into three great racial stocks and created highly detailed, if somewhat fanciful, maps to show their distribution. The Nordics dominated the north, particularly Britain and Scandinavia. This superior group, who were mostly Protestant, exhibited individualism, self-reliance, and skill as organizers, rulers, and adventurers, according to Grant. Alpines centered in mountainous central Europe arose from peasant stock, were generally Catholic, showed less initiative than Nordics, and submitted quietly to authority. Mediterraneans of the south, often superior to Nordics in artistic achievement, were nevertheless inferior in key traits of bodily stamina and aptitude for science. Grant deplored mixing across the earth's four or five primary races, but crosses between Nordics, Alpines, and Mediterraneans bothered him nearly as much. He argued that democracy might prove fatal when such unequal races lived together. The strength of the United States lay in the dominance of the blue-eyed, blond, Anglo-Saxon branch of the Nordic race, according to Grant. But he speculated that one of the two inferior, though fecund, races of Europe might gain electoral power over the Nordic element, a variation of Roosevelt's race-suicide thesis. Grant even drew parallels between the perils of Black-White race mixing in the South and the threat posed by New England's "indigestible mass of French-Canadians," who came from mostly inferior Alpine and Mediterranean stock, according to his system.[22]

Grant and Stoddard wrote at the fringe of the racialist consensus in the United States, taking immutable differences among white "races" further than most social commentators. However, some popular textbook writers clearly sympathized with their views. In his *American History*, Roscoe Lewis Ashley expressed anxieties over "great numbers of immigrants pouring into our cities" from southern and eastern Europe. They were, he wrote, "people of different races, ideals, and capacities from those of the Teutonic and Celtic races that founded and developed this republic." Reflecting popular prejudices among the native-born elite, Ashley suggested it might be necessary either to restrict immigration or to eliminate progressive political measures like the referendum and recall, which gave power to the mass of voters at the expense of the patrician classes.[23]

In a book first published in 1912, Columbia professor David Saville Muzzey wrote that immigration had only recently become a "race"

David Saville Muzzey in 1912. *Courtesy of Columbia University Archives—Columbiana Library.*

problem: "Before 1880 over four fifths of all the immigrants coming to the United States were from Canada and the northern countries of Europe, which were allied to *us* in blood, language, customs, religion, and political ideas. They were a most welcome addition to our population, especially in the development of the great farmlands of the West." But the Germans, Irish, Swedes, and English were being replaced, Muzzey continued, "by Hungarians, Poles, Russians, Italians," and other such alien peoples. They caused congestion in urban slums, formed breeding places for disease, and contributed to municipal corruption by selling their votes to the highest bidder.[24]

With their suggestions of different racial capacities among Whites, and their placement of New Immigrants outside the direct racial address of "us," Ashley and Muzzey adopted a strongly racist stand—one more typical of Southern textbooks published at the turn of the century. Most writers were more circumspect. They hesitated to characterize Europeans of any origin in starkly negative racist terms, either because they did not believe recent immigrants to be innately inferior to the old stock or because they decided that airing such views in schoolbooks might imperil sales. Immigrants active in municipal government in many Eastern and Midwestern cities had considerable say in what sort of texts their children would read. It was best not to offend them. When John Fiske assumed the presidency of the Immigration Restriction League in 1894, he called the New Immigrants "beaten men from beaten races." But in his *History of the United States for Schools,* published the same year, Fiske and his editors eliminated overt nativism, calling Americans a "European people transplanted to the soil of a new world." Of the citizens who voted in the elections of 1892, Fiske continued, almost in a hymn to the melting pot, "some were born in Europe, many were the children of European parents who had migrated to America, nearly all were descended from ancestors who three centuries ago were dwelling in the Old World." Discretion was the better part of salesmanship. Fiske learned that lesson early; others would confront it later.[25]

Discussion of the problems mass immigration presented to the nation was limited in books published before nativist anxieties reached their peak during and after World War I. When the subject did arise, most writers strove for at least the appearance of balance. They noted immigrants' contributions, particularly their labor that fueled industrial growth, and their alleged drawbacks. Among the latter were a willingness to work for low wages, which undercut native-born White workers, and their support of labor radicalism. Several authors blamed

Race and the Limits of Community

strikes and social disturbances like Chicago's Haymarket Riot of 1886 on unassimilated immigrants, for instance. Interestingly, writers often made no attempt to explain the contradiction in these alleged immigrant tendencies toward political extremism *and* meek acceptance of sweatshop wages. Other problems with these newcomers included their lack of familiarity with republican traditions and their more general cultural foreignness. One writer offered a fairly typical assessment of recent immigrants in a history published in 1923, one year before Congress severely restricted their entry into the United States:

> Favorable and unfavorable have been the effects of this immigration; it has given us millions of eager hands for mill, mine, and factory without which many of the "miracles" of this age would not have been possible. On the other hand, the unsettling effects of cheap labor, the crowding of thousands of aliens in our cities and mining towns, the lack of interest on the part of many for American traditions (as for the "American" against the "Continental" Sunday) have given rise to serious problems.[26]

Here the writer fit recent immigrants into the dominant theme of economic progress, albeit with some reservations. The reference to the "Continental" Sunday hinted at immigrants' lack of appropriate decorum on the Sabbath and at their broader threat to Protestant cultural dominance in the United States. Likely to avoid offense that might hurt sales, the author chose not to elaborate.

The biggest problem newer European immigrants created, according to most writers, was their reluctance to part with Old World ways. Willingness and ability to assimilate determined whether immigrants could be depicted as real or potential Americans. Even Muzzey and Ashley, who made the most disparaging remarks about the New Immigrants, argued that the newcomers' greatest threat lay in their propensity for creating "race clusters" in big cities and thereby imperiling the "unity of national life." The texts' role for European immigrants, whatever their national or racial origin, was to depart the urban ghetto to integrate themselves seamlessly into an "American race" dominated by the old stock and their descendants.[27]

The European race or people, whether authors included the New Immigrants in it or not, was the protagonist in the American story these books told. And the greatest action the race undertook was westward expansion. Though Frederick Jackson Turner never wrote a school history, the central ideas of his seminal 1893 essay, "The Significance of the Frontier in American History," permeated textbooks for decades.[28] Turner argued that settlers' experience on the ever-receding line between civilization and wilderness forged the national character. To the frontier, he wrote, "the American intellect owes its striking characteristics. That coarseness and strength combined with acuteness and inquisitiveness; that practical, inventive turn of mind, quick to find expedients; that masterful grasp of material things, lacking in [the] artistic but powerful to effect great ends; that restless, nervous energy; that dominant individualism." And with those traits, he added, came love of liberty and commitment to democracy.[29]

Turner, soon to be appointed professor of history at the University of Wisconsin, made these claims in part as a corrective to more overtly racial explanations of the American past. Most scholars at the time looked to Europe to explain the national character. Advocates of the Teutonic "germ theory" thought Americans' political ideals and institutions, which Turner tied to the frontier, could instead be traced back in a straight line to the forests of ancient and medieval Germany. Liberty-loving Germanic tribesmen, who menaced the more autocratic Romans, handed their democratic ways to their Saxon descendants in England, who passed them on to the seventeenth-century settlers of New England and Virginia, who then bequeathed them to the American republic. Depending on one's perspective, the endowment might be cultural or biological. Political ideas had simply been transmitted across generations and might be adopted by any people. Or, perhaps the "Teutons" and their modern offspring in Britain, Canada, Australia, and the United States had been given an innate genius for self-government that other races lacked. Most proponents of the germ theory, including textbook writers John Fiske and Alexander Johnston, tended to blend the biological and cultural explanations.[30] No matter what they emphasized, however, these scholars looked to Europe to understand the American condition.

By making the United States the product of its own unique environment, Turner opted for a much more nationalist approach. His focus on the frontier in an ill-defined "West" also allowed Turner to explain American history without returning repeatedly to sectional conflict and slavery, issues that still bitterly divided historians and the country at large. Turner's frontier stripped the polyglot populations of Europe of their old identities and molded them into Americans. Because it did not rely primarily on descent from common ancestors, his story also had some potential to detach national identity from race. But the frontier Turner imagined only partially resembled the real one. His West was not torn by conflict over slavery expansion, like 1850s Kansas. It did not have much of a role for Mexican-Americans, who populated the Southwest, or for the Chinese along the Pacific coast. Native Americans contributed somewhat more to the culture of the initial frontier in Turner's scheme, but they had little role over the long term. In short, Turner made his frontier implicitly White. And when textbook writers adapted his theory to their narratives, they made it even more explicitly so.

Roscoe Ashley placed great emphasis on the West in his history and borrowed heavily from Turner. In the "cosmopolitan West," Ashley wrote, "a new race was developed that was the blending of the colonial types which still existed on the Atlantic border. Here was the beginning of the really new nation, the American people." Another writer found "national character in the making" in the West. Still another declared the West the "most American part of America," a place where people were "crude, ungainly, lacking the poise and repose and dignity of older societies; but buoyantly self-confident, throbbing with rude vigor." David Muzzey praised the "rugged democracy of the pioneer community" and found the Westerner "rough and elemental, hardy and self-reliant."[31] Textbook writers all but lifted these passages from the "Significance of the Frontier" essay.

Turner stressed the power of the frontier to transform settlers. Most text writers who borrowed Turner's ideas, however, presented the West as a place of continuity, particularly of racial traits. The hardiness, egalitarian spirit, and industriousness of the pioneers largely replicated the qualities writers attributed to English, Scotch-Irish, or Dutch settlers when they departed from the Old World. The writers thus combined the language of Turner with much of the substance of Teutonic germ theory. The inclusiveness of the West as an idea was carefully circumscribed. When Muzzey claimed that Texans displayed the "chief traits" of Americans, particularly their "restless activity," he made no mention of native Tejanos or the Black slaves that American pioneers brought with them to the Mexican province. Andrew McLaughlin, like many of his peers, dreamed of the West as a place consecrated to Whites. "Feeble, excitable" Mexicans could not hold such territory over the long term, he wrote. "The Far West, which soon proved to be golden, belonged perhaps by a manifest destiny to the Anglo-Saxon man." Elsewhere, McLaughlin declared that the "trusty long-barreled rifle," axe, and hoe "were the weapons by which the West was won for the White man." Charles and Mary Beard praised the "Anglo-Saxon" genius that turned much of the arid West into farmland. Quoting the explorer John Wesley Powell, the Beards declared that "nowhere has the white man fought a more courageous fight or won a more brilliant victory than in Arizona," where he had carried law, order, and justice into a region that "never had so much as a speaking acquaintance with the three." The heroes of the Southwest, "thank God, are Americans"—by which Powell and the Beards meant White Americans.[32]

In textbooks and popular contemporary literature, one rarely encountered a typical Westerner or frontiersman who was not White or even more specifically Anglo-Saxon. From dime novels to popular religious tracts like Josiah Strong's *Our Country,* expansion of national space was bound up with race. Even progressive thinkers sometimes could not resist the lure of American history as racial destiny. Thomas Wentworth Higginson was an ex-abolitionist who wrote the most racially inclusive school history of the 1870s and 1880s. But when a critic assailed a popular fiction writer for churning out adventure stories that led children away from wholesome study, Higginson rallied to the writer's defense with a call to race pride. "It is not a bad impulse but a good one which makes a child seek the reading you call sensational," he declared to the reviewer. "The motive that sends him to Oliver Optic is just that love of adventure which has made the Anglo-American race spread itself across a continent, taking possession of it in spite of forests, rivers, deserts, wild Indians and grizzly bears."[33]

In narratives dominated by themes of territorial growth and social progress, which were dependent to varying degrees on White racial strengths, people of color receded to the periphery of the national community. There they remained outside the direct address of the writers' "we" or "us" and often became obstacles on the path of national development.

"Lazy, Improvident, and an Inveterate Gambler": The Native American

Writing in the mid–nineteenth century, historians like George Bancroft, Francis Parkman, and William Prescott gave considerable attention to Native Americans. Indians served as a picturesque element of the country's past, one that counterbalanced the story of a new, practical-minded young republic. Native Americans were also helpful in distinguishing America from Europe, thus affirming its unique national identity.

Taking their cues from romantic historians like Bancroft and Parkman, textbook writers of that era also featured Indians prominently. The story of Pocahontas, for instance, appeared in virtually every schoolbook history: her rescue of John Smith; marriage to John Rolfe; and an early, tragic death that left a single son "from whom many of the illustrious families of Virginia are descended."[34] Textbook writers found this colorful myth of national origins irresistible, even when they expressed some doubts about the veracity of Smith's role in the tale. Much of the Indians' part in the history these writers told was not so peaceful, of course. Accounts of Indian battles filled dozens of pages in most textbooks.

Popular as historical subjects, Indians nevertheless presented a problem for any writer attempting to impart moral lessons to a young reader. If Indians did have virtues, then the founding of the United States and its westward expansion raised a troubling ethical dilemma. If Indians were unredeemable savages, they were not worthy of an epic, nation-building contest with White settlers. All writers had to confront this difficult question, and most equivocated. In their books Indians were not simple brutes. As the example of Pocahontas showed, Indians had many positive attributes. Charles Goodrich found them "quick of apprehension, and not wanting in genius. At times they were friendly, even courteous." Were Whites then at fault for dispossessing Indians of their land and driving them westward? "It is not for us to say who is to blame," declared one writer in a history published in 1871, five years before a party of Sioux and Cheyenne defeated George Armstrong Custer at the Little Big Horn. "It is true, the whites were not always just and true and prudent in their dealings with the Indians. But, apart from this, there seems to be hostility between the Indian character and civilization. And it is not to be doubted that in a few more years the Red Men will have disappeared from the American continent."[35]

Most textbooks published before 1875 cloaked the "disappearance" of the Indians in this author's somber tone of inevitability. It was a decree ordained by God, or chance, or both.[36] That such a fate was unavoidable, in fact, lent tragic power to the story of the noble savage who fought against it anyway. This stock character sometimes merited praise like that lavished upon White heroes. Samuel G. Goodrich, better known by the pen name Peter Parley, devoted a page of his 1846 history to the last days of Metacomet, a Wampanoag warrior also known as King Philip, who led the final resistance against settlers in New England during the seventeenth century. Struggling in vain against the White onslaught, Philip learned that the colonists had captured his wife and sold his son into slavery in Bermuda:

One cannot help pitying the poor man; for, though a savage, he had a soul. He could, perhaps, have borne the mere loss of a nation, but he met with a loss [of wife and son], soon after his return, which affected him more than the loss of a nation, and severed the last ties which bound him to the land of his fathers.[37]

Tecumseh, who led an Indian alliance committed to blocking the expansion of settlers into the Mississippi Valley and Great Lakes region early in the nineteenth century, was, like Philip, depicted as an especially worthy Indian. George Quackenbos gave this leader perhaps the greatest textbook tribute accorded any Indian in his *Illustrated School History of the United States:*

> Tecumseh was the most formidable of all the Indian warriors that ever fought against the United States. He was nearly six feet high; his frame was muscular, and capable of great endurance. A high forehead, piercing eyes, and gravity of expression, gave an air of command to his whole person. Strict morality and adherence to truth from his earliest years, added to talents of a high order and eloquence rarely equalled, made him not only a ruling spirit among the tribes of the wilderness, but also an object of respect to the nation whom he opposed with undying hatred.[38]

In both passages, the noble savage rises above common stereotypes of Indians as primitive and sadistically cruel. Philip and Tecumseh are intelligent, powerful, brave, and moral. Their formidable opposition to White expansion provides drama for the narrative and honor to settlers who contend for their land. Most importantly, both men *die* in battle, along with their lesser compatriots. Having played their roles, these characters leave the scene with the plot resolved. The savage can earn nobility precisely because he is no longer a threat to, or continuing moral responsibility for, the nation. The tragic end of the noble savage thereby foreshadowed the "melancholy doom" awaiting all the native inhabitants of the country. Like the Indian hero Chingachgook in James Fenimore Cooper's 1826 novel *The Last of the Mohicans,* they would slip sadly, though eloquently, into an irretrievable past.

Authors writing before the late 1870s rarely considered the eventual fate of Indians who found themselves within the territorial bounds of the United States, defeated in battle but still very much alive. None considered Indians a real or potential part of the national community.

Race and the Limits of Community

Those seeing history, as Marcius Willson did in the 1850s, as the story of the "onward progress of the Anglo-Saxon race," would likely have found such inclusion disturbing. Quackenbos thought it necessary to explain to his readers that the first inhabitants of America were, in fact, human beings with the same anatomy as Europeans. His attempt to refute the claims of extreme scientific racists who thought Indians belonged to another species seemed only to underscore their alien presence in the new nation. Quackenbos made that foreign nature even more apparent when he declared that in all the Indians dialects, "there was not a single term for justice, temperance, or virtue"—the prerequisites for citizenship in the republic.[39]

The expectation of wholesale Indian extinction, at least in the near term, grew less tenable by the 1880s. An organized military threat by tribes in the West had finally disappeared. For the federal government and the states, the decades-old reservation system had once promised racial enclosure for the remaining Indians, essentially excluding them from the larger nation. But that system now came under attack—by tribes who fought against virtual imprisonment; speculators who wanted their land; and White reformers who condemned the long history of war, treaty-making, and treaty-breaking that had first led to the establishment of reservations. Helen Hunt Jackson, who drafted a scathing indictment of federal policy titled *A Century of Dishonor,* advocated full Indian assimilation into the dominant White culture.

Congress cautiously directed national policy toward the goal of assimilation with the Dawes Severalty Act of 1887. The act divided tribal lands into smaller units, granted some of those tracts to families or individuals, and offered the rest for sale to Whites. Congress also set up schools to hasten the Indians' Americanization. Under the plan, Indians were to become private landowners much like the White settlers around them. They would be saved from destruction by losing their Indian-ness. As one recent historian has noted, assimilation combined the ideals of sympathy for Native Americans, however condescending, with faith in American progress. All that undeveloped reservation land would now become productive; all the Indians would be reconstructed as citizens.[40]

Most tribes did not embrace this assimilation program, whose most immediate effect was a significant loss of reservation land. And it also divided Whites. Even would-be reformers grew to question the Indians capability for self-improvement. Daniel Dorchester, already noted here for his hope to mold Catholic immigrants into proper citizens (see chap. 3), was appointed by President Benjamin Harrison to the post of superintendent of Indian schools. He began the job hoping to lead his young charges "towards civilization and self respect." But during the course of his work, he wearily admitted that "no class of people" more readily fell from "progress."[41] There were other objections to the new policy. While offering a potential solution to the question of what was to become of the Indians, integration threatened the nation's supposed racial homogeneity, whose value was now buttressed by the tenets of scientific racism. The depth of some settlers' antipathy to Native Americans had become apparent in brutal conflicts of the 1860s and 1870s. In 1864 Colorado militia leader John Chivington had ordered a massacre of men, women, and children. "Nits make lice," he said. The killings sparked angry protests and a congressional investigation, but they also demonstrated that racism among Whites would not dissipate quickly.

Nevertheless, passage of the Dawes Act forced textbook writers to think of Indians' place in America's future, not just its past. "The belief that the American Indian is dying out is a common error," declared the author of one schoolbook. Indians, he continued, "will doubtless exist as long as the Caucasian race."[42] With this realization, the noble savage began to disappear from histories, and the once exotic Indian grew more mundane. By the 1890s textbooks had taken an increasingly "anthropological," and less romantic, approach to Native Americans. One history first published in 1893 informed its young readers that the federal government, through its Bureau of Ethnology, "employs scientific men, eminent scholars, and trained experts to ascertain in a comprehensive way all that is to be learned about the historic and prehistoric races of America." Stories of scalping and action-oriented illustrations of tomahawk-wielding savages gave way to detailed renderings of artifacts like wigwams, peace pipes, headdresses, and canoes. Authors and illustrators frequently introduced Indians in so-called typical poses or situations. Edward Eggleston's *New Century History of the United States,* for instance, showed "Indians at Home" and "Making a Fire." Such books resembled contemporary museums, replete with instructive displays and "authentic" diagrams and photographs. Many schoolchildren likely found the new approach less compelling than the old emphasis on Indian raids. But the new professional historians praised the abandonment of such sensational renderings of the past.[43]

Following the example of scholars such as Lewis Henry Morgan and John Wesley Powell, most authors placed past and present tribes on an ascending cultural scale, from savage (mostly hunters and gatherers) through barbarous (partially nomadic but capable of raising some crops) to semicivilized (defined by fixed residence, farms, and complex social organization). This system of stepping-stones to civilized life clearly left open the possibility of social advancement that underlay reformers hopes' for assimilating Indians into the nation. John Fiske still presented stereotypes of Indians in his book—they were "unsurpassed for cruelty"—but he made distinctions between more primitive and sophisticated tribes. Like many authors, he also introduced Indians in the past tense. That suggested both the former model of Indian extinction and the newer one of racial uplift that promised the cultural disappearance of Native Americans. A question at the end of one chapter invited readers to "imagine an Indian passing from a savage to a civilized state. When does he cease to be savage? To be barbarous? To be half civilized?"[44]

Most books dutifully noted, and some praised, the new policy of assimilation. Many authors showed compassion for Indians thrust into modern, industrial life. But continued presentation of past and present Native Americans as simple and brutish revealed underlying suspicions that they might forever be racially and culturally ill suited for full citizenship. For these writers, the Indian seemed the antithesis of bourgeois norms they associated with progress. One could define Indian society only with a series of negatives: "He built no cities, no ships, no schoolhouses. He constructed only temporary bark wigwams and canoes. He made neither roads nor bridges, but followed footpaths through the forest. . . . His highest art was expended in a simple bow and arrow." Later the same author revealed visceral disgust with the Indian, noting that at "home he was lazy, improvident, and an inveterate gambler. He delighted in finery and trinkets, and decked his unclean person with paint and feathers."[45]

Henry Elson found that the Indian never aspired to improve his own or his tribe's condition. "What was good enough for his fathers is good enough for him," Elson concluded dismally. General descriptions of "the Indian" almost always referred to men, though women shared the problems of the race. Using White, middle-class standards, many writers condemned the unnatural division of labor among Indians, in which women worked as "drudges," tilling land, carrying water, and taking on other tasks better left to men.[46] Common terms and phrases used to describe contemporary and historical Indians emphasized their incompatibility with White society. They were vengeful, stupid, lazy, treacherous, superstitious, and exhibited a wild love of liberty and utter intolerance of control. Even their supposed intimacy with nature, a virtue in the mind of earlier romantic historians, had grown less appealing decades later. The Indian that Europeans encountered, said one writer, was as "wild and cruel as the beasts around him." Even a relatively progressive historian like Albert Bushnell Hart occasionally used expressions likening Indians to vermin. The Apaches, "a brave and ferocious tribe," he wrote, "infested" trade routes in the Southwest.[47]

Turn-of-the-century writers usually portrayed plans for civilizing and assimilating Indians as a new federal policy, thrust upon the country by the closing of the frontier. However, a significant precedent for the Dawes Act had been set more than fifty years earlier. President Jefferson and other like-minded statesmen of the early republic had encouraged certain tribes to emulate White culture in return for guarantees of land ownership and tribal autonomy. By the 1820s the Cherokees had met most of the criteria of a "civilized" society. On territory centered in northwest Georgia, they achieved economic self-sufficiency through farming, operated a government under a written constitution, ran schools, and published a newspaper. Most had converted to Christianity. Some even owned Black slaves. When White Georgians coveted their land, the Cherokees appealed to the federal government and won a decision handed down by Supreme Court Chief Justice John Marshall. No friend of Indians, civilized or not, President Andrew Jackson refused to enforce Marshall's verdict and gave federal blessing to the expulsion of the tribe beyond the Mississippi. More than one-quarter of the Cherokees died from disease and exhaustion during a forced march known as the Trail of Tears.

The story of the Cherokees revealed how race determined eligibility for membership in the nation during much of the nineteenth century. The tribe's experience plainly contradicted repeated claims in some books that "the race seemed incapable of civilization" and undermined assurances in others that once Indians "were weaned . . . from the shiftless, roaming, cruel life of the tribe" they could become full citizens. Writers were reluctant to expose this example of moral and legal hypocrisy to their young readers. So their treatment of this historical episode became a touchstone to both their intellectual honesty and their underlying views about race.[48]

Many prominent writers, including John Bach McMaster and Edward Channing, simply ignored the history of the Cherokees. Others withheld critical information, such as Cherokee adoption of "civilized" ways and the Supreme Court decision in their favor. Hart told readers that Indians of the South and West, including Cherokees, were

Race and the Limits of Community

"fierce and warlike" and "wandered about the settlements and had no notion of taking up farms and living among the whites." The remnants of eastern tribes, he noted euphemistically, "were carried" west of the Mississippi. "The Indians had many good qualities," Hart concluded, "but they and most of the white people could never learn to live together in peace and friendship."[49] A few writers gave generally accurate, though dispassionate accounts of this nineteenth-century example of what we would now call ethnic cleansing but avoided mention of the death toll on the march to Oklahoma.

Taking the role of apologist, a popular Southern author, Susan Pendleton Lee, mixed obfuscation and outright lies in her textbook from the 1890s:

> You may think it was cruel to remove the Indians to new far-off lands. But they never learned civilization from the white men. Idleness, drunkenness, and other vices constantly increased among them. They did not really own the land, did nothing to improve it, and were a perpetual torment and menace to the whites, who punished their offenses with little mercy. To remove them seemed therefore the kindest and best policy for both races.[50]

Faced with a complex, troubling issue, Lee reached for a familiar palette of racial stereotypes. To her, Cherokees and all other Indians were idle, drunken, menacing—qualities that seemed fixed. The Indians *never* learned the arts of civilization. And presumably they never would, for her answer to conflict between them and Whites was complete separation.

The campaign to assimilate Native Americans culturally made it reasonable to assume that they might mix their blood with Whites as well. That prospect disturbed many writers. Though they praised the benefits of mixing among the peoples of northern Europe, they grew anxious about crosses between what they considered primary racial groups like Whites and Indians. The generally positive account of Pocahontas's marriage to John Rolfe was the one, anomalous exception to this viewpoint in nineteenth-century histories. However, by 1900 this tale appeared less frequently, a casualty of mounting anxieties over miscegenation and the professionals' effort to eliminate allegedly frivolous, storybook history from texts for older students. Several early twentieth-century historians openly questioned the wisdom of such interracial unions. David Muzzey credited much of the British victory

161

in the French and Indian War to the "unnatural alliance" between Whites and natives. Referring to French inland traders, the celebrated coureurs de bois, Muzzey declared, "These wild Frenchmen often sacrificed their native tongue, their religion, even their very civilization itself, and joined the aboriginal American tribes, marrying Indian squaws, eating boiled dog and mush, daubing their naked bodies with greasy war paint, and leading the hideous dance or murderous raid." He counted it fortunate that these "aggressive French rivals" had been subdued and that America had been won for "men of English speech, blood, tradition, and law." Nonetheless, Muzzey made it clear that the fully White French could still be assimilated into American society. The "blood" that had to be excluded was that of the pure Indian and the misconceived métis.[51]

Contemporary scientific racism held that mixing between members of distinctly inferior and superior races did little to improve the former and much to degrade the latter. Muzzey and several other writers concurred. The "one great blunder" of the French, said Henry Elson, was their failure to "diagnose" the Indian character: "The Frenchman spent himself to lift up the Indian, but more frequently the Indian dragged him down to barbarism; he married the squaw and raised a family, not of Frenchmen, but of barbarians." Another writer criticized the French in Canada for showing little interest in royal shipments of prospective French brides.[52]

Writers drew similar lessons from Spanish colonial policy. Conquistadors and their descendants blended their blood with enslaved Indians "until their own nationality was lost," noted one writer. According to another text, when the Spanish married natives they revealed their willingness "to descend from their European standard of civilization" and to corrupt their religious and political institutions. The authors concluded that "we have here one of the reasons the Spanish-American peoples have not progressed more rapidly." Edward Channing also labeled Spanish-Americans a "weak and indolent race."[53] Though books rarely addressed mestizos living in the United States, it seems safe to assume the authors believed they suffered from the same racial deficiencies.

Whatever conflicted feelings they harbored toward Native Americans, professional historians at the turn of the century deemed these people mostly irrelevant to the ongoing American story. The Indians' conflict with the Whites, now shorn of much of its old bloody but romantic aura, steadily receded in more "objective," institution-based text narratives. With it went the Indians themselves. Emma Willard opened the 1828 edition of her history with a fourteen-page chapter, "Concerning the Aboriginal Inhabitants of America." Readers could also find a three-page appendix devoted to Indians; and numerous references to different tribes throughout the book, mostly, of course, in the context of wars with White settlers. By the time Andrew McLaughlin published *A History of the American Nation* in 1903, things had changed dramatically. The separate chapter on Native Americans was gone, replaced by an introductory one on "Discovery and Exploration," in which McLaughlin summed up their culture and history in five short paragraphs. He discussed Indians in passing only nine more times in his book, a frequency fairly typical in writings of his scholarly peers. It was as if the story of the melancholy disappearance of the Indians had actually come to pass—not in the real world, but in the odd, parallel realm described by textbooks.

Separate, Unequal, and Mostly Invisible: The African-American

African-Americans presented even greater problems than Indians for historians who linked White nationalism with economic, social, and political progress. Demographically, Blacks were harder to ignore. While some racial Darwinists latched on to 1870 census data that seemed to show the post-emancipation Black population might be declining relative to that of Whites, thereby obeying the "beneficial" laws of race competition, it soon became clear that the supposition was flawed. The 1880 census showed the African-American population rising steadily, clouding the fiction that the United States was, or ever would be, a nation of Europeans and their descendants exclusively.[54]

For the new professional historians, the problem was not simply the mixed population of their own day. Slaves and free people of color had played such pivotal roles in the nation's past, particularly in the political and legal history the professionals favored, that it was even more difficult for writers to neglect them than to ignore Indians. African-Americans had contributed significantly to the country's industrial growth, providing raw material like cotton for Northern factories. Southern states, in particular, still depended heavily on their labor. After emancipation, most African-Americans also rightly conceived of themselves as full members of the nation. They actively sought integration into the body politic and equal rights as citizens, whereas Native Americans were more divided on these issues. Despite such factors, historians generally excluded Blacks from popular schoolbooks as assiduously as Southern Democrats kept them from the polls. When they did emerge from obscurity, African-Americans usually appeared as voiceless appendages to the main story of Whites, as the fugitive slave Dred Scott did in accounts of sectional disputes in the 1850s. Concern for the sensitivities of textbook committees in the South helped to determine what sort of narrative treatment Blacks received (see chap. 2). But much was simply the product of the authors' attitudes on race.[55]

Removal of Blacks from American history and the national community began with the language writers employed, at times probably without conscious intention. One textbook celebrated the expansion of the franchise in the early nineteenth century, noting that by the time of Jackson's presidency, "every man was a voter." The author ignored not only slaves in that cheerful assessment but free Blacks in several Northern states without the right of suffrage and, of course, Native Americans. Another historian writing of the crisis following Lincoln's election in 1860 stated that "almost all the Southern people believed that any State had the right to withdraw from the Union when it pleased." He later claimed that "the South was much disturbed" over the question of how to manage the freed slaves so that they "would not bring harm to the public."[56] For most writers, references to the South or the Southern people meant Whites only, unless Blacks were specifically included. Similarly, several textbooks explained the illegal toppling of Republican state governments in which Blacks had actively participated as the return of "home rule."

There were times in all textbooks when African-Americans had to appear for the narrative to make any sense. In many of these cases, authors chose to show Blacks in passive roles. During the Revolutionary War, for instance, British generals had promised freedom to slaves who rallied to the king's side. Several thousand cast their lot with Britain (other slaves and free Blacks fought with the rebels). When the Revolution succeeded, they naturally chose to leave America with the departing British. It was a daring, successful bid for freedom. But in Allen C. Thomas's *History of the United States,* and a number of other textbooks, the episode received only cryptic mention. As Thomas tallied America's claims against its former enemy, he noted that Britain refused to compensate the United States "for negroes carried off at the end of the war."[57]

Many books suggested that slave rebellions like the one led by Nat Turner in 1830 were not inspired by a genuine desire for freedom or the example of revolution in Haiti. Instead, White abolitionists from the North had provoked them to advance their own political interests.

Such passages were part of a larger narrative strategy of depicting much Black and Indian resistance to White rule as the result of outside influences. In some books, the Spanish in Florida provoked slave unrest in Georgia, while British forces in Canada inspired tribes in the Great Lakes region to war against settlers—as if both groups were incapable of acting on their own.[58] Such assertions reinforced the appearance that Blacks, in particular, were naturally submissive. Textbooks popular in the South made the point more clearly than those generally used in the North. One writer noted matter-of-factly that the twenty African captives that Dutch traders brought to Jamestown in 1619 "were docile, easily managed, and made excellent field hands." Another claimed that Spaniards found African slaves far easier to control than Indian ones.[59]

Leading historians from outside the South also left the impression that slaves and free people of color were oblivious to the implications of the Civil War for their lives. After discussing the successful efforts of Harriet Tubman to carry fugitive slaves along the Underground Railroad, Charles and Mary Beard maintained that the war and subsequent Constitutional amendments "did not enfranchise a class that sought and understood power, but bondmen who played no part in the struggle." To their credit, the Beards were the only widely read authors to name Tubman; the vast majority of books completely ignored Blacks in the abolition movement.[60] Thus through both omissions and direct statements, popular textbooks lent support to the belief that Africans and their descendants in America were naturally faithful and simpleminded. They generally affirmed views common among both romantic racialists and scientific racists of the era.

The caricatures of African-Americans emerged most clearly in discussions of Reconstruction. Most textbooks published in the 1870s and 1880s dealt briefly and noncommittally with this period, noting little more than the passage of the Thirteenth, Fourteenth, and Fifteenth Amendments and the dispute between President Andrew Johnson and Republicans in Congress on how to readmit the Southern states. By the late 1890s and early 1900s, however, a consensus formed among professional historians that Reconstruction had been a tragic error. Led by James Ford Rhodes and William Dunning, these scholars argued that Republicans had acted vindictively when they disfranchised leading Confederates and imposed military rule. Granting the vote to ex-slaves, while perhaps a well-intentioned policy, had needlessly antagonized Whites and corrupted state politics. Textbook writers, whether they were accredited historians or amateurs, generally adopted this view of Reconstruction. Narratives grounded in popular ideas of "Negro" racial inferiority and civic incompetence pleased several groups (see chap. 2). Professionals in the American Historical Association, who were eager to show a united front to the public, liked the compromise it offered between positions of White scholars in each section: The North had been right on the question of slavery and secession, but the South had been right on the question of home rule after the war. Text publishers liked this version of events because it kept White Southerners happy without antagonizing large numbers of people in the North.

Reuben Gold Thwaites and Calvin Noyes Kendall's *History of the United States for Grammar Schools,* like virtually all schoolbooks of the period, approached Reconstruction from the perspective of Southern Whites. After reviewing the economic and emotional hardships they faced when the Confederacy collapsed, the authors noted that Whites then faced the "still more serious" question of "what to do with the negroes." Ever since "these poor blacks had been living under civilized conditions, they had been dependent on the white men who owned them." They were so "ignorant and inexperienced that they hardly knew what to do with their freedom. Large numbers of them desired to see the world, so they traveled from place to place and swarmed into the towns, where they were often disorderly and committed many crimes." Hundreds of thousands of former slaves, said another text, "drifted aimlessly about the country for months. To many of them, freedom chiefly meant idleness." Caught up with the "strange delusion" that the federal government would provide each of them with forty acres and a mule, they formed habits that "led to much violence and crime."[61]

Ill equipped for freedom, the ex-slaves proved even more incompetent as voters and politicians, according to these books. They easily fell prey to "rascally Northern men," the Republican carpetbaggers. Under their tutelage, the freedmen plundered state treasuries, mismanaged public affairs, heaped indignities on the Whites, and orchestrated what two authors called "the most complete travesty on popular government the nation has known." One text noted that corruption in South Carolina was rampant, with state legislators ordering great quantities of wine and liquor. "Watermelons were furnished the members at the expense of the State," a passage concluded, "and at one session the watermelon bill was $1800."[62]

When discussing Reconstruction, many authors reverted to racial stereotypes, the reference to an appetite for watermelon being the most

Race and the Limits of Community

obvious. The pattern repeated, on a grander scale, the way that many writers approached the Cherokees' forced march to Oklahoma. Racial traits simplified explanation of complex historical events. Various textbooks referred to the freedmen as superstitious, ignorant, childlike, emotional, excitable, incapable of self-control—and, alternately, dishonest, shiftless, criminal, vain, and insolent. All in all, as William H. Mace remarked, "a strange body of men to make laws for states." Unable to think or act by themselves, they were again led by White men, this time carpetbaggers instead of plantation owners and overseers.[63]

In these texts Reconstruction became a case study in Teutonic constitutionalism, the creed that only Whites possessed the intelligence and inclination for politics and that the rest of world was destined to be ruled by them. The "white race labored for centuries to attain self-government," said Henry Elson, explaining why a newly enfranchised Black electorate naturally doomed Reconstruction to failure. Echoing Herbert Spencer's theories regarding the social evolution of different racial groups, David Muzzey concluded that "Negroes are, as a race, perhaps centuries behind the whites in civilization." Muzzey believed it fortunate that federal efforts to guarantee African-Americans their right to vote had failed at the end of the century. Success "would have only fanned into flame the embers of sectional bitterness."[64]

Few writers, except those catering specifically to the Southern market, repudiated biracial democracy as openly as Elson and Muzzey. Several textbooks blamed the alleged corruption among Black voters at least partly on environmental influences. Slavery, after all, had been a poor school for good citizenship. A small minority actually condemned the poll taxes and literacy tests that former Confederate states used to disfranchise African-American voters in the 1890s.[65]

Most authors, however, saw Black subordination in the South as necessary for the foreseeable future, because of a combination of racial incapacity and the lingering effects of slavery. Charles and Mary Beard said barring Black men from the polls violated the letter and spirit of the law. But they described disfranchisement as a product of impersonal forces, claiming that "nothing could prevent it"—much as other writers characterized the conquest of Indian lands as inevitable. Two leading professional historians, Charles Kendall Adams and William P. Trent, thought denying Blacks the right to vote had the positive effect of reducing racial tensions in the South. Another author predicted optimistically in the 1880s that the franchise would be granted again "as the negro shows himself worthy of it." Many linked the recurring theme of economic progress in the "New South" to the political powerlessness of African-Americans. Through schooling provided by White benefactors, Black men and women would be steered into useful occupations as sharecroppers, small farmers, or manual laborers.[66] Taking the "moderate" position of liberal accommodationists to Jim Crow, Adams and Trent condemned brutal acts by the Ku Klux Klan during the 1860s and 1870s, when Black men were still able to vote in significant numbers. At that time, they wrote, "something like a reign of terror" existed:

> Gradually, however, a better feeling was developed; but this was not until both whites and blacks came to see that the welfare of the negroes would be better served by industrial and educational than by political methods. The belief was slow in coming; and it was not until the administration of Hayes [1877–81] . . . that order and some measure of prosperity were established.[67]

Muzzey argued that the dominance of White men, particularly the "Southern gentlemen who realize that neither cruelty nor repression is going to make a good citizen of the negro," would lead to the "greatest efficiency of both races." Only misguided Southern leaders, he told readers, would deny the "colored race" public schooling and "force it to remain uneducated and inefficient." Looking to the years after President Hayes recalled the last federal troops from the South, Philip A. Bruce, a prominent historian in Virginia, reported that "the progress which the Southern people were making under white supremacy was extraordinary."[68]

Several writers neglected to mention that Black men effectively lost the right to vote as the twentieth century began. Maybe they thought the matter unimportant. Some probably hesitated to show their young readers such brazen assaults on American ideals of liberty and equality. Liberal, universalist understandings of democracy had not entirely collapsed under the weight of scientific racism. But many writers showed no such qualms. The continuing "Negro Problem" mentioned at the close of their textbooks was not the dilemma of how to assure African-Americans equal rights. Instead, it involved the question of how they could be peaceably relegated to second-class citizenship and channeled into economically productive work. Some texts written after the Spanish-American War linked the status of Blacks not to their fellow citizens in the United States but to the "alien races" in the new colonies and dependencies. The textbook Adams and Trent wrote in

Race and the Limits of Community

1903 explained the Senate's failure to approve annexation of San Domingo (today the Dominican Republic) in 1869 by citing the example of the South. "The opposition to the treaty was based principally upon the fact that the people of San Domingo were chiefly ignorant negroes," they wrote, and "public opinion seemed not to favor an addition to the number of negroes giving trouble to the government." Again, Muzzey was even more direct. He declared Puerto Rico racially unfit for statehood: "Its million inhabitants of mixed Spanish, Indian, and negro blood are not qualified for the responsibilities of an American commonwealth."[69] In general, then, schoolbooks portrayed African-Americans as a people distinct from the "American race." Blacks in these texts were often handicapped by racial and cultural backwardness but might be educated to play a productive part in the nation's future, though one separate from Whites.

The most remarkable dissent from the prevailing views on race came from the pen of an ex-slave named Edward Austin Johnson. Born near Raleigh, North Carolina, in 1860, Johnson attended Atlanta University in Georgia. He later earned a law degree and became active in Republican politics in his home state and, after Whites imposed Jim Crow, in New York. Early in his career, however, Johnson worked as a teacher and school principal. Convinced that history textbooks then on the market were inadequate for Black children, Johnson vowed to offer a remedy. In 1891 he published *A School History of the Negro Race in America.*[70] It opened with a critique of other writers who promoted racial prejudice, intentionally or unintentionally, in their work:

> I have often observed the sin of omission and commission on the part of white authors, most of whom seem to have written exclusively for white children, and studiously left out the many creditable deeds of the Negro. The general tone of most of the histories taught in our schools has been that of the inferiority of the Negro, whether actually said in so many words, or left to be implied [*sic*] from the highest laudation of the deeds of one race to the complete exclusion of those of the other.[71]

Johnson saw that putatively national histories then in schools examined only part of the American nation, the White part. By ignoring Black accomplishments, he reasoned, these textbooks reinforced negative racial stereotypes and rhetorically isolated Blacks from the American story of territorial, economic, and intellectual growth. How "must the little colored child feel," Johnson asked, after he or she completed an assigned course in American history that did not include a "favorable comment for even one among the millions of his foreparents, who have lived through nearly three centuries of his country's history[?]"[72]

Johnson sought to fill some of the gaps. He dwelt at length on African-Americans' long-standing struggle for freedom and attempted to dispel the claim in many other schoolbooks that emancipation came in 1865 unearned and unappreciated. Nat Turner, the slave-rebellion leader mentioned only in passing in other books and sometimes labeled delusional, was "undoubtedly a wonderful character," to Johnson, and he must have had "immense courage" to undertake such a "bold adventure." This author also recounted battles in the "War of the Rebellion" (the term showed his disdain for the argument that the conflict had been fought over legitimate claims to state sovereignty) in which African-American soldiers played pivotal roles. His version of the far West boasted Black "Buffalo Soldiers" who helped to subdue Indians and tame the wilderness. Johnson thus took qualities such as bravery and love of liberty, which other texts associated with Whites like the Scotch-Irish or English, and applied them to Americans of African descent. He even set some of their exploits on the symbol-laden frontier.

While Johnson expressed outrage over continuing racial discrimination, he remained a fervent patriot and apostle of economic opportunity. He frequently employed republican rhetoric and legendary national figures to attack slavery and its legacy. In his textbook, a defiant escaped slave in Florida declared, "Give me liberty, or give me death," echoing Patrick Henry. In his history the Marquis de Lafayette claimed he never would have aided the American cause in the Revolution if he had thought he were helping to found a land of slavery. In one passage, Washington doffed his hat to Black troops in the Continental Army. Elsewhere Johnson praised a number of Black statesmen, orators, teachers, ministers, and "far-seeing" businessmen. "A self-made man is a worthy description of a Saxon," he told his readers. "But a knowledge of the facts will teach us that nine-tenths of all the leading Negroes were and are self-made." Except in its call for race pride for African-Americans, Johnson's narrative reproduced much of the content and many of the moral lessons about self-sacrifice, hard work, and love of country common in other nineteenth- and early twentieth-century schoolbooks.[73]

Johnson paralleled contemporary writers in another way as well. He believed different races had unique traits. His views tended toward romantic racialism like that expressed by Harriet Beecher Stowe earlier in the century, which emphasized the positive qualities of people of color. The "Negro," he wrote, is "largely endowed by nature with affection, affability, and a forgiving spirit" and is "proverbially religious." His willingness to work long and faithfully made him "far superior" to the Indian.[74] White racists usually claimed that innate characteristics of Blacks marked them as outcasts or, at best, as junior partners in a country based on individualism and progress. Johnson said just the opposite; those traits made African-Americans ideal citizens who deserved full economic and political integration into the nation.

Its generally optimistic call for Black self-help and White respect put the *School History of the Negro Race* somewhere between the politics of Booker T. Washington, who questioned the wisdom of combating Jim Crow directly, and W. E. B. Du Bois, who advocated confrontation. Editions of the text after 1900 showed Johnson's increasing frustrations over segregation and racism. He bitterly attacked the alleged motivations for the Spanish-American War, noting that White Southerners harkened to the call to liberate mixed-race Cubans even as they denied basic rights to African-Americans at home. Surprisingly, Johnson's subversive messages did reach at least some Black students in public institutions. In 1903, for instance, North Carolina adopted the book as a supplementary text for Black schools. The fact that the volume went through eight editions by 1911 suggests other schools outside the state used it as well. Among textbook writers popular after 1900, however, Johnson stood almost alone in his demands for African-American rights.

Two of Johnson's White peers did express some of his sentiments. Willis Mason West made attempts to understand Reconstruction and Jim Crow from the perspective of Blacks and, like Johnson, used a more respectful upper-case "N" in the term "Negro." Albert Hart went further. Perhaps influenced by Du Bois, his former student at Harvard, Hart devoted considerable space to African-Americans in his *School History of the United States,* first published in 1918. He claimed that Americans were not a "race," but a people comprising diverse elements, including Africans and Asians. He noted contributions of African-Americans in the Revolutionary War and counted them in the ranks of nineteenth-century abolitionists. He even concluded that the Civil War had been so close in 1864 that Black troops likely tipped the scale and led to Union victory. Yet when Hart condemned the errors of the slave trade, he listed among its legacies that it "brought into America a strange and then savage race that otherwise would never have come." West, in turn, called the colonization plan to ship Blacks to

Schoolbook Nation

Africa during the antebellum era, a scheme meant to rid the country of both slavery *and* freed slaves, a "wise plan." The suggestion that America would have been better off without Black men and women was unmistakable in both books. While a few White writers might cautiously champion civil rights for all Americans, regardless of race, an understanding of African-Americans as a natural and integral part of the nation required too great a leap of the imagination.[75]

The representatives of one other of the "primary races" who appeared very briefly at the close of these books occupied a more ambiguous position than Blacks, Native Americans, and most Whites. Asians presented a paradox for writers who closely linked Whiteness with national progress. Popular stereotypes depicted Indians as only partially capable of civilization and African-Americans as shiftless and feebleminded. But Chinese immigrants came from a region of Asia with a history of civilization older than Europe's. Even their detractors admitted that the Chinese worked diligently in railroad construction, mining, and other industries of the West. Therefore, in narratives centered in part on economic opportunity and expansion, the Chinese and the smaller number of Japanese immigrants seemed to be model Americans in almost all ways but one; they were not White.

In the hands of some writers, the stereotype of Chinese industriousness became not an asset to the nation but a threat to its political and economic institutions. In explaining opposition to these newcomers, David Montgomery noted that "cheap labor was believed to be hurtful, rather than helpful," to the country. Another text quoted a California governor who claimed that "Mongolian" laborers were not really immigrants at all but sojourners and "virtual slaves" of foreign capitalists who sent them to America. Thus some textbooks drew connections between the Chinese and the New Immigrants from southern and eastern Europe, both of whom were blamed for low wages and class tensions in America. Other writers were clearly uncomfortable with such economic and cultural attacks on Asians. One woman reported charges that the immigrants' "habits of heathenism" might prove injurious to national morals. But she was dubious: "It can not be said, however, that the noisiest opponents of the Chinese are the most orderly or most Christian part of the population; while the 'heathen' very often set a worthy example of quiet industry and obedience to law." A pair of authors agreed that "shiftless citizens" actually led the anti-Chinese movement. Another writer noted that the Chinese played a "great part" in the development of the West.[76]

Why, then, did federal law turn such newcomers away? Faced with that question, many writers offered confusing non-explanations that expressed a latent xenophobia. One declared of the Chinese that there "seemed to be no limit to their number," though, in fact, streams of immigrants from Europe dwarfed those from eastern Asia. Charles and Mary Beard raised the specter of a "horde" of laborers, who were "accustomed to starvation wages and indifferent to the conditions of living," descending on California.[77] Clearly uneasy with the topic, Albert Hart explained a California law of 1913 forbidding Japanese immigrants from acquiring land in this way: "Chinese and Japanese students and business men were welcomed, but there was strong objection to receiving Asiatics in large numbers. Doubtless there would be just such objections in Japan if thousands of American laborers were to settle down there and compete with the native laborers."

Perhaps. But Hart discreetly avoided the fact that the United States usually welcomed such workers from Britain, Germany, Ireland, and other nations of Europe without complaint. Other historians were more open in declaring that Asians, whatever their virtues, had no place in the nation. Natives of eastern Asia "belong to a radically different race from that of Americans," maintained Roscoe Ashley. "Absolute prohibition of immigration of Chinese and Japanese laborers may seem unfair and contrary to the spirit of American institutions; but it is certainly the simplest solution of a great problem, and perhaps the only solution that it is wise for America to attempt."[78]

Discussions of Asian immigration consumed only a tiny portion of textbooks published at the turn of the century. But these passages are important for understanding racist conceptions of American history because they reveal how "reasonable" arguments about racial tests for membership in the nation were riddled with contradictions. Science and history had established the biological, or at least cultural, inferiority of Africans and Indians, according to many historians. But some of these writers sensed it had done so less convincingly with the Chinese and Japanese. To oppose their immigration or full citizenship seemed a capitulation to prejudice. And prejudice was wrong. Even Henry Elson, one of the more enthusiastic racists among these writers, agreed on that point. He was, he said, "as nearly without race prejudice as a normal white man can be," by which he meant he treated no members of a nonwhite race as any *more* inferior than they actually were.[79]

Despite the contradictions of scientific racialism and popular prejudice, and often in the face of demographic facts that showed otherwise, most authors confidently depicted the United States as a nation of European-Americans. And despite vague calls for an end to racial prejudice from historians like Elson, it was clear they fervently hoped it would remain so.

As nationalism swept Europe in the latter half of the nineteenth century, a few prominent thinkers on both sides of the Atlantic questioned the way nationalists coupled ideas of race and nation. In the United States, Elisha Mulford and Frederick Douglass advocated complete citizenship for African-Americans. In France, Ernest Renan wrote that the search for "pure" races would prove fruitless. He found the "national principle" guiding the formation of modern nation-states like France and Germany just. But Renan wrote that employing race, in its biological sense, as a determinant in nation-building was both unjust and dangerous. He conceived of the nation as a "soul, a spiritual principle," reconstituted on a daily basis by the consent of its citizens.[80]

Renan's understanding of the criteria for inclusion in a national community approximated the liberal ideals embodied in the Declaration of Independence and, after the Reconstruction amendments, the Constitution. To varying degrees over time, such thinking influenced popular conceptions of the United States. But most White Americans at the turn of the century also conceived of the nation in racial terms. Professional and amateur historians were no different. In stories of the country's past that they recounted for students in elementary and high schools, these writers often equated Whiteness with national citizenship. They lauded the industry, tenacity, and democratic impulses of various White races they claimed had founded America but often showered only the English, Scotch-Irish, Dutch, Germans, Scandinavians, and their "fellow kinsmen from Northern Europe" with that praise. Their textbooks sometimes openly discussed supposed biological and cultural infirmities of other races that lived in or threatened to immigrate to America. More often, these textbooks excluded nonwhites from the nation simply by ignoring their roles in America's past.

It is not especially surprising that publishers produced such racist volumes or that large numbers of schools used them. Textbook committees and teachers chose these books because they accurately reflected popular prejudices. In the 1920s, however, the professional historians who dominated the textbook market would find some of their attitudes on race out of sync with a large segment of the American public. Their emphasis on the English basis of American civilization and their celebration of Anglo-Saxon racial achievements would help to precipitate a wave of attacks on their textbooks and their vocation and to spur a new effort to define the national community and its past.

5. Anglo-Saxonism and the Revolt against the Professors

In the autumn of 1927 the new mayor of Chicago put the city's superintendent of schools on trial. The charge was treason.

William McAndrew had engaged in a plot to destroy American patriotism and "de-nationalize" students, according to William "Big Bill" Thompson. Proof of this claim against the sixty-four-year-old administrator centered on several allegedly pro-British textbooks in American history then used in Chicago's grammar and high schools. Written almost exclusively by professional historians, the books were said to slander Revolutionary patriots—branding John Hancock a smuggler, for instance—and to ignore all racial groups in America except the Anglo-Saxons. Mayor Thompson declared that the histories formed but one element in a plan orchestrated by English propagandists and their supporters in America to deliver the former colonies into the waiting arms of the British Empire. Sympathetic witnesses from Chicago and elsewhere in the country earnestly backed his charges against the "treason textbooks." Weeks turned into months as the unusual proceedings gained worldwide attention.

"Trial" was something of a misnomer. McAndrew sat before the city's school board, not a judge and jury in civil or criminal court. The superintendent faced neither imprisonment nor fines, only dismissal and loss of pay. In essence, the affair amounted to an extended public hearing on several of the country's most popular textbooks and their authors and, secondarily, on McAndrew's job performance. But participants as well as newspapers opted to label the affair a "trial." The term lent drama to the story, and it also recalled the recently concluded trial of John Scopes, another educator accused of introducing subversive ideas to students. "When Thompson gets through throwing out books with a bias in favor of England, in the end he'll have nothing left but fairy tales," joked Clarence Darrow, who had defended Scopes for teaching evolution and was thus no stranger to controversy in the classroom. Rabbi Louis L. Mann of Chicago's Sinai Temple echoed the famed attorney's sentiments. "The mayor has made Chicago in its intellectual humiliation second only to Dayton, Tennessee," he grumbled.[1]

The textbooks' authors and their colleagues gladly acknowledged parallels to the infamous "Monkey Trial." Such comparisons allowed historians to portray their vocation as a science, like biology, and to cast their critics as narrow-minded reactionaries who would take the history curriculum away from experts and hand it over to mobs and political opportunists. Thompson, wrote one of the writers' allies, "has committed himself to the denunciation of seekers after truth" and "gentle purveyors of information to school children." The historian Arthur M. Schlesinger admitted during the trial that his colleagues had not done enough to present their side in the controversy, for they had "felt that the disinterested quest for truth needs no defense."[2]

At times sanctimonious, often heartfelt, these assertions only partially explained the clash of ideas and social forces that underlay the episode. The conflict revolved around different understandings of what constituted national history and who had played primary roles in it. It pitted historians against two sets of opponents, each with different critiques of the textbooks. One wanted a return to the patriotic orthodoxy of the nineteenth century; the other sought a more inclusive version of the nation's history to reflect its growing ethnic and racial diversity.

The orthodox groups challenged the validity of what was loosely termed the New History.[3] Begun in the 1880s, the New History marked an effort by scholars to create more objective accounts of America's past. It relied less on the heroic exploits of virtuous soldiers and statesmen and more on temperate analyses of the long-term development of social, political, and economic institutions. To the country's first generation of professional historians, this new approach to writing and teaching history represented progress, the same kind that was bringing Darwin into the modern classroom. By the turn of the century the New History had come to dominate colleges. After university-trained historians wrested much control of textbook authorship from amateurs, it also made inroads into public schools.[4] There it met firmer opposition. Organizations led by the Sons of the American Revolution (SAR) resented the way historians were tampering with the old and familiar histories penned by popular nineteenth-century writers like Emma Willard, Samuel A. Goodrich, and George Payn Quackenbos. These

Anglo-Saxonism and the Revolt against Professors

critics saw modern histories, with their diminished attention to traditional heroes and villains and their more nuanced look at those characters that remained, as a threat to patriotism. They demanded a return to the older style.

The professors, in turn, argued that more realistic history provided a better foundation for honest love of one's country than the whitewashed accounts of the past. They defended themselves against these self-designated "patriots" on grounds of historical accuracy and intellectual honesty. Here the analogy to the Scopes trial seemed to work. Textbooks *had* been assailed by conservatives or, as one writer put it, the "forces of reaction and obscurantism."[5] The critics' uncompromising stand on textbook content, regardless of new research and evidence, paralleled the position taken by activists in the anti-evolution movement.

The second set of detractors, however, did not fit the Scopes model. They did not question the goal of objectivity. Instead, they took issue with how textbooks depicted various racial groups and how these groups had assimilated, and continued to assimilate, into the national community. Professional historians, who were overwhelmingly White, middle-class, Protestant, and of British descent, often saw issues of race and Americanization in similar ways. At times they were openly racist, constructing a hierarchy of human stocks. Many questioned the African-American capacity for self-government. Others expressed concern about welcoming immigrants from the alien "races" of eastern and southern Europe. More progressive historians did not present races as innately unequal but did see distinctions in the value of the cultures that such races were said to produce. In their histories they tended to offer disproportionate praise for the accomplishments of Americans with northern European, particularly British, ancestry. Progressives did not object to immigration but often demanded that newcomers shed the trappings of the Old World and embrace a superior, Anglo-American culture.

Not surprisingly, Americans of these "inferior" races and cultural backgrounds looked at Americanization quite differently. They opposed what came to be called the "cult of Anglo-Saxonism," whether they saw it as rooted in virulent racism or in somewhat more benign ethnocentrism. They argued that all racial groups had contributed to the formation of America's national identity, and they wanted their children's textbooks to reflect that view. References to the United States as an Anglo-Saxon country or emphasis on its racial and cultural ties to Great Britain deeply offended these critics. Like White

Southerners before them, they began to challenge historians and demand changes in books written for public schools. Begun at the end of the nineteenth century, the conflict simmered for over two decades. But the unique political climate of the 1920s spurred an open, bitter revolt against the professors and their books. Critics of Anglo-Saxonism searched for an outlet for their frustrations over the wartime and postwar surge of nativism, with its frenzied Americanization drive, hunt for alien subversives, and ultimately successful call to restrict immigration.

When these critics targeted textbooks, they briefly found themselves allied with the "patriotic" organizations. The latter groups found few problems with racial and cultural bias in the books but did fear that professional historians' more critical approach to America's past, particularly in schoolbook accounts of the Revolution that seemed to offer sympathy for England, imperiled national unity. And so the stage for the drama of the pro-British conspiracy was set.

Once begun, the revolt against the professors spread across the country. It became most intense in America's two largest cities, each with ethnically diverse populations and annual textbook sales near or over one million dollars.[6] New York City conducted two separate investigations of its history books between 1921 and 1923. Chicago began its trial of William McAndrew four years later.

The chain of events that led to New York and Chicago's textbook hearings can be traced back at least as far as 1895. In that year President Grover Cleveland intervened in a long-standing border dispute between British Guiana and Venezuela, demanding a resolution on American terms. War fever briefly gripped the country. The British, however, quietly backed down and submitted the question to arbitration. The brush with conflict had two interesting results. First, it elicited an outpouring of affection between the two nations, with Britons and Americans espousing blood kinship and common cause in international relations. A writer for the London *Spectator* chided his countrymen for their traditionally anti-American views. "We are told, for example, that what little Englishry they once possessed has long ago been bred out of them by foreign intermixture and that the new American is a compound of a hundred races with hardly a dash of the true English-speaking strain," he began. He quickly added that such a notion was "preposterous." The leading citizens of the United States were Anglo-Saxons, its law operated on Anglo-Saxon principles, and its "religious proclivities" and literature were distinctly Anglo-Saxon.[7] The blurring of linguistic, racial, and cultural boundaries made the term "Anglo-Saxon" difficult to define, a fact the writer readily admitted. But its very ambiguity aided rapprochement between the two countries. Advocates of Anglo-Saxonism on both sides of the Atlantic cheerfully ignored the real diversity in the United States and Britain. Together, they reveled in their conviction that the White, English-speaking nations of the world, led by these two countries, shared a heritage of intelligence, thrift, industry, and genius for self-government and an obligation to oversee the affairs of those peoples who lacked such virtues. American audiences applauded the calls for racial brotherhood from Edward Freeman and other English scholars. Britons, meanwhile, cheered the victories of their fellow Anglo-Saxons in the Spanish-American War.[8] Their government, alone among the great powers of Europe, had sided with the United States in the conflict.

The Venezuela Crisis also prompted people to ask why the United States and Great Britain, if they had so much in common, had nearly come to blows. Some answers were not hard to find. The nations had fought two wars, wrangled over Canada's boundary, and engaged in decades of economic and diplomatic rivalry. Farmers in the South and Midwest resented London and Liverpool's control of commodity prices. Politicians regularly "twisted the lion's tail," railing against British ownership of American land and industry.[9]

Many commentators, however, found a simpler cause for the bad feelings—history textbooks. Biased accounts of the Revolutionary War and the War of 1812 had inspired hate for the mother country, they said. Prominent writers, the governor-general of Canada, and several historians in the United States agreed that school histories distorted the past and bred ill will. Textbook author John Bach McMaster declared that in his competitors' volumes students were "taught to hate the only people on the face of the earth to whom we are bound by ties of race . . . the only people with whom it is possible to ever form a lasting alliance."[10]

The charges had some validity. Many popular school histories of the 1870s and 1880s oversimplified the causes of the Revolution and sometimes cast the Americans' foes as brutal tyrants. George Quackenbos detailed "acts of savage cruelty which too often disgraced British troops in the course of the war." They included British complicity in the massacre of American settlers on the frontier, a soldier's bayoneting of a boy who hid under his sick mother's bed during an attack, and, most prominently, horrendous conditions endured by American prisoners. Many captured soldiers were held at sea just beyond the piers of New York, a city the British held for most of the war:

> The prison-ships were moored chiefly in Wallabout Bay. On one of these, the *Jersey,* a thousand men were sometimes confined. Their food consisted of mouldy bread, spoiled meat, and other unwholesome and refuse articles. Such a diet, added to foul air and want of exercise, brought on a variety of diseases which swept them off by hundreds. Every morning the command was heard, "Rebels, bring out your dead." The bodies of the deceased were carried ashore and buried near the bay, in graves so shallow that they were often washed bare by the waves.[11]

Such passages likely inspired in children little respect for British political motivations or military tactics. But they must be read in context of the author's generally graphic style. American reprisals for attacks by Indian allies of the British were just as cruel in Quackenbos's book. American soldiers showed no mercy "but the firebrand" to whole villages, and even George Washington earned the ignominious title of "the Town-destroyer" from his army's victims. It is also important to remember that other text writers showed more generosity to the British than Quackenbos. John J. Anderson carefully explained their point of view on taxation in his histories. John Clark Ridpath, like most of his peers, noted that "eminent statesmen" in England, led by William Pitt, championed American principles. Mary Elsie Thalheimer, another popular text writer, made careful distinctions between Britain's leaders during the Revolutionary era and that nation's more enduring political ideals. "Though hard things must be said of the British government," she wrote, "we ought never to forget that our fathers had the spirit and ability to repel English injustice precisely because they had been trained to the rights and duties of Englishmen."[12] Even Quackenbos tended to stress Yankee idealism in the Revolution far more than British perfidy.

Two years after the peaceful conclusion of the Venezuela Crisis, Goldwyn Smith, a writer for the middle-class-oriented *North American Review,* set out to test the theory that textbooks had caused Americans to hate the British. Predictably, authors took the American side in the Revolution and the War of 1812, argued Smith. But their books were hardly "venomous." He had to go back to 1850 to find a history that exhibited what he saw as genuine bitterness toward England. And that book was a trade history, not one intended specifically for schools. Smith concluded that the further one advanced from 1776, the less Anglophobic histories became. A report issued by the New England History Teachers Association (NEHTA) in 1898 concurred. "Under the influence of deeper study and a keener sense of justice," wrote the teachers and historians on the NEHTA committee, "the element of bitterness which so often entered into the discussion of this subject [the Revolution] has largely disappeared."[13]

By the turn of the century, the charge that commonly used histories threatened progress in Anglo-American relations had grown less tenable, even for those who made the dubious assumption that students directly absorbed and retained the allegedly anti-British sentiments in their schoolbooks. Yet past and present histories still came under attack, particularly by professional historians. In a 1911 essay Albert Bushnell Hart dusted off an old edition of Quackenbos, a book used rarely, if at all, in schools of his day, along with Emma Willard's *History of the United States; or, Republic of America,* out of print for thirty-five years. Again came the charge that nominally "patriotic" schoolbook authors had regularly distorted history in the service of nationalism. "School histories have usually been written by people who knew very little history," wrote Hart. They had "thought it necessary to provide strong meat for little minds: hence the lurid pictures of the past which are forced upon the attention of millions of young people, and which leaves [sic] an impression that often lasts through life." Hart contended that such writers, untrained in modern techniques of scholarship, portrayed the Revolution as an "unprovoked attack upon the American people by the British people."[14]

Hart and his colleagues' fixation on this issue suggested more was at stake than a mere correction of specific errors and more general bias. There was. For the first generation of academic historians, criticism of popular schoolbooks served as a way to differentiate professional work from that by writers who lacked a doctorate in history or an appointment at a respected university. Hart underscored Quackenbos's status as an amateur by noting that he also penned schoolbooks on science and rhetoric. That was a gentle way of declaring the author unfit to write history. Changing times, Hart wrote, had rendered Quackenbos's "lurid pictures of the past" obsolete. "The historian," and here Hart meant the trained scholar, "is seldom called upon today to inspire national hatreds by recalling the cruelties of the other side."[15] Scientific objectivity distinguished the professional.

Not coincidentally, many historians who belittled amateurs had already written or would soon draft schoolbooks that competed with theirs. Hart finished his a few years after writing the critique of Willard and Quackenbos. Some of his peers had entered the market, and begun bashing the amateurs, considerably earlier. In a text first published in 1903, William P. Trent of Columbia University listed three "reasons for wishing to add to the long list of school histories of the United States" that had motivated him and coauthor Charles Kendall Adams of the University of Wisconsin. Second among them was the need "to treat the Revolutionary War, and the causes that led to it, impartially and with more regard for British contentions than has been usual among American writers." Willingness to overturn sacred myths of the past became a badge of professionalism. As a recent critic has remarked, the revisionist view of the American drive for independence served as a "magnificent advertisement" for the new standard of objectivity.[16]

The call to reexamine national history also reflected a new intellectual climate among American elites, including scholars, diplomats, novelists, artists, and the middle and upper classes generally. That shift was apparent in Hart's essay. He called for educators not only to reexamine the Revolution but also to transform the underlying objectives for teaching history and other subjects:

> The true principle in writing text-books ought to be to dwell upon our glorious heritage of all of England down to the Revolution, and much since that time. Shakespeare is our dramatist; Elizabeth was our queen; Tennyson is our poet; Dickens is our novelist. We ought to recognize the fact that the English have been working out a magnificent system of popular government on their own lines . . . that of all the nations of the world Great Britain is that one which is nearest to the United States in kinship, in institutions, and in aspirations.[17]

Hart, like many of his peers at the start of the twentieth century, increasingly conceived of America's national identity through its ties to the Old World, Britain in particular. This new perspective marked a major departure from views one hundred years earlier, when cultural leaders had hoped schools could save young citizens from the "infection of European vices."[18] Americans in the republican and antebellum eras had deliberately tried to remove themselves from the European orbit. They had tried to heed Washington's call to avoid "entangling alliances" in diplomacy and had extended that spirit to the cultural realm as well. But by 1900 many Americans eagerly sought to return to

Anglo-Saxonism and the Revolt against Professors

the "Anglo-Saxon family." Novelist Henry James spoke about a new English-American world, American students flocked to Oxford University, and several magazines sprang up in Britain and the United States celebrating Anglo-Saxon ties across the Atlantic.[19]

Several factors lay behind the new romance with Britain. Many Americans at the start of the nineteenth century had believed the United States lacked the cultural prerequisites of nationhood, but that sense of inadequacy steadily declined. As the country's elites gained confidence in their American identity, they grew more comfortable in acknowledging debts to England and, to a lesser extent, the rest of Europe. Racism also played a critical role. After gaining an overseas empire in 1898, significant numbers of Americans felt greater affection for a mother country that had also assumed the "White Man's Burden." The new mood also reflected nativist fears that southern and eastern Europeans flocking to the United States were contaminating the nation's culture and bloodlines. The popular textbook writers most sympathetic with England, including John McMaster, David Saville Muzzey, and Roscoe Lewis Ashley, usually exhibited the most suspicion toward the so-called New Immigrants.[20]

Evidence of this tilt toward Britain surfaced in several educational reports at the turn of the century. It was already evident in 1892, when the National Education Association's Committee of Ten released its report on the teaching of history, civil government, and political economy in the schools. The committee, which included Harvard president Charles Eliot and Princeton historian and future president Woodrow Wilson, carefully assessed the merits of studying various aspects of the ancient and modern past, given the unavoidable time pressures in the classroom. They advised that schools devote eight years to history. During that time, they concluded, a student had to learn English history, for it offered essential lessons in how to achieve a free and stable constitutional government. Committee members strongly recommended the study of France, the only other modern nation mentioned by name, but they eliminated the subject in their alternate, six-year plan. General European history, they decided, provided a useful *contrast* to "the development of the Anglo-Saxon race which is the main thought of British and American history." A report on history in the schools by the American Historical Association suggested that "Englishmen and Americans are of one blood" and that they shared the "individualistic spirit of the race." Another study affirmed that "English history is in some ways our history."[21]

Sentimental calls among educators for emotional reunion with the mother country increased when the United States declared war on Spain in 1898. At the NEA convention that year, a resolution celebrating the lofty motives of the war and the increasing "solidarity of both the American people and the Anglo-Saxon races" passed unanimously.[22]

Anglo-Saxonism crept into the professional historians' textbooks in two ways. As part of the broader increase in concern over race, writers began framing America's accomplishments through its past and present ties to England. Andrew C. McLaughlin, in his *History of the American Nation,* noted the "pure English blood" of New England, implying that the region's success, along with that of Virginia, sprang in part from its superior racial heritage. Willis Mason West pointed out that the celebrated Scotch-Irish settlers of the frontier were neither "Scotch nor Irish, but Saxon English." Many popular authors, including McLaughlin, Charles and Mary Beard, and Allen C. Thomas, saw a specifically Anglo-Saxon impulse behind the successful settlement of the frontier. While he harbored doubts about the propriety of seizing Mexico's northern provinces in the expansionist war of the 1840s, Thomas nevertheless believed "it has been far better that the large territory should be under Anglo-Saxon control." McLaughlin cited the Anglo-Saxon's "manifest destiny" in the American West, and several historians frequently used "Anglo-Saxon" interchangeably with "American." The United States at the close of eighteenth century was not English per se, noted another writer, but it was still "predominantly Anglo-Saxon." Familial terms and metaphors underscored blood and cultural ties to Britain. David Muzzey called the English "America's kindred." Edward Eggleston described the disputes leading to the Revolution as a "family quarrel."[23]

As Eggleston's example suggests, Anglophilia's other major effect on the books was a more sympathetic portrayal of Britain before and during the Revolution. While almost all writers found the Americans' resort to arms justified, they equivocated more than their predecessors had in previous decades. Hart thought the colonists had not been "desperately oppressed" before the war but had been "alert to resist the encroachments of tyranny." The author of another popular textbook agreed that the Americans began their rebellion against "tyranny anticipated." Charles and Mary Beard concluded that there was "much justification" for recent scholarship arguing that the colonists gained more from Britain's trade laws than they lost and that they "owed much of their prosperity to the assistance of the government that irritated them."[24] Other writers began to question long-held assumptions about the tyranny of "taxation without representation."

Anglo-Saxonism and the Revolt against Professors

From the British point of view, the colonists had been "virtually" represented in Parliament because individual members spoke for the interests of all British subjects in the empire. Muzzey went further than any other textbook writer in finding a middle ground between the positions of Britain and the colonies on such disputes. Echoing Hart, he wrote that the Americans' bid for independence

> has too often been represented as the unanimous uprising of a downtrodden people to repel the deliberate, unprovoked attack of a tyrant upon their liberties; but when thousands of people in the colonies could agree with a noted lawyer in Massachusetts, that the Revolution was a "causeless, wanton, wicked rebellion," and thousands of people in England could applaud Pitt's denunciation of the war against America as "barbarous, unjust, and diabolical," it is evident that, at the time at least, there were two opinions as to colonial rights and British oppression.[25]

As they acknowledged greater complexity in the origins of the Revolution, several text writers also delved into the motivations and actions of American patriots. McLaughlin disapproved of some attacks on British property and Loyalists in the colonies. "There were many acts of violence in these years," he wrote, "and we need neither excuse nor commend them." In another book, vigilante members of the Sons of Liberty stirred up "riots," intimidated colonists, and sacked and burned the residences of British officers during the 1760s. That organization had "carried their operations to such excesses that many mild opponents of the stamp tax were frightened and drew back in astonishment at the forces they had unloosed." Others noted that under British law, prominent colonial leaders like John Hancock had been smugglers. Everett Barnes claimed that the Second Continental Congress presided over by Hancock became a "scene of petty schemings" as individual colonies jockeyed for power. One book pointed out that many Pennsylvania farmers gladly sold supplies to the British in Philadelphia while Washington's army suffered at Valley Forge.[26]

The turn toward institution-based history accentuated this newly critical attitude. While professional historians began to present some of the Founders' flaws, they also dropped some of the traditional stories of American heroism that fit poorly in explanations of political, social, and economic development. In the new histories, Nathan Hale did not always regret having but one life to give for his country, and

185

Molly Pitcher did not always drop her water bucket and replace her fallen husband at his battlefield cannon.

Change in the Revolutionary narrative was not as drastic or sudden as these examples might suggest. Rather, it built cumulatively over several decades, even in books by the much maligned amateurs. The older histories were never as glowingly patriotic, and anti-British, as scholars imagined, nor were the newer books entirely groundbreaking. But the professional historians had a vested interest in emphasizing the extent of the transformation. It validated their ideal of objectivity and showcased the strides they had taken to achieve it. They gladly acknowledged that their books placed the War for Independence in a more evolutionary perspective and traced the quest for greater liberties to English precedents as old as the Magna Carta. Willis Mason West described the Revolution as "part of a thousand-year-long contest between the English-speaking people and their kings for more political liberty." A few writers approached Hart's ideal of portraying the contest as a "deep and broad Anglo-Saxon movement, in which both sides had some right and both had some wrong." A willingness to flaunt their iconoclasm, and the Anglophilia that often underlay it, would later come back to haunt the historians.[27]

In the near term, however, Anglo-Saxonism in textbooks fed the growing resentments of two important constituencies, Irish- and German-Americans. In 1907 their two largest ethnic organizations, the Ancient Order of Hibernians and the German-American Alliance, agreed to work together for common goals. These included preventing closer political ties to Britain, blocking passage of legislation to restrict immigration, and undertaking a "systematic investigation of the share all races have had in the development of the country." The Hibernians' president, Matthew Cummings, complained that in "all of our current school histories, and most others, in fact, the Anglo-Saxon has been glorified and exalted to the exclusion of those others who did so much for this country, like the Irish and the Germans and the other countries." The call for more inclusive history appears to have been genuine, though the passing reference to "other countries" suggests where priorities lay. The two organizations mostly sought to correct sins of omission, seeing that textbooks at least mentioned historical figures like John Barry or Baron Von Steuben in their treatment of the Revolution, for instance. They also wanted greater coverage of more general German and Irish contributions to American civilization.[28] The Hibernians and the Alliance already wielded considerable influence over the content of histories for Catholic schools, but they aspired to adjust historical credit in books for public institutions as well.

In 1909 the Germans took their case to the American Historical Association, which was drafting another list of suggestions for teaching history at the primary and secondary levels. Feeling rebuffed, they opted to go directly to publishers. They wanted to influence either a revision of some book already on the market or the creation of a new one. An outline of the plan appeared in *Mitteilungen,* the Alliance's official bulletin, in the summer of 1914:

As soon as we have a good book, which meets our requirements and is excellent also in other ways, so as to please other nationalities, with a smart publishing house behind it and with its organization, together with our organization, we will probably have turned the trick. When other publishers see that they are at a disadvantage in selling their books written in strict conformity with the American Historical Association pattern and disregarding the Germans, it is to be expected that in future editions these books will be "corrected" accordingly. If you want to do anything with an American you must attack his pocketbook. Having once started the thing, when we have proved to publishers that they must reckon with our influence, the thing will run itself. Then we shall no longer have to bother with the recommendation of the American Historical Association.

The Alliance dangled the prospect of official endorsement for a book that met its specifications and indicated that its branches would seek its adoption at the local level. At least two publishers showed interest. D. C. Heath already had one title, Henry Bourne and Elbert Benton's *History of the United States,* that nearly met the organization's needs. Alliance leaders remained confident of success until the war in Europe derailed the project.[29]

When the United States entered the conflict three years later, many German-Americans' dissatisfaction with current texts, and hostility toward the AHA, only deepened. Leaders of the German-American Alliance were hauled before a congressional subcommittee. Investigators cast their earlier efforts to curry favor with publishers in a sinister light. Instead of encouraging German-Americans to look at the "common heroes" of the nation's history, said one witness, "they pick out the German ones." Samuel Harding, a history professor at Indiana University, told senators how the Alliance had threatened to sponsor a boycott of his textbook on European history, written in 1915, for its treatment of the Great War.[30] Whatever the current political situation, it was extraordinarily unwise for a schoolbook writer like Harding to air his grievances against a large, well-organized group already experienced with lobbying for changes in the history curriculum. One can imagine sales agents at his publisher cringing as they learned of his activities. Fortunately for them, but unfortunately for the history profession, Harding was not the only scholar to entangle himself in wartime politics.

When hostilities broke out in Europe in 1914, American historians argued that their colleagues in the belligerent nations, particularly Germany, had become tools of extreme nationalists. Once the United States became directly involved in the war, the professors faced a dilemma. Would they remain impartial, or would they lend their scholarly hands to a war to make the world safe for democracy? In the battle between national service and objectivity, many historians made their compromises with the latter. Several prominent textbook writers chose to write propaganda, including Hart, McLaughlin, Beard, Claude H. Van Tyne, William Bagley, and Carl R. Fish.[31]

Scholars who undertook such work had three outlets for their efforts. The National Board for Historical Service (NBHS) published *History Teachers Magazine,* distributed to schools nationwide. The NBHS also worked closely with the official U.S. propaganda agency, the Committee on Public Information (CPI). Guy Stanton Ford, head of the history department at the University of Minnesota, directed the CPI's Division of Civic and Educational Publications. Dozens of scholars contributed work to Ford's division or other CPI projects. The CPI also published a regular bulletin, the *National School Service,* which Bagley edited. Further outside the government sphere was the National Security League (NSL). Formed before U.S. entry into the war, it took more strident stands than either the CPI or the NBHS, particularly on the threat of German influence in America. Hart and Van Tyne joined the NSL.

The three organizations published a variety of propaganda that centered on explaining American war aims, exposing Germany's threat, extolling the Allies, or presenting tips on what citizens could do to aid the war effort. Most work was relatively benign. Bagley wrote and edited children's verse, including:

Anglo-Saxonism and the Revolt against Professors

Hush little Thrift stamp,
Don't you cry;
You'll be a War Bond
By and by.[32]

Other literature proved more troubling. In depicting Germany, propaganda writers had initially tried to distinguish between its allegedly malevolent rulers and its generally innocent people. Over time the distinction was lost. One of the most famous CPI posters featured a helmeted German soldier, bloody bayonet in hand, looming over a burned-out village (see fig. on p. 190). The caption read, "Beat back the HUN with LIBERTY BONDS." Some scholars who wrote for the CPI blurred the line between the enemy abroad and the German-American at home. Germany, declared Stuart P. Sherman, a professor of English at the University of Illinois, was struggling to capture the American soul. Ostensibly American poets, novelists, and professors

attack everything in America that is due to English influence; praise everything in America that is due to German influence. Accordingly, they sneer at the ideals and professions of democratic government; they sneer at the Pilgrim Fathers and at all the Puritans who since the seventeenth century have constituted the moral backbone of the nation; they set themselves against every movement of moral reform; they sneer at those works of American literature that we recognize as classical.[33]

Sherman's diatribes revealed how the war had lain bare a bitter contest over the meaning of American national identity. On one side stood White, largely old-stock, English-speaking groups who sought to preserve what they saw as the dominant Anglo-American culture. On the other were recent immigrants and others who did not consider themselves or their country Anglo-Saxon. The pressures of war strengthened the conservatives, allowing them to forge closer links between nativism and popular understandings of nationalism. Anglophilia had its natural counterpart in Germanophobia.

In one CPI publication, Earle Sperry of Syracuse University condemned German-American newspapers, clubs, schools, and churches and argued that "national life" would be "stronger, sounder, and healthier without them." Princeton history professor and NSL writer Robert McElroy declared that the German soul was "perverted, and

A poster for the Committee on Public Information (CPI) by illustrator Fred Strothmann. After lending their services to the CPI, professional historians would come to be associated with the most xenophobic work it and other wartime propaganda agencies produced. *Courtesy of the Library of Congress.*

black as hell itself."[34] Suspicion of German-Americans, which propaganda writers stoked, was readily transferred to other immigrants. A furious wartime drive to impose cultural and political conformity on foreign-born citizens and aliens became, for many, a means to assure national security. Though he deplored the extremes to which this quest for unity would be taken, Guy Stanton Ford still thought CPI propaganda should create what he enthusiastically termed an "Americanized, nationalized American nation." Many of the country's native-born citizens asked on which side of the hyphen all newcomers, not just German-Americans, placed their loyalty. The hyphen, as industrialist Henry Ford put it, was a "minus sign."[35]

Schools became important venues for the Americanization campaign. The CPI and other agencies inundated teachers with propaganda. Educational spokespersons on the local and national level offered advice and often veiled threats. In a 1918 article in *Education* the president of the University of Maine, Robert Aley, declared that every teacher in the country should be a citizen and that any born outside the United States "should be so completely naturalized that all trace of the hyphen has been removed." By the time Aley's article appeared, many schools had already dropped the teaching of German. That change, he advised, "probably ought to be permanent." Aley also thought it important for students to unlearn the importance of German civilization. The war provided "a good time to review the origins of learning and culture, and fix in our minds the fact that much of it did not come from the Teuton." He suggested that teachers ask students to make a list of "world-revolutionizing" inventions, from the telegraph and electric light to the sewing machine and airplane. "Singularly enough," he concluded, "not one of them is credited to a German." Aley, like many historians, wanted to use the crisis of war to impress upon American students their indebtedness to Britain:

Today for the first time the soldiers of America are fighting side by side instead of face to face with the soldiers of other English speaking nations. The English speaking people of the world are responsible for the ideals we hold most dear. The English speaking people have stood for and developed personal liberty, law, order, individual opportunity, and national responsibility. The best things in our government and institutions are of English origin. The high school has a fine opportunity to revise the teaching of American history so that these fundamental origins may be understood and appreciated.[36]

Schoolbook Nation

The war revived claims that biased school histories had prejudiced generations of schoolchildren against England. The charge resulted not only in journal articles but in an entire book, *The American Revolution in Our School Text-Books,* prepared by Charles Altschul, a businessman who also wrote for the CPI. Altschul, like Aley, was a committed Anglophile. He saw the task of apportioning historical credit in histories as a zero-sum game. Appreciating Britain's role in the formation of the American nation required dismissing that of other countries. "The contribution of all other nations in our melting pot," he concluded, had been "negligible compared to England."[37]

Recommendations by Aley, Altschul, and others like them had some effect on history textbooks already on the market. Wartime editions paid tribute to British statesmanship. They addressed the United Kingdom's conduct in coverage of the present war, for which many writers relied heavily on CPI documents, and its behavior in other episodes like the Venezuela Crisis. Text author William Backus Guitteau even found something good to say about an episode that had once led to Anglo-American discord. During the Civil War a British shipyard had constructed a Confederate cruiser, the *Alabama,* which destroyed millions of dollars worth of Union shipping. The United States later demanded reparations. Great Britain agreed to discuss the issue. She "paid the money promptly," noted Guitteau, "and the Geneva Award gave the world a splendid example of arbitration as a means of settling disputes between nations."[38] Greater accounting of America's British heritage appeared in some books. McLaughlin and Van Tyne added a fifteen-page chapter, "How Europe Influenced America, 1607–1815," in the 1919 edition of their *History of the United States for Schools.* They discussed, among other issues, how British principles had influenced the Declaration of Independence and the Constitution.

Pressure for writers and their publishers to keep pace with shifting politics remained intense until the armistice in November 1918. California demanded a review of its history textbooks, fearing pro-German propaganda had infiltrated its schools. Montana expelled a book that mentioned the Teutonic origins theory, which postulated that American democratic traditions could be traced back to the forests of ancient Germany. The theory, which had largely fallen from favor among professional historians, suddenly appeared seditious once the United States entered a war to topple Prussian autocracy. James Harvey Robinson saw his *Medieval and Modern Times* dropped from Des Moines for insufficiently harsh condemnation of Germany's war guilt. Similar incidents occurred throughout the country.[39]

Anglo-Saxonism and the Revolt against Professors

Occasionally, historians took a stand against impulsive historical revisionism. However, for the most part, textbook authors, and more especially their publishers, capitulated to the zeitgeist. Critics had attacked West for pro-Germanism in one of his texts. He had little to fear from them when the 1918 edition of his *History of the American People* appeared. In it, he called Germans a "docile race," in the sense that they were "organized and obedient to the word of command," even if it meant mutilating captives. He also implied that German immigrants might pose a threat to national security. Nor could West be called critical of the war aims of America's allies. They were, he wrote, "waging *our* war, battling and dying to save our ideals of free industrial civilization, of common decency, from a militaristic despotism." West, like many of his peers, drew connections between the lessons of the Revolution and the responsibilities of the Great War. Quoting an English historian, West said that older conflict had split the English-speaking race but doubled its influence: "Not least among its results, the Revolution helped start England herself upon her splendid march to democracy. Now, after a century and a half, the two great divisions of the English-speaking race are coming together once more in sympathetic friendship, again, to 'double their influence.'"[40]

Not all historians displayed West's level of devotion to England, and only a few showed open hostility to German-Americans or other recent immigrants in their professional work. But many prominent scholars had joined the CPI, NBHS, and NSL, and they came to be associated with the worst propaganda the agencies produced. Historians made themselves highly visible during the war. They went on national speaking tours in support of America's entry into the conflict, for instance. McLaughlin even undertook a well-publicized goodwill trip to Great Britain. They testified before Congress. Print runs of their CPI pamphlets soared into the millions. Through the words and actions of leading historians, the profession aligned itself conspicuously with the aims of a Democratic administration led by one of its own. When disillusionment with the war and its unrealized goals set in, professors became a focus of public recriminations.

It did not take long. In December 1918, one month after the armistice, congressional hearings on the NSL began. One congressman scornfully read aloud some of Van Tyne's suggestions for promoting better relations with Britain by revising the teaching of the Revolution. Van Tyne, he said, was "not a safe man to go around the country and educate the youth of the country."[41] In the *New Republic,* columnist Henry L. Mencken mocked the "Star-Spangled Men" and their now tattered claims to objectivity.[42] Critics began to direct much of their anger toward the historians' textbooks. That choice was natural; they were public documents, purchased by taxpayers and subject to public oversight through state and city adoption boards.

These books and their authors came under heavy but generally disorganized attack in the first two years after the war. While different groups shared dissatisfaction with frequently used texts, they lacked a common explanation of the books' flaws or a prescription for remedying them. Broadly speaking, the historians' opponents fell into two camps. "Patriotic organizations" led by the Sons of the American Revolution and the American Legion objected to writers' attempts to render history objectively whenever that effort sullied the nation's reputation in foreign and domestic policy or emphasized long-standing rifts in American society, particularly those involving class. They favored a dramatic, episodic narrative patterned around heroic figures who would serve as models for youthful readers.

The second set of critics belonged to organizations affiliated on racial (a category that today would include ethnic) or religious lines. These included the historians' old adversaries in the German-American Alliance, renamed the Steuben Society after the war, and the Hibernians, along with the Catholic Knights of Columbus, the National Association for the Advancement of Colored People (NAACP), and similar groups. They usually advocated greater mention of, and tribute to, their constituencies in school histories. They also tended to oppose disproportionate lionizing of Anglo-Saxons in America and celebration of the country's ties to Britain.

There was some overlap in membership and ideas between these two broad communities, but they generally remained distinct. Sometimes individual organizations became openly hostile toward one another. During the war patriotic organizations had led the charge against pro-German books, a policy that hardly endeared them to German-Americans. After the war a writer for the Masons' national publication *New Age* claimed he saw "Jesuitical trickery" in positive treatment of Irish-Americans in histories published for Catholic schools.[43] The kind of sustained, vitriolic attack on textbooks that arose in the 1920s required some platform to bring these organizations into a loose alliance.

Edward McSweeney, head of the Knights of Columbus's Historical Commission, began constructing it in 1920 in a fifteen-page pamphlet entitled *America First*. Like many Americans of Irish descent, McSweeney resented his country's rapprochement and eventual alliance with a nation that had crushed Irish bids for independence for centuries. He also detested Anglo-Saxonism, seeing the theory that America's success could be attributed to its English ancestry as myth. "The Anglo-Saxon impulse was not, and is not, in the least responsible for the progress of the United States," he wrote. "It had nothing to do with the Spanish in Florida; the Huguenots in Virginia; the Swedes in Delaware and New Jersey; the Dutch in New York and Pennsylvania, and the Celts in Maryland and Pennsylvania."

McSweeney did not open his essay with either sentiment, however. Instead, he raised the specter of "unassimilated America" and its effects on industrial unrest, which was the "greatest problem facing America." It seemed like a familiar argument: Immigrants failed to understand or appreciate American political and social ideals and institutions. They thus easily fell under the sway of socialists, anarchists, Bolsheviks, and other radicals. Violent labor strikes and acts of terrorism, like the Haymarket Riot of 1886, inevitably followed. This rationale, in fact, helped to galvanize the movement for immigration restriction during the "Red Scare" that followed the war.

But McSweeney, unlike the nativists, did not see immigrant's wishes to retain their religious faiths or mother tongues as the threat to assimilation. The threat, instead, came from historians' attacks on the "sacred ideals" embodied in the Declaration of Independence and traditional understandings of the Revolution as an uprising against tyranny. If immigrants did not learn respect for the political principles of Washington, Hamilton, and the other Founding Fathers, they could never become loyal Americans. Historical revisionism endangered that respect. In fact, argued McSweeney, new interpretations of the Revolution reflected a "stupendous plot" carried out by British propagandists to undermine the foundations of national life:

> Text-books in use in the primary schools are already beginning to show the influence of the propaganda campaign. . . . Teachers of primary grades in which more than 90 per cent of the pupils are children of foreign-born parents, or are themselves foreign-born, are told pleasantly that whatever is good in this country is English, and not a word of explanation in defense of the United States. These children are at the age when they are beginning to think. How far will our national Americanization get with this competition?[44]

McSweeney's linking of assimilation, British propaganda, and the Revolution provided the glue that would hold disparate groups of textbook critics together. As rhetoric, it was masterful. He exploited a broadly held consensus that schooling, and especially history teaching, was critical in transforming immigrants into Americans. He invoked nativist anxieties but remained respectful toward immigrants. He also appealed to nationalist pride rooted in ideas of American exceptionalism. McSweeney described the American as "the highest product of civilization," a "composite" of various cultures and races, not a mere Englishman in the New World.[45] He also relied partially on facts. Between 1914 and 1917 the British *had* orchestrated a propaganda campaign to bring the United States into the war, though its effect on history teaching was minimal. On their own and through the CPI, NBHS, and NSL, historians and other educators *had* played up America's cultural indebtedness to England. There seemed to be just enough evidence to make his seemingly far-fetched conclusion—that the British were using schoolbooks to soften up Americans for eventual reintegration into the empire—appear credible to many people.

McSweeney's charges deeply influenced a newspaper columnist from New York City named Charles Grant Miller. In the summer of 1921, Miller wrote a series of articles, distributed nationally through papers owned by media tycoon William Randolph Hearst, repeating and elaborating on McSweeney's conspiracy theory. Behind the plot, he said, lay the accumulated wealth of Scottish-American millionaire Andrew Carnegie and Anglo–South African Cecil Rhodes. Carnegie Foundation money infiltrated putatively American schools and libraries while Rhodes Scholarships sent recent American college graduates to study in Cambridge, England, turning the cream of the nation's intelligentsia into British lackeys. Many historians had already become turncoats, he warned. They had eagerly agreed to rewrite the Revolution and other episodes in return for British gold and the social prestige their English connections could confer.

Miller named several members of this scholarly fifth column. Because he had little proof of the ludicrous charge of payoffs, beyond some historians' acceptance of invitations to attend an academic conference in London, he relied on passages from their textbooks to prove his theory. At times he accurately represented an author's views, for Anglophilia was not difficult to detect in many texts. Often he employed a more sensational style, making an incredible charge and then following up with little real evidence, perhaps only a short quotation taken out of context. "THE DECLARATION CENSORED," read the heading of a short chapter in *Treason to American Tradition,* a booklet prepared from his early newspaper columns. Below we learn that the

Anglo-Saxonism and the Revolt against Professors

book in question, McLaughlin and Van Tyne's *History of the United States for Schools,* merely traced many of Jefferson's ideas to John Locke and precedents in English law. Under the headline "AMERICAN HISTORY ANGLICIZED" Miller wrote that West's textbook taught "That Only England's Heroic Support Saved Our Union in the Civil War." West had actually written that workers, and the "English masses" in general, suffered under the embargo of Southern cotton. Despite that hardship, they sensed that the North was fighting for a just cause, the end of slavery, and they pressured the British government not to recognize the Confederacy. West never claimed England had somehow won the war for the Union.[46]

Allegations of British subterfuge found a receptive audience. They dovetailed with Republican attacks on the League of Nations, another scheme said to endanger national sovereignty. They played upon popular unease surrounding alleged Bolshevik conspiracies, which had led many Americans to support the illegal raids and deportations orchestrated by Attorney General A. Mitchell Palmer in 1919. The story of wealthy foreigners engaged in anti-American intrigue also manipulated class tensions. Miller subtly encouraged readers to make such shadowy connections. There existed, he said, "a vast net-work of imperialistic, capitalistic, scholastic and pacifist influences in support of the treason texts." Many Americans had also grown weary of the steady drumbeat of speeches, articles, and other propaganda in favor of the nation's wartime allies. Foreign-born populations in major cities often saw praise for England tied to overzealous Americanization campaigns, particularly those in public schools. Teachers wrote to the *New York Times* complaining that lessons on British literature or history often brought threatening notes from parents and protests from students. "It is not only students of Irish parentage who show these reactions, but immigrant children of other races," grumbled one such letter writer.[47]

Miller's claim that professional historians defamed Revolutionary patriots or omitted their inspiring stories to conform to the dubious ideal of "scientific exactness" also brought the support of political conservatives. The Sons of the American Revolution, Veterans of Foreign Wars (VFW), American Legion, Daughters of the American Revolution, United Spanish War Veterans, Grand Army of the Republic, and Descendants of the Signers of the Declaration of Independence all eventually endorsed Miller's views.[48] While its greatest supporters would be race-based and patriotic organizations, there seemed to be some aspect of the conspiracy story to appeal to almost everyone.

Politicians gravitated to the issue. James Graham, a former congressman from Illinois, devoted an Independence Day speech to the issue. He found a disturbing irony in the conspiracy: The British had borrowed millions of dollars from the United States during the war, only to use it "to pay for de-nationalizing us." He concluded grimly that if "they succeed it will not be necessary to repay" the debt. The *Illinois State Register* responded in an editorial: "When a man of Mr. Graham's standing, character and ability, charges 'falsification of history' and backs his charges with a very startling array of comprehensive data, his utterances demand more than passing attention." Textbook publishers heeded the *Register*'s advice. George W. Benton, editor-in-chief of the largest textbook publisher in the United States, the American Book Company, directed editors and authors to study the criticisms carefully. No book seemed safe, not even those penned by Irish-Americans. Officials at ABC feared a rival publisher was planting accusations of English bias in Charles H. McCarthy's *History of the United States for Catholic Schools*. They likely suspected Macmillan, publisher of a competing history by John P. O'Hara. O'Hara had recently come under fire in Miller's newspaper articles and thus could have benefited from a more liberal distribution of indictments for pro-Britishism.[49]

In 1921 New York became one of the first cities to mount an official investigation of the texts. Superintendent of Schools William Ettinger formed a research committee that included ten teachers, nine principals, and one principal's assistant. The committee, which was chaired by Edward Mandel, a district superintendent, sought to establish fundamental principles for teaching history, set standards for textbooks, and investigate charges against specific volumes. Committee members held public hearings on the issue from November 1921 until January 1922 and released their 171-page final report in the spring.[50] The Mandel Committee found no evidence of a British plot but did believe several books overemphasized English contributions to America, needlessly dropped inspiring stories, or gave too much attention to controversial topics. They also believed historians' judgment to be "reprehensible" in some cases. McLaughlin and Van Tyne's history earned the greatest censure for referring to John Hancock as a smuggler without sufficiently stressing that his lawlessness was a commendable blow against unjust British trade laws. The committee further declared that history must not be taught for its own sake, but as a means to good citizenship, which it defined as love of law and order, respect for authority, and reverence for American institutions.

Authors could not include facts that undermined that purpose on grounds of historical accuracy. Truth, said the report, was "no defense to the charge of impropriety."[51]

Relative to the mounting hysteria, the Mandel Committee's critique of ten texts then used in New York's schools appeared moderate. The same could not be said of a concurrent investigation mounted by City Hall. Mayor John Hylan saw that the textbook issue was ripe for exploitation. But Hylan had poor relations with school officials, and he likely concluded that their independent inquiry would offer him little political gain. So in December 1921 he ordered his own investigation and selected his commissioner of accounts, David Hirshfield, to oversee it. Hirshfield plunged enthusiastically into his work, telling reporters, "I'm 101 percent American, and this is going to be a 101 percent American investigation." He vowed to do a "great deal of research," examining not only the texts but original historical documents on which they were based. He indicated that he might write his own schoolbook, as other duties permitted. Hirshfield held five sometimes quite colorful public hearings. At one, a fistfight broke out over a dispute concerning the origin of the melody to the "Star-Spangled Banner."[52]

Over a year passed between the final hearing and the release of Hirshfield's report in May 1923. A story in the *New York Tribune* later revealed the cause for the delay. The mayor's office had paid a man named Joseph Devlin two thousand dollars to write the report. But Devlin, like the committee headed by Mandel, found no evidence of a British conspiracy. Further, he commended the books under investigation as generally excellent, though they might be improved. Hirshfield quietly shelved Devlin's report. He then turned to Miller, the original popularizer of the conspiracy theory and now also a paid consultant to the city. Writing under Hirshfield's name, Miller reiterated the charges he had made in the Hearst papers. He recommended that five textbooks already criticized in Mandel's report be barred from the schools: West's *History of the American People;* Hart's *School History of the United States;* McLaughlin and Van Tyne's *History of the United States for Schools;* Guitteau's *Our United States;* and Barnes's *American History for Grammar Grades.* To them Miller added Muzzey's *An American History;* another history by Barnes; the *Short American History by Grades;* and a supplementary book, C. H. Ward's *Burke's Speech on Conciliation.* Never willing to pass up free publicity, Hylan and Hirshfield included full-page photographs of themselves in the report. They made a good call. The document generated passionate

At the request of Mayor John Hylan, David Hirshfield led the second of two highly publicized New York City inquiries into allegedly treasonous schoolbooks. Here he is pictured in the 1923 *Report on Investigation of Pro-British Text-books.*

debate across the country, and the city had to print a second edition to keep up with demand.[53]

While the *Tribune*'s revelations of fiscal mismanagement soon discredited New York's hunt for treason texts, similar inquiries continued in other cities, including Newark; St. Louis; Somerville, Massachusetts; Washington, D.C.; and Evanston, Illinois. In Boston a city councilman even branded a dictionary pro-British. Officials at a public library in California removed two books by Hart and Van Tyne from their shelves, on the grounds that their treatment of the Revolution would hinder an Americanization program. Wisconsin and Oregon passed "pure" history laws. Wisconsin's measure banned from schools any text "which falsifies the facts regarding the War of Independence, or the War of 1812, or which defames our nation's founders . . . or which contains propaganda favorable to any foreign government." Once a book had generated complaints from five citizens, the state superintendent was obliged to schedule a public hearing.[54]

No episode arising from the alleged pro-British conspiracy, however, gained as much notoriety as Chicago's mayoral election of 1927 and the subsequent "trial" of superintendent William McAndrew, described at the opening of this chapter. As the Republican challenger to an incumbent Democrat in the mayor's office, William Thompson needed an issue to jump-start his campaign. He had already declared himself "wetter than the middle of the Atlantic Ocean," a stand that endeared him to bootleggers like Al Capone, reputed to have donated heavily to Thompson's coffers. His decision to target textbooks made sense for several reasons. The anti-British theme played well in wards dominated by Irish and German voters and, to a lesser extent, Italians. In casting McAndrew as the villain of the textbook conspiracy, Thompson also allied himself with the superintendent's many enemies, particularly the teachers' union. Thompson had also been tarnished by scandal during his previous tenure as mayor, from 1915 to 1923. As one commentator at the time noted, by making the American Revolution a central issue Thompson took the campaign into a mythical realm where his no-nonsense opponent, who ran on a good-government theme, was ill prepared to contend.[55]

Thompson's slogan became "Down with King George and the King's stool pigeon, McAndrew." To the delight of his critics, the ex-mayor often seemed to confuse George III, the Americans' antagonist in the Revolution, with the United Kingdom's current sovereign, George V. In March 1927 Thompson took out a full-page advertisement in the *Chicago Tribune,* inset with a picture of George Washing-

Schoolbook Nation

ton. "Why America First?" read the copy. "Because the American who says 'America Second' speaks the tongue of Benedict Arnold and Aaron Burr." The call to eliminate disloyal texts, it continued, "should stir to action every red-blooded man and woman in Chicago until the city is rid of pro-British rats who are poisoning the wells of historical truth."[56]

Thompson won the election and quickly fulfilled an earlier promise to bring McAndrew up on charges of insubordination. While the grounds for potential dismissal rested on a minor point of civil service law, the hearings focused almost exclusively on the unrelated questions of textbooks and pro-British machinations in the schools. McAndrew's trial in Chicago repeated patterns set by Hirshfield's investigation in New York. A parade of witnesses testified. Miller, who had worked for Hirshfield, now offered his services to Thompson. In New York, Miller and others had claimed that Columbia University harbored pro-British professors; now the treasonous school became the University of Chicago.

Both Hirshfield and Thompson finally overplayed their hands. Journalists castigated Hirshfield for wasting taxpayers' money once they discovered he had buried Devlin's report and paid Miller to write a more inflammatory one. Thompson, meanwhile, felt pressure to maintain the momentum of McAndrew's trial over several months. Essentially, the mayor was using the affair to run out the clock on the superintendent's contract. To liven things up, Thompson sanctioned a plan to find more seditious material at a city library and then to burn it publicly in Grant Park. His representative on the library board found four objectionable books and prepared to carry out the mayor's wishes. Opponents, however, immediately filed suit to stop the bonfire, and public opinion turned against the mayor. He retreated, declaring that he had never wanted a book burning, only segregation of the objectionable volumes from the main collection. The trial continued, but Thompson never recovered. The board ruled against McAndrew, only to have a judge reverse the decision.[57] By the spring of 1928 the Chicago episode had sputtered to a close. The drama of a British conspiracy against history in the schools, which had captivated the nation on and off since 1920, was over.

Once McAndrew's trial had devolved into what the progressive weekly the *Nation* labeled a "continuous vaudeville show," it was easy to forget the larger issues that lay behind the revolt against the textbooks.[58] Critics had raised fundamental, and often legitimate, questions about how historians presented the national community to stu-

Always eager to take the spotlight, Chicago mayor William Thompson joins a supporter singing "Big Bill the Builder," a tribute to his accomplishments in office. A photographer snapped the image in early 1928, as the city's textbook investigation was coming to a close. *Courtesy of the Library of Congress.*

dents in public schools. It was not a coincidence that these debates occurred while Congress passed the most sweeping limitations on immigration in America's history. Proponents of the 1924 National Origins Act wanted to halt change in the country's demographic composition. Many of them thought of the nation in racial terms, associating it with a northern European, often called Aryan or Nordic, identity. Those who did not fear biological contamination in immigration from the "races" of southern and eastern Europe still saw in the newcomers a threat to the dominance of a social order based on the English language, Protestantism, and a culture they believed the country had inherited primarily from Britain.

Not all of the historians labeled pro-British during the 1920s held such nativist views. Nevertheless, the backlash against textbooks still represented an attack on a national identity conceived in narrowly racial or cultural terms. Immigration quotas for Ireland and Germany were relatively generous under the National Origins Act, but Irish- and German-Americans, in particular, had long feared this sort of ethnically exclusive nationalism. That anxiety, coupled with group pride, had first provoked critiques of Anglo-Saxonism in schoolbooks in the early 1900s, well before McSweeney and Miller concocted the British conspiracy.

The textbook writers and their allies in the 1920s often missed the progressive element in the assault on textbooks—its effort to detach national history, and thus popular ideas of the American community, from any single racial or cultural bloc in the United States. In the same way, the texts' defenders tried to ignore the ethnocentric nature of many schoolbooks and much of the wartime propaganda with which historians had become associated. That is why they preferred the Scopes analogy. They wanted to believe the authors faced uncompromising zealots who, if given their way, would turn back the clock of progress in the historical profession and the schools. Applied to many critics in the patriotic organizations, the evolution-vs.-creationism parallel was accurate. New York's Mandel Committee had, after all, recommended banning controversial topics from the curriculum, no matter how relevant they might be to understanding U.S. history. Applied to the racial- and religious-based organizations, however, the Scopes argument failed. These groups wanted to include more people in the country's history, not censor it.

Oddly, many people who backed the embattled authors accused their adversaries of provoking racial antagonism. An association of history teachers voted to "deplore" agitation that would promote "animosities between classes or nations." George Counts, a leading scholar in education who had just left the University of Chicago for Columbia, said that Thompson "cultivated the rich soil of racial and national divisions." He pointed to Thompson's campaign advertisement in the *Tribune.* It read, in part:

> In the schools of this great city, with one fortieth of the population of the United States, the children—the future men and women who must carry on—are being taught that the American Revolution was an act of villainy against a benign King—that Washington was an ungrateful rebel—that Von Steuben, Kosciusko, Pulaski and other heroes who came to America to fight with Washington the battle for human liberty—were a lot of "undesirables" and merit scorn rather than the gratitude of the nation.[59]

Counts called the charges "pure balderdash." On a literal level, he was correct. No book argued that Washington was a traitor, except in the eyes of the British, and none scorned the foreign volunteers who aided the American cause. Several of the modern texts had excluded them, however, as space devoted to Revolutionary battles shrank. And while authors did not brand these soldiers "undesirables," several did characterize recent immigrants from Poland and other nations of southern and eastern Europe in just that way (see chap. 4). In *An American History,* Muzzey claimed that they threatened American living standards and "debauched" city politics. He questioned whether such immigrants could ever be molded into good citizens or would become an "ever-increasing body of aliens, an undigested and indigestible element in our body politic, and a constant menace" to free institutions. Another book described an increase in the "undesirable classes," particularly radicals, among recent immigrants. Charles and Mary Beard detailed problems presented by Italians, Poles, Magyars, Czechs, Slovaks, Russians, and Jews who came from countries "far removed from the language and traditions of England whence came the founders of the Republic." Even Germans, heretofore desirable immigrants, seemed less so to some authors during and immediately after World War I. One text referred to the disdain for ethics "bred into the bone of the Teuton."[60]

All popular texts did not label immigrants undesirable, but most, like the Beards', spoke of the "problems" they presented, especially in large cities like New York and Chicago. And, like Muzzey, several authors openly questioned whether people from races outside northwestern Europe could ever assimilate. Suspicion of immigrants and condescension toward nonwhites, whether it originated in schoolbooks or society at large, bred resentment. It rankled even more when combined with praise for Britain and Anglo-Saxons in the United States. Nativism and racism in these histories were mild compared to sentiments one might find in popular volumes for adult readers, like Madison Grant's *Passing of the Great Race* or Lothrop Stoddard's *Rising Tide of Color.* But because the selection of textbooks was subject to political control, they endured a disproportionate share of public reaction against the nativist climate of the 1920s.

Charles Grant Miller tried to tap that indignation in his newspaper columns and the pamphlet and full-length book, entitled *The Poisoned Loving-Cup,* adapted from those columns. Historians espousing the "Nordic complex," he wrote, had even slurred Christopher Columbus, choosing to ignore him and emphasize "vague myths of earlier discoveries by Norsemen . . . for no discernible reason but that there shall be no recognition of any contribution whatever from the Latin races in the making of America."[61]

Evidence for that charge was not entirely compelling. Professional historians did apportion less space to Columbus than their amateur predecessors in the nineteenth century had, but that was because stories of discovery and exploration were less important in institution-based history than narrative history. Contemporary textbooks, designed partly to please Scandinavian communities in the Midwest, did devote a few paragraphs to Vikings who had arrived in the Americas before Columbus. In his *History of Our Country for Higher Grades,* Reuben Post Halleck devoted a whole page to America's debt to these "Northmen," noting their heritage of "(1) unconquerable energy and determination, (2) the desire for free assemblies of the people to decide questions that many other races left to their king, and (3) a new idea of the personal independence and importance of each individual."[62]

This passage was a variation on the now taboo Teutonic theory, and Halleck, writing in the early 1920s, carefully avoided terms like "Teuton" or "Germanic tribes" in his explanation. But stories of Leif Erickson and his Viking companions had appeared in popular textbooks for more than fifty years. Miller, however, was less concerned with accurately accounting for textbook content than he was with exploiting it to support a theme he thought would resonate with readers. The same pattern occurred in his discussion of the Revolution:

Anglo-Saxonism and the Revolt against Professors

A striking phase of all the Anglicized revisions is the elimination of German, Irish, Italian and Polish assistance in the Revolution, as well as that of the Dutch of New York and Pennsylvania, the French of Carolina, the Swedes of New Jersey and Delaware, and the Negroes in all the colonies.

Almost uniformly throughout his book Everett Barnes calls the colonists "Englishmen in America" and "Britons fighting for liberty"; and he, as well as West, Ward and McLaughlin and Van Tyne, class the Revolution as an English "civil war" waged between English political parties on both sides of the sea, "neighbor against neighbor."[63]

Again, Miller overstated his case. The authors he cited tended to describe Americans of the 1770s as Englishmen, but elsewhere they noted that various ethnic groups had originally settled and later immigrated to the colonies. Because all the colonies were British, and the people in them British subjects, calling them "Britons" seems understandable. There was no "striking elimination" of foreign assistance in the Revolution, except in a few cases the dropping of a character like Casimir Pulaski or Thaddeus Kosciusko or of an American officer of Irish descent like John Barry. None of the nineteenth-century schoolbooks Miller, Hirshfield, Thompson, and others held up as models of exemplary history ever mentioned Italian assistance in the war.[64] Significantly, however, there was a large population of first- and second-generation Italian-Americans in New York and Chicago in the 1920s, and they voted.

Predictably, historians challenged Thompson and Miller on such points. "This race issue is one of fact," countered Albert Hart in an article in *Current History.* "It is absolutely established that at the time of the Revolution the main non-English elements in the American Colonies were the Germans, the Scotch-Irish Protestants and the Africans," and also "some thousands of Catholic Irish." Historians did not ignore Poles and Italians in their textbooks, Hart argued; those groups simply were not in America in significant numbers during the war.[65]

Trained to seek verifiable facts, a scholar like Hart missed how text critics employed a discourse grounded more in symbol. Miller appealed to opponents of Anglo-Saxonism by using schoolbook treatment of the Revolution as a metaphor for contemporary debates over national diversity. Throughout his writings on the British conspiracy he appropriated the language of extreme nativists, essentially turning their own weapons against them. Sounding like a champion of immigration restriction, Miller declared that pro-British doctrines had to be cast out of schools "if America is to remain American." From the more extreme racists Miller also borrowed language redolent of physical contamination. A history "alien in spirit" had begun to "appear bodily in our textbooks," he wrote. Long-established truths had been "incontinently reversed" in the "insidious effort to denationalize America." History in the schools, intoned Miller, must no longer be subject to "perversion, distortion and pollution." *America First* author McSweeney also saw the "pure streams of American history" being "polluted" at the source. Another Miller ally agreed that historians guilty of these crimes were "de-natured Americans."[66]

Thus the true threat to Americanism did not lie with recent immigrants in urban ghettos, according to this assessment, but with representatives of America's long-established native stock who rejected the principles of the nation's Founders. The hyphen remained a danger in America, but Miller pinned the threat on traitors who wished to "sacrifice the traditional national spirit on the newly erected altar of *British-American* hyphenation." His charge that a few wealthy British industrialists conspired to deliver the United States to a foreign power might initially seem outlandish. In fact, he had simply reworked popular, decades-old stories of papal plots to topple the republic, which the Ku Klux Klan and other opponents of Catholic immigration had recently revived. Nativists portrayed immigrants as physical, political, and moral threats to the nation. Miller reversed the equation, making White, middle-class, and largely Protestant historians, with their "unamerican doctrines," the real threat to the "virile American national spirit." Miller's views differed radically from those of nativists, but he skillfully adapted themes from their rhetoric. The very familiarity of such arguments probably lent strength to the backlash against historians and their books.[67]

Textbook writers may not have always deserved Miller's carefully choreographed wrath. Only David Muzzey and Roscoe Ashley adopted a clearly nativist tone in their histories. Nevertheless, many writers did extol Anglo-Saxon civilization and make it the standard by which potential Americans would be judged or made to conform. Consider the discussion of British victory in the French and Indian War in Reuben Gold Thwaites and Calvin Noyes Kendall's *History of the United States for Grammar Schools:*

Anglo-Saxonism and the Revolt against Professors

The fighting with the French united the English colonies, and prepared them for ultimate union in defense of their liberties. But quite as important was the fact that now the English race, with its ideas of liberal government, was to be allowed the opportunity to expand far westward into the interior of the North American continent; and to establish here a home for such of those people from other lands as wished to live under these laws, carry out these ideas, and help make our country a still greater and better nation.[68]

The passage applauded the English race in a way that glossed over diversity already present in the colonies in the 1760s, the sort of omission that often incensed critics. But at the same time Thwaites and Kendall appeared remarkably broad-minded. They endorsed the melting pot, welcoming "those people from other lands," and concluded that immigrants could make the United States a "greater and better nation." They did not call for restricting immigration by race or national origin. Their only qualifications were that newcomers agree to live under the laws of the land and carry out the ideas of the original English settlers. Of course, the authors' inclusiveness hinged on how one defined "ideas." One could read "ideas" narrowly, as a limited set of political principles, or see it representing a spectrum of English cultural practices to which immigrants would be expected to adhere.

Because textbook language was sometimes ambiguous, it can be helpful to look at historians' other work to better understand how they viewed Americanization. No author who came under fire in the 1920s supported the idea of the United States as a nation of immigrants more enthusiastically than Albert Hart. The sentiment appeared throughout his *School History of the United States.* In the frontispiece, usually reserved for an illustration of George Washington or Abraham Lincoln, Hart conspicuously placed "an immigrant ship entering New York harbor." In his reply to Mayor Thompson in *Current History,* he referred to the "many races which have combined to make the country great." Yet how did Hart see the role of the immigrant? He offered one answer with a 1911 article in the mass-marketed *Munsey's Magazine.* In "Is the Puritan Race Dying Out?" Hart reassured readers who feared immigrants might overwhelm New England and the rest of the nation. His use of the phrase "Puritan race" instead of the more common "Anglo-Saxon," "native American" (not to be confused with the more recent designation of American Indians), or "English race," suggested he would look at the issue in cultural rather than biological terms. The impression was borne out in the essay. Hart was no eugenicist. He had no anxieties about foreigners degrading national bloodlines by outbreeding native-born Whites—the demographic dilemma usually called the "race-suicide theory." Hart said that while descendants of seventeenth-century English settlers might dwindle proportionately in the American population, the stamp of their culture would remain dominant. Already, he wrote, "New England is peopled in part by Puritan Irishmen and Puritan Scandinavians; in another generation or two, at the most, there will be Puritan Italians, and perhaps Puritan Canadian French."[69]

Such arguments might have soothed nativists. But Hart ignored the possibility that large numbers of Italians, Irish, and French-Canadians might have had no desire to become Puritan, a term that connoted fealty both to English heritage and, unmistakably, to Protestantism. Hart welcomed immigrants, but he did not believe that they had much to contribute to the national culture, at least not until they had fully absorbed the country's heritage and outlook. It was in the gap between those two positions that historians like Hart found themselves vulnerable to attacks from Miller, McSweeney, and Thompson.

Anglophile historians who adopted an institutional approach to their textbooks tended to portray American culture as firmly Anglo-Saxon. The country's legal, political, and artistic institutions had been established on an English foundation in the seventeenth and eighteenth centuries, they said. That is why, elsewhere, Hart could refer to Elizabeth I as America's queen and even to a nineteenth-century English writer, Alfred, Lord Tennyson, as the country's poet. In this model, American institutions would continue to evolve, but their essential character would not change. Foreign-born Americans would adapt themselves to preexisting Anglo-Saxon forms, and the newcomers' cultural differences would mostly evaporate. As Willis Mason West wrote in his textbook, non-English peoples had played a great part in the making of the national life, "but after all, *the forces that have shaped that life have been English.*" Many native-born Americans, including some scholars, carried this belief in the virtue and necessity of assimilation to extremes during World War I. Propagandist Stuart Sherman, for example, saw German-Americans "sneering" at American literature, democratic government, and especially the Puritans who had long "constituted the moral backbone of the nation." But even in milder form, the belief that the United States had a fixed national identity essentially inherited from Britain infuriated textbook critics.[70]

Anglo-Saxonism and the Revolt against Professors

People dissatisfied with textbooks on the market in the 1920s did not always agree about how the national community should be depicted. Generally, however, the critics who organized on race and religious lines were American exceptionalists. They believed the United States had a unique national identity that could not be traced ultimately to Britain or any other country. And they wanted individuals from various backgrounds presented in schoolbooks and identified as contributors to that American identity. Politicians like Hylan and Thompson capitalized on those desires, and their campaigns against textbooks provided a forum for traditionally underrepresented groups to challenge their depiction in texts. Two representatives of the National Association for the Advancement of Colored People attended one of the Hirshfield hearings in New York. William Pickens, an NAACP field secretary, told those assembled that histories used in city schools should note that Crispus Attucks, a man of mixed race, was the first to fall in the Boston Massacre of 1870; that five thousand Americans of African descent had fought under Washington; and that large numbers of Black soldiers had served in the War of 1812, the Civil War, and the World War. Julius Hyman, representing the Jewish Welfare Board, requested that schoolbooks mention the role of Haym Saloman in the Revolution. Saloman had lent four hundred thousand dollars to the patriot cause, going broke in the process.[71] Neither Pickens nor Hyman appeared much interested in the alleged British conspiracy, but the structure of the hearings allowed them a voice, anyway.

In Chicago members of the Steuben Society repeated their earlier demands for greater inclusion of Americans of German descent in the texts. Irish, Italian, and Polish groups in the city also backed Thompson's charges against the historians. An Italian organization, for instance, officially protested against teaching that "the spirit and institutions of the country are English." During the trial Thompson also met with a council of American Indians representing the Chippewa, Winnebago, Sioux, and other tribes. "You tell the white men 'America First.' We believe in that," council members declared solemnly to the mayor. Then, like Miller, they inverted popular rhetoric about Americanism and assimilation. "We are the ones, truly, that are 100 percent. We therefore ask you while you are teaching school children about America First, teach them the truth about the First Americans. . . . We do not know if school histories are pro-British, but we do know they are unjust to the life of our people—the American Indian."[72]

The well-publicized meeting with the council reflected Thompson's fondness for political showmanship more than his pedestrian hope for a payoff at the ballot box (after all, there were just not that many Chippewa votes in the Windy City). Perhaps the mayor might also have been genuinely concerned about, or at least interested in, portrayals of American Indians. Either way, his willingness to consider their views provided a welcome contrast to the attitude of McLaughlin and Van Tyne. A few years before the pro-British controversy enveloped them and their schoolbook, they refused their publisher's suggestion to "give a little more space" to Indians, who received a total of approximately 170 pages in the high school–level history. They had fully covered, said Van Tyne, the "effect of the Indians wherever their existence changes the forward movement of the white man." They would not use Indian stories "merely to amuse the boys."[73]

This exchange shows how the professional historians' understanding of institutional history marginalized or rendered irrelevant certain groups in American history. Indian tribal cultures had contributed virtually nothing to America's legal, political, and other institutions, said these scholars, and so they could be safely ignored except in recounting where their resistance had impeded White expansion. A similar principle applied to immigrants. They remained a historical subject or "problem" only until they had fully assimilated. After that they often disappeared into a narrative dominated by English "forces."

Embracing Diversity: The Irony of Reform

Historians generally missed the legitimate charge of ethnocentrism because, to them, the alleged British conspiracy looked mostly like a simple attack on their profession and the integrity of their ideals. Since the 1890s they had tried to play a decisive role in fashioning the curriculum at the precollegiate level. Individual scholars might have disagreed about certain issues, but they shared the conviction that historians trained to the rigors of objective scholarship had the right and responsibility to oversee history in the schools, a responsibility they shared with teachers.

Critics in the 1920s demanded specific changes in textbooks, as other groups, like conservative White Southerners, had done for decades. But they also fundamentally challenged professorial authority. Charles Grant Miller mocked the alleged precision of "higher historical scholarship" and the "self-assumed superiority" of the AHA and its members. David Hirshfield publicly spurned the academics. Asked if he would consult professional historians for advice during his investigation, he responded: "Let me say this about experts. I am not strong on

Anglo-Saxonism and the Revolt against Professors

experts. I would rather have the judgment of the average man with a fair education than the man who has developed himself into an expert." William Thompson cheerfully ridiculed the historians, particularly those at the University of Chicago. Even members of New York's relatively restrained Mandel Committee concluded that historical objectivity had little place in public schools. "The usefulness of some of the books examined is impaired because the authors have written from the point of view of a critical historian," they wrote, rather than a "teacher," who they assumed would not be guided by the same dubious ideal.[74]

Faced with that kind of criticism, historians circled their wagons and sometimes furthered the impression that they were arrogant and elitist. Claude Van Tyne labeled his antagonists "ignorant fault-seekers." James Truslow Adams said that historians generally write their work in laymen's language, without the difficult formulas of more abstract sciences. As a result, "the common man constitutes himself a judge of its truth, and we have the spectacle of a municipal commissioner of accounts [Hirshfield] attacking the validity of the scholar's work while a town chamber of commerce defends it." Questioning the principle of public oversight of the schools, an associate professor of history at Smith College wondered whether "the rule of the people inevitably means the rule of the ignorant." Harry Barnes, a historian more willing to challenge the profession's supposedly sacred truths after his own participation in propaganda work during World War I, still saw history as the prerogative of trained academics, not the "accountants, plumbers, druggists, blacksmiths and lawyers who constitute our school committees."[75]

In that spirit, the AHA resolved in 1924 that no "self-respecting scholars" would stoop to censoring or otherwise altering their textbooks just to placate critics and salvage sales.[76] But by then many had already begun to do just that. Writers had to bend to the critics' will, at least partially, because publishers refused to champion their cause. When the Mandel Committee released its report in 1922, a spokesperson for D. C. Heath said his firm and others would try to conform to its recommendations. At the Hirshfield hearings the following year, representatives of several publishers sat silently as witnesses assailed their authors and books for lack of patriotism. American Book Company publisher William Livengood sided privately with Charles H. McCarthy, who had endured heavy criticism. But a letter Livengood wrote in 1921 revealed the delicate position in which his firm's employees found themselves, buffeted by assaults from various critics and struggling to keep their books in line with the shifting political climate of the 1910s and 1920s:

> You understand we can go a good way with our authors but we cannot go to the extent of deliberately changing their material. In spite of the fact that McCarthy is a good Irishman he insists that he will not make historical blunders to meet the criticisms of a recognized group of propagandists. It is a serious question . . . how far we dare go. . . .
> Well, the trouble isn't a new one. We jump out of the German frying pan into the British fire.[77]

How far *would* ABC, D. C. Heath, Ginn, Allyn and Bacon, and other publishers go? It soon became clear that while they sympathized with historians' desires to maintain professional integrity, they would not risk sales by deliberately antagonizing groups with the power to shape adoption decisions. Textbook writers soon found themselves pruning more overt expressions of Anglophilia from new editions of their books while retouching accounts of the Revolution. David Muzzey eliminated a passage in *An American History* declaring that "there were two opinions as to colonial rights and British oppression" and partially absolving the British for wrongs leading to the Revolution. Willis Mason West dropped a paragraph from his history that linked American and British destinies and praised the "two great divisions of the English-speaking race." William Guitteau, one of the few writers who came under fire who was not a professional historian, no longer mentioned how the Americans' decision to burn Toronto in the War of 1812 inspired the British to set the torch to Washington, D.C. More importantly, writers also began to embrace more inclusive versions of the White melting pot that made Anglo-Saxons, at best, only the first among equals.[78]

The flexibility shown by writers and editors helped to avert one outcome to the 1920s controversies that both feared—the production of schoolbooks by text critics. Thompson's threat that Chicago would create its own histories turned out to be mostly bluster. In 1928 it resulted in a meager sixteen-page supplement containing brief biographies of Casimir Pulaski, Bon Von Steuben, Thaddeus Kosciuszko, and other Revolutionary heroes, along with two pages devoted to the words of "Yankee Doodle Dandy." The author, a political ally of the mayor, received thirty-five hundred dollars for his efforts. The Knights of Columbus were somewhat more successful. In 1921 they embarked

Anglo-Saxonism and the Revolt against Professors

on an ambitious program to publish a series of historical pamphlets drafted by writers of various racial and religious backgrounds. But the expected conclusion of the endeavor, a single school history synthesizing the material, never appeared.[79] The American Legion, however, did create the two-volume *Story of Our American People* in 1926. Legionnaires gathered the support and endorsement of over twenty patriotic groups and educational societies, from the Boy Scouts and the Benevolent Protective Order of Elks to the Veterans of Foreign Wars. However, with no reputable historian willing to break ranks, the Legion had to recruit Charles F. Horne, a professor of English at New York's City College, to write the text. Historians and educators lampooned Horne's sugary prose, edited to varying degrees by the project's sponsors. In *Harper's Monthly* one historian called the texts a "bombastic eulogy for all things American, a teleological interpretation of the development of God's chosen people." Van Tyne, savoring the chance to reverse roles with his attackers, called *The Story of Our American People* "maudlin and sentimental."[80]

Such attacks did little to help the books' dismal sales, but Legionnaires themselves probably consigned the venture to failure well before publication. They failed to recruit the Hibernians, Steuben Society, Knights of Columbus, and other race- and religious-based organizations—their erstwhile allies in attacks on the professional historians. While the books overflowed with the heroic stories the patriotic organizations demanded, they showed a remarkable insensitivity toward recent immigrants from southern and eastern Europe. Horne praised Europeans who had built America over several centuries but added that the flow of "high grade" immigrants had ended before the close of the nineteenth century. Without mentioning Italians, Russians, Poles, Hungarians, or Jews by name, Horne suggested that subsequent newcomers included a large number of "'undesirables,' that is, people of whom Europe wanted to be rid." Horne was even less charitable to the Chinese ("We could scarcely hope to turn these oriental peoples into 'Americans'") and African-Americans.[81] While prejudice toward the latter groups was still fairly common in texts in the 1920s, Horne's failure to embrace a pluralism that included all Europeans made his books unacceptable to large numbers of Thompson's supporters in Chicago and Hirshfield's in New York.

The assault on history teaching had been only partly about racism and ethnocentrism, of course. Slander against America's heroes had been an equally important charge against the historians. Hearst columnist Charles Grant Miller objected with particular vehemence to mention of the heated rivalry between Alexander Hamilton and Thomas Jefferson in books by Muzzey, McLaughlin, Van Tyne, and others. Most troublesome were discussions of partisan charges that Jefferson was an "atheist, liar, and a demagogue" and inclusion of Hamilton's infamous assessment of the American electorate: "Your people, sir, is a great beast."[82] Miller claimed that unflattering treatment of these figures arose from British efforts to undermine American patriotism. But authors had actually included this material to explain to readers how the Founders differed in their understanding of republican government, particularly as it related to social class. The aristocratic Hamilton equated democracy with mob rule. Jefferson, in contrast, appealed to masses of White, male voters and so became a demagogue in the eyes of his Federalist critics.

Miller's reproach of the authors on these points may have represented a tactical decision. Patriotic organizations that backed him tended to favor elimination of any explicit discussion of class tensions, which had begun to appear in school histories after the turn of the century. Muzzey, for instance, had come under heavy fire for encouraging "class hatred" with his straightforward discussion of labor strikes, trusts, populists, and the presidential election of 1896.[83] His critics preferred a more seamless American story of political consensus and economic progress. Miller, who had made attacking textbooks an almost full-time job for seven years, knew that he had to appeal to these patriotic organizations, along with race-based ones, to keep the controversy alive. But Miller's commitment to a version of history in which flawless leaders have no fundamental disagreements with one another seems to have run deeper. "The history that truthfully presents our nation's annals in such a sympathetic, virile, patriotic spirit as to inculcate in our children pride in the birth and development of our republic, honor to its heroes, devotion to principles and progress, and zest in its ideals and purposes," he wrote in *Treason to American Tradition,* "this is true history." Hero worship, according to Miller, was healthy. Far more than historical accuracy, it served the national interest. A passage in an essay by Mayor Thompson, but likely ghostwritten by Miller, developed this theme:

> The Christian church rests upon the divinity of Christ. To attack that is to assail the spiritual life of the Christian church. . . . The nobility of heroes, with belief in their causes and ideals, is to the nation, what divinity is to religion. . . . Nations have their shrines to patriotism, as churches have their altars of divinity.

Anglo-Saxonism and the Revolt against Professors

The patriot must guard the one, as the devout must protect the other.[84]

Miller (or Thompson) presented history as dogma and the revisionism by professional historians as heresy. Here his line of reasoning closely resembled that of the Tennessee legislators who banned the teaching of evolution and precipitated the Scopes trial. He even drew the parallel between protecting patriotism and safeguarding Christianity, suggesting that facts that challenged either belief system had to be suppressed.

Miller's stand presented a curious irony. At the turn of the century, the rise of Anglo-Saxonism had helped to reunite White Northerners and Southerners under the banner of White supremacy, easing Southerners' demand for their own histories. The work of David Muzzey, the most maligned historian during the 1920s, grew out of that tradition. Because Muzzey conceived of the nation as fundamentally united, racially by its Whiteness and culturally by its English heritage, he more readily explored its divisions along lines of class and politics. Miller, however, attacked race-based nationalism. He claimed that America found its true commonality in dedication to the Founder's ideals of "liberty" and "freedom." But these principles amounted to little more than glittering generalities for Miller and many of his followers. In practice, demands for intellectual and political orthodoxy accompanied their embrace of racial diversity. That was the spirit behind Thompson's ill-fated call for book burnings, the recommendations by New York's Mandel Commission for a history free of controversial topics, and Miller's endorsement of censorship in the passages cited earlier. Like the salutary calls for more representative texts, that spirit of censorship also determined how writers subsequently revised their texts.

Today, many educational critics on the right tend to lump together proponents of greater diversity in history teaching; left-leaning historians who came of age in the 1960s; and, more generally, those who approach the activities of Americans and their government with a critical eye. To someone like Rush Limbaugh, the multiculturalists and "Tenured Radicals" (the phrase comes from a best-selling book by Roger Kimball) are one and the same. The examples of Miller and Muzzey show that such an alignment is not inevitable and, in many contexts, not even likely.

The attack on pro-British books during the 1920s was thus a complex episode. It complicates our understanding of history wars today, and eighty years ago it defied the simple labels many historians and educators wished to apply to it. But the professors who thought of themselves as "seekers after truth" and "gentle purveyors of information" had a point, and they rightly feared its long-term consequences for textbook publishing and teaching in the schools. More than any other episode of the twentieth century, the alleged British conspiracy and the Scopes case determined how modern textbooks would be planned, written, edited, and marketed to schools. The 1920s accelerated the development of "managed texts" in history, biology, and other subjects. Political calculation by publishers, as much as the expertise of scholars and scientists, began to exert ever greater control over the presentation of potentially contentious issues, from primate evolution to the nature of America's revolt against Great Britain.

The 1920s left a bitter taste in the mouths of many historians. The writer of one popular American history told a researcher that resisting the "sins of omission and commission" was now impossible: "And, if any author tells you he is not influenced by such pressure, that he tells 'the truth, the whole truth, and nothing but the truth' as far as he knows it, don't you believe him. He is a conscious or unconscious liar." James Harvey Robinson, a prominent scholar and for many years history advisor for Ginn and Company's textbook department, understood the dilemma well. In the 1920s Robinson remarked, "No publishers of text-books for the schools would venture to permit a writer to give children the best and most authoritative knowledge that we have today."[85]

Yet soon after he uttered these words, one publisher was allowing a writer to try to do just that. And the publisher was Ginn.

6. Harold Rugg vs. Horatio Alger
Social Class and Economic Opportunity,
1930–1960

At the start of 1939, Harold Rugg was the most widely read author of social science textbooks in the United States. In the decade since he finished the first full-length volume in the Man and His Changing Society series, his publisher, Ginn and Company, had shipped more than five million of his texts and workbooks, reaching students in approximately five thousand school systems.[1] Rugg's frankness, left-of-center politics, and underlying optimism about America's destiny struck a chord with a country devastated by the Depression. As a delighted Midwestern sales agent for Ginn put it, "Everybody wanted the Rugg books."[2]

But within months, Rugg became the subject of the most celebrated case of censorship in the nation's history. After critics accused him of corrupting youth with subversive, even communist, propaganda, this education professor at Columbia University's Teachers College watched his reputation and the sales of his books plummet. By 1951 Rugg's fortunes had changed irrevocably. His texts, long since removed from the classrooms of public schools, gathered dust in storage basements and library shelves. Nearing retirement, he prepared to give an address at Ohio State University, only to have the American Legion mount a vigorous protest and successfully pressure school authorities to impose a gag rule to block appearances by "disloyal" speakers. Hundreds, perhaps thousands of the university's students had once cradled Rugg's books in their arms. Now, it seemed, his ideas were simply too radical for them to consider as adults.[3]

What led to Rugg's undoing? Was he a would-be revolutionary foiled by the Legion and a host of other critics or, as many of his supporters continue to claim, the hapless victim of a right-wing conspiracy? Neither depiction captures the real spirit of this progressive educator, though there are elements of truth in both. Rugg is best understood as a dedicated social critic and teacher who, with like-minded educators, dreamed of using schools to reform American society. His particular interest was the social studies curriculum, and his tools for civic betterment included a series of texts for elementary and junior high school students. What brought these books acclaim in educational circles for most of the 1930s, and infamy among conservatives soon afterward, was their author's willingness to touch on a usually taboo topic.

Until the 1930s, social class had been one of the most sensitive issues in textbooks on U.S. history. Acknowledging that there had long been stark disparities of income and wealth among Americans was awkward enough for writers. Explaining how those differences had inspired competing economic philosophies and political programs was even more treacherous. Throughout much of the nineteenth century, and into the first decades of the twentieth, civic groups and politicians demanded that textbook authors promote national unity and encourage patriotism among young readers. But nationalism, as one scholar has put it, is animated by the conviction that all citizens share a "deep, horizontal comradeship."[4] Social inequality and economic exploitation ran counter to that national myth, and so, not surprisingly, many of the men and women who drafted books destined for the nation's classrooms tried to avoid these subjects. Once professional historians began to replace amateurs in the textbook-writing trade, however, they found that such self-censorship clashed with their own dedication to objectivity. Led by David Saville Muzzey in the 1910s and 1920s, they slowly and cautiously began to address the role of class in the country's past.

Rugg chose to explore class even more assiduously. Personal temperament guided that decision, but so did academic training. Rugg was not a professional historian, and he was not guided by the disciplinary ideal of objectivity—of rendering the past dispassionately, just as it had happened. He was a scholar of education committed to progressive ideas and methods. While some of his fellow textbook authors were willing to discuss contentious issues as they arose naturally in their narratives, Rugg actually built his books around them. As a progressive educator, he hoped that a focus on unresolved social issues would make schoolwork individually and socially relevant for students and thereby more compelling. He began the writing process for Man and His Changing Society by identifying the most important problems he believed young Americans would face as adults and then tried to explain how these problems had arisen and how they might be solved in the future. The persistence of material inequality in America especially interested Rugg. Like his fellow writers, he praised the nation's record of economic accomplishment. But unlike many of his predecessors, he delved into murkier topics—the pernicious influence of money in politics; the class bias of revered statesmen; and, most noticeably, the apparent failure of laissez-faire economics, which had, at the time his books rolled off the presses during the Depression's worst years, produced millions of destitute farmers and industrial laborers along with a handful of those he termed the "idle rich." Rugg's heroes were middle- and working-class Americans who endured hardship as they struggled to reform and perfect their society, a theme suggested by the title of one of his books, *America's March toward Democracy*. Rugg's focus on everyday people made the texts especially readable. They had an appeal akin to John Steinbeck's *Grapes of Wrath* and photographer Dorothea Lange's sympathetic portraits of migrant laborers.

The texts were so popular that Rugg became a convenient target as political winds began to shift at the end of the 1930s. For his discussion of poverty and claims that some sort of national economic planning would be needed to prevent another collapse, critics branded him un-American. A few suggested that he and other progressive "REDucators" were doing Moscow's bidding. The critics included familiar faces from the 1920s battles, including the American Legion and the Daughters of the American Revolution. But powerful corporate interests also joined these groups, arguing that Rugg's emphasis on the defects of industrial capitalism would sow disorder and weaken children's commitment to free enterprise. Well funded and guided by fervent leaders, the campaign routed Rugg from the schools. By 1944, sales of his books had dropped 90 percent from their peak in the late 1930s.[5]

The story did not end there, however. Like earlier textbook battles, Rugg's ordeal helped to define the acceptable limits of discourse in America's public schools. The successful attacks on Man and His Changing Society spurred publishers to release books in the 1940s and 1950s with far more glowing images of the United States and its pageant of economic progress. Class conflict as a factor in American history grew more muted in postwar texts, and poverty—what was shown of it—was safely relegated to the past. Students saw a present-day America united across class lines, and sometimes one that appeared entirely middle-class in make-up.

221

When he began writing for schools, Rugg very intentionally inserted himself into a long-standing, often bitter feud about how Americans should conceive of themselves as a national community. In one camp were liberal nationalists, "liberal" being used here in its nineteenth-century, European sense, not in its modern American one. As liberals, they championed political freedom, property rights, and free markets. As nationalists, they saw Americans united by a devotion to liberal philosophy, particularly individualism and the conviction that all citizens had essentially equal opportunity to exploit their liberties for economic gain. American liberals were the heirs of Abraham Lincoln, their most eloquent advocate.

Aspiring to national office in the 1850s, Lincoln had confronted slaveholders who argued that the peculiar institution was relatively benign. It was far better for the slaves, they claimed, than the industrializing economy of the North was for White workers, who were forced into dead-end poverty with none of the security for old age or sickness that slavery provided. Rebuking the slaveholders, Lincoln sketched out a hopeful, and very liberal, picture of national progress, one illustrated by his own rise from poor backwoods farmer to congressman. Relations between capital and labor were fluid in the North, he argued, and workers were not fixed into any position for life. "Many independent men . . . a few years ago were hired laborers," he told a Wisconsin audience in 1859. Their cases supported the general rule:

> The prudent, penniless beginner in the world labors for wages a while, saves a surplus with which to buy tools or land, for himself; then labors on his own account another while, and at length hires another new beginner to help him. This . . . is free labor— the just and generous, and prosperous system, which opens the way for all—gives hope to all, and energy, and progress, and improvement of condition to all. If any continue through life in the condition of the hired laborer, it is not the fault of the system, but because of either a dependent nature which prefers it, or improvidence, folly, or singular misfortune.[6]

In a flexible economy anchored by both farming and industry, an enterprising laborer could always go into business for himself or purchase good soil out West, declared Lincoln. No "fault of the system" condemned one man to groveling subservience under another, only poor planning, foolishness, or extraordinarily bad luck. Steering clear of those, the hard-working individual could not only substantially better himself but, in so doing, improve "the condition of all" in the nation. Because liberals believed unfettered capitalism was fundamentally sound, they saw a very limited role for the state in the economy, at least in principle. Beyond securing the rights of property, one of its few duties was to provide public education, which would prepare citizens for productive work and propel the wheel of social mobility. Additional state intervention in the economy could be justified only when it served a higher, *national* purpose. Liberals could therefore support tariffs because, they reasoned, protection of industry benefited the growth of the American economy and thus the country at large. They opposed legislation recognizing the right of workers to organize, mandating an eight-hour workday, or supporting an inflationary monetary policy because these measures, from the liberals' perspective, benefited some groups (laborers and debt-ridden farmers) at the expense of others (industry owners and creditors).[7]

Simplify the philosophy sufficiently, and turn from the economy as a whole back to the individual in Lincoln's address, and you end up in the company of Horatio Alger Jr. That Massachusetts-born writer charmed young readers with stories of Ragged Dick, the penniless shoeshine boy who struggles to make his way in New York City. After many colorful adventures, Dick transforms himself into Richard Hunter, Esquire, through a combination of honesty, thrift, self-denial, and the kindly attention of an older man who sees his promise. Alger had not originally intended his work to become an emblem of laissez-faire economics. He had exploited the rags-to-riches theme, in part, to lure readers to what might otherwise have been too grim a subject for juvenile fiction—orphaned boys living in the streets of the country's largest city. The stories might then, he wrote, "have the effect of enlisting the sympathies of his readers in behalf of the unfortunate children."[8] As the myth that has grown around Alger's name shows, however, the effect was just the opposite. The ability of Dick and his fellow shoeshine boys to climb to bourgeois respectability suggested that while wide gulfs might seem to separate the street urchin from John Jacob Astor, upward mobility was always possible in America. In short, the system worked.

Ragged Dick found his literary and philosophical counterpart in Julian West, the hero of Edward Bellamy's 1888 novel *Looking Backward*. West is a wealthy, somewhat neurotic Boston bachelor transported over one hundred years into the future. Convinced that the poverty, economic inequality, and labor unrest of his day would haunt the country indefinitely, West is startled when he awakens in an industrial utopia overseen by an all-powerful but benevolent state.

The driving force behind his country's transformation, West discovers, is the same concentration of capital that had ignited and then sustained industrial growth during the nineteenth century. Small firms grew into larger ones, evolved into corporations, and then colluded with other corporations to form trusts, which then spread to other industries, and so forth. Eventually, a single national monopoly, the Great Trust, grew to encompass the whole economy and operate for the benefit of all citizens. There is no room for individual enterprise in this utopia, in the sense of investment outside the state, because the Trust operates with an economy of scale that shuts out any competitor. But, West learns from his guide in 2000, the spiraling consolidation of capital had already limited individual opportunity more than one hundred years before, especially for the working classes.

"Before this concentration began," says West's host, "the individual workman was relatively important and independent in his relations to his employer." With a new idea and a little money, a laborer could start a successful business, and thus there were no rigid barriers between social classes. "But when the era of small concerns with small capital was succeeded by that of great aggregations of capital, all this changed," he continues. "The individual laborer, who had been relatively important to the small employer, was reduced to insignificance and powerlessness over against the great corporation, while at the same time the way upward to the grade of employer was closed to him."9

The liberal hope of social mobility outlined by Lincoln and dramatized by Alger had become a tragic anachronism by the 1880s, according to Bellamy. The author of *Looking Backward* did not see smashing the monopolies as a solution. As the success of his utopia showed, they should be encouraged to grow until they evolved into instruments of a nationally planned economy. Unlike some of his Marxist contemporaries, Bellamy did not call for violent revolution—the utopia of the novel arose peacefully—or link the country's hopes for a better future with the worldwide movement of the working classes. Bellamy's ideas were socialist, but he expressed them in the familiar, soothing language of nationalism. His economy was national in scope, not global, and his citizens were intensely patriotic. Tormented by the social inequalities of his day, Bellamy wanted to harness the vast emotional and political power of nationalism and direct it to humanitarian ends. But his economic philosophy made his nationalism look much different than that advanced by the liberals; it was economically collectivist, not individualist, and it relied on state regulation and planning of industry, not lais-sez-faire.

Looking Backward became a wildly successful novel, surpassed in popularity at the turn of the century only by *Ben-Hur* and *Uncle Tom's Cabin*. Devotees of the book and its classless society formed over 150 "Bellamy Clubs" across the country, started a magazine, and formed an important wing of the Populist Party. The book also inspired other utopian fiction, along with more practically oriented magazine articles that introduced middle-class readers to socialist-oriented nationalism.[10]

By the 1890s these competing strains of nationalist thought—liberal and humanitarian—provided a set of poles between which American politics would pivot for decades. Business leaders and social conserva-tives appealed to national loyalty when they opposed labor unions and welfare legislation as expressions of a divisive, class-based philosophy that threatened the economic liberty of capital. A Brooklyn minister, for instance, suggested in 1885 that the National Guard be put to patri-otic use crushing strikes. Politicians heeded such calls. In 1892 federal troops stopped a walkout by silver miners in Idaho, and two years later President Grover Cleveland sent several thousand deputies to end a strike of Pullman railroad workers in Illinois. Cleveland championed a society held together, ironically, by its self-reliant and often atomistic nature. Despite his willingness to use federal power to resolve labor disputes, he claimed to be committed to limited government. He once rejected a call for federal aid to victims of a Texas drought because such help would weaken "the sturdiness of our national character" and discourage the private charity that "strengthens the bond of a common brotherhood."[11]

To the left of liberals were Americans who argued that the rise of monopoly capitalism demanded more activist governments. Accord-ing to these critics, if the state were given sufficient powers, it could protect farmers and workers from exploitation while safeguarding con-sumers from monopolists' high prices and frequently unsafe products. The Populists came closest to building a political platform around humanitarian nationalism, but the same ideas also influenced more moderate Progressives and inspired politicians like Woodrow Wilson. Nevertheless, liberal thinking tended to dominate federal policy until the start of the 1930s.

In the half-century before Rugg burst upon the publishing market, textbooks in American history also aligned firmly with the liberals. Back in the 1830s, Emma Willard had warned her young readers that the selfish pursuit of wealth would weaken the social bonds that made a republic possible. But as industrial growth seemed to confirm some of her fears, Willard's sense of foreboding slowly faded from later histories. Wary of entangling themselves in controversy, writers sketched a peaceful America in harmony with Horatio Alger, only without the vivid depictions of poverty that gave his books a slightly subversive edge. In one text, for instance, there is only a "supposed conflict between capital and labor."[12] Schoolbooks praised Cyrus McCormick, Andrew Carnegie, Thomas Edison, and other self-made entrepreneurs, holding them up as models for students. Rather than dwelling on economic inequities, they extolled the virtues of unrestrained industrial growth—marveling at inventions like the telephone and skyscraper, ticking off national progress through gains in the gross national product or miles of railroad track laid—in page after page of text and illustrations.

The 1897 edition of John Bach McMaster's *School History of the United State*s epitomized the buoyant spirit of many texts. "Every class of society was benefited by these improvements," McMaster noted, "but no men more so than those who depended on their daily wages for their daily bread." The author even brought readers on an imaginary ride in a modern locomotive, a welcome change, he reminded his audience, from primitive means of travel early in the nineteenth century: "Now we step into a beautifully fitted car, heated by steam, lighted by electricity, richly carpeted, and provided with most comfortable seats and beds, and are whirled across the continent from Philadelphia to San Francisco in less time than it took Washington to go from New York to Boston." McMaster carefully avoided mentioning that large numbers of Americans could not have afforded such luxurious travel. He also failed to discuss the bitter and violent strike by Pullman workers who manufactured the kind of plush cars he discussed. Though McMaster and other text writers offered an aside or two on the plight of less fortunate Americans, real poverty rarely crept into their halcyon depictions of the country in their own day. All Americans were metaphorically and literally free to ride his train of progress.[13]

That tidy depiction of laissez-fair capitalism grew a bit tarnished in the first two decades of the twentieth century. David Muzzey was the most daring revisionist among textbook authors, but his *American History* was more nostalgic than radical. He saw both labor unions and great corporations, each products of the industrial revolution, as somehow inimical to national interests. Muzzey's philosophy often seemed Jeffersonian, full of longing for an individualist past of yeoman farmers and craftsmen who either worked alone or bargained as equals with their employers.[14] He never fully wrestled with how industrial growth had fundamentally changed the country or explored alternatives to prevailing social and economic norms. What changed the politics of both the nation at large and schoolbooks in particular was, of course, the Depression. The economic reversal that began in 1929 revived interest in Edward Bellamy and his ideas. When the historian Charles Beard and the educational philosopher John Dewey independently composed a list of the most influential works published since 1885, both put *Looking Backward* in second place, after Karl Marx's *Das Kapital.* After Franklin Roosevelt's election, newspapers began to draw parallels between *Looking Backward* and the new president's economic plans. A 1934 headline in the *Christian Science Monitor* proclaimed, "Bellamy Went to 2000 for New Deal, Part of Which Is Being Put into Use Today."[15] Such stories tended to exaggerate the radicalism of the New Deal, but it was clear that FDR's brand of nationalism found a distant cousin in Bellamy's novel, a kinship perhaps unintentionally encouraged by the title of Roosevelt's 1933 book, *Looking Forward.*

Operating in an atmosphere of perpetual crisis during his first years in office, Roosevelt repeatedly invoked the sanctity of the nation to justify the expansion of federal control over the economy and the creation of a vast, overlapping network of short- and long-term social programs. He sometimes even capitalized the "N" in "nation" for printed copies of his speeches, including the one he delivered at his second inaugural. In that well-known speech, Roosevelt claimed he saw one-third of a nation ill housed, ill clad, and ill nourished. "It is not in despair that I paint you that picture," he told listeners:

I paint it for you in hope—because the Nation, seeing and understanding the injustice in it, proposes to paint it out. We are determined to make every American citizen the subject of his country's interest and concern. . . . The test of our progress is not whether we add more to the abundance of those who have much; it is whether we provide enough for those who have too little.[16]

More than any president before him, Roosevelt acknowledged how capitalism generated systemic poverty. Through his New Deal programs, both those focused on simple recovery and those devoted to broader economic reform, he argued that minimal standards of living and true equality of opportunity could be assured only through a far more significant government role in the economy. Eager to present his ideas as both modern and rooted in traditional American ideas, Roosevelt and his associates appropriated the word "liberal" to describe them, thereby edging the word toward its modern social and political definition. In a confusing bit of semantic evolution, the old-style "liberals"—champions of free market and limited government—were now usually thought of as "conservatives."

Business leaders, alarmed by Roosevelt's embrace of some aspects of humanitarian nationalism in legislation such as the Social Security Act of 1935, led a backlash against the New Deal in the 1936 election. As Roosevelt's vision of a limited welfare state and partial retreat from laissez-faire capitalism gained coherence over the next two years, his opposition grew stronger. That bitter partisan debate set the stage for the attacks on Rugg's Man and His Changing Society, and they cannot be fully understood apart from it.

Roosevelt, the product of an elite New York family with a tradition of public service, was carefully groomed for the crucial role he would play in national politics. Rugg, in contrast, followed a less predictable path toward his own destiny as one of the great innovators in the social science curriculum. He was born in Fitchburg, Massachusetts, into a relatively prosperous working-class family descended from settlers who had arrived in America in the seventeenth century. He attended public schools that reflected what he later described as the narrow, nervous conformity of his hometown. Out of frustration, curiosity, and perhaps a bit of boredom, Rugg postponed college to take a job as a weaver in a textile mill. Firsthand experience taught him sympathy for industrial workers and skepticism about the virtues of unregulated capitalism. After his stint at the factory, Rugg attended Dartmouth College and earned a degree in civil engineering. He worked as a railroad surveyor and taught engineering for a few years but decided that precollegiate education was his calling. He finished his Ph.D. in 1915 and had something of an intellectual awakening as he devoured the works of contemporary social critics and intellectuals, including Van Wyck Brooks, Waldo Frank, James Harvey Robinson, and John Maynard Keynes, the economist whose work on fiscal policy would help to guide the New Deal. To Rugg they were "specialists on the frontier of thought," and he soon began to believe that the contemporary social issues and problems they explored could be introduced to students in the public schools, even at the elementary and junior high levels.[17]

Two historians in particular, Frederick Jackson Turner and Charles Beard, deeply influenced Rugg's understanding of America's past and present.[18] From Turner, Rugg borrowed an emphasis on the West as a key determinant of the American character, which he saw as democratic, individualist, and self-reliant. Such sentiments had appeared in dozens of popular histories in the early twentieth century. But Rugg also wanted to explore the question left open at the end of Turner's 1893 essay "The Significance of the Frontier in American History." How would Americans safeguard their democratic values in an increasingly complex, interdependent, industrial society that no longer had an expanse of open land that continually renewed the American spirit?

While Turner provided Rugg with a reverence for the West, Beard offered a model of how class-based interests, and often class conflict, shaped historical change. That model, in turn, partly determined how Rugg answered Turner's question about how democracy would meet the challenge of the new era. When Rugg was finishing his doctoral work, Beard was already gaining fame, and in some circles infamy, for *An Economic Interpretation of the Constitution.* In it Beard claimed that the framers of the federal government represented the wealthy, propertied citizens of the infant republic, not the masses of people who had supported and died for the Revolutionary cause. Predictably, he argued, statesmen like Alexander Hamilton and James Madison organized the new national government to protect their own interests and those of others in their social class. To critics of Beard, however, *Economic Interpretation* slandered the Founding Fathers and suggested they had snatched away an early chance for Americans to develop a true, popular democracy.

Accepting much of Beard's thesis, Rugg wanted to show young people how democracy had actually expanded on the foundation laid in 1787 and how it might continue to do so now that the United States had completed the transformation from an agrarian to an industrial economy. Rugg's approach to social studies was thus grounded in his belief in ongoing social change, and in the responsibility of schools to prepare children for it instead of forcing them to imbibe the sort of outdated knowledge and truisms he remembered from his own school days in Fitchburg.[19]

An experimental school at Columbia's Teachers College proved to be the ideal setting for Rugg to begin his work in curricular reform. Opened in September 1917, the Lincoln School was to be, according to a founding document, a "laboratory for the working out of an elementary and a secondary school curriculum, which shall eliminate obsolete material and endeavor to work up in usable form, materials adapted to the needs of modern living." Rugg hoped to craft learning aids that would both build on knowledge Lincoln's students already possessed and have them "learn by doing." True to progressive principles, Rugg expected young people to debate ideas he adapted from "frontier thinkers," not memorize a textbook. With a touch of the arrogance that sometimes slipped into his work, he dismissed social science texts then on the market as "veritable encyclopedias." The claim had some justification. In 1920 schools were still using tomes like David Montgomery's *Leading Facts of American History,* whose title neatly captured its organizing principle. But many good narrative histories had already appeared, particularly for high school students. Rugg did not aspire just to write history, however, but to fuse history with civics, geography, and other disciplines to create a more complete picture of the origins of present-day society. More than any other single educator, he would end up creating the modern academic subject of "social studies."[20]

Rugg began designing materials on mimeographed sheets. They quickly proved cumbersome, so he hit on the idea of printing a series of pamphlets. Using connections with colleagues and former students, he raised funds for the project from a network of schools across the country. They underwrote production costs and, in turn, received the pamphlets as soon as Lincoln's students did. By the summer of 1922 Rugg had four thousand orders from participating schools, and demand increased steadily as he revised existing pamphlets and created new ones. Over three hundred schools were using them by 1926, prompting several publishers to express interest in turning the pamphlets into books. Rugg chose to work with Ginn and Company, and in 1929 his first book's initial print run of twenty thousand copies sold out in four months.[21] It was a harbinger of brisk sales that would continue even as the Depression squeezed school budgets.

Man and His Changing Society explored world history and culture, but Rugg devoted much of his energy to examining the United States, particularly in two volumes for junior high students: *America's March toward Democracy: A History of American Life, Political and Social* and *The Conquest of America: A History of American Civilization, Economic and Social.* As his subtitles suggest, Rugg reached well beyond narrow political history. But what really set his books apart from others on the market was their emphasis on conflict—between individuals, between governments and governed, and especially between social classes. Conflict gave these books for elementary and junior high students a clear narrative trajectory and made them far more compelling and readable than nominally more "advanced" books for high school students. Rugg's style was unmistakable almost from the first page. In the introduction to *America's March toward Democracy,* he asked readers to analyze the story of a fictional town called Franklin, where a governor calls out troops to "maintain order" during a labor strike. He then pointedly defined political history as the "continual struggle between groups of people, each of whom desired to control government." Disparities in wealth and income often propelled this struggle in his books, either implicitly or explicitly. The guided airplane tour that opened *The Conquest of America* began in the South, where readers flew "over poor hill farms where the farmers can hardly get a living." Further on they viewed a shantytown for textile workers, whose lot Rugg understood from personal experience: "'Can people live in such houses?' we ask. 'They can't afford anything better on eight or ten dollars a week,' our guide answers."22

As readers continued, traveling backward from the 1930s to the late eighteenth century, they found a history that differed much from what their parents or older siblings had read in school. Borrowing from progressive historians like Carl Becker, Rugg asked students to think of the Revolution not merely as a contest between the British and Americans but as a struggle among social classes on both sides of the Atlantic. Acknowledging that social divisions were less rigid in America than in England or the rest of Europe, Rugg nevertheless stressed that the colonies were far from the unstratified society that most earlier writers had depicted. *Conquest* explained that "the division of America into classes was largely on the basis of money, possessions, and family position. The few members of the wealthy class insisted on their right to govern the more numerous 'lower' class." Later Rugg noted that "from the very first years in America the mass of people struggled against the control of the wealthy property owners." When the British imposed the Stamp Tax and other measures, it was the "laboring classes" who protested by boycotting goods, tarring and feathering tax collectors, and dumping tea into Boston Harbor.23

In Rugg's books, the colonial elites were nearly as distressed by the patriot uprising as the British themselves:

But a movement had started which they [the wealthy] could not stop. The skilled workers and laborers of the cities, the frontiersman and the small farmers, and a few intelligent leaders were actively bringing about a revolution. They frequently forced hes-

itating merchants to act. From that time on, the rebellion proceeded largely against the wishes of the upper classes. There was
more and more opposition from many well-to-do people who
sympathized with England.

Rugg did qualify such sweeping statements. For instance, he noted
that some of the Tories came from the ranks of the "common people"
and that some of the Revolution's most able leaders, including Jefferson and Washington, were wealthy landowners. On "the whole, however, the aristocrats were more anxious for peace with England than
were the common people."[24]

Like writers who had come under fire in the 1920s, Rugg reinter-
preted the Revolution, the story of national creation, to support his
own vision of the American community. Authors like David Muzzey
and Willis Mason West had stressed the links between the two
branches of the "English-speaking race" in Europe and North America.[25] For some writers, that stance reflected a desire for cultural rapprochement with Britain and suspicions that recent immigrants did not
measure up to their Anglo-Saxon predecessors. Rugg was neither an
Anglophile nor a nativist, however. He never equivocated on the question of whether the split with Britain was justified. What distinguished
his account of the Revolution was a foregrounding of class issues in the
colonies' dispute with the mother country and the claim that disparities
in wealth had divided the nation from its beginning. For Rugg, the
world of the 1770s was not *that* much different from the present, in
which the families of textile workers huddled in shacks.

Rugg continued to use class as a historical lens when he turned to
the years after the war. In other books, the story of the United States
under the Articles of Confederation amounted to a brief lesson in the
perils of political disorder: the love of liberty, which had defeated
British tyranny, sowed economic and social chaos when it proceeded
unchecked. Rugg complicated and enriched that story, delving into
monetary policy in language an eighth-grader could understand.
Debtors wanted the states to print more money so that they could
more easily pay off loans, claimed Rugg, but the rich opposed currency
inflation because they were not eager to be paid back in depreciated
dollars. The impasse paralyzed the economy. The poor struggled to
survive through the crisis, but what, he asked pointedly, "was the condition of the well-to-do? Some of the people seem to have been doing
quite well. A Boston merchant speaks of the demand for such luxuries

as French silks and cambrics. He says in one letter: 'I would observe that people dress as much and as extravagantly as ever.'"

The solution to the disorder, in all histories, including Rugg's, was a more powerful national government. But Rugg questioned whether the creation of this government represented only good sense and civic virtue. Again, he looked to social class, now drawing on Beard and his *Economic Interpretation*. While poor and middle-income Americans favored a stronger central state to create a national currency and stabilize commerce, Rugg argued, wealthy speculators in western lands had a more selfish reason for favoring the Constitution. When the newly invigorated federal government surveyed the land and established army posts, the value of the speculators' investments soared.

A group of even less reputable investors also proved eager to cash in on the new order, according to Rugg. In 1790 Treasury Secretary Hamilton drew up a plan to redeem old Continental bonds and paper money at full value. Patriotic citizens had originally purchased and used these notes during the war, but in the slump that followed they had been trading at a few cents on the dollar. "Congress had no sooner heard of Hamilton's plan than some of the members of the Senate and the House of Representatives and well-to-do friends who were in on the secret began their dishonest work," Rugg noted in a conspiratorial tone in *America's March toward Democracy*. The speculators hurried to backwoods communities and purchased the bills from unsuspecting farmers who still believed them to be nearly worthless. To dramatize the swindle, Rugg provided a half-page illustration of one such scene: A stylishly dressed man in a top hat sits outside a log cabin tallying up his purchase as a buckskin-clad settler looks on. The frontiersman's curious wife peeks out from an open doorway.

Rugg chastised such "clever people" who would manipulate politics for personal gain:

These two classes of speculators were gambling in public lands and public money. They added in no way to the country's wealth. They produced nothing from the earth, manufactured no new goods, suggested no new ideas to benefit the people. They were simply making money by gambling. But to make their speculations profitable a strong central government was necessary. It is easy to understand, therefore, that they would be among those who worked hardest to establish such a government.

Readers went away from Rugg's books with the message that the Constitution and the political system it created were mixed triumphs. Most Americans enjoyed the advantages of greater political and military stability. But a wealthy minority benefited more than others. And that was precisely the aim of the "prosperous, intelligent, even brilliant Americans" who drafted the Constitution. That class of people advanced their own interests and provided checks and balances, such as the Electoral College, that partially insulated federal power from the direct will of the people. The "merchants, the landowners, the manufacturers, the shippers, and the bankers were given what they wanted," concluded Rugg. "They obtained a government which would keep money and trade in sound condition, preserve order within the country, and defend the nation against foreign enemies."[26]

Like the drafting and adoption of the Constitution, the rise of industry provided Rugg an opportunity to weigh social gains against losses. The half-century from 1850 to 1900, the era of the country's great industrial expansion, "was indeed the most important single period in the raising of the common man's standard of life," Rugg wrote. His readers learned that Americans of their own time were "living far more comfortable lives than their forefathers of even two generations ago." Yet he clearly sympathized with the working classes, noting that a majority of nineteenth-century factory laborers were "condemned to a life of poverty and long hours of hard toil." Almost always, he asserted, "the wages of the worker were too small to meet the increasing costs of living. Almost always slight improvements were won only by fighting and suffering. Almost always the conditions of many workers remained bad, even though improvements were made." Rugg occasionally discussed economic exploitation as a moral and personal issue. At one point, for instance, he condemned some "miserly, wealthy landlords" who managed urban tenements. More often, however, Rugg suggested that the problems of poverty were systemic. Addressing the conflict between capital and labor, he characterized the "evils of the factory system" as unexpected and largely unavoidable by-products of a new economic system. Rugg also sometimes praised industrial pioneers for their temerity and genius. Railroad baron Cornelius Vanderbilt was not a villain, for instance, but a "far-seeing businessmen."[27]

The American histories in Man and His Changing Society were complex works that defied simple characterization, and a few carefully chosen quotations can distort them. Rugg did see America divided into four groups—farmers, often poor; the "great American middle class"

Harold Rugg vs. Horatio Alger

of towns and cities; destitute tenement dwellers; and men and women of leisure. And by stressing how "utterly differently the four classes" lived, he raised questions about national unity and deliberately subverted myths about equality of opportunity. He asked readers of his books to let the problem of material inequality "be constantly" in their thoughts as they studied America's history and contemporary life.[28] While class conflict enlivened his narrative, it did not overwhelm it. Glancing quickly through the books, one might have seen little to distinguish them from others on the market. Rugg painted a romantic picture of the West; praised the melting pot; and showed delight in cataloging recent advances in transportation, communication, architecture, and other fields. He also strove for a sort of "balance" by examining controversial issues from multiple perspectives. But he did not struggle to avoid all appearance of bias. He was far more interested in engaging students, getting them to grapple with ideas, and sometimes leading them toward his own views, than in letting the facts of history somehow "speak for themselves." His politics and social philosophy deeply influenced his textbooks, a fact he never denied.

Rugg belonged to a school of left-leaning progressive educators called social reconstructionists who believed that laissez-faire economics had failed America and had to be abandoned. The problem for reconstructionists was not merely that mostly unregulated capitalism had led to huge gaps in wealth between the rich and poor. They argued that the materialist and individualist ethos that underlay the system had also poisoned political, cultural, and intellectual life in the United States. The reconstructionists hoped to reform that system and undo the damage, humanizing industrial civilization through some combination of central planning and government regulation of the economy. Further, they believed that progressive educators should employ schools to change popular attitudes and misconceptions that supported the status quo, thereby accelerating the expected economic and social transformation. Rugg, in particular, believed that American schools suffered from a "cultural lag." Remembering his childhood in Fitchburg, he concluded that most schools were conservative institutions where teachers trundled out a shopworn curriculum that did little to prepare students for a changing world. He wanted his textbooks to help close the gap between school and society.[29]

In the hands of its more enthusiastic supporters, reconstructionism veered toward indoctrination. George Counts, whose research in the 1920s examined how schools perpetuated inequalities along class, race, and ethnic lines, took a fact-finding tour of the Soviet Union in 1927.

He came back impressed. Counts did not endorse all of the Communist Party's goals, but he did admire how the party used the schools to achieve them. The subtlety of that distinction did not entirely allay anxieties of moderates in the movement, nor did Counts's provocatively titled 1933 manifesto, *Dare the Schools Build a New Social Order?* Particularly during the early 1930s, the more militant reconstructionists flirted with revolutionary rhetoric and displayed an often uncritical enthusiasm for Soviet models. Editors of the movement's semi-official journal, *Social Frontier,* also printed the work of genuine radicals, including Earl Browder, the general secretary of the Communist Party in the United States.[30]

Reconstructionist ideas occasionally crept into *Man and His Changing Society.* Rugg praised the "wise educational philosophers" then reforming the country's schools, for instance, and showed a distinct fondness for the "scientific planning" of society and for the sophisticated people he thought could best undertake it. In one book, he introduced readers to five typical Americans: Mr. Very Poor Man, Mr. Average Worker, Mr. Average White Collar Man, Mr. Prosperous Business Man, and Mr. Cultured Man. Though his income was modest, Mr. Cultured Man was happy and content. He, his wife, and his children watched avant-garde films, visited art galleries, and read challenging literature (unlike the "standard" or middlebrow fare perused by Mr. Average White Collar Man). "How much courage could the people of America take if they could see this house and realize what could be done with education and careful thought!" concluded Rugg in a passage about Mr. Cultured Man, who seemed like a stand-in for the author himself.[31]

Did Rugg's books cross the line between merely discussing and openly promoting the sort of social reform needed for the "Great Society" he advocated in his professional writing? At times, yes. In his scholarly book *The Great Technology,* Rugg called for replacing what he saw as the pell-mell of laissez-faire economics with careful planning by the state. In the 1931 edition of the textbook *An Introduction to the Problems of American Culture,* in turn, Rugg informed students that after implementing programs for social security, unemployment relief, and other immediate needs, the United States should undertake "nation-wide plans for co-operative control" of transportation and communication and for the production of basic foodstuffs, clothing, and housing. Elsewhere in the text he speculated that if adequate strategies were implemented, poverty could be eliminated and all the "necessities and comforts" Americans needed could be produced in a

Harold Rugg vs. Horatio Alger

twelve-hour workweek—a utopian scenario that owed much to Bellamy's *Looking Backward.*[32]

In *The Conquest of America,* Rugg partially justified his high hopes for state planning by citing what he saw as the happy precedent of government control of prices and the takeover of some industries during World War I. While wartime economic policy merited only a sentence or two in most histories, Rugg called it, in bold print, a "Lesson in Cooperation and Government Regulation." Americans gained critical experience from the episode, according to the author: "First, they learned that in our kind of interdependent world the people have to cooperate with one another; second, they learned that the government may have to step in and take charge of our lives." It was, editorialized Rugg, "the greatest effort that the American people had ever made to do things together as a people."

Rugg also used this passage to hammer in another key theme from his professional work: that individual freedom in America would have to be balanced against the larger good of society, with the state as arbiter. Farmers, workers, and business corporations had all benefited from federal control, Rugg pointed out, but they had to give something up as well. They had to become "used to having the national government step in and tell them what to do. This was something new in America, for each man had always believed he could do largely as he pleased—as long as he obeyed the law." In Rugg's version of events, businessmen refused to accept the lesson, demanding a return to prewar policies once the armistice had been signed. "'Give back the railroads to their private owners,' they said. 'Let us run our affairs by ourselves. We don't need you,' they cried."[33]

This account had a distinctly tinny quality, at odds with the usually intelligent tone of the books. Rugg claimed that he tried to ensure that every "bit of history" he put into his texts had a "clearly established functional justification."[34] When he wanted to use history to demonstrate an argument, however, to make it "functional" in the crudest sense, he lapsed into melodrama. The rogues to boo here are business owners who "cry" for government to "take its hands off their operations" in the 1920s, thereby setting the stage for the crash of 1929. If this was not indoctrination, it came perilously close.

As the excerpt on government planning suggests, Rugg departed from previous textbook writers in another way. He explained recent events in a bold, direct manner. The general rule of writing history for the schools had been that the closer authors came to the present, the less freedom they could exercise in interpreting events or even mentioning potentially divisive issues. History in the living memory of teachers and textbook boards simply aroused too many passions.[35] That practical sales strategy, however, directly contradicted the philosophy of progressive educators in the emerging field of social studies. Eager to make schooling relevant to students' lives, they wanted the curriculum to *focus* on current social problems. With that strategy guiding his work, Rugg could hardly ignore the Depression, clearly the biggest "social problem" of the 1930s.

Building on his books' emphasis on social class, he explained that the primary cause of the economic collapse was unequal distribution of income. Had America really been prosperous during the 1920s? "Those who thought about the 60,000,000 to 70,000,000 poorer people said: No!" There was, he wrote, a "tremendous difference in the income of the 'rich' and 'poor,'" and with such inequity, "it is clear that many of our people could not buy the fine things which were available." He then presented a daunting array of statistics to prove his point. But poverty was not simply bad for the poor; by leading to underconsumption, Rugg explained, it endangered the economy as a whole. When workers and farmers could not purchase the growing numbers of shoes, cars, toasters, and washing machines, unsold items piled up on showroom floors and factory shelves. But many Americans "closed their eyes" to these facts. "In the summer of 1929," Rugg concluded ominously, "it seemed that they were really living 'in the best of all possible worlds.'" Teachers and students who knew from personal experience what happened next must have appreciated the ironic suspense, even if they missed the reference to Voltaire's *Candide*.

Rugg simplified the economics of the crash a bit, as he had to for his young audience, but the underconsumption argument was fundamentally sound. However, Rugg was not satisfied merely with overturning the myth of the prosperous 1920s. He went on to paint President Herbert Hoover as a callous leader keen on denying responsibility for the economic downturn and keeping the burden for relief squarely at the state and local levels. And then Rugg sided unabashedly with the current chief executive and his New Deal:

> We see then that the Roosevelt Administration decided that the relief of the American people from distress is a national problem, not merely one for state, local, or private charity. It said that in times of distress the Federal government should step in and, if need be, give billions of dollars for relief! Relief for the unemployed, relief for distressed homeowners, relief for

Harold Rugg vs. Horatio Alger

stranded youths, relief for impoverished farmers, relief for ailing businesses. In short, it must give relief to every needy group within the nation.[36]

In its departure from the rule about approaching recent history in a blandly neutral way, Rugg's discussion of the Depression was little short of incredible. He vilified a living ex-president only five years out of office. He endorsed a partisan economic policy still working its way through Congress. He championed a president loathed by critics on the right. Condemning the laissez-faire philosophy of the Republicans, he embraced humanitarian nationalism, which was anchored by the conviction that the people, acting through government, were responsible for the welfare of all citizens. Most daringly, Rugg returned again to the issue of class, tying previous struggles for economic and social justice to the unresolved political questions of the 1930s.

How did Rugg get away with it? Why did his publisher not demand a "balanced" textbook, particularly after weathering the textbook wars of the 1920s?

Two factors unique to the 1930s, and one unique to Rugg, explain this apparent mystery. First, there was the wrenching experience of the Depression itself. With almost a quarter of workers unemployed and most of the rest living on reduced incomes, the political and cultural consensus that textbooks usually reflect had collapsed. At a time when a financially unbalanced plan to "Share the Wealth" propelled Huey Long onto the national stage, and Father Charles Coughlin enraptured radio listeners with increasingly anti-Semitic explanations for the country's troubles, Rugg's version of American history looked comparatively tame, even if it was directed at impressionable young people.

Second, a scandal had recently erupted when several American corporations were found trying to manipulate textbook content. During the 1920s many states and cities were considering increased regulation or direct control of their gas, electric, railway, and other utilities. To forestall such plans, an industry coalition led a national propaganda effort around the "public utility question." Corporations waged most of their campaign in the open, but when journalists found that they were also quietly pressuring publishers to revise schoolbooks to ensure positive treatment of private utilities, charges of censorship began to fly. The Federal Trade Commission began hearings on the issue in 1928. Understandably, corporations became skittish about any further involvement with schools or their curricula. With business leaders effectively recusing themselves, educators had what an observer at the time termed a greater "disposition to be experimental" in the teaching of "social-economic relations."[37] Rugg was not the only progressive educator to benefit from the changed mood. *The Building of Our Nation,* a history by Eugene C. Barker, Henry Steele Commager, and Walter P. Webb, endorsed a limited welfare state. The authors of another popular text, *The United States in the Making,* cited Charles Beard's work in their discussion of the Constitution. Even Beard himself sold a considerable number of the texts he coauthored with his wife, Mary. Still, why did no writer dare to go as far to the left as Rugg?

The explanation was fairly simple. Ginn and Company gave their author extra leeway because he had effectively test-marketed much of the books' content when he first released the pamphlets they were based on back in the 1920s. Rugg was also a flexible author, willing to revise as events warranted. When the horrors of collectivization under Josef Stalin became more widely known as the 1930s progressed, for instance, Rugg's books grew more critical of the Soviet Union. Man and His Changing Society also became more popular with each passing year, apparently validating Rugg's ideas and his approach to teaching. According to one Ginn editor, nobody at the firm predicted any especially bitter attacks would begin in 1939, after the series had already been in schools for a decade.[38]

Yet there had been a few signs of trouble. As far back as 1927 a corporation had objected to schools in one Appalachian city employing Rugg's pamphlets. The company backed down, but teachers were thereafter reluctant to use the materials. The mid-1930s also witnessed little-publicized complaints about his books in Montana, Illinois, Indiana, Massachusetts, and Iowa. Perhaps the greatest portent of conflict had nothing to do with his books at all. In 1933 Rugg spoke at a conference on "Youth and the World" sponsored by the *New York Herald Tribune.* He said nothing of political importance, but the *Daily Worker,* the official newspaper of the American Communist Party, covered the event and mentioned him in passing. A prominent anticommunist named Elizabeth Dilling spotted the story and added Rugg to *Red Network,* a field guide to alleged subversives much perused by red-baiting groups in the 1930s and 1940s.[39]

Rumbles of thunder finally gave way to rain in Englewood, New Jersey, in the spring of 1939. Bertie Forbes, publisher of *Forbes* magazine and a columnist for William Randolph Hearst's newspapers, took a seat on Englewood's board of education. This mostly affluent bedroom community across the Hudson River from Manhattan had already witnessed a quiet, behind-the-scenes effort to pressure teachers to drop Rugg's books.[40] Forbes now brought the campaign into the open, using his position on the board and access to the press to wage an unrelenting assault on Rugg that deeply divided the city. Attacks intensified as spring turned to summer. Inspired by Forbes, the New York–based Advertising Federation of America began criticizing Rugg's books for their claims that advertising raised costs and sometimes misrepresented goods. Sounding almost personally wounded, the organization's research director, Alfred Falk, said Rugg's *Introduction to Problems of American Culture* "built up" a picture of advertising "as a pretty rotten sort of institution." Ironically, Rugg had actually credited the federation for its work in eliminating unfair practices in the industry. Nonetheless, the federation sent a letter to members claiming that Rugg had given a black eye to their trade and capitalism in general. "Attacking business from every angle," it read, "Rugg sneers at the ideas and traditions of American democracy, making a subtle plea for abolition of our free enterprise system and the introduction of a new social order based on the principles of collectivism." The federation urged its sixty affiliated groups to wage local campaigns against Rugg.[41]

The advertisers' crusade was soon dwarfed by the efforts of the National Association of Manufacturers (NAM). Citing a "widespread and increasing" fear that un-American ideas had been creeping into schools in recent years, NAM funded a survey of six hundred textbooks in the social sciences, including history, economics, sociology, civics, and geography. That venture struck close to home for Rugg, for it was led by a colleague at Columbia, an economics professor named Ralph Robey. Released in January 1941, the report targeted Rugg more than any other writer for giving students a biased view of America's economic and political systems. NAM forwarded the twelve-hundred-page, single-spaced document to state boards of education, libraries at teachers colleges, and teachers' organizations. It also encouraged manufacturers to visit local schools to obtain lists of textbooks in use. Leaders disavowed charges of censorship. "It would be a grave mistake for any person," read an official statement, "whether a manufacturer or of any other calling, to seek to have the schools discontinue the explanation of any subject or any philosophy simply because it is inconsistent with a philosophy traditionally accepted in this country." Faced with criticism in the press, NAM then sent letters clarifying its policy to thirty-eight thousand teachers and ten thousand school administrators, an outwardly reassuring gesture that actually underscored how much money and time the organization was willing to expend in the cause.[42]

Several other conservative or right-wing organizations and individuals hopped on the anti-Rugg bandwagon. George Sokolsky, a publicist for NAM, wrote a series of articles on the subject for *Liberty* magazine and *Nation's Business*. An American Legion officer named A. G. Rudd teamed up with Alfred Falk from the Advertising Federation to form the Guardians of American Education. That group tried to ban Rugg's books from New York schools. The Guardians also published what was, relative to more hostile assessments of Rugg's work, a well-researched, forty-three-page critique called *Undermining Our Republic: Facts about Anti-American Schoolbooks and the Nationwide Scheme of Radical Educators*. Other Legionnaires also became interested in Rugg's case after a national committee in the organization declared that his books opposed the "American tradition" and were "not suitable" for schools. An influential article by O. K. Armstrong entitled "Treason in the Textbooks" appeared in the Legion's monthly magazine. A business executive with close ties to the organization also tried to get Rugg investigated by the Dies Committee, forerunner to the infamous House Committee on Un-American Activities (HUAC).[43]

Others played key roles in this loose coalition against the progressive educator. Merwin K. Hart, head of the self-styled New York Economic Council, wrote letters and pamphlets denouncing Rugg and was instrumental in getting the books removed from schools in Binghamton, New York. The Veterans of Foreign Wars and the Daughters of Colonial Wars soon entered the fray as well. Rugg also believed that publishing rivals of Ginn and Company stoked the controversy surrounding Man and His Changing Society. The claim may not have been far-fetched. The Advertising Federation of America, one of his fiercest opponents, was chaired by Mason Britton. Britton also happened to be vice chairman of the board at the McGraw-Hill Publishing Company, and that firm published a two-volume history called *Our American Heritage* that competed directly with books by Rugg.

Looming above all the critics was Hearst. Though rarely seen, Hearst was an unavoidable presence in the controversy, as he had been in the textbook battles of the 1920s, when his publications led the charge against pro-Britishism in the schools. The publishing magnate, who by the mid-1930s controlled twenty-nine newspapers in eighteen cities, took a considerable interest in protecting schools from what he thought of as subversive ideas.[44]

Harold Rugg vs. Horatio Alger

The nature of complaints against Rugg varied somewhat among critics. Many thought he was simply too forthcoming with unflattering truths about the nation's past. A corresponding secretary for the Daughters of Colonial Wars claimed that Rugg tried "to give the child an unbiased viewpoint instead of teaching him real Americanism. All the old histories taught my country right or wrong. That's the point of view we want our children to adopt. We can't afford to teach them to be unbiased and let them make up their own minds."[45] Others shared that conviction but chose not to express their hostility to critical thinking in the schools quite so baldly. A few of Rugg's antagonists believed he was a genuine radical, a Soviet agent committed to the violent overthrow of the U.S. government. Whatever individual axes they had to grind, the critics shared several misgivings about the author and his book series. Rugg, they said, unduly emphasized class fissures in America's past and dwelled too extensively on poverty. He suggested that unsavory financial motives guided the country's revered statesmen, business leaders, and corporations. He tried to undermine faith in free enterprise and individual initiative, thereby subverting patriotism and making children more susceptible to the lures of "collectivism." Finally, critics linked Rugg and progressive educators led by John Dewey with what they perceived as a dangerous leftward trend in American politics since the election of 1932.

The authors of the conservative pamphlet *Undermining Our Republic* argued that Rugg made American history "a drab story of selfishness, greed, imperialist expansion, exploitation, and class antagonisms." Armstrong agreed with that assessment in his essay in *American Legion Magazine* and suggested that teachers all too willingly parroted the themes in Rugg's books. He opened "Treason in the Textbooks" with an anecdote about his fourteen-year-old son returning from school curious to know whether George Washington had been a "big business man." Queried about what he meant by the question, the teenager said he had been learning such things from his teacher. Armstrong took quick action:

I went straight to the instructor. She told me, with evident condescension, that old methods of teaching were being supplanted by a more "realistic" approach to problems. It's all part of "progressive" education. For instance, the men who framed the Constitution *were* the "upper class," she insisted; they were the owners of land, shippers and moneyed men generally. They were particular to safeguard the capitalistic system, and school children should be taught that fact "as an intelligent approach to present-day problems."[46]

The claim that textbooks slandered heroes was old, a relic of the 1920s and earlier decades. But the connections between the historical revisionism begun by Charles Beard and the "present-day problems' at the end of the 1930s, when the United States struggled to shake off a decade-long Depression and gird itself for a possible war, gave the timeworn charge new relevance. Criticisms of America's free-enterprise system, warned Columbia's Ralph Robey, would tend to create discontent and unrest. Man and His Changing Society "planted the seed" of class hatred, according to Falk, Rudd, and their *Undermining Our Republic* coauthor Hamilton Hicks. The series was "clearly calculated" to "cause pupils to rebel against all authority," added Forbes. "The Rugg books tend to destroy unity and to cause distrust of the founding fathers of our country," declared an American Legion official in Port Chester, New York, soon after the Germans overran France. "At a time like this we need full national unity."[47]

Few Americans doubted the need for solidarity, least of all Rugg, whose appraisals of the world situation had grown increasingly somber by the start of the 1940s. The crux of the debate over his books was never about unity per se, however, but about how young Americans should conceive of that unity. Rugg's detractors argued that world crisis demonstrated the need for a return to economic and educational values that they believed had once bound Americans together, among them individualism, free enterprise, limited government, and an embrace of tradition for its own sake. Rugg argued, and arranged his history and civics texts to demonstrate, that America's political and economic ideology had to continue evolving to meet crises at home and the challenge of communism and fascism abroad. The welfare state would have to expand, claimed Rugg, and the government would have to take more direct control of economic development.

If the controversy over Rugg often sounded like a proxy war over the New Deal, that's because it was, at least in part. Accusations that sinister, foreign ideas lurked behind his books, the reconstructionists, and progressive education in general certainly raised eyebrows, but they made far less sense in 1940 than they might have in 1933. Even firebrand George Counts had grown disenchanted with Stalin, and he was elected president of the American Federation of Teachers after promising to end communist influence in the union.[48] The homegrown economic reform of the New Deal was not dead, however, and it continued to bedevil conservatives.

The authors of *Undermining Our Republic,* for instance, claimed Rugg's texts unduly emphasized poverty in Appalachia, thereby making the Tennessee Valley Authority look like a godsend to the region's inhabitants. They also complained that Rugg told students that the Supreme Court favored the wealthy, pointing to questions in the workbook for *America's March toward Democracy:* "From which economic class did the members [of the court] come? To what extent did they interpret the laws in the interest of all the people? In the interest of the well-to-do classes?"[49] Here, it was hard to miss a wry commentary on Roosevelt's ill-fated court-packing scheme. Beginning in 1935 the Supreme Court had begun declaring New Deal programs unconstitutional. Full of economic conservatives appointed by previous administrations, the court of the mid-1930s did embody the narrow class interests Rugg alluded to in *America's March.* Hoping to salvage his programs, the president tried to bypass the justices. He announced plans to appoint up to six new members to the court, ostensibly to improve efficiency, but in fact to dilute the power of the conservatives. The plan backfired, disappointing Roosevelt's allies and handing his enemies evidence for their oft-repeated charge that he harbored a dictatorial streak. But as war approached, direct attacks on administration policies began to look unpatriotic, and so Rugg became a useful substitute target for the Wizard of Hyde Park.

The growth of organized labor in the 1930s, and the New Deal's official encouragement of it, also colored critiques of Rugg's work. In December 1936, General Motors workers in Flint, Michigan, took over their plant, refusing to leave until the company recognized their union. When local police tried to force them to vacate the premises, workers pelted them with nuts, bolts, coffee mugs, and bottles. Bucking the traditional pattern set by their predecessors, neither Michigan's governor nor the president intervened on GM's behalf, and the strikers won. Law-and-order conservatives were furious. As the uproar over Rugg began, Rudd, Falk, and Hicks blamed school propaganda for what seemed to them an inexplicable public sympathy for the autoworkers. "When immature minds are constantly deluged with attacks on our economic system, the 'aristocrat owners,' and private property, and with similar appeals to class hatred," they asked rhetorically, "is it surprising that in later years they see nothing wrong with the sit-down strike?"[50]

Schoolbook Nation

The aversion to Rugg reached beyond contemporary politics, however. Advocates of a government hands-off policy for the economy argued that laissez-faire was just to all citizens, so what troubled them most about Rugg was his tendency to demystify individual economic opportunity. If a reader did not believe in the ubiquity of opportunity, they realized, then poverty looked like a problem built into the American system and not the result of personal failures. They understood that discussion of material inequality without the corresponding affirmation of social mobility made America look like those old, class-bound societies of Europe. For conservatives of the 1930s and 1940s (heirs to nineteenth-century liberalism), faith in opportunity cemented the national union; without it, the specter of division, chaos, or collectivism loomed. Thus Rugg's skepticism on the issue topped their indictment against his books. They returned to the question of opportunity repeatedly in their attacks, often distorting Rugg's positions in the process.

Armstrong's article in the Legion's magazine included an illustration of a nearly demonic-looking teacher, presumably Rugg, in a rumpled jacket and tie (see fig. on pgs. 248–49). As his hands drip muck on books labeled "U.S. History," "U.S. Heroes," "Constitution," and "Religion," he gestures to a chalkboard where he has written, "AMERICA IS <u>NOT</u> A LAND OF OPPORTUNITY." Students look on in reverential confusion, one scratching his head, another clasping his hands together as if in prayer. Like other critics who attacked Rugg for his treatment of this topic, Armstrong cited a passage from a student workbook that asked if America provided opportunity for all its people. Rugg's suggested answer appeared in the teachers' guide: "The United States is not a land of opportunity for all our people; for one fifth of the people do not earn any money at all. There are great differences in the standards of living of the different classes of people." Here was a concrete example of what Armstrong referred to elsewhere in his article as a doctrine "so subversive as to undermine [students'] faith in the American way of life." Rugg and his allies were "intent upon breaking down respect for individual effort and initiative."[51]

Other critics drove home that point. In an essay fittingly entitled "Is Your Child Being Taught to Loaf?" George Sokolsky argued that it was not just Man and His Changing Society that was sapping the work ethic. The whole philosophy of progressive education was to blame. Homework had recently been decreased, he warned; once-rigorous books had been dumbed down. Less capable students were being advanced to the next grade. Sokolsky explained why:

Harold Rugg vs. Horatio Alger

A new theory is motivating promotions. It is the theory that it is *socially* evil to leave a child behind; that it is *socially* sound to promote a child whether the child is bright or dumb, hard-working or lazy, honest or sneaky. In a word, it is a doctrine of sacrificing the competent, efficient, and hard-working child in the interests of the incompetent and lazy child. But is it really in the lazy child's interest? Is he not being kidded into believing that life is just a bowl of cherries—and that all he has to do is slide along? Would you want your child to gain that conception of life?

It was not difficult to make the jump from the classroom to the nation at large, from the frustrated or lazy child to the slow or disgruntled laborer on the assembly line. Sokolsky helped readers make that connection. Children, he wrote, had to be "trained to believe" in a competitive world where "men and women must work hard to get on," presumably without sit-down strikes or the aid of a "collectivist" state.[52]

Rugg and other progressives had never meant to discredit the idea of opportunity in America, at least not to the extent Sokolsky imagined. John Dewey, like the conservatives, linked opportunity closely with America's national identity. But when he talked about "nationalizing education," Dewey argued that schools had to place a real chance for success in the hands of all students, not blithely claim that it was already there. For his part, Rugg celebrated opportunity where he found it in America's past. In *The Conquest of America,* he wrote that to immigrants the United States was a "land of promise." Although their lives might have been "hard and disagreeable at first, they were usually glad that they came."[53] Elsewhere, he recounted the success stories of entrepreneurs. However, Rugg did question whether Americans at the bottom and top of the social scale truly had equal prospects for success. That sentiment lay behind the oft-quoted passage from the teachers' guide that suggested America did not provide opportunity "for all our people." Rugg's books argued that the comforting moral of Horatio Alger's *Ragged Dick*—that even a motherless shoeshine boy had a shot at the American dream—was deceptively simplistic. More than the debunking of heroes, the critique of the Constitution, or the attribution of base motives to advertisers, this was the kind of claim that made Man and His Changing Society so dangerous.

And interesting. Unlike many educational writers, Rugg had genuine ideas and the courage to express them. He openly bragged that "among the schoolbook authors of America" he alone "refused to

The "Frontier Thinkers" are trying to
sell our youth the idea that the American way of life has failed

Treason

"DADDY, was George Washington a big business man?"
The question, asked by my fourteen-year-old son,
gave me a bit of thought.
"What do you mean?" I asked.
"Well, our teacher says the men who wrote the Constitution
were landowners and business men."
"What did she mean by that?" My son's explanations from
that point on were hazy. He hadn't quite grasped the reasons
for emphasis upon the economic status of our Founding Fathers.
But it was evident the discussion by his teacher had raised
doubts as to these patriots being all they were cracked up to be.
That started me off on a study. My son's class was known
as "Democratic Living." Good enough. But what did George
Washington and his business interests have to do with that?
Plenty!
I went straight to his instructor. She told me, with evident
condescension, that the old methods of teaching were being
supplanted by a more "realistic" approach to problems. It's
all a part of "progressive" education. For instance, the men
who framed the Constitution *were* the "upper class," she insisted; they were owners of land, shippers and moneyed men
generally. They were particular to safeguard the capitalistic
system, and school children should be taught that fact "as an
intelligent approach to pres-
ent-day problems."
Legionnaires are parents—

most of us. Our children average from four to fifteen years. The
older groups are in junior and senior high school. It's time we
learned that our children are being taught, in the name of
civics, social science and history, doctrines so subversive as to
undermine their faith in the American way of life.
My eldest son is still a little vague about it. But give him
three years more, and he'll be convinced that our "capitalistic
system" is the fault of selfish fellows like Benjamin Franklin
and Thomas Jefferson who wanted to save their property; that
the poor man wasn't given proper consideration, that in Russia
the youth are engaged in creating a beautiful, new democratic
order, that modern business is for the benefit of the profit-
makers, that advertising is an economic waste, that morality
is a relative value, and that family life will soon be radically
changed by state control.
All out of textbooks and courses adopted by public high
schools in the good old U. S. A.—by state and local school authorities that likely do not know they have been taken for a
ride by the most insidious attack of un-Americanism yet per-
fected by the Trojan horsemen.
It's a case for the Dies Committee on Un-American Activities, and with the vigorous coöperation of The American Legion
the Dies Committee has turned its attention to these subversive
activities in our schools. But it's more than that. It's a case for
the personal attention of every parent who would like to preserve American ideals and institutions.
"Catch 'em young!" That's the motto of the radical and
communistic textbook writers who all too evidently have been
in control of the field. You expect college and graduate students
to delve into controversial social and political theories. But it's

By O. K. ARMSTRONG

8

An illustrator for the *The American Legion Magazine* depicts a progressive educator, likely meant to be Harold Rugg, corrupting America's youth. *Illustrations and text reprinted with permission of* The
American Legion Magazine, September 1940.

in the TEXTBOOKS

the junior and senior high school years that provide the lasting impressions. Teach a boy or girl of twelve to sixteen that George Washington might have been a land-grabber, James Madison a shady trader, the Constitution a protector of the economic royalist, and modern business an oppressor of the poor man, and the idea sticks.

It's time to cite chapter and verse. Obviously, long and detailed quotations are impossible in a brief article.

The best we can do is to select a few samples, list the textbooks now under scrutiny by the Legion's Americanism Commission and urge parents to proceed with their own investigations of textbooks and reference material used in their own schools.

By far the most prolific of the social science schoolbook writers is Professor Harold O. Rugg of Teachers College, Columbia University, New York City. In 1933 Professor Rugg produced a book called *Great Technology*. The whole underlying thesis of this book is that our American way of life is a failure and must be replaced by a new order based upon some type of state socialism.

"Our task is nothing short of questioning a whole philosophy of living—the philosophy of capitalism and *laissez-faire*," says Prof. Rugg. He declares candidly in this book that the public schools must be utilized to "change the climate of opinion" so that traditional American ideals and motivations will be abandoned.

With considerable vigor he set himself to this task, turning out some sixteen textbooks used widely in high schools all over America. Some dozen other authors have succeeded in having textbooks, similar in content and purpose to the Rugg courses, adopted by state education boards.

Together these courses form a complete pattern of propaganda for a change in our political, economic and social order.

The trick has been to consolidate what used to be separate studies of history, geography, civics and social science, all in one course and call it "Democratic Living," or something similar. The

---

See list of "Frontier Thinking" schoolbooks on page 71

---

westward movement of our pioneers, for example, can thus be used to teach the geography of the country, the history of the times, the social problems encountered, and other aspects of westward expansion, with whatever "interpretation" the textbook plus the instructor might care to give them.

Major Augustin G. Rudd, a Legionnaire parent of Garden City, New York, whose curiosity was aroused—as was mine—by questions asked him by his children, made a study of all the textbooks used in his home town schools. His report of this study, now in the hands of the Americanism Commission, is a tribute to one man's determination to get to the bottom of subversive activities in the schools. In his report on the Rugg textbooks we find:

"In *Pupils' Work Book* the question is asked: 'Is the United States a land of opportunity for all our people? Why?' This is the answer the child should give, according to (Continued on page 51)

Schoolbook Nation

dodge the question of public and private ownership." He *wanted a* debate on social and economic problems, and it surely gratified him to see critics of his textbooks, eager to gain ammunition against him, forced to slog through and to dissect his more "serious" works like *The Great Technology.* Most of Rugg's supporters, however, did not want to engage in that kind of debate, probably because they feared it would play to conservatives' efforts to brand him an ideologue out to corrupt young people. Like backers of historians in the textbook war of the 1920s, they preferred to cast the debate as one of fidelity to the historical record (Rugg) versus censorship (his opponents). A statement from a committee of supporters in Philadelphia epitomized this deliberate, reasoned, and altogether boring strategy: "Our examination of the Rugg books has not discovered any statements which taken with the complete context can be regarded as subversive of American ideals and principles. We have not found any statements which criticize our government, its policies, or our distinguished representatives, which are not truthful statements of facts."[54]

Extremist tactics employed by a few of Rugg's opponents aided this effort to portray the educator as a beleaguered, misunderstood author of schoolbooks. Residents of Bradner, Ohio, for instance, made headlines when they tossed his texts into a school furnace.[55]

Early in 1942 Rugg found another ally in the American Committee for Democracy and Intellectual Freedom, an organization founded in 1939 by some of the country's leading scholars. The group, whose executive committee included the atomic physicist J. Robert Oppenheimer, had already run afoul of conservatives for its critique of the communist-hunting Dies Committee. Now several of its members published an extensive review of Rugg's textbooks intended to rebut the NAM abstracts compiled by Columbia's Ralph Robey. The authors trotted out the usual shibboleths about accuracy and objectivity, but Robert S. Lynd, already famous for his sociological study *Middletown* (which Rugg had cited in his texts) offered a bit of a dissent. At the start of his review of *Changing Government and Changing Cultures,* Lynd declared that he was not an entirely impartial reviewer because he believed "in democracy" and "the broadening social control over property." If that constituted bias, then, yes, Rugg was biased too, Lynd implied. Every book, "if it is not to be an intellectual shambles, orients itself to certain selected problems and relevant events in the universe of experience with which it deals; and if one dislikes the problems and feels they should not be discussed in schools, one can accuse an author of bias because he writes about them."[56]

Harold Rugg vs. Horatio Alger

Lynd admitted the obvious. The real conflict did not revolve around the truth of Rugg and the propaganda of business executives and the American Legion, or vice versa. That kind of paradigm had long since grown stale in debates over teaching history. Rugg had a distinct social and political philosophy, including a critique of unfettered capitalism and a vision of how a more powerful state could promote national welfare and provide greater opportunity for all citizens. Those views structured but did not completely dominate his books. Rugg's opponents, by singling out and condemning certain text passages, articulated an opposing ideology. Academic freedom and censorship were still central to the uproar over Man and His Changing Society; after all, zealots were burning his books. But the more interesting clash was between conservative and humanitarian understandings of American nationalism—each no less impartial than the other—and how they would be embodied in the social studies curriculum. In that contest, participants knew, the sort of textbooks published in the ensuing years would serve as the yardstick of victory.

Neither side won.

Rugg had the good fortune to attract numerous supporters, including the National Education Association, the American Civil Liberties Union, the *New Republic,* many newspapers, and countless professors, teachers, superintendents, clergy, and parents. Together, they won several battles. Bertie Forbes's crusade to drive Rugg's books out of Englewood failed. After earning the ire of many of the town's residents, particularly after shifting his attacks from Rugg to teachers, Forbes lost his seat on the board of education. Other towns and cities appeared to be following Englewood's lead. In the spring of 1941, the journal *School and Society* reported that the storm over Rugg had begun to subside, a sentiment echoed in *Publishers' Weekly.* Representatives of Ginn and Company told *Time* magazine that since the assault on their author had begun, they had actually been receiving *larger* orders for his books.

Officials at Ginn must have known they were whistling in the dark, however. Controversy sells trade books, but it dooms textbooks by making them politically costly to use. Some teachers and administrators backed Rugg even to the point of losing their jobs, earning his gratitude in his account of the affair, a book with the somewhat pedantic title *That Men May Understand.*[57] But many other educators did not. When a fervent corps of local business leaders or Legionnaires called for the ouster of Rugg's texts, they quietly acquiesced instead of mounting a protracted defense. More and more districts, from Los

Angeles to suburban New York, quietly retired the series. If sales of books in the Man and His Changing Society series are considered in isolation, Rugg clearly lost this contest.

It would be a mistake to assume that public pressure alone accounted for the disappearance of the books. Forbes recognized another reason in his 1941 essay "Does This Smell of Sovietism?" The texts were "written a decade ago," he argued, and "misrepresent, in my judgment, the economic conditions now existing in America."[58] Forbes was right. Rugg produced most of his books in the depths of the Depression, but at the start of the 1940s his critiques of income disparities and laissez-faire capitalism had grown less relevant. By that time the federal government had established oversight or control over significant parts of the economy while also setting up a limited welfare state. The Securities and Exchange Commission (SEC) monitored Wall Street, while the Federal Depositors Insurance Corporation (FDIC) stabilized banking. Price supports and crop controls managed farm production. The Wagner Act guaranteed workers the right to organize, and the Fair Labor Standards Act (FLSA) set a minimum wage and maximum hours for the workweek. In addition to old-age pensions, the Social Security Act granted aid to families with dependent children (now usually called "welfare"), payments to the disabled, and unemployment insurance. The world of 1929 was gone. The New Deal fell considerably short of the socialist utopia imagined by Edward Bellamy, or even the planned economy of Rugg's *Great Technology,* but it had moved the country to the left. And what the New Deal failed to achieve—an end to the Depression and the rebirth of economic opportunity for millions of unemployed Americans—government spending for World War II did.

In *America's March toward Democracy,* Rugg devoted three pages to an earnest discussion of socialism, giving roughly equal space to arguments for and against it. "There is one conclusion we can agree on, however," he intoned. *"The questions raised by the socialists and their opponents are of the greatest importance."* By 1947 that observation seemed prophetic when applied to foreign policy, as the United States and the Soviet Union began waging the Cold War, but it looked almost quaint relative to domestic affairs. The earlier sense of crisis had passed, and the nation seemed to have found the magic formula for averting future downturns—an economy combining the tonic of free enterprise, increased regulation, and the kind of massive state spending advocated by the British economist John Maynard Keynes (one of Rugg's "frontier thinkers"). The creator of Man and His Changing

Harold Rugg vs. Horatio Alger

Society even found kind words to say about this new mixed economy, likely because he saw it lending credence to his ideas.[59] Now that the polarizing turmoil of the 1930s was over, America as a whole sought a new political center. So did the writers of U.S. history for schools. They tried to balance the views of Rugg and his opponents to create a newly harmonious, unified picture of the nation. For just over fifteen years, the effort mostly succeeded.

Into the 1950s

Authors of postwar schoolbooks took some of their cues from professional historiography, which came to be dominated by the "consensus school." Left-leaning historians like Charles Beard and Carl Becker, who had analyzed social class and organized their work around clashes between the haves and the have-nots, or the "people" and the special interests, increasingly fell from favor. Chastened by fratricidal war and genocide in Europe, and disillusioned with radical politics after learning the extent of Stalin's atrocities in the Soviet Union, a new generation of historians eschewed conflict in their work. Instead, they sought to understand the common values and ideals that they believed had united Americans throughout their history. Perry Miller, best known for his books on New England's Puritans, assailed Beard for what he thought was an overly simplified economic determinism in the elder scholar's work on the Constitution. After taking a beating in the 1930s, the stock of nineteenth-century captains of industry went up; that of populists and other past critics of the status quo went down.

Extremism of any sort became suspect. Arthur M. Schlesinger Jr., whose father had defended his peers in the textbook battles of the 1920s, championed the "vital center" in American politics. The sociologist Daniel Bell wrote about the "end of ideology." In the same vein, Daniel J. Boorstin, a university-trained historian who amassed a wide readership among the general public, argued that America's governing ideology was a *rejection* of the kind of political passion that had plunged Europe into terror. Other leading scholars expressed similar convictions. Studies in U.S. history with the sort of socially critical tone pioneered by Beard, who died in 1948, became far less common. While the transformation can easily be exaggerated—some labor historians, for instance, refused to join the general march toward the center—the overall trend in the profession was still plain.[60]

The rise of the consensus school limited the political range of scholarship text writers would draw upon, but it involved no coercion. The postwar hunt for communist influence in the schools did, and it contributed to a growing spirit of self-censorship initially triggered by the Rugg controversy. The House Committee on Un-American Activities and its state-level counterparts like the Tenney Committee in California targeted both colleges and high schools. Teachers grew reluctant to question the country's economic system and its government policy or to encourage students to think too critically themselves, because a whiff of subversion could bring a subpoena to appear before such committees. In New York City and Los Angeles, teachers who invoked the Fifth Amendment and refused to testify about their political affiliations or to "name names" automatically lost their jobs.[61]

Investigators scrutinized schoolbooks with as much ardor as they questioned teachers. Richard Combs, a lawyer with another California legislative committee investigating communist influence in the schools, found a time-saving technique to scan for inappropriate material in a book series called "Building America." He simply cross-checked names in the index with lists of suspected radicals. But when he found what even he deemed "plain, forceful, and direct" denunciations of communism in the books, he concluded that someone had simply inserted them to offset more subtle left-wing bias. In a catch-22 worthy of Joseph Heller, the books were thus still "unfit for use in our schools." In Indiana, a member of the state textbook board vowed to drive any mention of Robin Hood from approved titles. She was sure communists were exploiting the take-from-the-rich-and-give-to-the-poor theme to corrupt America's youth.[62]

Alabama put the greatest effort into cleaning up its curricular materials. In 1953 its legislature passed Act 888, which required publishers supplying texts to schools in the state to certify that none of the books' authors, or even writers cited for additional reading, was "a known advocate of communism or Marxist Socialism" or had belonged to the Communist Party or a "Communist front organization." The act would have hamstrung authors trying to write about radical politics, social class, or virtually anything else, but it was so sweeping that courts struck it down. Nevertheless, the act brought a chill to the publishing industry. And Alabama did not act alone. Between 1958 and 1962, well after the height of McCarthyism had passed, legislatures in over one-third of the states mounted probes of texts or attacked them in some other way.[63]

Many of the individuals and groups leading the assault on texts in the 1950s were veterans of the campaign against Rugg. Their complaints had not changed much. They objected to explicit discussion of social class and depictions of poverty. Critics testifying before a text-book committee in Texas, for instance, complained about how one book reported that prosperous people in the antebellum South had once looked upon small farmers as "poor white trash." A political cartoon they wanted removed from another text for leaving an "extremely unwanted impression" showed a destitute family in the Panic of 1893. The Daughters of the American Revolution found fault with "uncomplimentary" photographs of slums and Depression-era lines of the unemployed.[64]

Critics on the right also returned to the charge that histories promoted collectivism, pointing to coverage of government antipoverty programs or simply the growth of state power in general. The catalyst for Alabama's textbook law of 1953 was not the inclusion of radicals but, apparently, the mention of public housing, which annoyed Birmingham real-estate interests. The leader of Texans for America objected to allegedly favorable remarks on the federal income tax, farm subsidies, and welfare programs. Another Texan protested that a popular textbook called *America: Land of Freedom* failed to state that Social Security was "evil."[65]

Many publishers were eager to placate the right. Told by critics in the Lone Star state to drop the names of seven alleged subversives from their junior high American history, representatives from the firm of Lyons and Carnahan answered that if the charges were true, they were "not only willing but anxious to delete any references to such persons in *Freedom's Frontier* or any of our publications." But if failure to denounce programs like Social Security as creeping socialism was somehow biased, even the most pliable publishers found themselves in a quandary. As the education editor of the *New York Herald Tribune* remarked in 1952, it "frequently turns out that the charge of *advocacy* of change results from a *recording* of change that has already taken place." The exasperated vice president of Macmillan's education department made the same point. "To a stout defender of *laissez-faire*," he wrote in *Phi Delta Kappan*, mention of "the most even-tempered facts of past history or of contemporary life may brand [an] author as a 'collectivist' or a 'subversive.'"[66]

Could a textbook dealing with recent American history just sidestep the New Deal? Not really. And now that economic reforms of the 1930s had become institutionalized, supported even by the moderate Republican Dwight Eisenhower, text writers could not condemn them without appearing to attack the federal government and the will of voters. That, of course, would have amounted to "subversion." So textbooks generally shoehorned the New Deal into a narrative of American progress. One such book included a series of one-page features illustrating "Milestones of Democracy." It included a double tribute to "The Right of Working People to Organize," recognized under the Wagner Act of 1935, and to "Social Security." Accompanying photographs showed a meeting of the International Ladies Garment Workers Union and a smiling, elderly couple holding a government check, their figures backlit by soft, soothing light.[67] Much to the frustration of critics on the right, the activist state and the cause of humanitarian nationalism had made significant gains in popular textbooks, even though Rugg had gone down in defeat.

Despite the risks involved, a few authors and editors also consciously chose to grapple with class. In *History of a Free People,* Henry W. Bragdon, a teacher at a private school in New England, dared to explain how Americans split along class lines during the Revolution and the debate over ratifying the Constitution. Though his tone was considerably less strident than Rugg's had been, the essence of the account was the same. The book included a discussion of Jefferson's disputes with Hamilton, along with the latter's desire for a government of the rich and well born that would keep the "swinish multitude" under control. Editors tried to fortify the courage of history instructors who must have been tempted to treat the two Founders with bland reverence, rather than to explore their philosophical and frequently personal conflicts. Bragdon and his editors also juxtaposed photographs of a Vanderbilt mansion and a turn-of-the-century tenement, its residents staring hollow-eyed at the camera. The two authors of another book openly addressed the "problems" that industrial capitalism engendered. The rise of corporations, they wrote, "gave a few men power over millions of workers and consumers. They often used their power to keep wages down and prices up, to crush attempts of labor to organize, and to dictate to state legislatures and even Congress itself."[68]

Textbooks writers and editors could never afford simply to ignore complaints from conservative critics, however. Instead, they tried to blend liberal and humanitarian ideas and to restore the faith in economic opportunity and class mobility that Rugg had challenged. In their new synthesis, one critical element in Rugg's books—the importance of class and conflict between classes, particularly in recent history—partially faded away. The revised story of America did not always please the American Legion or critics like E. Merrill Root. Root, a curious figure who balanced careers as a poet, respected scholar on the work of Robert Frost, and hired-gun in right-wing campaigns to clean up the schools, published a 1958 work called *Brainwashing in the High Schools* that argued that the United States was losing the Cold War due to a collectivist bias that histories implanted in young people.[69] He was especially vexed by textbooks' alleged favoritism toward the New Deal. Despite complaints from Root and others, however, it is clear that texts of the era still relied on several traditional, conservative themes.

First, they told students that contemporary relations between labor and management were based mostly on consensus and mutual respect, not antagonism. The 1952 edition of Gertrude Hartman's *America: Land of Freedom* prefaced a discussion of strikes in the nineteenth century with a note that many "employers *in the early days* were opposed to labor unions," a verbal sleight of hand that ignored intense business hostility to unions under the New Deal. That ill will had led to repeated Republican attempts to overturn the Wagner Act and to undermine labor's gains. The GOP achieved a partial victory by rolling back some of the legislation's provisions in 1947 under the Taft-Hartley Act. Politically messy as the conflict over Taft-Hartley had been, it was too significant for Hartman to ignore outright. So she slipped into the passive voice. "During the period of labor unrest after the war," she informed her young readers, "it was felt that the Wagner Act had given labor unions too much power." *Who* felt that way? *Which* unions had gained too much power? Hartman avoided giving her young readers specific answers. Accompanying illustrations failed to clarify issues, offering instead staged images of satisfied workers and peaceful labor-management negotiations. They included a photograph of two smiling men preparing to punch their time cards. The caption told readers that American workers "now go to their jobs each day knowing exactly the hours they are going to work and the pay they will receive." Other authors were more honest when discussing Taft-Hartley and labor-management disputes, but the general pattern of minimizing recent social conflict was unmistakable.[70]

In their 1954 text *Our Nation's Story,* Everett Augspurger, a Cleveland high school teacher, and Richard A. McLemore, a professor at Mississippi Southern College, showed an almost Orwellian tendency to omit troublesome facts of recent labor history. A 1937 strike "accompanied by some violence in Chicago led to the recognition of the United Steel Workers Union," according to the authors.[71] The account is accurate to a point, but euphemistic, neglecting to explain what sort of violence or even what company was involved. Republic Steel had, in fact, enlisted the support of local police, who then fired on a peaceful crowd, killing ten people, an event known in labor circles as the Memorial Day Massacre. The book's abbreviated account, however, served several purposes. It allowed the writers to hew to the narrative of progress, one that relied, to the annoyance of conservatives, on gains by unions. But it also obscured underlying class conflict, which generally pleased those same critics. The story of the strike was thus "balanced" in a way that avoided offending adoption boards, particularly in Illinois, where memories of the strike were still fresh. But faith in progress is inherently conservative, for it makes committed struggle or radical alterations in the status quo unnecessary. Books like *Our Nation's Story* implied that, given the chance, time solves all social problems.

In books of the 1950s, the federal government also solved them. Textbooks typically treated the government as a benevolent, disinterested force acting on its own initiative to protect the interests of labor, business, and other groups. The historian Allan Nevins prefaced Hartman's book with the claim that American history "is a story of how a passion for social justice led American statesmen, one after another, to try to make sure that no one would be ill-fed or ill-housed, no one would be hungry, no one would lack a chance to work and use his talents." That theme surfaced repeatedly in Hartman's text, as in this typically soporific passage:

> Because of the importance of the working people in the life of
> the nation, the government became interested in their welfare.
> As early as 1884 a Bureau of Labor was organized to collect and
> publish information on labor matters, and in 1913, during the
> administration of President Wilson, a Department of Labor was
> established to "foster, promote, and develop the welfare of
> wage-earners of the United States, to improve their working
> conditions, and to advance their opportunities for profitable
> employment."[72]

As statesmen or a disembodied government took center stage in the narrative, social activists receded. Solutions to poverty or social conflict descended from above in Hartman's book, or, at least, the federal government earnestly searched for them. Unlike Rugg, Hartman downplayed physical and political conflict as a route to progress. So, while she devoted this paragraph to the creation of the Department of Labor in 1913, she omitted the better-known and perhaps equally important story of striking miners and their families who were killed by company agents the following year in Ludlow, Colorado. Textbook authors rarely suggested that violence could provide the necessary constructive tension to sway public opinion and produce change, as the deaths at Ludlow did. *Our Nation's Story* implied that violence retarded reform. "*Despite* outcroppings of industrial violence" at the turn of the century, its writers concluded, "workers' benefits such as the eight-hour day, which we now take for granted, were introduced."[73]

Textbooks in the postwar era made massive government intervention in the economy seem both natural and, as Nevins argues, humanitarian. Rugg, however, had justified centralized economic reform by showing readers contemporary poverty and lack of opportunity. His successors removed those elements from their discussion of the United States at midcentury, fostering an impression that no economic reform beyond what had already been accomplished by the New Deal was necessary.

"The most notable fact about the nation's increased wealth is that it has come to be shared by more and more people," claimed the authors of one history. "Never before had so many Americans enjoyed so much prosperity," added another. Americans had gained "a standard of living such as the world had never before known," said a third. Poverty appeared in the books only as an ill-defined problem that was being overcome through existing government programs. *The Making of Modern America,* written by professional historian Leon H. Canfield and social studies teacher Howard B. Wilder, paired pictures of an urban slum with a new housing project. "Light, air, and cleanliness," read the caption, "have begun to replace the dinginess and squalor of earlier low-cost houses."[74]

There were a few exceptions to this policy. Canfield and Wilder's text, first published in the more experimental 1930s as *The United States in the Making,* allowed that not "all American families have sufficient income to provide them with acceptable standards of living." But in the 1958 version, that concession came with a Cold War–inspired preface that showed, with text, graphs, and a seemingly endless parade of tractors, that even the poorest American workman was far ahead of his Soviet counterpart. "He needs to work far fewer hours than a Russian citizen works to buy food and clothing for his family," the authors assured young readers. "Because of this advantage the American can afford to enjoy many things that are beyond the reach of workers in many other lands."[75]

The University of Wisconsin endured as a redoubt of conflict-oriented labor historians and freethinkers even during the McCarthyist 1950s, but one would never guess so when reading *Living in Our Amer-*

ica, a text by Wisconsin's Edward Krug. In the book's concluding chapter, Krug and Stanford coauthor I. James Quillen took an extraordinarily gentle look at problems like poor housing, inadequate health care, and unequal opportunities. Easygoing cheerfulness characterized much of their tone, as suggested by an excerpt they included from comedian Bob Hope's 1946 book *So This is Peace:* "There's an endless string of new things coming along and old things growing more mellow just as there has always been and always will be." Yet Quillen and Krug also took the issue of social and economic progress quite seriously. For them, such progress was both inscrutably mystical and undeniably concrete. In *Living in Our America,* the country's history culminated in a scene that illustrated the optimistic, socially unified fantasy of the 1950s—a massive, low-slung automobile plant where vehicles in the parking lot stretched toward the horizon. The editors even included a poem in free verse to explain the photograph:

> In the United States can be found factories
> with parking lots full of automobiles—
> not just cars of officials and factory owners,
> but cars of the workmen, too.

The cars are more than simple "pieces of machinery," according to the poem:

> They are symbols, too, that their owners are free—
> free to live in city, town, or country,
> free to move on to other work,
> free to seek other ways of life,
> free in body and spirit.[76]

In sentiment, this passage recalled one from John McMaster's history from the 1880s, when he invited readers to imagine themselves careering across the country in a luxurious train—only now the railroad car was replaced by the privately owned automobile. Quillen and Krug thus reaffirmed a textbook theme that stretched back several decades. Technological progress benefits all Americans, "not just officials and factory owners," and because its fruits are shared more or less equally, it undermines the very idea of class itself. When Rugg began writing his books in the 1920s, he wanted to explore how industrialization challenged key American beliefs in social justice and political equality. In the 1950s, these postwar histories declared, such challenges had finally been overcome, in large part during the critical era encompassing the 1930s and World War II.

In a section that began with the bold-faced heading "Social and economic problems interest Americans," two authors summed up the lessons of the previous thirty years:

> The mid-century American was sensitive to the problems of society. The Great Depression had taught him how interdependent Americans in every walk of life were. He had learned, from bitter experience, that suffering in one part of the nation affected the whole nation. He had come to believe that when people were not prosperous, it was the task of all the people to discover the cause and eliminate it.[77]

Here, we see the middle-class bias that pervaded the texts. The epiphany that this hypothetical citizen achieved is probably *not* that he and others like him needed the aid of the rest of the nation. Despite a reference to "all the people," the statement suggested a sense of charity; acting through the instruments of the state, he would now help others. Like much in the books, it smoothed over some of the rough edges of social conflict that lead to progress. It also invited all readers to imagine themselves as middle-class, blurring social divisions tied to income, wealth, and education. Again, the contrast to Rugg, with his portraits of Mr. Very Poor Man and Mr. Prosperous Business Man, is unmistakable.

Images of America as middle-class, or simply classless, recurred frequently in texts from the 1950s. The middle class of the early twentieth century, noted Canfield and Wilder, "gave America its real tone and quality" and provided "those who made real contributions to American life and culture." When they addressed labor issues in contemporary America, writers avoided the term "working class." Bragdon and McCutchen maintained that even in the 1930s there had been "few class distinctions in America," a claim at odds with much of their own, generally straightforward text. A less sophisticated book argued that the "absence of class distinctions" marked colonial America and that "this characteristic has continued to be one of the finest features of American life." Another book showed a White mother preparing a meal for her two children in a spacious, modern kitchen, its countertops and numerous appliances buffed to a silvery sheen. "The kitchen scene above gives some indication of the modern American standard of living," read the caption. Illustrations of "typical" dress at different periods of American history, a motif in the books, invariably showed men and women of middle or above-average income. Where depictions of variations in wealth and income of contemporary Americans did appear, they were usually accompanied by cheerful reminders about equality of opportunity, the prime leveling force in society. Critics of Rugg had claimed that he "deliberately pursued" the "building of class consciousness" in his schoolbooks. It would be difficult to make the same charge against books of the 1950s, unless they made children conscious that they were part of the great American middle class.[78]

These rosy pictures were accurate to some degree. Americans did enjoy unprecedented prosperity in the 1950s. Labor consolidated its gains from earlier decades, and the federal government, working with the states, undertook modest efforts to help the poor. Those factors led to a more even distribution of the nation's wealth, especially when contrasted with conditions in the 1920s and early 1930s. But the story of progress missed critical facts. The New Deal tended to benefit those groups, like organized labor, that already had some access to governmental power. For instance, relatively prosperous farmers benefited more from aid than poor ones. In a paradox that deeply troubled some of Roosevelt's advisors, federal programs actually made it more profitable for large landowners in the South to drive out their share-croppers.[79] Few textbooks mentioned such facts, leaving the impression that the noble impulses of humanitarian nationalism had largely solved the riddle of inequality in the 1930s. Now that citizens knew that "suffering in one part of the nation affected the whole nation," that chapter of domestic history seemed over. The hopes of benevolent statesmen had been fulfilled.

There was still plenty of inequality in the 1950s, of course, but students would not see it in their histories. Pictures of unheated Appalachian shacks, crumbling urban tenements, or impoverished Indian reservations would have shown the persistence of poverty over generations, directly challenging the myth of Horatio Alger that still filled these books. The dearth of such scenes reflected both the limited knowledge of some writers and a conscious decision to avoid offending adoption boards. The shock brought on by the "discovery" of poverty after the publication of Michael Harrington's *The Other America* in 1962 stemmed from its erasure from the popular imagination. The textbooks used by a generation of middle-class students played an important role in that forgetfulness.

It is easy to lampoon the monotonous self-assurance of so many aspects of popular culture from the 1950s, from magazine advertisements for washing machines, their knobs and dials caressed by attentive models, to television programs like "Father Knows Best," which dispensed platitudes in a convenient, half-hour format. Textbooks, too, offered generally positive messages steeped in visions of material plenty. Yet while the books distorted the national story through a combination of evasion and political compromise, they still retained a certain ideological coherence. The story they told about America, as they told it, generally made sense. That sense of order would not last. The shape of things to come could be glimpsed one day in 1962 as J. Evetts Haley, the leader of a conservative watchdog group, lectured a committee of the Texas legislature.

A successful rancher and businessman, Haley and other members of his organization shared views typical of right-wing critics who had gravitated to the textbook issue in the years after Rugg's defeat, though he was, perhaps, a bit more colorful (he had once slugged a professor who criticized HUAC). They wanted books to devote more space to traditional military, political, and business heroes and to remove muckrakers and social critics like Ida Tarbell and Upton Sinclair. They preferred that histories not present Social Security and labor unions favorably, and they did not want texts to dwell on disparities of income and wealth. After Haley finished his litany of such complaints and recommendations, one member of the legislature, Mexican-American John Alaniz, wanted a clarification.

"You object to the mentioning of social classes in these books?" he asked.

Exactly, Haley replied, because the lack of class distinction was "why your people and mine came to this country."

Alaniz stared back at him for several seconds, betraying no emotion. Then, "Mr. Haley, part of my people were here already."[80]

The committee room erupted in laughter. Even Haley's supporters joined in, seeing how unconscious assumptions about race, class, and U.S. history had suddenly made the man look foolish. Over the next decade, similarly awkward scenes would play out across the country as people of color, particularly African-Americans, demanded larger and much revised roles in textbooks. The America imagined by histories of the 1950s—united across class lines, tolerant, blessed by equal opportunity for all, and ever looking forward—would threaten to unravel as authors and publishers were forced to confront the legacy of race. It began in Detroit.

7. The Narrative "Unravels," 1961–1985
A Story in Three Parts

"A people who began a national life inspired by a vision of a society of brotherhood can redeem itself. But redemption can come only through a humble acknowledgment of guilt and an honest knowledge of self."
—Martin Luther King, Jr. *Where Do We Go From Here: Chaos or Community?* (1967)

"We do not believe you can improve race relations by emphasis on injustices of the past. This book does just that. Neither do we feel that a generation of white students should be made to feel guilty over the past over which they had no control and about which they knew nothing. This book imparts that feeling of guilt."
—Undated letter by Mr. and Mrs. Serge R. Ballif, regarding California's proposed adoption of *Land of the Free*, an American history for eighth graders (1966)

The civil rights movement had several turning points. They were moments when suppressed rage borne of segregation and discrimination crystallized into dramatic gestures of defiance—Rosa Parks refusing to relinquish her seat to a White passenger on a Montgomery bus in 1955; four African-American college students occupying the lunch counter at the Woolworth's store in Greensboro, North Carolina, in 1960; Stokely Carmichael leading a chant of "Black Power" on the march from Memphis to Jackson, Mississippi, in the summer of 1966. To these newsreels of our collective memory should be added the image of Detroit resident Richard Henry telling his son to stay home from school on a fall day in 1962.

The Narrative "Unravels," 1961–1985

Frederick Henry was an eighth-grader at Durfee Junior High, and that calculated act of truancy marked a new strategy in a campaign by Blacks to force city schools to suspend use of the history *Our United States: A Bulwark of Freedom*. Eventually successful, this effort broke the ideological grip that conservative Southern Whites had kept on educational publishers since the turn of the century. The demands of a newly powerful constituency of urban Blacks now sent writers, editors, and sales agents scrambling to revise textbooks.

In some ways, history appeared to be repeating itself. The struggle to integrate Blacks into largely all-White textbooks paralleled earlier battles to force publishers to abandon "Anglo-Saxonism" and to include the Irish, Germans, Italians, Jews, and other groups in the national story. African-Americans had, in fact, played important roles in those battles.[1] But where White ethnics had made considerable gains in representation since the 1920s, Blacks had not. White Southerners had been the most visible obstacle to the racial integration of schoolbook history, but the problem went deeper.

Once nativism and narrow ethnocentrism among some text writers had been tempered, White immigrants and their descendants could be mixed into preexisting storylines without undue difficulty. Authors simply emphasized some narrative elements less, and others more. Attention to the country's strictly English heritage declined while books put more stress on the ongoing creation of the national community by centuries of immigration. Stories of recent newcomers to America actually strengthened myths of the country as a land of opportunity and a refuge from political tyranny and religious intolerance, key themes in texts written in the shadow of World War II and the Cold War.

Blacks, however, presented far more difficulties. Their presence almost anywhere in the texts—from the hold of a Dutch ship selling Africans into forced labor in Virginia in 1619 to the doors of Jim Crow schools in the 1950s—cast doubt on many of the patriotically uplifting sentiments that had sustained and given meaning to the American story. It was virtually impossible to integrate them into these books without a fundamental rethinking of text content. Other nonwhites posed challenges too, of course. American Indians, the target of often openly genocidal warfare, hardly served as a testament to the benevolent course of westward expansion. Mexican-Americans, who had been incorporated into the country in 1848 and subsequently stripped of much of their lands through legal chicanery, fit awkwardly into tales of immigrant success. So did Japanese-Americans, so recently imprisoned in camps in the Western interior. Blacks, however, raised the most obstacles to authors of the 1960s, who were called to make their books better reflect the country's multiracial past. That challenge stemmed from African-Americans' status as the nation's largest racial minority, their recently awakened political power, and their critical role in virtually every aspect of the country's history.

Calls to integrate African-Americans into history textbooks stirred passions to an intensity not seen since the 1880s and 1890s, when Catholics and White Southerners began writing their own books, thereby splitting the national market. That sort of passion was especially troubling for publishers. They had worked for decades to put that market back together by painstakingly crafting a consensus version of the nation's past, one that offended the fewest people possible but tended to satisfy none completely. Over time, that strategy of harmonizing the concerns of different groups generally worked, most recently in the 1950s' blending of economic philosophies that had once divided supporters and opponents of Harold Rugg. Educational critics regularly disparaged the result as history of the lowest common denominator. But it clearly sold books, helping to make educational publishers attractive targets for corporate buyouts in the postwar years.[2] By the early 1960s, however, the consensus story and the profits it produced seemed to be on the verge of falling apart.

When Blacks in cities like Detroit demanded revisions, even cosmetic changes to existing books, they provoked a backlash among some Whites. Yet it soon became clear that conservatives could not stem the tide of racial integration in schoolbooks, but only influence how the waters would flow. The episode that most clearly revealed its new course occurred in 1966 and 1967, after California tentatively adopted the first mainstream history written expressly to include African-Americans in the national story. *Land of the Free* proved to be the most daring departure from political orthodoxy since Rugg's series Man and His Changing Society, and it soon generated controversy up and down the state. Debate over the book's proposed use in schools centered on the question of how its three writers' discussion of Black history would either support or subvert the goals of history teaching, some written directly into California law.

The contest echoed history wars of the past even as it raised new issues. Should the history of Blacks focus more on the contributions they had made to America or on the suffering they had endured? Should textbooks, in the well-worn phrase of the 1960s, "tell it like it is" even if more factual accounts of slavery and racism troubled students and teachers? Would the new history promote harmony among different racial groups in society or exacerbate discord? Would it encourage or discourage patriotism? Because these questions and their potential answers were complex, the problem of integrating history did not divide people neatly into opposing camps. Nevertheless, the debate in California came to be embodied in two very different figures. One was the state's flamboyantly conservative superintendent of public instruction, Max Rafferty, who had genuine objections to *Land of the Free* but also wanted to parlay public opposition to it into support for his own reelection and a possible run for the U.S. Senate. The other was John Hope Franklin, a respected historian, tireless advocate for frank examination of the country's racist past, and coauthor of the textbook. After months of wrangling, California officials chose a fate for *Land of the Free.* But the underlying conflict between Rafferty and Franklin could not be resolved so easily. It continued to dominate debate in the state and across the country for more than a decade, coloring decisions over what sort of texts publishers would be willing to produce and what states and cities would agree to use them. Begun amid a final dismantling of Jim Crow that has been called the Second Reconstruction, the debates recalled the history wars a century earlier that had pitted ideological allies of Thomas Wentworth Higginson and Alexander H. Stephens against each other. This time, publishers' search for balance, for a new narrative equilibrium, largely failed. By the 1980s, books had expanded dramatically in size, their running text, sidebars, questions, and activities showcasing a new interest in the previously neglected history of African-Americans. At the same time, the books had lost the confidence of their 1950s counterparts. Authors grew hesitant and unsure as they tried to tell a story that linked the experiences of all Americans or even attempted to show that Americans *were* a single people. Critics on the right were quick to blame "multiculturalism" for this new textual uncertainty. Publishers, they said, were all too willing to add historically superfluous material to appease African-Americans and a host of other groups, while the story of the nation itself withered. But that critique was, at best, only half correct. The overstuffed incoherence of these revised textbooks sometimes had less to do with what publishers were adding and more to do with what they were studiously leaving out.

African-American Protest

Detroit was a natural flash point for the emerging conflict over race and history. At the start of the 1960s, it was America's fifth-largest city, its population fed over previous decades by an expanding automobile industry in southeast Michigan that had drawn both Blacks and Whites to the region. Race relations were often tense and sometimes violent, most tragically in the wartime riots of 1943, which left twenty-five Blacks and nine Whites dead. After the war, African-Americans gained clout in city politics, a change due both to their organizational skills and to the steady exodus of Whites to Oak Park, Livonia, and other communities in the city's expanding ring of suburbs. In those trends, Detroit mimicked patterns in urban areas across the country.[3]

Among Black organizations based in the city, the Group on Advanced Leadership (GOAL), headed by Richard Henry, became especially influential over school policy.[4] GOAL members demanded that Detroit's school system become more responsive to the needs of African-Americans, citing problems with discrimination in hiring, for example, and pushing for court supervision of school desegregation. In March 1962, Henry turned his attention to the exclusion of Blacks in textbooks, which had been an issue in the city since the late 1950s. Members of the board of education expressed sympathy with GOAL's desire for texts that better reflected the city's racial diversity but argued that better books were simply not available. Members of the organization were unwilling to let the situation rest there, however. James Hurst, the chair of GOAL's Committee for Racial Justice in Curricula, demanded that Detroit issue an ultimatum—if national publishers would not provide appropriate schoolbooks, the city would find a way to produce them locally. Failure to issue an ultimatum, Hurst wrote to the board, would result in the "needless continuation of a situation in which the Negro is made to pay tax dollars for his own debasement because some publisher deems it 'too costly' or 'too much trouble' to change a few illustrations." Over the summer, the superintendent of schools, Samuel Brownell, promised to find curricular materials "more suited" to Detroit, but real progress seemed elusive.[5]

As Hurst's comments suggested, the general problem with books, from readers and geographies to histories and math texts, was the absence of Blacks. Invisibility clearly amounted to a form of debasement, but it lacked the drama to galvanize the city, especially because the problem was spread across hundreds of books used by the schools. To press their case, GOAL needed a more overtly offensive book, one that combined a general absence of African-Americans with caricatures of those that did appear. When Henry flipped through the text his son began using in his junior high history class that September, he knew he had found just the book.

The Narrative "Unravels," 1961–1985

Little about *Our United States: A Bulwark of Freedom* suggested the pivotal role it would play in this controversy. First published in 1959 by the Illinois-based firm of Laidlaw Brothers, it had three authors: Harold H. Eibling, a superintendent of schools from Ohio; Fred M. King, director of instruction for the public schools of Rochester, Minnesota; and James Harlow, a social studies teacher living in California. A typical history usually listed a professional historian among its authors, but the lack of one in the approximately seven-hundred-page *Our United States* hardly made it unique.

The one relatively unconventional feature of the text was its series of fictional sketches designed to flesh out more general historical information in the rest of the text. The book's subtitle came from a modern-day vignette in which a man, George Allen, brings his young niece and nephew on a trip to the nation's capital. Once there, they take in the sights and hear repeated affirmations about the country's democratic spirit. "A bulwark of freedom, that's what the United States is," declares Allen as he slaps a table for emphasis. "Yes, a regular bulwark of freedom. Always has been." The tome's didactic and earnestly patriotic tone was leavened occasionally by attempts at humor, as when a gruff, unnamed member of the Lewis and Clark expedition, told to make note of flora and fauna, responds "Flora and who?"[6]

African-Americans occupied little space in *Our United States.* They appeared in the book's numerous illustrations only three times, and always as slaves. Their contributions to the nation were limited mostly to music, and here the mentions were brief and, in one case, strangely decontextualized. "The lonely slaves sang what they felt in their heart," Eibling, King, and Harlow informed their readers. "Doing so, they gave us the Negro spiritual, a form of music peculiar to America. Spirituals have a quality of rhythm and melody that has made them one of the best known forms of American music."[7] That the inspiration for this music might have included more than a mysterious "loneliness," and that what slaves "felt in their hearts" might have been a bitter longing for freedom, were left unexplored.

Following the pattern set by this discussion of spirituals, the authors glossed over hardships Blacks had endured throughout American history. Slavery appeared as generally benign, and readers were asked to imagine it through the eyes of Whites, particularly slave owners. "Life in the Southern colonies was not just one big picnic; it had its serious side too," they declared. "Plantation owners had to be good managers and supervisors. They were personally responsible for the welfare of a good many human beings." They provided "all these people with the necessities of life and some of the comforts." A question at chapter's end asked students to imagine they were members of a wealthy slave-owning family that summered in Charleston. "Write a letter to a close friend of yours," the text suggested, and make "him feel the excitement of your kind of life." When the authors broached the delicate issue of the peculiar institution's unpleasantness in a short aside on *Uncle Tom's Cabin,* they retreated to qualifiers. Harriet Beecher Stowe had written about what she "*thought* must be the miserable condition of all slaves." In the chapter on Reconstruction, they made passing note of voting restrictions on Black men, some of which "are still in force," but then never returned to the subject. Only this erasure of Black experience allowed the writers to knit the American story together on the superficial "bulwark of freedom" theme.

In the book's concluding pages Eibling, King, and Harlow assured readers that the right to vote "is guaranteed to every native-born and naturalized American." Oblivious to the violence that kept Blacks from the polls in states like Mississippi until the mid-1960s, the fictional George Allen reinforces that civics lesson before departing for Washington. He tells his niece and nephew that in America "all men are equal under law." His nephew responds, "Gosh, Uncle George, you've done a lot of thinking about this!"[8]

What Richard Henry and other Detroiters would find most disturbing about *Our United States* were several pages that dealt with a fictional Tennessee plantation called Idlewild and its owners, the Austins. At the start of the Civil War, the family patriarch takes a company of slaves with him to work as laborers near the front lines. He soon dies, leaving the battle against the Yankees to his eldest son. Meanwhile, back at the plantation, the remaining Austins and their slaves scratch out a living as best they can. Some slaves run away "during the confusion and fighting" in the vicinity of Idlewild. Twenty-year-old Henry Austin longs to join the war, but a young field hand named Cicero reminds him that his dying father's wish was that Henry "stay here and take care of your mother and sister and us!" Suddenly, there is a "shriek" from Cicero: "'Master Henry,' he cried, 'The Yankees are coming!'"

Reaching the house, a Union officer questions Mrs. Austin about reports that she has been harboring Confederate soldiers, a charge she does not deny. The lieutenant gives her ten minutes to empty the house before his men burn it to the ground.

The Narrative "Unravels," 1961–1985

The Austins and their house slaves carried out the few valuables they still possessed . . . Around the corner came the other slaves—women, children, old folks, and a few young men—herded along by a squad of soldiers. The children were crying as they clung fearfully to their mothers. When they caught sight of Mrs. Austin, they broke away from the soldiers, came to her, and crouched behind her as though asking her for protection.

The officer then mounts his horse, explains why President Lincoln believes slavery is wrong, and reads the Emancipation Proclamation.

When he had finished reading the presidential order, the lieutenant folded the paper and placed it inside his tunic. To his surprise, the Austin slaves showed no joy over their new freedom. They stood still, eyeing the soldiers suspiciously. Finally Old Uncle Josephus stepped timidly forward.

"Please, sir," he said, cap in hand, "may we go back to work now?"

"Drat it, man!" the lieutenant had lost his patience. "Didn't you understand what I've just said? You're free! You can do anything you want, go anywhere you want."

Mrs. Austin intercedes, explaining in simpler language what freedom means. The slaves remain unmoved.

The passage boasts a proud mistress, marauding Yankees, and infantalized Black males ("shrieking" Cicero is actually a twenty-year-old man)—stereotypical figures that would be equally at home in *Gone with the Wind*.[9] Since the only conflict here lies between Union soldiers and Southerners, Black and White, who want to maintain the old ways of slavery, the story also robs the most pivotal moment in African-American history of any real significance.

With this account of the Austin plantation topping an indictment of the publishing industry's racial insensitivity and the city's collusion in it, the months-old push for better textbooks gained new life. The local branch of the NAACP, often at odds with the more militant members of GOAL, eagerly joined the campaign and called for an immediate withdrawal of *Our United States* from classrooms. According to an NAACP review of the book, the "image of the Negro projected by the authors is that of a dependent, servile creature" who had contributed little to the development of the country and "is incapable of functioning as a responsible person." Other objections included the book's casual approach to the early history of slavery in America, its implicit endorsement of slaveholder paternalism, and its absence of any discussion of the Black struggle for civil rights. The book was "an insult to every Negro living in Detroit," according to one NAACP official.[10]

Henry's decision to pull his son out of school drew attention to the issue, helping to land stories in several newspapers—first the Black weekly *Michigan Chronicle,* then the dailies *Detroit News* and *Detroit Free Press,* and finally the *New York Times.* The tactic also rattled school officials. Leonard Kastle, acting president of the school board, complained that Henry was "using" his son unfairly. In fact, Henry had sent Frederick back to school fairly quickly, likely to avoid prosecution, but he continued to keep him out of the history class where *Our United States* was used. On that point he remained firm. "I'll go to jail before I allow my son to return," he announced at the end of November. He also promised to enlist ten thousand of Detroit's Blacks in the cause. Despite that mounting pressure, city officials continued to oppose throwing out the book, which had been adopted only a year before. Superintendent Brownell fell back on the defense that, despite its faults, *Our United States* was still the best text available for junior high students. He exaggerated, but not by much.[11]

The Laidlaw book was the product of an ideological bargain almost all major publishers had struck with conservative Southern Whites earlier in the century. In return for Southern purchases of nationally distributed books, the firms would defer to White sensitivities on a range of issues regarding race. An unwritten system of rules nearly as complex as the Jim Crow laws themselves governed what histories, or any textbook, could present. The Civil War had to be called the "War Between the States," an endless source of frustration for grammarians because the term literally meant a conflict involving only *two* states. No African-American soldiers could be pictured or, ideally, even mentioned. Blacks could appear in illustrations with Whites, but generally only in subordinate positions. Black and White children were never to appear together. Vague pronouncements about equality and democracy of the sort *Our United States* included would pass muster with adoption committees, but direct attacks on de jure segregation would not.

When a few publishers challenged these provisions in the 1950s, they did so at their peril. In 1952, for instance, Alabama governor Gordon Persons personally intervened to block his state's adoption of *The Challenge of Democracy,* a McGraw-Hill textbook. One of the chapters of *Challenge* dealt at length with the Fair Employment Practices Commission (FEPC), a federal agency set up in 1941 to guarantee equal rights for Blacks working in factories with war contracts. The FEPC had been the brainchild of African-American labor leader A. Philip Randolph, who had forced it upon a reluctant Franklin Roosevelt only by threatening a one-hundred-thousand-man march on the capital. Discussion of the FEPC, therefore, broke several rules. It presented Blacks outside stereotypical roles; it suggested they suffered from unfair discrimination; and, most importantly, it implied the national government should intervene to advance integration. In a letter he fired off to Alabama curriculum officials after reading the book, Governor Persons wrote, "I know of no one who treasures Southern tradition who will ever agree to the break down of our segregation laws and the acceptance of the principles of the FEPC." An editor from McGraw-Hill, who apparently sped to Montgomery to save the adoption, consented to the changes the governor demanded.[12]

The FEPC virtually disappeared from history textbooks after the incident. When two publishers did dare to break the silence at the start of the 1960s, they avoided mentioning Randolph's role in creating the commission. The FEPC was just another example of the state's paternalistic concern for its nonwhite citizens. "The interest of Americans in social problems caused the government to become more sensitive to minority group problems," one book explained euphemistically, and as a result of *Roosevelt's* action "a wide range of jobs was opened to Negroes which had previously been closed to them."[13]

Because of popular prejudice and the threat of reprisals by Southern Whites, text treatment of African-Americans in the first fifteen years after World War II was therefore not much different from what it had been during the 1910s and 1920s. Popular books still condemned slavery as an economically backward institution but rarely considered its morality or examined it from the perspective of the slave. "Without making apologies for the system, one may say that on the average plantation the slaves were not harshly treated. Many of the owners were kindly, humane men," wrote Ralph Volney Harlow in the 1953 edition of *The United States: From Wilderness to World Power,* a history used at colleges and more advanced high schools. "Plantation owners" believed conditions were better for the slave than the factory worker, continued Harlow. Working outdoors was "at least healthful," especially with a restful, two-hour break at midday. Passing quickly over the issue of discipline, the writer quoted a master who gladly slaughtered twenty-eight head of cattle for his slaves' Christmas dinner. "I can do more with them [the cattle] in this way than if all the hides . . . were made into lashes," the thoughtful owner declares.[14]

The yuletide holidays also figured prominently in I. James Quillen and Edward Krug's *Living in Our America,* a junior high text also published in the early 1950s. After noting that plantation life had its "work-a-day side and its colorful side," the authors quoted extensively from a cheerful account of a Christmas celebration penned by the popular novelist and White supremacist Thomas Nelson Page. Slaves gather with the master, mistress, and their children, some of whom have been away at school. Here, even the fact of bondage is smoothed away by playful references to the busy mistress as a "slave" in her home and to her young scholars as "slaves of the school-room." A few pages later Quillen and Krug do mention in passing the few harsh masters and cruel "overseers who whipped the lazy and severely punished those who disobeyed their rules." The tension breaks quickly, however. In a sketch at chapter's end the stereotypically lazy slave is fodder for comic relief. A slim, well-dressed planter, cold drink in hand, is befuddled when he finds a barefooted field hand loafing behind a bale of cotton, strumming a banjo.[15]

Other books approached the topic more soberly but replicated *Living in Our America*'s general technique: Any discussion of cruelty would be carefully balanced with a more positive view of the institution. Brevity aided many writers, Mabel B. Casner, a teacher at a private school in Connecticut, and Ralph H. Gabriel, a professor nearby at Yale, summed up the subject of how slaves lived with essentially four sentences in their *Story of American Democracy:* "These laborers worked on the plantation fields in gangs. The planter fed, clothed, and cared for his slaves. He took care of the old people when they could no longer work. Slavery made life in the South very different from life in the North."[16]

For the era of slavery, writers rendered African-Americans as historical objects, their destiny tossed about by slave owners, abolitionists, politicians, and ultimately the Union and Confederate armies. In reporting on Reconstruction, authors altered their perspectives only slightly. Discussion about the period continued to be dominated by the work of the historian William Dunning (see chap. 4). Dunning and his followers saw Reconstruction as a "tragic era," the title of an aptly named book about the period, when the doomed but still noble social order of the South was torn asunder by bitter Republicans who gave unprepared ex-slaves the right to vote. State governments supported by Blacks and led by unscrupulous Northern carpetbaggers and their Southern-born allies, the scalawags, then plundered the war-ravaged region. According to this interpretation, the chaos ended only when a better class of Southern Whites toppled the Republican regimes, "redeemed" their state governments, and restricted the freedmen's voting and other rights. Reconstruction, according to Harlow, was thus a "farce" of "extravagance and plunder" in which Whites who paid most of the taxes "could do nothing but look on." In *The Making of Modern America,* Leon H. Canfield and Howard B. Wilder called it an era of "shameful dishonesty and misrule." Even the 1961 edition of Lewis Paul Todd and Merle Curti's *Rise of the American Nation,* which was relatively progressive on racial issues, still referred to Reconstruction as "one of the darkest chapters in the life of the nation."[17]

In popular culture, racist stereotypes tend to appear as paired opposites, and this sort of binary opposition deeply influenced how historians in the Dunning tradition depicted African-American males. They were either timid, credulous pawns of the carpetbaggers or rapacious beasts bent on seizing power and subjecting Whites, particularly women, to their domination. Both stereotypes had appeared in textbooks published since the 1890s, but the image of the predatory Black man unloosed from the social control provided by slavery receded over time. In the 1944 edition of *The United States in the Making,* readers learned that the "more vicious" freedmen became "a menace to society." In the 1958 edition of the text's successor, *The Making of Modern America,* that passage was gone, though the authors still maintained that the "attempt to force Negro rule upon the South" caused friction between the races and delayed sectional reconciliation.[18]

The elimination of one-half of a doubly negative stereotype hardly amounted to an improvement, for it led to increasingly condescending depictions of Blacks that reinforced an image of their powerlessness and incompetence. *Our United States* compared the freed slaves to children: "Suppose you were awakened from sleep tonight and told that your parents were gone and that you must look after yourself. What would you do? If you think about such a problem for a while you can better understand the biggest problem of Reconstruction."[19]

Most textbook authors in the 1950s blamed the failure of the postwar governments squarely on carpetbaggers and scalawags, since they must have been the only real actors in them. "Most of the Negroes became tools of these unscrupulous men," lamented Gertrude Hartman in *America: Land of Freedom.* "Through no fault of their own they were incapable of exercising the powers thrust upon them," agreed another author. An illustration for a third book made the point visually. It showed a crafty-looking, mustachioed politician, carpetbag at his feet and derby on his head, gesturing to two slack-jawed Black voters to sign their "X" on a ballot.[20]

The story of Reconstruction as a dreadful assault upon the rights of White citizens began to show cracks by the start of the 1960s, in part due to new scholarship and the declining influence of the Dunning school among professional historians. Some textbooks began to note achievements of the Republican governments, such as the establishment of public schools, and others discussed the terrorism the Ku Klux Klan employed to suppress the Black vote, though usually in very general terms and often with underlying sympathy for the organization's cause. "No matter how good its [the Klan's] purpose may have seemed to its members," admonished one writer, "its evil methods cannot be defended."[21] That admission was a considerable improvement over many books, which attributed the success of the Klan to its mysterious regalia and nighttime ritual, which frightened the invariably "superstitious Negroes."

Publishers still catered to conservative White Southerners, however, tossing in photographs and sidebars that extolled myths of the Lost Cause of the Confederacy, even when they strained belief. *Rise of the American Nation* extended a tribute to war hero Nathan Bedford Forrest so rich in obfuscation that it is hard to believe the book's respected authors wrote it and didn't leave that responsibility instead to an editor or consultant. Forrest "demonstrated that he could be as honorable in defeat as he had been courageous in war," claimed one passage. He told his surrendering troops in 1865: "You have been good soldiers; you can be good citizens. Obey the laws, preserve your honor." It was a curious bit of praise for Forrest, one that neglected the best-known detail of his resumé: helping to found the most infamous extralegal organization in American history. Other publishers who were less circumspect in dealing with the Klan and other elements of White Southern mythology had to pay for their indiscretion in sales. An illustration of a menacing pair of armed, hooded Klansmen in one textbook annoyed Texas critics and contributed to a largely successful effort to block use of the volume throughout the state.[22]

Their part in Reconstruction complete, African-Americans largely departed from textbooks, appearing infrequently or in awkward contexts. The authors of *Living in Our America* returned to them in passing only five more times, mostly outside the main text in recommended readings, two of which were from *Readers' Digest*. The book closed with a lukewarm defense of racial concord that managed to avoid mentioning "Negroes" by name. "Perhaps a part of the problem of race or minority-group relations will be solved by you when you are grown up," it remarked hopefully, the tone suggesting the need for reform was not too pressing. "Perhaps your children will solve part of it." *Our United States* provided about the same level of coverage, including a brief discussion of how jazz originated "with the music of the Negro" before going on to influence "serious music" by White composers like George Gershwin. Writing in the early 1960s, the authors could not avoid the *Brown vs. Board* decision of 1954 that outlawed school segregation. But the brief note of the court's ruling was rendered meaningless because the authors never explained what segregation was or how it worked.[23]

Other texts proved somewhat more forthcoming, especially when compared to *Our United States,* but they tended to obscure how African-Americans challenged segregation and racism and usually wrapped all allusions to Blacks in a reassuring narrative of progress. Historian Paul F. Boller recorded the *Brown* decision and the 1957 Civil Rights Act in *This Is Our Nation* but failed to note that political organizing in the African-American community led to both. Another book commented favorably on recent accomplishments by Blacks and mentioned their accomplishments in sports and music.[24]

The figure that epitomized the limited integration of texts at the end of the 1950s was George Washington Carver. An African-American botanist at Alabama's Tuskegee Institute known for his work with peanuts, Carver appeared in book after book. He provided a vivid example of Blacks' upward mobility along with their contributions to American life. The Carver the books portrayed was also nonthreatening to Whites. He taught and conducted research at an institution with an all-Black student body, and he was not associated with militant demands for racial equality. Photographs showed him as an elderly, amiable scientist, the happy product of Booker T. Washington's Atlanta Compromise of 1895, which linked advancement for Blacks to their disengagement from protest and politics.

Such piecemeal and stilted attempts at inclusion should not obscure the more general absence of Americans of African descent in books published before 1962. In language and illustrations, Blacks were systematically imagined out of the nation's story. In *America Is My Country,* a history used by eighth-graders in California, authors listed a series of "Documents of Freedom." They omitted the Emancipation Proclamation, the Reconstruction amendments to the Constitution, and the *Brown* ruling, all of which would have moved African-Americans toward the center of their narrative. The publisher did not even include an entry for "Negroes" in the index.[25]

At the start of the century, text writers had regularly used Blacks as foils, tools to define what Whiteness and, with it, "American-ness" meant. Most crudely offensive racial stereotypes had vanished from textbooks in all school subjects by the late 1950s, a testament to the work of the NAACP and other groups, but the pattern of racial contrasts and simultaneous exclusion from the national community continued. A telling example occurs in *Living in Our America.* One chapter contains a sketch of a formally dressed George Washington, standing erect, hands behind his back, speaking at Mount Vernon with a White groundskeeper, who is hunched over a wheelbarrow. Accompanying it is this paean to the retired president:

Men, he kept saying to himself, are free.
That is the way they are meant to be,
And the world will always remain askew
Until they are all like me and you.[26]

It would be an unsurprising, even banal instance of yet another textbook venerating the father of his country were it not for two elderly slaves, a man and a woman, standing in the background. Visually, they help center Washington in the frame. Clearly pictured, they are both seen and unseen, for the homely song of freedom clearly does not apply to them, but to Washington, the groundskeeper, and the implied White reader ("me and you"). The effect is startling to a present-day reader, and one is tempted to think the editors at Scott, Foresman, and Company intended this ironic juxtaposition of liberty and slavery. But from the context of the rest of the book, it is clear they were oblivious to the paradox. These two Black figures, strangely marooned in the illustration and surrounding text, thus stare mutely from the page like the schoolbook equivalent of the "invisible man" of Ralph Ellison's novel.

What Richard Henry and other activists in Detroit were trying to do in 1962 was to make such distortions painfully visible to school officials, publishers, and the public at large. They were not the first to try. African-American educator Edward Austin Johnson had addressed the issue as far back as the 1890s, and his calls for reform were echoed by the Association for the Study of Negro Life and History, founded in 1915 by Black historian Carter G. Woodson. African-Americans pressed for change during the 1920s, when the British conspiracy craze created a flurry of interest in history texts. In the 1930s and 1940s Charles Edward Russell continued the NAACP's program to improve schoolbooks. Much of that work was, of necessity, reactive in nature and modest in its goals—shaming publishers into removing terms like "nigger" and "darkie" from storybooks and song lyrics, for instance.[27] The blatant hypocrisy of fighting fascism abroad while permitting Jim Crow at home, discussed forcefully in Gunnar Myrdal's influential *American Dilemma* in 1944, allowed a broadening of the call for reform in the years after World War II. A milestone came in 1949 when the American Council of Education published a review of school histories that was highly critical of their portrayal of African-Americans.

In the wake of that report, New York City became a center for further challenges. In 1951 the teachers' union complained to the board of education about books that were "insulting and derogatory" to minority groups. The following year, the board responded by dropping eight books from its approved list. In 1959 it issued a statement to one hundred publishers calling for more diversity in book illustrations. Real change was stymied by at least two factors, however. The impact of reform efforts dissipated as they worked their way through the city's educational bureaucracy, legendary then and now for its inertia and byzantine complexity. A case in point: Eibling, King, and Harlow's *Our United States* clearly violated the spirit of New York's policy on minority representation in textbooks, yet it still found a place on the roster of acceptable texts when more racially inclusive alternatives were available. But the city's attempts to force change in texts during the 1950s clearly had some influence, because activists in Detroit patterned their proposed ultimatum to publishers on a similar one in New York.[28]

The more important roadblock to change remained the Southern market. Publishers had been cool to New York's 1959 call for more racially diverse schoolbooks. Representatives at some firms politely suggested that, since the city's share of the nation's school population was relatively small, more voices would have to be heard before they undertook serious revisions. Austin McCaffrey, executive secretary of the eighty-five-member American Textbook Publishers Institute (ATPI), said his organization would urge serious consideration of reform but added euphemistically that books had to go into areas of "great sensitivity." The managing director of the high school division at Prentice-Hall was slightly more direct. Taking his firm's policy of "nondiscrimination" too far, he said, would invite hostile responses in some areas. As if to prove his point, that same year the Daughters of the American Revolution (DAR) attacked forty-four schoolbooks for promoting progressive causes, with the group's Mississippi chapter especially upset by desegregation. Soon afterward, Governor Ross Barnett capitalized on the mood. Responding to calls from the DAR, the American Legion, and White Citizens Councils, Barnett took direct control of text adoption in the state, an unprecedented move even in the South. "All of us ought to be against anything in our textbooks that would teach subversion or integration," he railed. "Our children must be properly informed about the Southern and true American way of life."[29]

Events in Detroit, however, finally provided a critical mass for the kind of changes Barnett and his allies wanted to stop. Richard Henry and others applied the political pressure that kept officials in Detroit, a city with a considerably smaller school system than New York's, from either smothering the campaign with platitudes and promises of future action (although they tried) or sinking it in a bureaucratic quagmire. The Detroit activists also benefited from increasing public sympathy for their cause. The Anti-Defamation League of B'nai B'rith published another influential study of textbooks in 1961, a move emblematic of the role liberal Jews played in reforming textbooks and advancing the cause of civil rights in general. Amid the violence spawned by recent efforts to desegregate schools in the South, the study's finding that books ignored Blacks and treated racial inequality with "complacent generalizations" struck home. A headline on the editorial page of the *Detroit News* soon declared that *Our United States* was a "Bad Textbook," and the accompanying story called the fictional vignettes that gave readers the upright, slave-owning Austins "pedagogical abominations." The book, said the *News,* "manages somehow, in what it says and what it doesn't, to reinforce all the old Negro stereotypes, at best patronizing and often cruel."[30]

Detroit's board of education acknowledged the public outcry by approving plans for a supplement on Black history that would correct some of the distortions in *Our United States*. It was to be an interim measure before the city officially abandoned the book, a move that would come almost exactly a year after the protests started. Written by Detroit teachers and edited with the help of Black leaders and a scholar from Wayne State University, the fifty-two-page *Struggle for Freedom and Rights: The Negro in American History* contrasted sharply with the original textbook. In place of the politically vacuous tribute to Negro spirituals, for example, the writers explained that slaves "sang about their misery" and their desperate quest for freedom, quoting several songs to back up the claim. Elbowing out helpless Cicero and deferential Uncle Josephus, who wanted only to return to work upon hearing the news of emancipation, were dynamic historical figures—rebellion leader Nat Turner, "determined to help as many slaves as possible," and Frederick Douglass, the "great speaker" and "first-class" writer who escaped slavery in Maryland and fought for the abolitionist cause. The authors' profile of Harriet Tubman, a key figure of the Underground Railroad who packed a pistol on her raids into the South, was especially dramatic: "If any slave whom she was conducting to freedom lost his nerve, she drew her gun and said, 'You'll be free or die!'"[31]

Black leaders in Detroit generally liked what they saw. Henry pronounced himself "delighted" with the supplement. An official with the NAACP said it "seems to be a conscientious effort to set the record straight" and proclaimed it "basically a fair start" in the much larger task of integrating the American history that all students would learn in school. Detroit officials also agreed to send a letter to their text suppliers demanding schoolbooks that would "contribute significantly to understanding and good will among different racial, religious, and minority groups," thereby meeting virtually all of GOAL's demands.[32]

Publishers knew which way the wind was blowing. Large cities like Detroit, Newark, New York, and Cleveland had growing percentages of minority residents who were forming an ideological bloc with a book-buying power to rival that of White conservatives in Texas, Mississippi, and other states in the South. Publishers could delay revisions no longer. Within a year after the storm over *Our United States* began, one firm after another addressed the issue. They began internal reviews of their policies, met with educators and civil rights groups, began hiring more racially diverse staffs, and issued new statements about how African-Americans and other minorities would be treated in their curricular materials. That change came as a great relief for many editors and sales representatives, who had bitten their tongues when Southern adoption committees began interviews with questions like, "You got any niggers in your book?"[33]

Other states and cities quickly followed New York and Detroit's lead by establishing their own policies for racial diversity in textbook content. The drive to integrate the virtual world of schoolbooks, particularly those in history, began to mirror the real-world desegregation of school buildings begun in earnest with the *Brown* decision ten years earlier. Then, the Supreme Court had purposefully reached beyond narrow legal precedent, calling in social scientists to testify on the long-term effects of Jim Crow schools. In their unanimous decision, the justices declared that segregation denied Blacks equal protection of the laws and thus violated the Fourteenth Amendment. But they went on to argue that legal separation of the races in schools "generates a feeling of inferiority" that would affect African-American students' "hearts and minds in a way unlikely ever to be undone."[34]

In a parallel fashion, critics now faulted textbooks both for historical inaccuracies and, more broadly, for perpetuating that same feeling of inferiority. Citing a Philadelphia study of early childhood education, a writer for the *Negro History Bulletin* argued that textbooks had helped "to create images of Negro children which make it more difficult for them to be regarded as worthy human beings either by themselves or others." In Detroit, the NAACP claimed *Our United States* "gives little justification to the Negro child to consider himself or his heritage as worthy and significant." Forced to look elsewhere to refute the stereotypes and exclusions advanced by the book, and finding little support through the schools, "he is forced to adjust to a self-image he instinctively rejects but cannot easily invalidate." New York City's board of education called inadequate textbooks "psychologically damaging." A Black teacher in California accused history books of scarring "countless thousands," some deeply, some superficially. "The force of caricature is overwhelming," he remembered later. "Like polluted air, we inhale it without any significant conscious awareness of what is happening, or how harmful the effects may be."[35]

Many commentators moved on to the natural conclusion that racial bias in schoolbooks and the larger society were mutually reinforcing. The superintendent of schools in Berkeley, California, called texts used in his state a "perpetuating force in racial discrimination." One of the most articulate advocates of this claim was Lerone Bennett Jr., an editor at Chicago-based *Ebony* magazine. Blacks were "Orwellian nonpersons in the symbolic world projected by textbook writers," he said. "The average text does not tell these students who they are and how they got that way. It does not give them an image of their hope and of their condition. It does not corroborate their reality. They do not live in the country described in the book." For Bennett, symbolic segregation justified spatial segregation and represented another technique to exclude Blacks from American life, a claim amply supported by intense opposition to text integration in the same regions where de jure segregation had been most entrenched.[36]

Responding to the critique from Blacks, and the new threat to sales, publishers made some changes almost immediately. Dick and Jane, protagonists in the long-running elementary readers, found several new, nonwhite friends, including the African-American twins Pam and Penny. The pace of integration for history books was mixed. Short, relatively inexpensive supplementary books on Black history began to appear in significant numbers by 1965. But the standard narrative histories used by junior and senior high school students, the behemoths of the industry, took longer to retool. First to arrive were hasty revisions of long-running volumes. Though much content remained the same, writers and editors made the appropriate genuflections to the cause of racial equality and added some racially integrated photographs to the final chapters. Coverage of the postwar drive to end Jim Crow, once handled with an awkwardness that rivaled presentation of full frontal nudity in hygiene textbooks, turned into a selling point, at least in certain venues. In a February 1964 advertisement in the educational journal *Social Studies,* Houghton Mifflin touted its latest edition of *This Is America's Story* as fully up to date with the Cuban Missile Crisis, the assassination of John Kennedy, and recent "civil rights demonstrations."[37] In the cautious world of textbook publishing, that change was breathtaking.

Despite their enthusiasm, however, publishers still had not answered a nagging question. Would fully integrated texts ever sell in the South? Signs remained discouraging. Alabama segregationists fumed when they found a text showing a former secretary of state shaking hands with the president of Nigeria. Mississippi rejected an 815-page literary anthology because it contained a three-page essay by Black novelist James Baldwin. A Florida teacher had her car tires slashed and her windows chalked with warnings after she used a supplementary history that showed African-American troops battling Confederates in the Civil War. Given that environment, many publishers were glancing nervously over their shoulders to see what would happen to the first histories written from scratch after the uproar over *Our United States.* The expected showdown came not in the South but in California.[38]

The Debate over *Land of the Free*

John Hope Franklin's personal and professional lives seemed to lead inexorably to the sort of rendezvous between race and history that *Land of the Free* brought to that state. He was born in the all-Black town of Rentiesville, Oklahoma, in 1915. His family's move to Tulsa six years later was delayed by Whites who rampaged through the city's

An undated photograph shows John Hope Franklin early in his career. *Duke University Archives.*

Black neighborhood and, when its armed defenders were dead or fleeing, finished burning it to the ground. Six-year-old Franklin watched as his distraught mother waited for news of her husband, who had gone to Tulsa ahead of them. Fortunately, he was not among the dozens, perhaps hundreds of Blacks killed, the exact number concealed for decades by city officials not eager to have Tulsa known as the site

The Narrative "Unravels," 1961–1985

of the bloodiest race riot in American history. Franklin graduated from the city's segregated high school, attended Fisk University, and then began graduate studies at Harvard.[39]
Filled with a love for history, the young scholar endured numerous indignities. One of his mentors at Harvard was Samuel Eliot Morison, who fancied himself free of racial prejudice and bragged of his family's abolitionist roots. But, perhaps to prove that family history had not affected his objectivity, Morison and Henry Steele Commager began a discussion of slavery in their college textbook this way: "As for Sambo, whose wrongs moved the abolitionists to wrath and tears, there is some reason to believe that he suffered less than any other class in the South from its 'peculiar institution.'" Beginning research that would puncture the folly in such claims, Franklin found segregated state archives in the South unprepared to accommodate an African-American scholar. He had to refuse Saturday lunch dates with colleagues while working at the Library of Congress; the only nearby restaurant refused to serve Blacks. "In the face of forces that deny him membership in the mainstream of American scholarship and that suggest that he is unable to perform creditably, the task of remaining calm and objective is indeed a formidable one," Franklin wrote with characteristic reserve in "The Dilemma of the American Negro Scholar." He maintained quiet composure in public and in his professional writing but "blew off steam," as he put it, by drafting bitter essays on his experiences. He also lent his considerable talents to the cause of abolishing Jim Crow. Responding to a request by Thurgood Marshall, he coordinated historical research that the NAACP used in *Brown vs. Board.*[40]
Franklin's scholarship defied the sort of racial separation he found around him. While much of his work focused on African-Americans in the South, his goal always remained creating an interracial synthesis of regional and then national history. He studied Black history not only because it was worthwhile in its own right but also because American history made little sense without it. In his most influential early work, *From Slavery to Freedom: A History of Negro Americans,* published in 1947, he meticulously assembled and interpreted a vast body of data to show the centrality of African-Americans in the national story and to undermine racial stereotypes. He combined a celebration of Black accomplishments with a frank discussion of slavery and racism, and their negative effects on all Americans. Discussions of racial violence pervaded his work, particularly in *Reconstruction: After the Civil War,* which appeared in 1961 as the demand for integrated textbooks began to heat up. His tone was often strangely dispassionate, the better to

By the 1960s, John Hope Franklin was making history as well as writing it. Here, he joins other scholars in the celebrated civil rights march from Selma to Montgomery, Alabama, in 1965. From left to right: Franklin, Mark Haller, John Higham, Bradford Perkins, Arthur Mann, and William Leuchtenburg. Dennis Hopper, "Selma, Alabama (U.S. Historians)," 1965. Courtesy of the Artist.

conform to expectations of objectivity and to avoid charges of bias that always hovered over scholars who were not White, Protestant, and male. That stance helped to make him, as one writer has put it, the "model Negro historian for white liberals."[41]

That professional standing and, of course, Franklin's own racial background suddenly transformed him into a hot commodity among educational publishers. Reeling from attacks by African-Americans across the country, they were eager to update their books with a voice that they hoped would be both "authentic" and acceptable to most Whites. Starting a review of its textbooks in 1963, Silver, Burdett brought Franklin in as a consultant. Doubleday hired him as a general editor of Zenith Books, its new line of multiracial history supplements. Ginn and Company tapped him to help update the chapter on Reconstruction in the latest incarnation of David Saville Muzzey's history. That last task was an ironic, yet curiously appropriate role for Franklin the revisionist. When it had originally appeared in 1912, Muzzey's book was one of the most unapologetically racist ones on the market. Tamed somewhat over time, Muzzey's pen could still sting enough fifty years later to cost Ginn its contract with the schools of Washington, D.C., the situation that likely inspired the firm to update the text. Franklin was happy to oblige publishers, calling the common distortions and omissions of Blacks in texts "sinister and misleading."

Giving him his greatest potential influence on the educational market, Benziger Brothers asked Franklin to serve as one author of a new history for eighth-graders. He was joined in the venture by Ernest R. May, a diplomatic historian at Harvard, and John W. Caughey, a professor at the University of California at Los Angeles. The trio marked a sharp break from the mostly politically innocuous writers of the previous decade. In 1950, for instance, Caughey had lost his job for refusing to sign a loyalty oath (California's supreme court later reinstated him). He had also vocally championed desegregation in the public schools of Los Angeles. It was a measure of Benziger's trust in their authors, and the firm's uncertainty about the best way to navigate through the brave new world of integrated textbooks, that editors gave them uncharacteristically broad leeway in designing *Land of the Free*. "We didn't write it with some publisher looking over our shoulders saying, 'Oh, no! You can't write that,'" remarked Franklin proudly in early 1966, after they had completed what they expected to be an essentially final manuscript.[42]

When members of California's State Curriculum Commission (SCC) pored over book submissions to their offices, they noticed several qualities that distinguished *Land of the Free* from its competitors. First was the ubiquity of African-Americans in the history it told. They were no longer simply objects, but actors, particularly in the twin struggles to crush slavery and then to secure equal rights after 1865. The book's section on abolitionism noted the work of David Walker, William Wells Brown, and Sojourner Truth, while Frederick Douglass and Harriet Tubman both earned a "Stand for Freedom." That series of biographical portraits also honored more traditional figures like Thomas Jefferson and Roger Williams.

Breaking with most earlier books, Franklin, Caughey, and May discussed racial oppression in a relatively straightforward manner. They did not divorce conditions of slavery and Jim Crow from human agency, as other writers were wont to do, but showed them as part of a deliberate policy of racial exploitation initiated and supported by Whites, often through violence. From the beginning, they tackled slavery as both an economic and a moral issue. A diagram of a slave ship showed Africans "stowed away" like cargo:

> Into the cramped and stuffy space below deck, they [sailors] crowded people from many tribes. The practice was to load more than a full cargo, because it was taken for granted that many would die on the slow voyage across the Atlantic. In airless, steamy holds, jammed in with strangers, fed little, and bound with chains, these Africans made their unwilling journey to America.
>
> Once in America, the Africans went where they were forced to go. Exhibited at a market, they were sold to the highest bidder. Threats, whips, and chains made them go where the new owner wanted them to go.

Two paintings suggested the breakup of families. One depicted the African shore, where a slave trader prepared to strike a man calling forlornly to his wife and children; the other showed a slave auction in antebellum America. Careful to balance portrayals of African-Americans as victims with images of them as engineers of their own liberty, the authors and editors also included a dramatic scene painted by Eastman Johnson of a man, woman, and young child on horseback. The caption read, "Trying to make it to freedom."[43]

Day-to-day life for slaves appeared bleak in *Land of the Free*. For clothing, "no more was provided than was absolutely necessary." Housing "was poor and uncomfortable." Slaves were regularly whipped, the authors reminded readers: "The system, as Thomas Jefferson said, encouraged cruelty." Adapting some of Franklin's own research, published in *From Slavery to Freedom*, the authors disassembled the myth of the slave as carefree roustabout: "Most of the slaves endured what they had to. If they loafed on the job, it was often a form of protest. Slaves pretended to be ill and unable to work. Sometimes they destroyed tools or other property or damaged the crops. A few slaves were so desperate that they cut off their own hands or committed suicide."

The authors also made it clear that a deliberate policy of brutality and humiliation survived the collapse of slavery and reached into contemporary times. A dramatic, half-page illustration of a nighttime cross burning included the explanatory caption, "The hooded nightriders of the KKK terrified, tortured, and often killed Negroes and their white sympathizers." A chart showed how Jim Crow separated the races in schools, streetcars, bathrooms, and graveyards. Black scholar and political activist W. E. B. Du Bois now appeared alongside Booker T. Washington. In a comparison of their strategies for racial betterment, Du Bois's policy of active struggle against the White establishment clearly trumped Washington's accommodationism. In coverage of the civil rights movement of the 1950s and early 1960s, the authors also addressed the cost of that confrontational approach for Blacks and their White supporters. Peaceful protesters "drew savage resistance" not only from White Citizens Councils and the Klan but also from police and other local officials who employed "dogs, fire hoses, cattle prods, gas, whips, and clubs." Violence included the "bombing of Negro homes and churches" and the "assassinations of literally dozens of persons." Advances by minorities, Franklin, Caughey, and May reminded the reader, are "won only by continual and often painful struggle."[44]

The interracial character of the abolitionist movement, the rise of Jim Crow, the *Brown v. Board* decision, and other aspects of African-American history had often been difficult to follow in earlier texts because Blacks showed up only intermittently. *Land of the Free* not only corrected this flaw but sought to connect conditions of Blacks in the 1960s to the broad sweep of the past. Under the heading, "A present problem with ancient beginnings," two questions at the end of one chapter linked the early history of slavery under Christopher Columbus and the colonial leaders of Virginia to the recent "struggle for equal rights and fair treatment" across the United States. Again departing from earlier histories, some of the book's questions directed readers to imagine themselves as Blacks struggling for freedom or justice.[45]

Despite its candor on racial issues, the book never veered toward cynicism. The tone remained resolutely patriotic. However, the authors generally tried to direct readers' emotional loyalty toward American ideals of fair play and political equality, not merely to the state or its administrative arms. Thus the authors could be critical of police complicity with White supremacists in the South and skeptical about the disinterested virtue of national leaders. That policy applied even to the authors' heroes. "Without the demonstrations," they wrote, John Kennedy and Lyndon Johnson "might not have called so effectively" for key civil rights legislation.

A similarly critical stance also characterized other aspects of the narrative, some unrelated to domestic issues of race. The authors questioned the wisdom of using atomic weapons against Japan, for instance, and the continued testing of new bombs. They also devoted two pages to what they characterized as the judicial railroading of Nicola Sacco and Bartolomeo Vanzetti, two Italian immigrants and self-proclaimed anarchists executed for murder in Massachusetts in the 1920s.[46]

In the 1960s, Sacco and Vanzetti were heroes among liberal-left thinkers, and their appearance here pointed to the last distinguishing characteristic of *Land of the Free*—its clear tilt toward left-of-center politics. Chapters on the twentieth century celebrated the accomplishments of Democratic presidents in both text and photos, while giving comparatively little space to Republican occupants of the White House or to GOP heroes like Douglas MacArthur. Two-time Democratic presidential nominee Adlai Stevenson provided the book's epigraph. Elsewhere, readers could spot a song by folk musician Woody Guthrie and a sidebar on Rachel Carson's groundbreaking environmental volume *Silent Spring*. Caughey, perhaps remembering his own politically charged dismissal from a university post, appeared to have written much of the book's attack on Joseph McCarthy, the House Committee on Un-American Activities, and the general hunt for subversives in the 1950s. In "the name of security we tried to keep freedom bright by turning off the lights one by one," editorialized the authors.[47] The book's politics could never really be separated from its approach to race, however. Democrat Johnson received so much attention, including a page and a half for his 1965 address to Congress urging adoption of the Voting Rights Act, largely because he dedicated much of his energy in office, up to the point of *Land of the Free*'s publication, to the cause of racial equality.

From its discussion of the country's early history to its depiction of contemporary times, the authors' clear voice provided a welcome alternative to the bland pseudo-neutrality of many texts from the 1950s. But abandonment of that appearance of objectivity would eventually pose the same sort of threat to Franklin, Caughey, and May that it had to Harold Rugg.

Nevertheless, the book's new honesty in presenting African-American history must not have appeared especially risky to officials at Benziger Brothers. Their authors had crafted the book keeping in mind California's big prize—a monopoly to provide the general American history textbook used by almost every eighth-grader in the country's most populous state, a guaranteed sale of 385,000 volumes in the first year alone. And the fresh outlook Franklin and his colleagues provided was just what recent events suggested Californians wanted.[48]

Not long after GOAL and the NAACP began calling for the removal of *Our United States* from Detroit schools, the Berkeley chapter of the Congress on Racial Equality (CORE) pushed for an examination of textbooks used in the state. The result was *The Negro in American History Textbooks,* a 1964 report published by the California State Department of Education and written by a panel of distinguished historians led by Kenneth Stampp, author of a groundbreaking study of slavery, *The Peculiar Institution.* In especially scathing language, Stampp and his collaborators condemned writers and publishers for systematically excluding African-Americans from their books and demanded that Blacks appear as integral parts of any text adopted by California in the future. The state's board of education subsequently drafted criteria mandating that any approved book portray "fully, fairly and factually the role of the Negro in American history."[49] A new state law backed up the policy. Editors at Benziger, like those at all major publishers submitting texts to Sacramento, were intimately familiar with the historians' report and the new criteria. In an effort to keep even more attuned to the California market, they also brought in two editorial advisors from administrative posts in the state's schools.

When Franklin, Caughey, and May finished the manuscript, Benziger decided to market it as a consciously revisionist textbook. An advertisement praised the authors for "refusing to deal with the history of the United States as one continuous episode of progress free from mistakes and social injustice" and for "candidly treating a number of subjects which other texts desperately avoid." *Land of the Free,* it declared, showed "what can be accomplished on all levels of education if only the will and the courage are present."[50]

The strategy worked. *Land of the Free* beat out its closest competitor in early 1966 and appeared on the tentative list of approved books, beginning a process that would include public review and perhaps minor revisions. But then at a May meeting, members of the State Curriculum Commission were handed a lengthy report written by Emery Stoops, a professor of educational administration at the University of Southern California. Stoops assailed *Land of the Free* on numerous grounds, but his most incendiary charge was that the book was "slanted in the direction of civil rights . . . with high praise for militant groups and condemnation for the great majority."[51] To back up this specific critique, he pointed to the book's alleged favoritism toward the

American Civil Liberties Union and the United Nations. Nobody on the SCC could miss the racially coded language, however. The man who distributed the report, and now sat silently, was Stoops's friend and political ally, the state superintendent of public instruction.

Like John Hope Franklin, Maxwell Rafferty was a son of the South. Beyond that accident of birth, most of the similarities ended. Rafferty moved from New Orleans to Los Angeles as a boy and then graduated from Beverly Hills High School before moving on to UCLA. He majored in history, joined the UCLA Americans, a conservative organization begun to counteract what members saw as the university's left-wing atmosphere, and graduated with a C+ average. The left's threat to public education grew even more menacing for Rafferty when he decided to become a teacher and so returned to UCLA for additional coursework. He found the school of education was a "hotbed of rabid John Dewey progressivism" where he had to conform to survive. After earning his doctoral degree in 1956, he declared war on what he saw as a misguided pedagogy that was leading California and the rest of the country toward ruin. He thereby joined a decades-old crusade that had already ensnared Rugg and his books. In 1961 Rafferty became superintendent of schools in La Canada, California, after working for six years in Needles. His administrative work generally drew high marks.[52]

Before a public meeting of La Canada's school board, Rafferty delivered a speech called "The Passing of the Patriot," the most memorable of his early salvos against progressive methods and curriculum content. He and his peers "had been so busy educating for 'life adjustment' that we forgot that the first duty of a nation's schools is to preserve that nation," he proclaimed. Clarity was the greatest value in education, according to Rafferty, and it was achieved through teaching grounded in the transmission of enduring, universal values that transcended the social and intellectual upheaval he saw all around him. "With everything blurred, with nothing clear, with no positive standards, with everything in doubt," he told the board, "no wonder so many [young people] welsh out and squeal or turn traitor when confronted with the grim reality of Red military force and the crafty cunning of Red psychological warfare."[53]

The superintendent drew his inspiration from many sources at or near the political fringe, including a book suggesting that biased history texts had rendered American prisoners of war in Korea susceptible to brainwashing.[54] Adapted into an essay for *Readers' Digest,* the speech endeared Rafferty to the state's right wing, which backed his run for the nominally nonpartisan post of state superintendent in 1962. Rafferty was a skilled campaigner. He knew how to use his brand of nostalgic populism to paint his opponent, a college professor, as a creature of the educational establishment. "Max was a spellbinder of a speaker," remembered his campaign director, "a rootin', tootin', hot dogs and ice cream, bunting and the flag kind of speaker."[55] Rafferty won the election by a slim margin. That was no mean feat in 1962, when California's leading Republican, former vice president Richard Nixon, lost the race for governor.

Once in office, Rafferty continued to expound his educational philosophy in a syndicated column and a series of books. For those who looked closely, that philosophy must have seemed fated to clash with the calls for textbook reform emanating from New York, Detroit, and now California itself. Rafferty believed that history teaching existed to cultivate patriotism. If some new element of the curriculum threatened that goal, it had to go. The debunking of historical myths or premature attempts to furnish young people with painful truths could not be countenanced. "Balancing virtues with vices, belittling the heroes, dwelling unduly upon the scandals of the past," he wrote, "these are the techniques that produce in the minds of the children a balanced, bland, tasteless, lifeless image of their country, and all in the sacred name of objectivity."[56] Impartiality was a sacred goal to a scholar like Franklin, who even fretted that his work for the *Brown* case might have compromised his scholarly detachment. For ex–history major Rafferty, it was a dangerous interloper in the curriculum.

In defining the content of history teaching, Rafferty drifted between the irreconcilable positions of stern disciplinarian and hopeless romantic.[57] History was at times a collection of undisputed facts that a student must learn and be able to assemble chronologically on command. History in that sense was like Latin grammar, which the superintendent prized as an emblem of order. Rafferty tended to champion "factual" history whenever he wanted to condemn its troubling cognitive cousin, "interpretive" history, which biased historians were always trying to sneak into schools. Despite that tough posturing over a just-the-facts approach, he actually prized a far more colorful version of the past populated by larger-than-life heroes engaged in dramatic adventures, like the Crusades. What constituted this nation's history? Rafferty answered that question in his 1965 book *What They Are Doing to Your Children*. It was

Lawrence carried dying from his shattered deck, rallying long enough to give the United States Navy its deathless slogan: "Don't give up the ship!"; Sam Houston at San Jacinto, reminding enemies for all time to come that Americans would forget attempts to enslave them only when Texans forgot the Alamo—these and a hundred more great stories cluster about our history, bulwarking and supporting it, mingling in a Red, White, and Blue mist, clamorous with voices out of our past, dramatizing American history and American institutions so that wide-eyed children will always remember.[58]

In his sentimentalized view of history, Rafferty resembled "patriotic" critics of the New History in the 1920s or, further back, nineteenth-century textbook authors such as Emma Willard and Charles A. Goodrich. Unlike many of those writers, Rafferty did not have a vision of American history, or the American nation, defined by race, at least overtly. After his advisor Emery Stoops attacked *Land of the Free,* the *San Francisco Chronicle* ran a cartoon of Rafferty as a medieval bookburner, his ample girth somewhat exaggerated, dancing about around a pyre where copies of the textbook burned (see fig. on p. 297). His caption read, "It's slanted toward CIVIL RIGHTS!" The lampoon captured some of Rafferty's personality—in 1963 he had led an assault on the *Dictionary of American Slang,* calling it a "practicing handbook of sexual perversion."[59] But as the cartoon imagined him as an opponent of racial integration, suggesting ideological kinship with Ross Barnett or Alabama governor George Wallace, who had personally interposed himself in a building doorway to block desegregation of his state's university, the *Chronicle* missed the mark.

Rafferty once wrote that schools need to inculcate into the "hearts and minds" of students the importance of "American principles of tolerance and equality of opportunity." He usually stood by that position. In his capacity as state superintendent, he had written a positive foreword to the 1964 report *The Negro in American History Textbooks.* Despite his many political differences with the authors, and scholars in the University of California system in general, he genuinely supported the panel's calls for greater representation of racial minorities in schoolbooks. Several months before the report was released, Rafferty had even met with leading publishers to address the problem. When a curious state legislator asked him about the meeting's agenda, Rafferty responded with a thoughtful letter noting the flaws in a typical history text: "Nowhere in the book are there any pictures of modern Negroes except on postage stamps or in the single person of the great vocalist, Marian Anderson. There are no mixed groups of Negroes and Caucasians shown. No mention is made of great Negro figures in our past." As the state's leading educational administrator, Rafferty appointed Blacks to senior policy-making positions.[60] He also worked closely with Ruth Howard, the first African-American to serve on the SCC.

Early in Rafferty's administration, race remained a quietly simmering issue in California's educational politics. Before 1965, most Whites in the state could tell themselves that the civil rights movement and the racial unrest associated with it were a drama unfolding back east. The morality tale pitted reactionary, mostly working-class Whites against well-dressed, nonviolent protesters epitomized by Martin Luther King Jr. Television images from Little Rock, Selma, and Montgomery helped to simplify and regionalize the story, masking its complexity and national dimensions. So when Congress passed the Civil Rights Act of 1964 and the Voting Rights Act of 1965, effectively ending de jure segregation, that story was supposed to come to a close, too. But it failed to do so, most vividly on the streets of the Watts section of Los Angeles. In August 1965 Black rioting left thirty-four people dead and approximately one thousand buildings damaged or destroyed. For many African-Americans, the violence signified ongoing frustrations over poverty, housing discrimination, and police brutality. For many heretofore moderate Whites, ominous images of Black men hurling stones and bricks while torching White-owned businesses suggested senseless violence. For Californians of all racial backgrounds, events in Watts called into question the apparent progress the nation had been making in race relations.

The violence made the cause of integrating textbooks look both more pressing and, in some ways, irrelevant. Nobody experienced the paradox more acutely than Mervyn M. Dymally. Dymally was a former fifth-grade teacher, and like many African-American educators, he had experienced frustration with his lily-white textbooks. When he gained a seat in the state legislature, he introduced a bill requiring that all history books used in California schools correctly portray Black history. The bill went down to defeat in 1963. But Dymally, who had campaigned for Kennedy in 1960, knew how to work the system. He met with school boards, civic groups, the state's board of education, and other legislators to build support for the measure. He reintroduced it as Assembly Bill 580 in January 1965. Six months later, Governor Edmund G. Brown signed the bill into law, a tribute to the ex-teacher's

California state superintendent of public instruction Maxwell Rafferty in an official photograph and as imagined by a cartoonist for the *San Francisco Chronicle* in 1966 (see pg. 297), as the battle over *Land of the Free* began. *Photograph courtesy of California History Room, California State Library, Sacramento, California. Cartoon © San Francisco Chronicle. Reprinted by permission.*

"It's slanted toward CIVIL RIGHTS!"

persistence. But only a month later, Dymally found himself on the streets of Watts, urging his constituents to keep calm. One man held out a bottle and told him, "If you're with the people, throw it."[61]

Like Dymally, Rafferty was an elected official intimately involved with the cause of textbooks and race. He, too, sensed a sudden shift in Californians' attitudes. In the spring of 1966 he must also have grasped how a campaign against *Land of the Free,* the country's first widely distributed history text to integrate African-Americans, could rally his conservative base and exploit the heightened anxieties of White voters he needed for reelection in the fall. That's not to suggest that the superintendent did not have real objections to the book's content, many unrelated to race. He did. But he was also shrewd enough to exploit the political opportunity.

Soon after presenting Stoops's critique to the SCC, Rafferty and his conservative allies were plotting ways to keep the textbook issue before voters for months, in newspapers and on television and talk radio. They would succeed in that scheme by short-circuiting the state's usual adoption procedures. Typically, the curriculum commission, whose members were appointed by the board of education, handled selection of texts for students in grades one through eight. The SCC then divided that task among subcommittees that often called in consultants. Their decisions then funneled upward to the commission as a whole, which assembled an initial list of approved texts. Copies of those books then went on display at public libraries across the state, allowing a chance for commentary and feedback. In some cases, minor revisions to the texts followed. Finally, the state board, which had ultimate authority over adoptions, signed off on the SCC's decisions.

After Stoops attacked *Land of the Free,* the commission reaffirmed its choice of the book even as members argued some revisions were needed. The state board appeared to stand by the commission but, in fact, undercut its authority by calling for an outside panel of historians to examine the text. The issue became steadily more embroiled in politics. Conservative members in the legislature threatened to block any funds for purchase of the book. Engaging in a similar tactic, Rafferty vowed to ask the governor, Ronald Reagan, to withhold funds for distributing *Land of the Free* unless Franklin, Caughey, and May made substantial changes.[62] Letters on the issue steadily piled up in the superintendent's office. Those letters, along with official correspondence, statements by Rafferty, the report of the historians' panel, and accounts in the press, provide a vivid account of how Californians wrestled with the idea of racially integrated history.

Charges leveled at the book varied. Some critics generally ignored race and focused on the alleged leftist bias of the book. Writer after writer condemned the authors for including several lines from the antinuclear folk song "What Have They Done to the Rain?" Many condemned the book because it had received positive notice in *People's World,* a communist newspaper. But much of the commentary returned, in one form or another, to race. A few critics expressed a visceral Negrophobia, an aversion to any kind of textual integration more characteristic of reactionary thought in the South. One group pointedly referred to Franklin as a "Negro professor," a designation meant to undercut his legitimacy. Its members also accused Allan Nevins, a historian who had had no role in writing the book but did serve on the state-appointed panel reviewing it, of favoring miscegenation. Revulsion over racial mixing also surfaced in a letter by a woman upset with *Land of the Free*'s praise for Reconstruction "Radical" Thaddeus Stevens, a villain in most histories published before the 1960s. Franklin and his coauthors had noted that Stevens, a White champion of civil rights, chose to be buried in a Black cemetery. "His mulatto mistress lived with him," the woman argued. "Where else would she bury him than in a Negro cemetery?" Stevens, she added, was a "scourge of humanity."[63] Rafferty did not share these extremist views, but he was not above capitalizing on them. In some of his public statements nominally about other issues, like the authors' treatment of American imperialism, listeners could easily choose to hear a validation of their racial prejudices. "I guess I'm getting just a little tired of today's historians second-guessing the past instead of just telling us what happened," he told attendees at a luncheon in August, three months before the election. "So we sent Marines to Haiti forty years ago to keep the voodooistic islanders from butchering one another. . . . You don't have to tut-tut loftily about gunboat diplomacy."[64]

Many critics argued that while including more African-American history in textbooks was fine, Franklin, Caughey, and May had done so in an unnecessarily gloomy, unpatriotic way. It was one of the most common complaints about *Land of the Free*. In the end, it would become the most powerful one. "Almost every other page deals with slavery," lamented one critic. "With the constant hammering about 'slavery' the authors are imbued with the importance of 'beating a dead horse.' Surely there are authors in this great land who are capable of writing a reliable . . . text that will include the great and heroic events [and] 'play fair' with the founding fathers."[65]

Others agreed that the sort of Black history Franklin and his coauthors presented maligned American heroes. One letter writer wanted the book to show that many prominent slaveholders, among them Washington and George Mason, also opposed the institution. "Isn't the main theme of this book Negro slavery?" she asked. "If so, the efforts of these three men might have been included." Another wanted a note of efforts to end slavery at the Constitutional Convention. Some critics thought it unfortunate that Patrick Henry's exhortation "Give me liberty or give me death" ended up buried in an excerpt from LBJ's address on civil rights. The members of the self-styled Land-of-the-Free Committee thought Johnson's speech ended the book on a "sour note." While some of the complaints were simply incorrect—Patrick Henry's aphorism also appeared, right on cue, in coverage of the Revolution—the underlying problem they addressed seemed quite real to the critics. "The entire feeling of this book is that of the complete injustice of the white race toward the negro," concluded one reviewer. A writer from Van Nuys did not like the series of sidebars that featured many African-Americans: "In what are titled 'Stands for Freedom,' glaring inferences [*sic*] lead the reader to believe that our society is less than a desirable one."[66]

For many, the problem with the book was that Franklin and his colleagues had simply profiled the *wrong* Blacks. The authors had chosen "negative thought models," which essentially meant people who fought racial injustice publicly. One was Martin Luther King Jr., "too widely known to need comment," and another Rosa Parks, who had "instigated" the Montgomery bus boycott. What had happened, asked a correspondent, to Booker T. Washington (now overshadowed by DuBois) and George Washington Carver, those standbys from 1950s texts? Even a relatively "safe" figure could still offend some people. Crispus Attucks was a well-known Revolutionary-era hero who faced down British troops in the Boston Massacre of 1770. He had appeared in a few texts before 1960 and was fast becoming a standard character. But in the aftermath of Watts, some Californians seemed to think Attucks looked a little too much like just another disaffected Black man in the city with a grudge against the authorities. He would be better "listed as a rabble rouser than patriot," one claimed. Many critics longed for apolitical African-American figures, or at least ones that could be depoliticized before insertion into the text. John Collier, a member of the state legislature who tried to block funding for the book, alleged that it was "slanted to talk about the political philosophy of minority races. It doesn't even mention the Negro sports heroes, and I resent this."[67]

Discussion of the violence used to maintain slavery and segregation was especially troublesome. One couple objected to an illustration of a whip-wielding overseer looming over a group of slaves. That scene, agreed another critic, "is not typical, is very exaggerated and gives a wrong impression. Delete it as bias." Others did not want the book's authors to claim that the campaign for civil rights had drawn "savage resistance" in the South. Stoops praised the runner-up for adoption, Houghton Mifflin's *This Is America's Story,* for its "objective reporting of what took place in Negro demonstrations," implying that *Land of the Free*'s approach was both inaccurate and inflammatory. Many critics thought that the book would needlessly burden young readers with a sense of responsibility for errors made long ago in the national past. The board of education in one county condemned the book in the thinly veiled language of race. "It's designed to build up a segment of the country at the expense of the rest of the country," members argued, "like they are trying to instill a guilt complex in us."[68]

The Narrative "Unravels," 1961-1985

Rafferty emerged as the most forceful exponent of this conservative view. History should be multiracial, he argued, but authors must try to accentuate the positive in their discussions of Blacks. In 1964 Kenneth Stampp and the other authors of *The Negro in American History Textbooks* had condemned accounts of the past that denied the "obvious deprivation" suffered by African-Americans. Rafferty had signed the report, but it did not reflect his views on this point. He wanted that deprivation hidden. "Don't keep hitting Negro children with their menial background," he advised Franklin and his colleagues, completely misinterpreting their aims. In a subtitle to the chapter on Reconstruction, the authors had written, "The Union is restored, and with it white supremacy." Rafferty wanted to delete the second half. He admonished the authors to just "write history and let the student make the judgment."[69]

At the start of a chapter on the antebellum period, *Land of the Free* included a full-page illustration with an outline map of the eastern United States (see fig. on p. 302). In the North lay a factory and a railroad, and in the South a plantation house. Superimposed on each section were images of children. In the North a group of White girls and boys were playing, while in the South a barefooted Black boy, obviously a slave, sat alone. The montage suggested how racial, economic, and cultural differences divided the country in the years *before* the Civil War. Rafferty would have none of it. He demanded that the publisher omit the picture "or incorporate this Negro child into the group. Don't suggest isolation and segregation because of color—defeats purpose of the book."[70]

Rafferty was thus guilty of the same offense that he generally blamed on leftist historians: deciding what ideological goal teaching should serve and then manipulating accounts of the past to further it. And what was the purpose of the book, according to Rafferty? Apparently, it should have aided the cause of integration by offering an idealized, post-*Brown* America of racial harmony and then, as much as possible, projecting that view onto the past.

Rafferty's ideas for improving *Land of the Free* contradicted other aspects of his educational philosophy as well. "Progressivism," he once argued, had bowdlerized the traditional classics read in schools, the better to serve the cause of "life adjustment" and intergroup harmony. "The results of this organized effort to create a brave new world of togetherness by filling children's minds with mush and pap are oftimes calculated to make the angels weep," Rafferty claimed in his syndicated column a few months before the textbook controversy began.

18. Section against Section

The nation is hopelessly divided

"We are not enemies, but friends. We must not be enemies."

ABRAHAM LINCOLN
First Inaugural Address

316

An illustration from *Land of the Free* that rankled Superintendent Rafferty. *From* Land of the Free, *by John W. Caughey, John Hope Franklin, and Ernest R. May (New York: Benziger Brothers, 1966). Reproduced with permission of Glencoe/McGraw-Hill.*

Yet he now wanted to drain the textbook of the moral and physical strife surrounding race so that students would be left with that same image of "togetherness." Conflict was fine in American history as long as it involved battles with outsiders. Thus Rafferty wanted more coverage of the Battle of the Alamo, where the opponents were Mexicans. But now that the textbook had incorporated African-Americans into the nation, patriotism required that conflicts between Blacks and Whites be concealed.

That kind of historical repression came naturally to the superintendent, whose ability to block out the unpleasantness of race relations in America transcended the apparent cynicism of his effort to censor Franklin's textbook. Elsewhere in his calls to get school curricula "back to basics" and to ground teaching in Judeo-Christian values, he championed what he characterized as traditional, reassuring literature, such as *The Wizard of Oz,* in which "Dorothy skipped arm in arm with the Scarecrow down the yellow brick road," and *Huckleberry Finn,* where a "battered raft floated to immortality upon the broad bosom of the Father of Waters, and Huck became the apotheosis of all boys everywhere." That Twain's novel was a complex work that also involved "Nigger Jim," Huck's awakening to the humanity of African-Americans that his fellow Whites denied, and a bitter denunciation of Christian hypocrisy in supporting slavery seemed, quite genuinely, lost on Rafferty.[71]

Conservative attacks on *Land of the Free* did not go unchallenged. Historians, teachers, and civil rights groups rallied to the defense of Franklin, Caughey, and May. The history professors whom the state asked to examine the book disagreed with the authors on some issues but strongly backed their overall approach, particularly their inclusion of the "violent antagonisms that stud our record." A "realistic rendering of the national experience, both pluses and minuses," would provide a "sounder basis for loyal and effective citizenship," they concluded. The book's portrayal of African-Americans had seemed "disconcertingly novel" to some Californians, the historians surmised, because that group had been ignored by texts in the past.[72]

Others agreed that undue frankness did not mar the book, directly contradicting Rafferty's claims. An eighth-grade teacher from Orangevale recounted her frustration with history books that led her students to claim that Blacks had been better off under slavery than freedom because they had been better fed and housed. Honest "presentation of issues like slavery," she wrote, "does not demean the American experience, but rather enhances the story of the extension of

303

freedom and democracy that is our true history." The president of the California Council for the Social Studies, which represented approximately two thousand teachers, called the book a "milestone" in the "battle for reality" in the state's classrooms. In a presentation before the state's board of education in May, a representative of the United Civil Rights Council praised the racially integrated authorship and content of *Land of the Free*. "Negro Americans for, lo, these hundred years have sought in vain to hear some faint echo of their achievement mentioned in the text books of the public schools," read the council's official statement. "Twenty million Americans wait with confident expectancy your adoption of this text."[73]

Recent events in Watts, along with other racial unrest in the state, affected the way both opponents and supporters looked at *Land of the Free*. But where critics argued that the book would create a "climate of hatred" and "add to the racial fire rather than heal it," others saw just the opposite. One writer thought it would aid the cause of "mutual understanding." A White woman from Los Angeles cited the "rewarding but far from troublefree lesson" she and her neighbors had learned about racial integration:

> We are confident that in the reasonably near future this lesson will have to be learned by many, many more Americans and we are certain that it will be less painful than ours if all American children are better taught about the contributions all people have made to the development of our nation. Respect for others and self-respect are very important foundations for understanding.[74]

The battle over *Land of the Free* thus revealed two very different programs for integrating American history. One tilted toward Franklin. His life had been defined in large part by race, from his experience in the segregated public facilities of Oklahoma in the 1920s to his sudden cachet among educational publishers seeking to conciliate Blacks they had so long neglected. He favored a rendering of African-American history for schools that reflected his own life's balance of oppression and accomplishment. It would also exhibit the essential qualities of his professional scholarship and public persona—measured, balanced, free from invective but always forthcoming. Franklin's supporters believed such a history would force young people to confront the troubled legacy in their country's past and, to paraphrase King, better live out the meaning of America's creed of equality and justice.

Rafferty, who in his brashness and indifference to historical objectivity often appeared the antithesis of Franklin, wanted students to forego much of that introspection and historical analysis. Schools were not the place for a candid discussion of current social problems or an exploration of their origins in the past. They existed, as he declared before becoming superintendent, to "preserve the nation" by celebrating its virtues. What Rafferty wanted was not history, but escape from it. He offered a comforting alternative to the burdens of the past that White Americans seemed to confront each time they turned on their television news or, windows rolled up and doors locked, drove through their inner cities. In return for jettisoning the past and its obligations, he and they would offer support for the current integration of schoolbooks and, perhaps, neighborhoods as well. One critic of *Land of the Free* neatly summed up that enlightened view. "I am particularly concerned with improving race relations," she wrote. "But I do not think it can be done by stirring up past injustices, or by repetition of the theme of the downtrodden negro." Here was an appealing vision for many Whites who wanted to see themselves as basically decent people free from prejudice. In time even some Blacks would be drawn to it. It was destined to be far more influential on textbook publishing than the knee-jerk racism represented by people like Ross Barnett, whose takeover of text selection in Mississippi was mostly a political stunt. Rafferty, to his credit, effectively communicated this new social contract, offering a selectively forgetful history as a moral salve to voters. In 1962 he had eked out a narrow election victory. Four years later, with debate over *Land of the Free* defining him politically, he won in a landslide.[75]

Franklin claimed his own victory. He, Caughey, and May won adoption without making many substantive changes to the book, and virtually none regarding race. But his historical outlook would not come to dominate subsequent textbooks. Neither would Rafferty's.

Half-Told History

When the Pacific Coast manager of Houghton Mifflin wrote to Rafferty in 1964 to publicize the recent revision of a history text, he pointed out that his company "subscribes to the principle that textbooks play a unique role in helping to unify the nation." All major educational publishers shared that outlook, which had not changed much since the mid–nineteenth century. But in the late summer of 1966 the furor over *Land of the Free* suggested that single textbooks might not be able to fulfill that role any longer. The first of the truly integrated histories had not only divided California; in a quieter way, it had split the country. Many large cities, particularly Northeastern and Midwestern ones like Cleveland, Philadelphia, Kansas City, and Milwaukee, had purchased the text. [76] But Southern states generally ignored it. That pattern suggested that the ongoing attempt to incorporate African-Americans and other minorities into books would divide the national market, just as many publishing executives had feared. As the conflict in California began to wind down, Congress addressed this issue in an unprecedented series of hearings.

The House inquiry into "Books for Schools and the Treatment of Minorities" was the brainchild of Adam Clayton Powell Jr., the combative and outspoken representative from Harlem. Powell had earned the moniker Mr. Civil Rights in Washington, particularly for his devotion during the 1950s to the so-called Powell Amendment. This plan to bar the transfer of federal funds to segregated schools was a political dead letter, but Powell, oblivious to defeat, kept introducing it anyway. By the mid-1960s, however, his fortunes had changed. The bill had effectively become law through the Civil Rights Act of 1964, and Powell was now chair of the House Committee on Education and Labor. Like many civil rights activists of the era, Powell had broadened his interest from the desegregation of schools to the integration of textbooks. In 1964 he called on the Office of Education to survey "curriculum materials" to see how, or even if, Blacks appeared. What soon made Powell's interest more than idle curiosity was passage of the Elementary and Secondary Education Act, which slotted over four hundred million dollars for state and local purchases of texts and library books.[77]

By the start of the hearings in late August 1966, Harlem's representative was musing about plans to extend a sort of Powell Amendment to schoolbooks, apportioning federal money to buy those deemed racially integrated but denying it for others. That threat would later turn out to be a bluff, but it still brought a parade of earnest publishers and appropriately deferential state and local officials to Washington. Anxious about federal intervention, they were eager to show that the integration of schoolbooks was proceeding smoothly, a fiction belied by the well-publicized fracas in California.

Aside from *Land of the Free,* the clearest evidence that text revisions were splitting the national market was the rise of "dual editions" since the early 1960s. These were alternate versions of readers, math texts, histories, and other books—one with Blacks and other racial minorities, one without. Dual editions, sometimes called star editions or, more colorfully, mint-julep editions to indicate their Southern origins, were an open secret in the industry. Publishers resorted to them because they found it impossible to reconcile the preferences of adoption committees in Cleveland and Detroit with those in Texas and Alabama. Scott, Foresman, for example, published a fourth-grade reader with a story about the African-American scientist Benjamin Banneker and a sixth-grade one with information on the slave trade; the star editions lacked them. But because buyers wanted to use the one, *national* version of the book, publishers often concealed the existence of dual editions in their catalogs. Then representatives simply presented only the version they assumed an individual state or city would want. The deception often worked well, at least until someone confused the copies, as happened when one firm inadvertently sent both editions to an NAACP member.[78]

Asked by members of Powell's committee about dual editions, some publishers sounded a bit like Claude Raines in *Casablanca.* They were shocked—*shocked!*—to learn that some firms would cater to racists by producing all-White versions of texts. Or, if not quite shocked, at least appropriately dismayed. All disavowed the practice. In a statement to the committee, Cameron Moseley, vice president of Harcourt, Brace and World, said his company had been forthright in discussing race relations in its social studies texts, especially since the *Brown* decision of 1954. Not only had the publisher "not made a practice of issuing separate editions of the same work," it had found adoption committees wonderfully receptive to the new titles. Not one, he said, "has ever informed us that our textbooks would not be considered because of multi-racial references in their content or illustrations."[79]

But, speaking with a reporter from the *Wall Street Journal* a year before, Moseley had told a different story. Officials in one Southern state had approved a new series of grammar and composition books and then grown enraged when they found illustrations of Black and White children playing together. "There was an unofficial, implied threat to cancel all our contracts in the state, not just for that series," Moseley remembered. Harcourt then went through the time and expense to produce a "deintegrated" version of the text. "It seems economically sensible as well as culturally desirable to have a single edition for the entire country," he told the *Journal.* "But the bigger the stakes, the more feasible a special edition becomes."[80]

Nobody on the committee questioned Moseley about this contra diction, though the *Journal* article was reprinted in the official House report on the hearings, and some members or their aides must have been aware of it. For the most part, the hearings steered clear of the truly contentious issues, whether in textbooks or the real world. Representative Roman Pucinski opened the inquiry with an earnest call for racial integration—in history books, anyway. As Chicago mayor Richard Daley's point man in Washington, Pucinski was also fighting a plan to cut off federal aid to Chicago schools, a rather drastic tactic some Johnson officials were considering to force the city to make an honest effort to overcome entrenched segregation.[81] After Pucinsk finished his self-serving homily about integrating history books, Powell tossed back a comment about racial tensions in Illinois. But Harlem's representative, embroiled in widening scandals that would soon end his tenure in the House, did not push the issue further.

Pressed gently on the question of dual editions, publishers did admit that older versions and newer, integrated books were being sold simultaneously, according to contracts negotiated with individual districts Thus a state like Texas might have adopted an all-White civics book in 1963 and kept receiving it for years afterward, even after a publisher had officially replaced it. Company representatives assured the committee that these old editions, star editions in all but name, would be retired as soon as the contracts expired. But completing that process in some cases might have taken six to eight years.

Compared with home economics or math texts, history books never made attractive candidates for dual editions. Histories are sold like newspapers, with only the latest edition retaining much value. Publishers typically hold publication, for instance, to squeeze in results of the latest presidential election. Hoping to sell a text five years out of date was impractical. So was tinkering with content to produce two concurrent editions. Why? In a literary anthology, editors could shuffle one or two contributions by Black authors with pieces by Whites fairly easily. But in a more fully integrated history like *Land of the Free,* where information on African-Americans was embedded throughout the text and not confined to separate chapters, tinkering with content to produce another edition was impossible. Preparing second editions of such books for the South would require writing essentially all-new ones, and that meant returning to the expensive and cumbersome split-market policies that publishers had been forced to adopt at the end of the nineteenth century.

That approach had been mostly relegated to the past by the 1960s, but not entirely. In the same year that members of Congress expressed deep concern over the prospect of breakaway texts for Dixie, Laidlaw Brothers, publishers of the much maligned and quickly revised *Our United States,* released a separate history for Catholic eighth-graders.[82] It was a measure of how seamlessly immigrant Catholics and their descendants had been integrated into the national fabric, in contrast to African-Americans of all faiths, that this book and others like it, which might have been perceived as threats to a nationally unifying history, never raised an eyebrow among members of Powell's committee.

A more likely impediment to the complete racial integration of history books was the proliferation of supplementary texts on African-American history. That subject received attention before, during, and after the congressional hearings. Supplementary books were nothing new. Edward Austin Johnson's *School History of the Negro Race in America* had appeared in the 1890s. In the 1930s, African-American educator Merle Eppse also wrote supplementary books, the best known of which, *The Negro, Too, in American History,* was used in some Black schools in the South and several cities in the North, including Chicago and Philadelphia.[83] A few cities also produced their own supplements. The market for such books expanded dramatically after Detroit's battle over *Our United States* began in 1962, however, as frustrations over racial exclusion in general histories finally forced publishers to act. It expanded further in the middle of the decade when the federal government provided funds for local schools to purchase the new multiracial books.

For those people still committed to the idea that Americans of all racial backgrounds should be choosing from a common set of schoolbooks, there were two ways to look at supplementary texts. They might be the first step in bringing Black history to students of color, and to at least some Whites, while allowing publishers sufficient time to write new narrative histories that more fully incorporated Americans of African descent. "Supplements are the bridge," claimed Wyatt Tee Walker, publisher of the Negro Heritage Library, which included titles like *Profiles of Negro Womanhood.* "I keep saying 'Freedom Now,' but I know in my heart it can't be freedom now. It'll be ten years before we have fully integrated textbooks," he argued in early 1966.[84]

The other way to view these texts was as a diversion, one that relieved pressures on publishers of more general books and kept African-American history out of White students' hands. There was considerable evidence for that theory. When Mississippi educators affirmed their commitment to using multiracial books, they presented

Powell's committee with an official statement listing titles "for" minority groups. In California, Rafferty advisor Emery Stoops had attacked *Land of the Free* for allegedly grievous errors and distortions. But then, revealing his underlying aims, he suggested it would still be perfectly acceptable as a supplemental book, purchased by the state in smaller numbers and likely targeted primarily to districts with a high percentage of African-American students. As far back as Detroit's publication of *The Struggle for Freedom and Rights*, some people feared that Black history not presented in standard books would be seen as peripheral to "real" American history. A writer for the *Saturday Review* worried that supplemental books might represent the same "separate but equal doctrine" in a new guise.[85]

The rise of Black studies courses in the mid-1960s, accompanied in some quarters by a more militantly separatist philosophy of education, did lessen the sense of urgency publishers experienced as they grappled with how to incorporate the African-American past in full-length national histories. Teachers in these courses relied more on supplemental books and often openly disdained traditional histories, which they saw as impervious to real change and mostly irrelevant to their needs. In one New York class, for instance, students took out the larger books only to study examples of bias and propaganda, a teaching method that actually worked best with tomes like the 1962 edition of *Our United States*.[86]

Supplemental books and, to a lesser extent, dual editions deflected some pressure for reform, but the push to revise national histories continued. However, it never completely split the market for those books along racial or geographic lines, as other forces had done eighty years before—no firm ever marketed *A History of the United States Prepared for African-Americans*, for instance. That breakup was averted in large part through the efforts of Blacks in the South. With official political power guaranteed by the Voting Rights Act, they demanded, and got, more inclusive books, ending several states' status as bastions of the all-White text. In the fifteen years after the release of *Land of the Free*, publishers steadily integrated their books, at least on a quantitative level, as a cursory examination of the mounting index references to "Negroes," "Blacks," and, in the 1980s, "African-Americans" attests. But producers of the most popular histories never resolved the question of how to do so—in the mold of conservatives like Rafferty, or in the more unsparing, intellectually honest style of Franklin? They opted for a muddled version that split the difference, offering enough Black history to make students question the simpler patriotic themes that structured most books before 1960, but not enough to establish a newer, more credible synthesis. In other words, the market for texts held together, but the story they told began to fall apart.

The least controversial and thus most popular means to include more African-Americans was through the "contributions" narrative. Authors spliced Black men and women into a preexisting storyline without significantly disrupting it, much like publishers had done in the early twentieth century when they began giving more attention to White ethnics. By the late 1950s, the contributions approach was already gaining popularity. When Henry W. Bragdon began work on his long-running *History of a Free People,* his editor advised him that the final book had to mention both Haym Saloman, a Jewish hero of the Revolution, and Crispus Attucks, a Black counterpart. When states and cities began drafting racially inclusive criteria for book selection after 1962, they frequently employed the language of contributions. The Michigan legislature, for instance, mandated that history texts "include an accurate recording of any and all ethnic groups who have made contributions to the world, America or the State of Michigan societies." Connecticut directed local school boards to find books that "present the achievements and accomplishments of individuals and groups from all ethnic and racial backgrounds." Publishers followed these recommendations and added African-Americans to their coverage of literature, science, politics, and other fields, giving readers now familiar figures like Benjamin Banneker and the poet Phillis Wheatley, along with some lesser known ones like Ben York, who accompanied Lewis and Clark, and William Henry Hastie, the first Black federal judge.[87]

Once a consensus had been reached that Americans of African descent belonged in histories in significant numbers, this model seemed to offer a solution to the thorny problem of integration. In California, both supporters and critics of *Land of the Free* had favored the approach, though the former sometimes wanted texts to include contributors to the cause of civil rights, like Frederick Douglass and Rosa Parks, while the latter fell back on less controversial figures in sports or the ever popular George Washington Carver. Because the contributions story could accommodate differing philosophies, it looked apolitical. In fact, however, it was deeply conservative because it generally piggybacked on an earlier narrative structure. The limits of the approach are painfully evident in a 1967 Texas proclamation marking

Negro History Week, which Governor John Connally issued in response to a request from the Association for the Study of Negro Life and History. It read like pure Rafferty:

> Our founding fathers, in their foresight and wisdom, made American citizenship a right and a privilege of all Americans regardless of race, religion or national origins.
>
> It is also proper that we recognize the contributions of minority groups that have had a role in making our great American culture.
>
> In the month of February there has been one week designated Negro History Week in tribute to eminent Negroes, living and dead.[88]

The proclamation welcomed African-Americans into the nation's story, but at the cost of historical accuracy. The first sentence was simply false. Race was an *explicit* criterion for full citizenship in many states for almost a century after the Revolution, and the Dred Scott decision of 1857 transferred that principle to the federal level. Of course, the Constitution also endorsed slavery for Americans of African descent, though its drafters skirted direct mention of race. This kind of patriotic forgetfulness appealed to many writers making initial attempts to integrate their books. As far back as the 1950s, for example, authors of one text had dared to extended a tribute to Dorie Miller, a Black sailor who fought off the Japanese during the attack on Pearl Harbor. But the writers had then failed to mention that the country's armed forces segregated Miller and other Blacks during World War II.[89]

Among its other drawbacks, the contributions approach could also reveal an underlying sense of noblesse oblige, a condescending sense of responsibility to usher the previously excluded onto the stage so they might utter a few brief lines in the American pageant and then depart. A letter writer in California neatly captured the sentiment. She liked *Land of the Free* because it showed "appreciation and understanding . . . toward all those poor, ignorant, and underprivileged people who in their humble ways have helped to make our country great."[90]

Understandably, critics quickly tired of heroic contributors who showed up dutifully in books but often seemed detached from larger streams of African-American history. Historian Louis R. Harlan termed many accounts of them "sugar-coated success stories," and another scholar derided them as a multiracial variation on the old

312

"cherry-tree history." Edwin Fenton, a professor at Carnegie-Mellon University, summed up many educators' frustrations: "A text full of men like Crispus Attucks is not enough."[91] Publishers got the message, and so they overlaid the contributions story with less uplifting but still cautious discussions of slavery, racism, and discrimination. But often the two narrative techniques clashed, undermining the coherence of the books.

In *These United States,* a Houghton Mifflin history first published in 1978, Blacks appeared frequently in the contributions mode. Deborah Sampson, a woman of color who disguised herself as a man to fight in the Revolutionary War, merited a sidebar. Readers also learned that "many Congregationalist ministers were activists in the cause of American independence" and found an attractive painting in color of African-American Lemuel Haynes, a Revolutionary soldier and clergyman who "served only white congregations in New England." Later Blacks were shown "contributing to the growing industrialization" of the United States:

> Elijah McCoy patented inventions that made possible the automatic oiling of machinery. Jan E. Matzeliger invented a machine that shaped and fastened the leather over the sole of a shoe. This process led to the mass production of shoes and greatly reduced their cost. And Granville T. Woods obtained some fifty patents during his lifetime. One of these patents was for an incubator which was the forerunner of present-day machines used to hatch eggs.[92]

All this material is accurate and fits the criteria for racial inclusion set by states like Michigan, but it does not necessarily promote a better understanding of African-American history, or American history in general, particularly when space in a single volume is so limited. Haynes does not typify Congregational ministers who supported the Revolution, nor does he adequately represent African-Americans of the era, few of whom were Congregationalists and almost none of whom were ministers in the denomination. The authors or editors seem to have chosen him mostly because he was Black and could be combined with existing artwork. McCoy and Woods are intriguing characters, but their inventions are fairly obscure. Because similar inventors of other racial backgrounds are not singled out by name, their appearance here is awkward. Interestingly, the historian authors of California's 1964 *The Negro in American History* had feared publishers would opt for just this sort of utilitarian inclusion. They had called for a "conscious effort to portray outstanding Negro figures," but with selection determined by the same criteria for all groups.[93]

Of all the characters mentioned here, Sampson, who appeared in several other histories as well, has the least claim to space. She hardly serves as a window to the experience of most Black women of the time. Nor do readers learn how she was able to pose as a man or why she chose to fight for a country that enslaved African-Americans. Answers to these questions might make Sampson more worthy of study, but they would complicate her role as a "contributor," one of history's interchangeable parts, a handy replacement for Molly Pitcher or Haym Saloman.

Though the authors of *These United States* often relied on contributors, the book lacked the sanitized tone and content of its counterparts from the 1950s. They addressed the brutality of slavery, the rise of Jim Crow, the false promise of the Horatio Alger myth ("In the 1950's those who worked hard and did their jobs well had every chance of getting ahead—if they were white"), even the Black Power movement.[94] But their discussion of racial oppression tended to be general in nature, treating African-Americans as an amorphous mass. People of color usually gained clear identities when they contradicted the general pattern of hardship. That was the case with contributors, like Lemuel Haynes and Elijah McCoy, or those who successfully fought against racism, like King. This pattern appeared throughout popular textbooks of the 1970s and 1980s, giving them a disjointed, confusing quality, especially when illustrations and running text are compared. Because most publishers hesitated to depict graphic scenes of Black poverty beyond the perfunctory shot of sharecroppers, African-Americans usually appeared in the well-dressed, middle-class forms of W. E. B. DuBois, Marian Anderson, Thurgood Marshall, and Ralph Bunche. Photographs of these figures told a reassuring story of progress up from slavery, a message refuted by much of the blander accompanying print explaining how racism limited Blacks' opportunities.

If heavy reliance on contributors sometimes left textbooks with muddled history, another method of integration promised both coherence and drama. Authors could depict African-Americans as protagonists in a centuries-long struggle to secure their freedom and rights as Americans, the technique favored by Franklin, Caughey, and May in *Land of the Free*. The stories of struggle and contribution overlapped to some degree. A text might discuss Langston Hughes, for instance, as a great American poet, a bitter critic of racial discrimination, or both.

The Narrative "Unravels," 1961–1985

As an author depicted African-American figures more as champions of racial justice, however, they could no longer be swapped as easily with preexisting White figures. DuBois could not be mixed indiscriminately with "prominent historians of the early twentieth century," for instance, nor could King be used as an example of "successful Protestant ministers of the postwar era," in the way that Attucks *could* take the place of another hero of Revolutionary times. So, the struggle for racial justice explicitly defined the textbook roles of DuBois, King, and others like them, distinguishing them from contributors.

Conservatives in California had tried to eliminate leaders of the civil rights struggle from *Land of the Free,* preferring apolitical contributors instead. But over the next twenty years, publishers mostly ignored their objections. Black abolitionists, Civil War soldiers, Reconstruction officials, and twentieth-century civil rights workers marched into textbooks that students read across the country, following the path blazed by supplemental works like Detroit's *Struggle for Freedom and Rights.* Newer books provided a startling contrast to those from the 1950s, and the difference was most apparent in depictions of Reconstruction. No longer were the freedmen the dazed, easily manipulated dupes of unscrupulous carpetbaggers. They were actors who understood their political and social goals and fought to achieve them as much as circumstances allowed. "They hoped that Reconstruction would bring them land and the chance for an education. These freedmen wanted to be able to vote and hold office in order to have an equal place in Southern life," explained the authors of *America Is,* a text popular in the early and mid-1980s. "To protect their interests, blacks generally voted for Republicans." Most African-Americans elected or appointed under Reconstruction governments "worked effectively and well," according to another text, and their record "provides a strong recommendation for the idea of democracy." Most books profiled, or at least mentioned, a few of these officials. Those who appeared most frequently included Blanche K. Bruce and Hiram P. Revels, U.S. senators from Mississippi, and Robert Smalls, a slave who pirated a Confederate ship in the Civil War, freed himself and his family, and then served in Congress.[95]

The new story of Reconstruction looked like a photographic negative of the old one, with light and dark reversed. It was no longer a "failure" because it imposed dishonest officials, backed by Black votes, on a prostrate White South. "The great *tragedy* of Reconstruction was not the corruption, but the failure to obtain a lasting equality in citizenship for the Negro," wrote high school teacher Jack Abramowitz in

315

his *American History.* "Basically, most white southerners simply could not accept the idea of a society where white and black were equal," one text explained, blaming recalcitrant ex-Confederates for the problems. "Southern *Whites* were not ready for emancipation," declared one set of authors, cleverly inverting the standard refrain in histories published before 1960.[96]

The "struggle" narrative worked fairly well in coverage up to 1877 because writers gave Blacks clear antagonists with concrete plans for exploiting them. Textbooks regularly discussed the Cotton Kingdom's need for cheap labor and often included detailed defenses of slavery by Southern politicians and intellectuals such as John Calhoun, James Henry Hammond, or Thomas Fitzhugh. In Reconstruction, books had the Ku Klux Klan. Texts usually did not mention Klan leaders by name but almost always included a photograph or other illustration of its hooded members, as Franklin, Caughey, and May had done in *Land of the Free.* After discussions of Reconstruction, however, White supremacists and their ideas grew steadily dimmer in many books, until, like black holes circling distant stars, they could be glimpsed only through the gravity they exerted against moving, visible bodies—A. Philip Randolph, King, Rosa Parks, the Supreme Court, Lyndon Johnson, Malcolm X.[97]

A few examples suggest the pattern. In *American History,* Abramowitz discussed how "Dixiecrats" split the Democratic Party in 1948 but strangely failed to note it was the party's controversial support of civil rights that inspired Strom Thurmond and his allies to go their own way. The Dixiecrats, he observed obliquely, simply considered Harry Truman "too liberal." In a sidebar on the school integration standoff in Little Rock in 1957, the writer failed to name the governor, Orval Faubus, whose battle of wills with the president finally forced Eisenhower to send army paratroopers to guarantee the safety of Black high school students. Eisenhower's "action was resented by some people in the nation, but it met the approval of those who believe that public education must be free of segregation," Abramowitz concluded flatly, stating the obvious. The American Book Company's *History U.S.A.* also managed to tell the story of the "slow but steady progress of the American Negro" after World War II without discussing *who* opposed that advance or why. Like Abramowitz, the authors did not identify Faubus in their account of Little Rock, a small omission by itself but one that, with others, made it difficult for readers to place names or faces to the cause of racism. What became the Civil Rights Act of 1964 "stalled" in Congress, but the text said nothing about which legislators opposed it. *The Free and the Brave,* written by Columbia University historian Henry F. Graff, was similarly vague.[98]

Other books described these events more clearly but frequently slipped into a passive construction that let the perpetrators of "massive resistance" recede into the page. One discussed the course of the year-long bus boycott in Montgomery: "During this time, the homes of several blacks were bombed." Greater clarity risked sales, especially in the South. When one author updated his text and blamed a series of bombings in Birmingham more specifically on "white extremists," city schools dropped the book.[99]

Segregationists had often been more than willing to explain and defend the "Southern way of life." But textbooks rarely mentioned figures like George Wallace or Ross Barnett and almost never quoted them. They did not explain how the system of racial separation worked and how integrated schools, restaurants, and movie theaters threatened not only the larger racial hierarchy but also a more personal sense of self-worth and identity for many Whites. More advanced histories for colleges probed these subjects fairly well, but the concepts were not difficult to grasp and could have been introduced more widely in the high school, even junior high school curriculum.[100] However, because the political sensitivities of Whites often meant the motivations of integration's foes (and usually the foes themselves) could not appear in precollegiate books, the civil rights movement lost its moral and emotional drama. In *American History,* its most celebrated leader took on a two-dimensional, almost cartoonish quality: "Dr. King was a man for all seasons, a man for all places, and a man for all men." King often did not fare well in books designed for other academic subjects, either. After the mid-1960s, publishers of literary anthologies for high schools finally responded to demands to incorporate African-American authors. Editors became especially fond of the "I Have a Dream" speech. But they often deleted King's specific references to racism in the South, making the overall address sound less like a call for reform and more like an insipid collection of truisms.[101]

This pattern of introducing Blacks into the American story but simultaneously muting racial conflict is especially clear in the illustrations most publishers chose. Back in the 1950s and 1960s, civil rights leaders had planned demonstrations they would provoke violent retaliation, particularly from state and local police. Brutal images, they knew, would appear on television and in print. Public demands for federal authorities to intervene would then build outside the South. That technique left a memorable visual record—mobs, unrestrained by police, attacking Freedom Riders trying to integrate Southern bus stations; police dogs lunging at marchers; members of the Birmingham Fire Department blasting peaceful demonstrators with high-pressure water hoses. Such photographs were familiar to readers of *Life* or *Newsweek,* but they rarely made it into textbooks of the 1970s and 1980s. Instead, editors chose less confrontational images—Kennedy delivering an address on civil rights; a distant view of people gathered for the 1963 March on Washington; Rosa Parks taking her seat in a newly integrated bus, a well-dressed White man behind her; a close-up of two Black hands casting a ballot.[102]

Publishers' reluctance to depict racial violence extended to their coverage of earlier decades as well. No books consulted for this study included photographs of the whip-scarred backs of ex-slaves, though these could be found in college histories. Only one showed a lynching, and it depicted Klansmen preparing to hang a *White* man (Klansmen did target Republicans of both races during Reconstruction, but this image, standing alone, plainly distorted the historical record). So, while African-Americans had begun to appear in texts in large numbers after 1965, a new set of rules, somewhat looser than the codes of the 1950s, still governed how they could be portrayed.[103]

The best way to understand the political boundaries writers had to work within is through a book that broke the rules. The most daring text of the post–civil rights era covered state rather than national history. Edited by James W. Loewen, a sociologist, and Charles Sallis, a historian, *Mississippi: Conflict and Change* departed from standard textbooks in a number of ways. The authors integrated significant amounts of cultural history into their narrative. When they addressed race relations, their prose was lively and engaging, shorn of the peculiar mixture of evasion and earnestness common in other texts. Along with biographical portraits of Mississippi's Black leaders from Reconstruction to the modern era, the writers also included complex examinations of White figures who either espoused racism or manipulated it for political gain. But the most remarkable aspect of the book lay in the editors' choice of photographs. One showed a White police officer striking a young Black protester at a Mississippi courthouse while a nearby officer clutches a confiscated sign reading, "No More Police Brutality." In another, civil rights leader James Meredith, shot during a 1966 march, drags himself to the side of the road while screaming in pain. A grainy photograph from earlier in the century depicted a lynching, with White bystanders gathered around a burning Black body, mugging for the camera. Nearby text explained in a simple, direct manner the "ideology of lynching."[104]

Educational publishers refused to touch the book, though it would go on to win a prestigious literary prize. A trade press, Pantheon, did agree to work with Loewen and Sallis, but in 1974 officials on the Mississippi Textbook Purchasing Board found the finished book "too controversial" and "too racially oriented." At this point, the editor/authors opted for a heretofore unique strategy to get the book on the list of approved texts; they sued the state. At the trial, White members of the adoption committee pointed to the lynching photograph, suggesting that it might lead to unruly classrooms and arguing that it would be best not to dwell on unfortunate episodes of the past. "It is a history book, isn't it?" responded the judge. Loewen, Sallis, and the other plaintiffs won their five-year legal battle, but the case did not set much of a precedent. Traditional textbook publishers knew initiating similar suits would only risk sales of their other books. What they gained from the case was a keen understanding of what sort of historical information was still unacceptable to large numbers of Americans.[105]

Conservative Whites were not alone in pressing writers and editors to approach racial issues with a caution that bordered on censorship. Though some African-Americans, like Franklin, favored a relatively blunt approach to teaching history, others were not eager to trade textbooks that once excluded Blacks for ones that seemed to portray them mostly as victims of poverty and injustice. That pattern began to emerge by the mid-1960s. In California, for instance, it was an African-American member of the state's board of education who killed a proposal to include in one text the image of a slave being beaten with chains. In Detroit, a researcher queried a group of civic-minded Black parents on their reactions to fifty-five illustrations that might appear in junior high–level histories. The parents expressed most approval for pictures of King, DuBois, Frederick Douglass, Booker T. Washington, and boxer Joe Louis. Those they liked least included children in a slum, farm laborers picking cotton, stokers shoveling coal, and a cartoon about slavery. The history these parents wanted their children to learn clearly favored what the researcher called "eminent individuals who enhanced the Negro image" over stories of hardship in the past or present.[106]

Sometimes publishers missed these cues. Thinking they were good corporate citizens responding to the demand for integrated books, Follett Publishing produced a reader that showed African-American children in an inner-city setting. Detroit purchased it only to have Black parents object. Follett then had to destroy ten thousand books and

replace them with readers that placed the children in a clearly suburban, middle-class environment.[107]

Other Blacks also felt potentially negative images should be weeded
from texts. Writing in the journal *Social Education* in 1969, Nathan
Hare of San Francisco State College called for a curriculum that would
not get "bogged down in history" but focus on creating a usable past
that could uplift the community and give young people the means to
repair their self-image and group consciousness. "Black history must
above all be a story of struggle and aspiration . . . not a catalog of the
white man's undernourished if not infected conception of the Black
race and its goals—a view endorsed in one way or another by Black
assimilationists," Hare argued. Such comments underscored tension
over the issue among African-Americans that led to bitter criticism of
John Hope Franklin and like-minded scholars.[108] For pioneers in the
effort to integrate texts, the irony must have been keen. When some
Black educators favored separatism or stressed Black historical agency
at the expense of White culpability, they found themselves odd bedfel-
lows with people like Max Rafferty and Emery Stoops.

Publishers struggling to integrate their textbooks thus faced a set of
conflicting demands that sometimes transcended the racial backgrounds of critics. A measure of their difficulties can be gleaned from
the adoption criteria issued by different states and local districts. In
California, individual cities chose their own books for students beyond
eighth grade, and Los Angeles told its reviewers to avoid historically
evasive texts. Among the questions they were to ask themselves: "Do
unresolved intercultural problems in the United States, including those
which involve prejudice and discrimination, receive candid treatment,
or are they rationalized, distorted, or ignored?" In the same vein,
Michigan called for books that presented "the forces and conditions
which have worked to the disadvantage of minority groups, so that the
student is led to make accurate and unbiased judgments regarding
intergroup conflict."[109]

A few publishers geared their histories to these expectations. Addison-Wesley's sophisticated high school text *U.S.A: The American
Experience* offered clear accounts of racist violence, which made its
discussion of the Black Power movement in the 1960s refreshingly
intelligible, in stark contrast to other, tamer books. The authors
quoted Malcolm X's defense of armed struggle: "If it is wrong to be
violent defending black women and black babies and black men, then
it is wrong for America to draft us and make us violent abroad in
defense of her." Later, they noted that police "appear to have 'hassled'

[Black] Panthers unnecessarily and attacked them with little cause." Though the book did not advocate Black militancy, it did consider its causes. At the end of a chapter on antebellum America, the authors asked if readers "believe violence is a justified reform tactic if peaceful means for bringing about change show few results."[110] The question had a distinctly modern ring.

The American Experience, with its authors' willingness to discuss critiques of government policy and possibly radical solutions to social problems, would not have been welcome in Arizona. In 1973 the state's board of education, reacting to years of unrest over race, the war in Vietnam, and other issues, tentatively approved a policy that would have effectively barred presentation of Henry David Thoreau's "Civil Disobedience," let alone the Panthers. It declared that textbook content "shall not interfere with a school's legal responsibility to teach citizenship and promote patriotism" and that it "shall not include sections or works which contribute to civil disorder, social strife, or flagrant disregard for the law."[111]

Texas, which influenced publishers more than Arizona because of the size of its market, had even stricter standards. Books used in public schools of the Lone Star state could not "include works which encourage or condone civil disorder, social strife, [and] disregard for the law" or, even more broadly, serve "to undermine authority." In addition, Texas required books to present "positive aspects of the United States and its heritage." Well into the 1980s the Texas Society of the Daughters of the American Revolution objected to discussions of Jim Crow, lynching, segregated schools, and race-based restrictions on voting, on the grounds that they would leave students with negative impressions of their country. Mel and Norma Gabler, a conservative husband-and-wife team who gained national attention for their lobbying before Texas officials, were especially effective in pruning discussions of racism from state-approved texts.[112]

Publishers who were not willing to write off large sections of the country, and most were not, had to find some sort of compromise between these different mandates. Even single states sometimes directed firms to integrate books in inconsistent ways. That had happened in California in the 1960s, giving both camps in the *Land of the Free* debate the opportunity to cite standards that seemed to support their views. When West Virginians became embroiled in a textbook war in the mid-1970s that mostly involved readers and literary anthologies, one county adopted conservative criteria out of step with the multicultural guidelines set in Charleston.[113] As many of the texts published after 1966 show, trying to balance between these directives led to jumbled, contradictory accounts of African-American history. But problems for the overall coherence of the books did not stop there. Even in its bowdlerized form, this new history of African-Americans began to unravel the narrative threads that held together the rest of the American story and that the authors had inherited from books published in the 1950s, 1940s, and, in some ways, as far back as the nineteenth century.

In the past, authors had organized their books by defining what bound Americans into a national community and then explaining how that nation advanced, more or less together, through time. Americans, they had argued, shared certain values. These included religious tolerance, belief in political equality, respect for human rights, love of learning, and desire for material gain. History then became a story of "progress," or the slow but steady realization of these ideals for all Americans. Progress encountered obstacles, such as the disparities of wealth initially created by industrial expansion, or intolerance that marred the experiences of some European immigrants, but it always overcame them. This narrative had been flexible enough to absorb essential parts of critiques by Catholic historians and White Southerners in the early and mid–twentieth century. In the first case, the text writers jettisoned Protestantism from the set of American commonalities and incorporated religious pluralism more firmly in its place. In the second, they made race a more explicit criterion of national identity, either overtly through celebrating Whiteness or covertly by ignoring the history of nonwhites, particularly African-Americans.

After 1962, textbook authors confronted a paradox. They had to find some way to place Blacks into an American story predicated, in part, on their exclusion from it. It was an awkward task. Most African-Americans had neither chosen to come to America nor descended from those who had. The uplifting story of the immigrant, enthusiastically embraced by writers since the textbook wars of the 1920s, did not apply well to their experience. Instead of progressing steadily, the status of Americans of African descent also tended to slip backward at irregular intervals. The military and ideological tumult of the Revolution weakened the institution of slavery, for example, but ratification of the Constitution strengthened it. So did the invention of the cotton gin, the kind of technological innovation that, elsewhere in history, was supposed to improve the lives of Americans. Even more troubling, the status of Blacks often seemed to be inversely related to that of Whites. As the right to vote expanded for White males in the 1820s and 1830s, for instance, conditions for slaves and free people of color worsened. When reforms of the Progressive Era broadened democracy for Whites, Jim Crow fixed African-Americans into second-class citizenship across the South. There were other problems as well. Throughout the country's past Blacks often had limited access to "opportunity," that long-running engine of narrative progress. Finally, the history of racial prejudice called into question those qualities, like tolerance and respect for liberty, that all Americans were supposed to possess.

Authors who incorporated African-Americans in the country's history could choose to address these problems in a few different ways, none of them mutually exclusive. They might ignore or downplay these contradictions. Some writers who made cautious attempts at integration in the 1950s took this route. Mabel Casner and Ralph Gabriel knit together their *Story of American Democracy* with a series of sidebars called "Milestones of Democracy," which celebrated achievements such as religious liberty and the rise of the party system. One, titled "Democracy Extended to Negroes," marked the Thirteenth, Fourteenth, and Fifteenth Amendments (which ended slavery and guaranteed, at least on paper, legal equality for Blacks) and included a sketch of several dignified-looking Black men, one a soldier, lining up to cast their ballots. Casner and Gabriel held on to their theme of democratic progress, however, only by neglecting to explain how Jim Crow soon stripped African-American men of their right to vote.[114] Flushing such large swaths of history down an Orwellian memory hole was no longer politically tenable after Detroit's attack on *Our United States,* but many writers found other, more refined ways to retain part of the old storylines, particularly through the story of Black "contributions" discussed earlier.

Yet even with some narrative jury-rigging, problems were inevitable. Henry W. Bragdon began the 1950s versions of *History of a Free People* with a list of ten "characteristics of Americanism"—economic opportunity, educational opportunity, wide participation in politics, concern for the welfare of others, and toleration of differences, among others. Such themes were typical in schoolbooks, but Bragdon was a skilled, thoughtful writer who qualified his statements as he thought necessary and, relative to his competitors, dealt with African-American history at some length. "It should be noted that many of the qualities described as typical of America have not been completely realized," he noted. "Negro slavery, which existed in this country until 1865, was an absolute denial of equal opportunity and respect for individual rights."[115]

A little over ten years later, Bragdon realized he had not gone far enough. His 1969 essay "Dilemmas of a Textbook Writer" offered a mea culpa of sorts. Bragdon saw how events of the previous decade had forced teachers and authors to examine their own prejudices. The "Negro revolution has educated us all," he wrote. For his part, Bragdon made his book more racially inclusive and, in a related move, toned down some of his ten themes. Yet he was far from willing to abandon them altogether in a slow slide toward nihilism. He concluded there was still "a mandate to a textbook writer to attempt to instill a sense of commitment to this country, free of condescension or false pride, a patriotism that looks to past traditions of America to attempt to right present injustices."[116]

All text writers after 1962 faced Bragdon's "dilemmas," and most adopted his solution: Keep most of the old narrative structure and argument (with a few exceptions, namely the Dunning account of Reconstruction), but note where the Black experience contradicted the more "general" story. Textbooks published after 1965 were thus full of historical asides of sentence, paragraph, or even chapter length. Describing the arrival of settlers on the Atlantic Coast, Abramowitz wrote that "while millions of people came to America in search of freedom and a new life, several million others, Black Africans, were torn from their homes, brought to the New World as slaves." *Land of the Free* described the common lot—or, more accurately, the lack of it— for later settlers: "With the exception of slaves—and that is a major exception—American society was not frozen into classes." African-Americans repeatedly introduced a discordant sense of retrograde motion in the books. The authors of *These United States* included a whole chapter on the experiences of nonwhites in the late nineteenth century entitled "Some 'Other Americans' Lose Ground." In *The American Experience* readers learned that most New Deal programs, which had been applauded in 1950s texts as expressions of Americans' deep commitment to the well-being of their fellow citizens, "did not help the majority of Negroes."[117] Every book's chapter on the supposedly *national* phenomenon of suburban growth after World War II had to note that most urban Blacks remained behind in the city (though texts usually lacked clear explanations of how racism, violence, and the policies of the federal government assured that outcome).

Because most texts did not entirely abandon old myths of opportunity and progress, Black history often had to be segregated spatially, placed outside the main running text. That policy suggested implicitly that African-Americans, and to some extent other nonwhites as well, were a people apart from the whole, that Americans did not form a single national community. At times, that idea became explicit. In the aftermath of urban rioting in the mid-1960s, Lyndon Johnson had formed the National Advisory Commission on Civil Disorders, commonly called the Kerner Commission. In their official report, commission members found that the nation was "moving toward two societies, one black and one white—separate and unequal."[118] Several textbooks published after the report's release in 1968 reported those findings. None tried hard to refute the two-nations thesis.

When authors or their editors *did* try to insert African-Americans into old storylines, the effect could be jarring. *America Is* opened with the unit "America Is Opportunity":

> Opportunity has been a way of life for people coming to America from the start. Thousands of years ago, people from Asia moved slowly overland into Alaska, hunting and gathering more food. Beginning in the fifteenth century, people from Europe and Africa traveled by sea to the New World. They believed that America offered a place to lead their own lives. With great areas of land and many natural resources, opportunities for people in America seemed to be unlimited.[119]

Before the 1960s, a passage like this one would simply have ignored Native Americans or Africans. As it is, the attempt to yoke prehistoric "people from Asia" into what remains, at heart, a story of European expansion is strained. The suggestion that America beckoned to Africans as "a place to lead their own lives" is simply preposterous. The error is clearly unintentional, the result of an attempt to apply a new, racially inclusive sensibility to an old, racially exclusive matrix. The rest of the book deals with Blacks and Indians in a much more realistic manner. Yet the mistake is all the more troubling because it appeared in the third edition of *America Is,* long after an observant reader should have caught it.

Older, apparently discarded narratives had a way of reasserting themselves, of speaking through writers who would, when confronted with the evidence, likely argue that they had not *meant* what the words seem to say. That some versions of the past are potent enough to produce this sense of contradiction, of consciousness split between genuinely individual thought and adherence to socially sanctioned ideas, is what cultural theorists mean when they talk about "hegemony." Few were exempt from its effects. Franklin, Caughey, and May dealt thoughtfully and methodically with African-American history in *Land of the Free,* but when turning to relations between Europeans and Indians, they sometimes slipped momentarily into a tone of moral detachment and suggested that the loss of Indian lives and lands was somehow inevitable. "These first Americans were the first to have their lands taken from them, the first to be segregated, the last to get the vote, and the last to share in the rewards of the American system," the authors declared somberly in an early chapter. But the sentence preceding it read, oddly, "In all probability, no human agency could have prevented the take-over by the Whites."[120] So, were Whites therefore absolved from responsibility? With an acute labor shortage in colonial America, was slavery equally inevitable? These suggestions, which so blatantly contradict Franklin's aim to have students wrestle with the moral legacy of the nation's founding and growth, lurk unquietly beneath the surface of the page.

A sense of confusion, of overlapping, incompatible ideas and purposes, suffused many textbooks of the 1970s and 1980s. The first half of Columbia historian Henry F. Graff's *The Free and the Brave* replicated the heroic, individualistic history of the late nineteenth century. Graff introduced the book with an account of Amerigo Vespucci and a confident affirmation: "One day Amerigo's America would stand for something more beautiful than the noblest statue or most wonderful painting. It would mean in every language of the globe 'individual freedom and opportunity for the many.'" Later, readers learned of Jamestown leader John Smith's admirable qualities. His "strong faith in final success, strict self control, and, above all, stout heart" would be "requirements for millions of future Americans."[121]

Black men, women, and children first appeared as unwelcome intruders into this sunny narrative, but they grew more insistent as the book progressed. At one point, Graff quoted an account by an African-American school principal working in the early twentieth century. The man asks a student what line of work he plans to enter:

"I am going to be a door-boy, sir."
"Well, you will get $2.50 or $3.00 a week, but after a while that will not be enough; what then?"
After a moment's pause he will reply: "I should like to be an office boy."
"Well, what next?"

A moment's silence, and, "I should like to get a position as a bell-boy."

"Well, then, what next?

A rather contemplative mood, and then, "I should like to climb to the position of head bell-boy."

He has arrived at the top: further than this he sees no hope. He must face the bald fact that he must enter business as a boy and wind up as a boy.[122]

It is difficult to imagine a sharper, more poignant critique of the myth of opportunity that structures the early chapters of *The Free and the Brave*. The first and second halves of the book seem to have sprung from the minds of different writers.

In some texts, that may well have been the case. Often several authors composed an initial text, only to have it massaged by editors, simplified by reading consultants, and clipped by sales agents wary of a word or passage that might offend adoption boards. A controlling authorial voice often got lost in the process.

Even in books generally dominated by a single perspective, unifying the narrative was not easy. Daniel J. Boorstin and Brooks Mather Kelley's *A History of the United States* was one of the most popular, and conservative, textbooks of the 1980s. In a throwback to volumes written decades earlier, the prologue simply excluded non-Europeans. "In the Old World people knew quite definitely whether they were English, French, or Spanish. But here it took time for them to discover that they really were Americans," they began, adding later, "This is a book about us." But, just as in Graff's book, African-Americans kept getting in the way of progress. To their credit, Boorstin and Kelley dealt fairly honestly with the oppression of Blacks, particularly in the twentieth century. So honestly, in fact, that by the end of the book they were struggling awkwardly to save that initially triumphalist narrative. "No other nation in history had been so conscience-stricken over the injustices to so large a group," they affirmed. "Nor had any other nation accomplished so much to help a particular minority. Once again, the United States was setting an example to the world."[123]

In short, the old textbook storylines were like a cracked and leaky bucket, with the experiences of African-Americans trickling, often spurting out the holes. Even with a patchwork of qualifiers, and the ladling of Black history into separate sidebars and chapters, American history could still look quite messy.

The disorder in the textbooks contrasted sharply with the national mood of the 1980s. Max Rafferty's old boss, Ronald Reagan, won the presidency in large part because he had been so effective in articulating reassuring myths about America's past. His campaign speeches resounded with stories of the immigrant's climb to success, the boundless opportunity of the frontier, even an American exceptionalism straight out of Emma Willard's histories, only now with a decadent, corrupt Old World portrayed by communist oligarchs instead of nineteenth-century monarchists. Rafferty lost his bid for the U.S. Senate in 1968 largely because of his abrasive personality, but Reagan did not suffer from that handicap. The president was also even less constrained by stubborn historical facts that might cast a shadow over his genial demeanor and generally upbeat worldview. American history was mostly White history to the president, who would nevertheless sometimes include Blacks in it, on his own terms. He was fond of telling the story of how Dorie Miller's heroism at Pearl Harbor instantly broke down segregation in the armed forces. Unfortunately, like so many of Reagan's anecdotes, this one was not true. The military remained highly segregated until well after the war, and Miller, still consigned to the U.S. Navy's Jim Crow role of cook, died when the Japanese sank his ship in 1943. For leaping on deck during the attack and manning an anti-aircraft gun, Miller had moved from mess attendant second-class to mess attendant first-class.[124]

But, like some individuals implacably opposed to his ideas, Reagan, too, did not want to get "bogged down in history." It was morning in America, as the slogan for his 1984 reelection campaign had it, and the dark night of national introspection and historical revisionism begun in the 1960s was supposed to be over.

For many educational critics, several with direct ties to the Reagan Administration, the current generation of textbooks was thus an affront to new national sensibilities. While the president's election had validated people's desire for certainties about the creation, growth, and future promise of the nation-state, school histories had grown less surefooted and more confused. Many critics blamed writers for adding nonwhites indiscriminately throughout their books, thereby upsetting the integrity of the story. That claim had some justification, as illustrated by publishers' sometimes strained efforts to include characters like Revolutionary soldier Deborah Sampson. But African-Americans generally had not been added to books out of proportion to their numbers or historical worthiness, the conviction underlying much of this critique. Blacks appeared peripheral because the themes at the center

The Narrative "Unravels," 1961–1985

THE BOONDOCKS   by AARON MCGRUDER

In the aftermath of 1960s protests, publishers began presenting African-American history through stories of generally noncontroversial "contributors" to national progress. The predictability of the formula still inspires satirists. BOONDOCKS © 2000 Aaron McGruder. Dist. By UNIVERSAL PRESS SYNDICATE. Reprinted with permission. All rights reserved.

of the story, shrunken and qualified though they were, still did not adequately address their experience.

The effort to bring African-Americans into textbook history, begun in earnest after Detroit's protest against *Our United States,* had succeeded in some respects, failed in others. On the positive side, Blacks were now unmistakably part of the American people and the American story, appearing in numbers that began to reflect their historical importance. A glance at schoolbooks from the 1940s and 1950s shows how much change text critics have wrought. But, like the civil rights movement of which it was a part, the drive to reform books and teaching fell short of complete victory. Political pressures from Whites, combined with tensions within the Black community, kept the *addition* of African-Americans to texts from evolving into true integration. Appealing to some, the often simplistic contributions approach also brought jeers from all sides (see fig. above). The attempt to orient Black history on a new narrative axis, the struggle for freedom and equal rights, suffered from publishers' wariness about fleshing out opponents of equality and conveying the depth of oppression. Equally unsatisfying was the obligatory-sounding discussion of African-Americans as unfortunate exceptions to the general story of progress.

The most logical way to integrate history was also the most difficult, politically and intellectually. It involved developing a new historical synthesis, one that showed how the experiences of Blacks, Whites, and Americans of other racial backgrounds were mutually dependent, inextricable parts of a larger story. It would explain, for instance, *why* slavery and racism flourished in a country dedicated to political democracy and equal rights. John Hope Franklin sought such a synthesis in his scholarly work and, to a degree, in *Land of the Free.* Most other text writers did not.

Conclusion

I taught American history at a small community college at the corner of Broadway and Reade Street in Manhattan from 1999 until the summer of 2001, when I took a leave of absence to finish this book. Students in my classes read a collection of essays and primary documents along with two fairly traditional textbooks, one of which had been used in many high schools. I left copies of them on a shelf in a second-floor office I shared with several other teachers.

On the morning of September 11, 2001, those books changed from teaching tools to historical artifacts. Six blocks away, events had suddenly, and tragically, overtaken them. The final chapters were now hopelessly out of date, of course. But, in many ways, so were the rest of the narratives. The debates over multiculturalism and "political correctness" in the 1980s and 1990s had shaped the books' treatment of American history. That social and political context had now shifted profoundly, but how? What issues of that earlier culture war had the ferocity of the attacks rendered petty or inconsequential? What unresolved questions still resonated with teachers, historians, students, and the public at large?

Americans would look for answers, as they had always done, in national mythology. During the last two decades of the twentieth century, a consensus had emerged on the right, and even among many liberals, that national myth had become faded and frayed, a casualty of broken promises in the war in Vietnam, the rise of radical politics in the universities, and an increasingly separatist philosophy among the country's minorities. Emblematic of the view was an essay by the historian William H. McNeill entitled "The Care and Repair of Public Myth," which appeared in *Foreign Affairs* in the fall of 1982. McNeill argued that when a people believe certain stories about who they are and how they got that way, they are able to act when circumstances "suggest or require a common response." Nations, in other words, live and die by their myths. At the start of World War II, Britons "'knew" from schoolbook history" that in European conflicts their island nation always lost the early battles but persevered to final victory. The story of bulldog tenacity proved prophetic, especially because people retained faith in it through the darkest months of 1940.[1]

The British had faced a daily threat of terror from the skies in the early 1940s. Americans in the early 1980s did not, but they nevertheless found themselves confronting their own crisis of myth, according to McNeill. He blamed much of the problem on his colleagues. They had spent two decades examining the past through the eyes of the poor and oppressed, and so the history they told tended to tarnish convictions about the unique virtue of American society. Discarding some old myths was normal and healthy, in McNeill's estimation, because they have to evolve to meet people's changing needs. But historians were failing to advance new myths. Worse yet, wrote McNeill, some scholars were substituting divisive for unifying myths, thereby "intensifying the special grievances of one group against others."[2]

This theory about the collapse of national mythology animated attacks on textbooks and teaching for nearly twenty years. In early 1994, shortly before the battle over the history standards began, Gilbert T. Sewall of the New York–based American Textbook Council published an article in the *Wall Street Journal* called "The Triumph of Textbook Trendiness." Sewall's target was the new edition of a decades-old volume, Lewis Paul Todd and Merle Curti's *The Triumph of the American Nation.* Editors and a new lead author had cut the text's narrative core in half, he claimed, replacing it with white space and extraneous illustrations. Revisionists had even bowdlerized the title, shortening it to *The American Nation.* The only triumph that remained, he concluded, belonged to liberal crusades, particularly in the final chapters, which were a "medley of racial and gender themes, radical gestures, and trendy global 'concerns.'"[3]

One did not have to agree with Sewall's assessment to see that textbooks published since the start of the 1970s *had* lost the confidence of their precursors from the 1940s and 1950s.[4] A chapter in a text from 1979 opened with a critical, demystifying tour of Disneyland's Carousel of Progress. Authors of another book wrote in an oddly self-referential way, a style that contrasted sharply with the omniscient cheerfulness of *Our United States,* the book that had first catalyzed reform in Detroit in 1962. "Textbooks on American history have usu-

Conclusion

ally emphasized the growth of democratic institutions rather than political and racial injustices," they explained, "the expansion of economic opportunities rather than the exploitation of the poor, whether black or white, and the despoiling of much of the land." Attempts to articulate new myths still seemed ensnared by the failure of old ones, as when one writer tried to offer a *counter*-counternarrative to Manifest Destiny. "The expansion of America was motivated as much by the desire for free land and personal freedom," he reassured readers, "as by the desire to expand slavery."5

Though he did not discuss textbooks directly in his essay, McNeill found this enfeebling of myth ominous. "A people without a full quiver of relevant, agreed-upon statements, accepted in advance through education or less formalized acculturation," he warned, "soon finds itself in deep trouble, for, in the absence of believable myths, coherent public action becomes very difficult to improvise or sustain."6

If we accept McNeill's hypothesis, however, then some unifying myths proved themselves fairly resilient in the fall of 2001. In the aftermath of the attacks on New York and Washington, D.C., the nation improvised and sustained a war against Al-Qaeda and the Taliban in Afghanistan with sober, patriotic resolve and barely a whisper of dissent. Americans hung flags from their windows, affixed red, white, and blue buttons to their clothes, and lined up to donate blood—sometimes consciously invoking the nostalgic myth of the self-sacrificing "Greatest Generation" of World War II celebrated in Tom Brokaw's bestselling book.

At the same time, September 11 also kindled an effort to revise old myths and to define new ones—ones that would help to explain why we were fighting and how the conflict fit into the larger pattern of national history. Some of these attempts, particularly at the outset, were reflexive and fairly simplistic, characterized by calls to defend "freedom" and "democracy" without explanations of precisely what those terms mean. A small portion of the discourse was openly divisive, particularly as talk radio crackled with references to American Muslims as a menacing fifth column. However, many such attempts have been careful and measured. Major newspapers, for instance, have printed thoughtful essays about the history of the country's legal separation of church and state and how it has stymied the development of the kind of political tyranny prevalent in much of the Middle East.

As they have at several times in their history, Americans are now struggling to reinterpret their past and forge a new consensus about it.

Schoolbook Nation

West Virginia senator Robert Byrd, a coal miner's son who remembers reading one of David Saville Muzzey's textbooks by the light of a kerosene lamp, recently joined a campaign to involve the federal government more directly in history teaching. He and other legislators were aroused by a study called *Losing America's Memory,* which bemoaned, once again, the alleged loss of historical literacy among young people. Following Byrd's lead, Congress appropriated fifty million dollars for grants to local and regional projects designed to improve instruction in the subject.[7] Begun a few months before the 2001 attacks, the program continued after them without triggering the kind of vitriolic confrontations that had befallen the national history standards less than ten years earlier.

The partisans in the history wars of the 1990s seem to have entered into an uneasy truce, awakened perhaps to a truth revealed by the terrorists. Much of the earlier conflict over multiculturalism had revolved around the issue of whether or not Americans, with their diverse backgrounds, really constituted a single nation. With the standards, that played out in the change of American "peoples" to "people." The hijackers of September 11 never considered such a question. The United States represented something quite coherent to them, and they made little distinction among Americans with regard, for instance, to class or race. If they could take the existence of a national community for granted, so, to some extent, could we.

That renewed sense of unity presents an opportunity for a more honest examination of the issues that have long divided Americans, for a more open debate about historical myths we hope textbooks and other teaching aids will present. This cultural and intellectual give-and-take will likely proceed more smoothly if we are able to steer clear of some pitfalls encountered in past battles.

Passions over history teaching tend to create false dichotomies. One of the least constructive is the belief that history is either "traditional" or "revisionist." Myths are not static, however, handed down from one generation to the next until an upstart historian decides to overturn them. Americans have continually renegotiated their myths, a process apparent in the changing content of textbooks. The Protestant nation of Emma Willard's histories in the 1840s gave way by the 1950s to a celebration of America as a tolerant refuge of Judeo-Christian pluralism. Myths of Anglo-Saxon cultural and racial superiority in books published at the beginning of the twentieth century mostly disappeared by the 1930s, replaced by a story of the nation as a melt-

Conclusion

ing pot of European immigrants. Changes to those *revised* myths
began in the 1960s and gave us contemporary tributes to multiculturalism. These observations may seem straightforward, even obvious,
but the traditional-revisionist paradigm has come to dominate
almost every textbook battle, from the campaign against Harold
Rugg to the more recent debate over the standards. Each time it has
choked off debate.

Another, sometimes false dichotomy pits historical "truth" against
the unambiguous evil of "censorship." Typically, critics will request, or
demand, that a fact or passage be removed from a textbook. That
material, which authors may have included originally without much
thought, then suddenly takes on the aura of great historical truth.
Think, for instance, of the numerous mentions of the Ku Klux Klan
and Joseph McCarthy in the early draft of the standards. Removing
such references under pressure looks like capitulation to censorship,
and writers are understandably reluctant to do so. Publishers, often
more willing to countenance such revisions, are still nervous about
being seen bowing to critics. That is why after hearings in Texas they
avoid releasing before-and-after versions of books they put up for
adoption.

Because it is easy to understand and tell, the truth-vs.-censorship
story often structures coverage of teaching conflicts in newspapers and
on television. Sometimes this narrative does capture the essence of
such contests, but often it obscures a more complex situation and tends
to polarize activists and textbook writers who might both gain from a
less heated exchange. Eager to maintain (publicly, at least) the ideal of
objectivity, many historians in the 1920s had willfully ignored critiques
of ethnocentrism in popular schoolbooks, giving political opportunists
like William Thompson and David Hirshfield an even greater chance
to exploit the absurd charges of a British "conspiracy" against the
country's schools.

In addition, the line between censorship and the unavoidable
process of choosing what material to exclude as irrelevant or peripheral can sometimes be difficult to track. During California's battle over
Land of the Free in 1966, conservatives called on the book's authors to
identify W. E. B. Du Bois as a communist. It was an old trick from the
1950s. Faced with such a stipulation, writers had generally been reluctant to taint the drive for racial equality with communism, so they had
deleted all references to leftists like Du Bois and the poet Langston
Hughes.

But this time, the California distributor for *Land of the Free* refused to budge. The firm sent state officials a letter, almost certainly approved by the authors, explaining why. "In a full-length biography of Du Bois it would be told undoubtedly that at 93 he renounced his American citizenship, went to Ghana, and became a Communist" as an "extreme gesture of protest." That kind of fact did not belong in an eighth-grade textbook, the letter writers explained, because it would amount to "character assassination." A similar policy applied to other historical figures, they wrote. "Thus we do not mention Washington's towering rages, Jefferson's slaveholding, Clay's rakish life, Grant's excessive drinking, the sordid details of the scandals of the Grant and Harding administrations."[8]

The authors and their editor had made some decisions that may appear to us today as judicious, unwise, or something in between. How important *was* DuBois's turn to communism? Perhaps not very. Discussing it would certainly have complicated *Land of the Free*'s presentation of him as a liberal hero. Avoiding it, however, can also distort history. Du Bois was not quite a last-minute convert to radical thinking, at least not to the extent this letter suggests. A Marxist approach to class and race structured some of his most important work, particularly *Black Reconstruction,* published in 1935. In the 1950s he became an apologist for Stalin. Perhaps a brief examination of the appeal that radical, even brutal ideologies had for some African-American intellectuals might have better revealed the depth of racial oppression in the country. But such a digression might also have confused young readers or unnecessarily detoured them around the more important themes of the chapter, or the book as a whole. The choice of what to leave in and what to take out is rarely easy.

Given over three decades of hindsight, it is easier to dispute the letter's writers on some other points. While Grant's penchant for whiskey might be no more than a footnote to American history, Jefferson's ownership of slaves surely is not. His slaveholding neatly symbolizes the complicity of the Founders, and their political philosophy, with the institution. The champion of local democracy, political and economic egalitarianism, and the (White) yeoman farmer is the same Jefferson who owned slaves and wrestled with his own racism. His personal dilemma, handled with honesty in the classroom, can shed light on what has been a great national dilemma. Too often, writers have tried to treat slavery and racism merely as unfortunate exceptions to the generally liberal philosophy of early Americans. In fact, as the histo-

Conclusion

rian Edmund Morgan showed convincingly in *American Slavery, American Freedom,* they were deeply entangled with one another as early as the 1650s.[9] Much of the drama in national history since 1776 has centered on the struggle to wrench noble ideas about freedom from popular ideas about race. It is sometimes a dispiriting story, beset with reversals like those that ended Reconstruction, but it needs to be told. Jefferson is one of the great, tragic figures in that story. Yet many textbook authors, from the first generation of professional historians onward, have been eager to whitewash his legacy. Even some scholars who did not write schoolbooks, and thus were unencumbered by the dictates of conservative adoption boards, were reluctant to confront growing evidence that he fathered children by one of his slaves, Sally Hemmings. Only recent DNA evidence that made his paternity all but certain could convince them.

We have moved far from the reverential approach to national heroes in nineteenth-century textbooks by Willard or Charles A. Goodrich. But a continuing reluctance to make those heroes fully human actually impedes the construction of historical myths that unite all Americans. If one wants to explore the country's multiracial character and its tortured progress toward equality and freedom, Hemmings and Jefferson probably deserve a place together far more than old icons like John Rolfe and Pocahontas. A stilted portrait of Jefferson as a saintly hero of democracy cannot effectively bring together Americans today, if it ever could.

Censorship of textbooks does remain a serious problem. But opponents of censorship can take comfort in the knowledge that the proliferation of new media, particularly the Internet, has made it increasingly difficult for individuals and pressure groups to control the flow of historical information into the classroom. The work of creating a new national mythology for our schools will increasingly take place outside overtly political adoption agencies, where the pressure to sweep away uncomfortable issues has often been intense. For that, we can be thankful.

"Forgetting, I would go so far as to say historical error, is a crucial factor in the creation of a nation," the French scholar Ernest Renan once observed.[10] That insight is important. A bit of historical amnesia can make it easier for people to imagine themselves as a single body, and dwelling upon mostly forgotten conflicts may not be healthy for any society. But the converse can also be true. Repressing truths about subjects central to a country's identity, as slavery and racism are to the

United States, makes it impossible to construct a version of the national past that doesn't collapse under its contradictions. Remembering, one might go so far as to say historical accuracy, is also a crucial factor in the maintenance of a nation.

As the story of September 11 passes into the history books, Americans will lose an alien "other" against which they can define themselves and the sort of cohesion that only a direct assault on the country can inspire. When they are gone, a deeper sense of unity will rest even more firmly upon an honest reckoning with our own past.

Notes

Introduction

1. David Oshinsky, "The Humpty Dumpty of Scholarship," *New York Times*, August 26, 2000, sect. B, p. 9.

2. Frances FitzGerald, *America Revised: History Schoolbooks in the Twentieth Century* (New York: Vintage, 1980), 73, 102–3.

3. Gary B. Nash, Charlotte Crabtree, and Ross E. Dunn, *History on Trial: Culture Wars and the Teaching of the Past* (New York: Knopf, 1998), 149–58; Diane Ravitch, *Left Back: A Century of Failed School Reforms* (New York: Simon and Schuster, 2000), 432–37; Carol Gluck, "Let the Debate Continue," *New York Times*, November 19, 1994, 23.

4. Nash, Crabtree, and Dunn, *History on Trial*, 151, 193.

5. E. D. Hirsch Jr., *Cultural Literacy: What Every American Needs to Know* (New York: Vintage, 1988), 9.

6. Hirsch, *Cultural Literacy*, 22–23.

7. Diane Ravitch, "Multiculturalism: E. Pluribus Plures," *American Scholar* 59 (summer 1990): 337–54; Diane Ravitch, "Tot Sociology; or, What Happened to History in the Grade Schools?" *American Scholar* 56 (summer 1987): 343–54; Diane Ravitch and Chester E. Finn Jr., *What Do Our Seventeen-Year-Olds Know? A Report on the First National Assessment of History and Literature* (New York: Harper and Row, 1987), 49; Nash, Crabtree, and Dunn, *History on Trial*, 109.

8. Arthur Schlesinger Jr., *The Disuniting of America* (New York: Norton, 1993), 16–17, 61–74, 86, 93. For an introduction to Afrocentric thought, see Molefi K. Asante, *Afrocentricity: The Theory of Social Change* (Buffalo: Amulefi, 1980).

9. Joan W. Scott, "History in Crisis? The Others' Side of the Story," *American Historical Review* 94 (June 1989): 682.

10. Newt Gingrich, *To Renew America* (New York: HarperCollins, 1995), 7, 30, 33. Nash, Crabtree, and Dunn's *History on Trial* first led me to this passage from Gingrich's book.

11. For an introduction to the intellectual debates surrounding the scholarship that grew out of the 1960s, and particularly the rise of cultural studies, see

Patrick Brantlinger, *Crusoe's Footprints: Cultural Studies in Britain and America* (New York: Routledge, 1991).

12. Schlesinger, *The Disuniting of America*, 67–69; Molefi K. Asante, "The Afrocentric Idea in Education," *Journal of Negro Education* 60 (spring 1991): 171.

13. Lynne Cheney, "The End of History," *Wall Street Journal*, October 20, 1994, 14.

14. *Phyllis Schlafly Report*, March 1995, quoted in Nash, Crabtree, and Dunn, *History on Trial*, 5; Ruth Rosen, "The War to Control the Past," *Los Angeles Times*, November 24, 1994, sect. B, p. 5; Jon Wiener, "History Lesson," *New Republic*, January 2, 1995, 9.

15. "Letters to the Editor: A History of All of the People Isn't PC," *Wall Street Journal*, November 21, 1994, 17.

16. Diane Ravitch, "Standards in U.S. History: An Assessment," *Education Week*, December 1994, 12; Diane Ravitch, "Revise, but Don't Abandon, the History Standards," *Chronicle of Higher Education*, February 17, 1995, 52.

17. Walter A. MacDougall, "Whose History? Whose Standards?" *Commentary*, May 1995, 41–42; Ravitch, *Left Back*, 436; Eric Alterman, "Culture Wars," *Rolling Stone*, October 19, 1995, 46; Gluck, "Let the Debate Continue," 23; Nash, Crabtree, and Dunn, *History on Trial*, 149.

18. A similar pattern would occur the following year in the even more bitter divisions over the Smithsonian Institution's commemoration of the end of World War II and the atomic bombings of Hiroshima and Nagasaki. See Edward T. Linenthal and Tom Engelhardt, eds., *History Wars: The Enola Gay and Other Battles for the American Past* (New York: Henry Holt, 1996).

19. Nash, Crabtree, and Dunn, *History on Trial*, 193.

20. FitzGerald, *America Revised*, 35.

21. John Leo, "The Hijacking of American History," *U.S. News and World Report*, November 14, 1994, 36. For a more thoughtful examination of the influence a generation of scholars who came of age in the 1960s had on the standards, see John Patrick Diggins, "Historical Blindness," *New York Times*, November 19, 1994, 23.

22. Nash, Crabtree, and Dunn, *History on Trial*, 16, 22.

23. Allen Lichtman, "History According to Newt," *Washington Monthly*, May 1995, 48.

24. For a sample of the dispute among historians, see the "AHR Forum" in the June 1989 edition of the *American Historical Review*.

25. For example, see Robert Lerner, Althea K. Nagai, and Stanley Rothman, *Molding the Good Citizen: The Politics of High School History Texts* (Westport, Conn.: Praeger, 1995), 81–83; and Schlesinger, *The Disuniting of America*, 61. FitzGerald also discusses what she sees as the sudden appearance of Attucks in *America Revised*.

26. Mabel B. Casner and Ralph H. Gabriel, *The Story of American Democracy* (New York: Harcourt, Brace and Co., 1950), 107.

27. John Leo, "Affirmative Action History," *U.S. News and World Report,* March 28, 1994, 24.

28. I borrow the question from John Leo, who wrote, "I think the problem is this: How can the story of minorities and women be told more fully and honestly without pulling the main story of America's development out of whack?" Leo, "Affirmative Action History," 24.

29. Schlesinger, *The Disuniting of America,* 122, 137.

30. Hirsch, *Cultural Literacy,* 104–7.

31. Nash, Crabtree, and Dunn, *History on Trial,* 83, 84, 192, 198, 204.

32. For example, Lawrence Levine has explored how the seemingly natural placement of cultural forms like opera or minstrel shows into "high" or "low" categories grew out of sometimes violent conflicts in nineteenth-century America. See *Highbrow Lowbrow: The Emergence of Cultural Hierarchy in America* (Cambridge: Harvard University Press, 1988).

33. Stuart Hall, quoted in Michael Apple and Linda Christian-Smith, "The Politics of the Textbook," in *The Politics of the Textbook,* ed. Michael Apple and Linda Christian-Smith (New York: Routledge, 1986), 12.

34. Edward Austin Johnson, *A School History of the Negro Race in America* (Raleigh: Edwards and Broughton, 1891), 9.

35. Edward Channing to George Brett, July 7, 1897, and December 26, 1897, Macmillan Company Papers, Author Files, Box 64, Manuscripts and Archives Division, New York Public Library, New York.

36. On the rise of educational professionalism, see David Tyack, *The One Best System: A History of American Urban Education* (Cambridge: Harvard University Press, 1974). For examples of pro-corporate bias in history and other textbooks during the 1920s, see Melville J. Herskovits and Malcolm M. Willey, "What Your Child Learns," *Nation,* September 17, 1924, 282–84.

37. Michael Apple, "Regulating the Text: The Sociohistorical Roots of State Control," in *Textbooks in American Society: Politics, Policy, Pedagogy,* ed. Philip G. Altbach et al. (Albany: State University of New York Press, 1991). For an argument about how the state actually channels private conflict into the schools, see Martin Carnoy and Henry Levin, *Schooling and Work in the Democratic State* (Stanford: Stanford University Press, 1985).

38. I adopt the phrase from Michael Apple's *Official Knowledge: Democratic Education in a Conservative Age* (New York: Routledge, 1986).

39. My focus on textbook content distinguishes this work from Jonathan Zimmerman's recent book *Whose America? Culture Wars in the Public Schools* (Cambridge: Harvard University Press, 2002). While we have examined some of the same controversies over history teaching, we have also reached significantly different conclusions about them.

40. For an intriguing but speculative example of this approach, see "American History and the Structures of Collective Memory: A Modest Exercise in Empirical Iconography," in Michael Frisch, *A Shared Authority: Essays on the Craft and Meaning of Oral and Public History* (Albany: State University Press of New York,

1990). For an insightful look at how young people of different racial backgrounds tend to interpret history differently, see Terrie Epstein, "Adolescents' Perspectives on Racial Diversity in U.S. History: Case Studies from an Urban Classroom," *American Educational Research Journal* 37 (spring 2000): 185–214.

41. Diane Ravitch and Arthur M. Schlesinger Jr., "The New, Improved History Standards," *Wall Street Journal*, April 3, 1996, 14; Arthur M. Schlesinger Jr., "History as Therapy: A Dangerous Idea," *New York Times*, May 3, 1996, 31; Lynne Cheney, "New History Standards Still Attack Our Heritage," *Wall Street Journal*, May 2, 1996, 14.

Chapter 1

1. Emma Willard, *Abridged History of the United States; or, Republic of America* (Philadelphia: A. S. Barnes and Co., 1843), 13.

2. Edward Channing, *A Students' History of the United States* (New York: Macmillan, 1898), xxxv. The passage appears in "Suggestions to Teachers," by Anna Boynton Thompson, a schoolteacher who collaborated with Channing on the book.

3. For an introduction to the terminology of nationalism, see Ernest Gellner, *Nations and Nationalism* (Ithaca: Cornell University Press, 1983), 1–7.

4. Samuel Beer, *To Make a Nation: The Rediscovery of American Federalism* (Cambridge: Belknap Press of Harvard University Press, 1993), 4.

5. Paul C. Nagel discusses the intellectual foundations of unionism in *One Nation Indivisible: The Union in American Thought, 1776–1861* (New York: Oxford University Press, 1964).

6. Nagel, *One Nation Indivisible*, vi. For more on the fear of republican decay and its relation to history writing, see Maris Vinovskis, *History and Educational Policymaking* (New Haven: Yale University Press, 1999), 4–8.

7. Benjamin Rush, "Thoughts on the Mode of Education Proper in a Republic," and Noah Webster, "On the Education of Youth in America," both in *Essays on Education in the Early Republic*, ed. Frederick Rudolph (Cambridge: Belknap Press of Harvard University Press, 1965), 10, 19, 65; Cathy N. Davidson, *Revolution and the Word: The Rise of the Sentimental Novel in America* (New York: Oxford University Press, 1986), 62–63.

8. Charles A. Goodrich, *A History of the United States of America, on a Plan Adapted to the Capacity of Youth* (Bellows Falls, Vt.: James I. Cutler, 1827), preface. Nina Baym argues that Emma Willard struggled to reconcile an endorsement of an "expansionist, entrepreneurial, and imperial vision of the American future" with the common fear that corruption would ensue when citizens pursued private gain instead of public good. See "Women and the Republic: Emma Willard's Rhetoric of History," *American Quarterly* 43 (March 1991): 1–23.

9. Willard, *Abridged History of the United States* (1843), 154. The cherry-tree story appears in readers by Weems and at least one history. For more on

the subject, see "The Mythologizing of George Washington," in Daniel J. Boorstin, *The Americans: The National Experience* (New York: Random House, 1965).

10. Charles A. Goodrich, *A History of the United States of America* (Boston: Jenks, Palmer and Co., 1847), 262.

11. Arthur Goldberg, "School Histories of the Middle Period," in *Historiography and Urbanization: Essays in American History in Honor of W. Stull Holt,* ed. Eric F. Goldman (Baltimore: Johns Hopkins Press, 1941), 19; Baym, "Women and the Republic," 18.

12. Not all wars proved equally popular in all sections. Many New Englanders, perhaps a majority, disapproved of the war with Mexico in the 1840s. But even Willard, a native of Connecticut with her own misgivings about the conflict, still portrayed the acquisition of California and General Winfield Scott's storming of Mexico City's fortified heights of Chapultepec in glowingly patriotic terms.

13. John Frost, *A History of the United States: For the Use of Schools and Academies* (Philadelphia: Charles DeSilver, 1856), 250. The first edition of Frost's book appeared in 1837.

14. Salma Hale, *History of the United States from Their First Settlement as Colonies to the Close of the War with Great Britain in 1815* (New York: Collins and Hannay, 1829), 245.

15. John M. Murrin adopts the expression from an early critic of the Constitution. See "A Roof without Walls: The Dilemma of American National Identity," in *Beyond Confederation: Origins of the Constitution and American National Identity,* ed. Richard Beeman, Stephen Botein, and Edward C. Carter II (Chapel Hill: University of North Carolina Press, 1987). For a discussion of literature's role in the process, see Benjamin Spencer, *The Quest for Nationality: An American Literary Campaign* (Syracuse: Syracuse University Press, 1957).

16. Hale, *History of the United States,* front matter; Benedict Anderson, *Imagined Communities: Reflections on the Origin and Spread of Nationalism* (New York: Verso, 1991), 63.

17. Emma Willard, *Abridged History of the United States; or, Republic of America* (New York: A. S. Barnes and Co., 1858), 404–5.

18. I am not including here textbooks written explicitly for schools in the South, which are the subject of the next chapter.

19. William M. Swinton, *A Condensed School History of the United States* (New York: Ivison, Blakeman, Taylor and Co., 1879), 240–41. For a discussion of historians' changing views on the causes of the war, see Thomas J. Pressly, *Americans Interpret Their Civil War* (New York: Free Press, 1965).

20. George Payn Quackenbos, *Illustrated School History of the United States and the Adjacent Parts of America from the Earliest Discoveries to the Present Time* (New York: D. Appleton and Co., 1868), 446–48; John Clark Ridpath, *History of the United States, Prepared Especially for Schools* (Cincinnati:

Jones Brothers and Co., 1876), 306. A few writers, most notably Thomas Wentworth Higginson, dissented, making slavery a central issue in their histories or declaring the war inevitable. For more on Higginson, see the next chapter.

21. Karen F. A. Fox and Jack C. Thompson, "To What End: The Aims of Two Centuries of American History Instruction," *Teachers College Record* 82 (January 1980): 34–37; John J. Anderson, *A Pictorial School History of the United States* (New York: Clark and Maynard, 1885), iv.

22. Fox and Thompson note that by "mid-century nearly half of the northern and western states had legislated national history courses into public schools in one way or the other. By 1896, all but eleven states had similar laws." See Fox and Thompson, "To What End," 4. Bessie Louise Pierce also discusses this nineteenth-century legislation in *Public Opinion and the Teaching of History in the United States* (New York: Knopf, 1926). For statistical evidence regarding changes in the history curriculum, particularly the ascendance of American history by century's end, see Arthur Woodward, "Teaching Americans about Their Past: History and the Schools, 1880–1930" (Ph.D. diss., University of Illinois at Urbana-Champaign, 1982).

23. Merle Curti, *The Roots of American Loyalty* (New York: Russell and Russell, 1967), 158.

24. Curti, *The Roots of American Loyalty,* 169; Nagel, *One Nation Indivisible,* 134; George M. Fredrickson, *The Inner Civil War: Northern Intellectuals and the Crisis of Union* (Urbana: University of Illinois Press, 1993), 57.

25. Curti, *The Roots of American Loyalty,* 167; Charles Sumner, "Are We a Nation? Address of Hon. Charles Sumner before the New York Young Men's Republican Union" (New York: n.p., 1867); Douglass, quoted in Pressly, *Americans Interpret Their Civil War,* 67–68.

26. Benedict Anderson, *Imagined Communities,* 10–12.

27. Elisha Mulford, *The Nation: The Foundations of Political Order and Civil Life in the United States* (New York: Hurd and Houghton, 1875), viii, 9.

28. Mulford, *The Nation,* 13–17, 21–22, 359.

29. For an early indication of this trend, see Robert Ellis Thompson's discussion of history's role in "national education," in his *Political Economy with Especial Reference to the Industrial History of Nations* (Philadelphia: Porter and Coates, 1882), 375–85. The first edition appeared in 1875.

30. Francis Newton Thorpe, *In Justice to the Nation: American History in American Schools, Colleges, and Universities* (Philadelphia: n.p., 1886), 1–9, 17.

31. In the 1870s, for instance, German-born historian Hermann Eduard Von Holst developed the thesis that the years leading to the Civil War presented a grand battle between nationality and freedom on one hand, and state sovereignty and slavery on the other. See Pressly, *Americans Interpret Their Civil War,* 47–50.

32. John Fiske, *A History of the United States for Schools* (Boston: Houghton Mifflin, 1894), 292–93. Frank A. Hill, a high-school headmaster, wrote the "Suggestive Questions" for the book.

33. William H. Mace, *Method in History for Teachers and Students* (Boston: Athenaeum Press, 1897), 63.

34. *Report of the Committee [of Ten] on Secondary School Studies Appointed at the Meeting of the National Education Association* (Washington, D.C.: Government Printing Office, 1893); Lucy M. Salmon, quoted in Peter Novick, *That Noble Dream: The "Objectivity Question" and the American Historical Profession* (New York: Cambridge University Press, 1988), 71.

35. John Bach McMaster, *School History of the United States* (New York: American Book Company, 1897), 183.

36. McMaster, *School History of the United States,* 178–79.

37. Fiske, *A History of the United States for Schools,* 315.

38. Earlier organic nationalists also stressed the role of economics and industrial growth. Robert Ellis Thompson made them central to his 1875 work, *Political Economy.*

39. Edward Channing to George Brett, July 2, 1897, Macmillan Company Papers, Author Files, Box 64; Channing, *A Students' History of the United States,* vii.

40. Jesse Olney, *History of the United States on a New Plan* (New Haven: Durrie and Peck, 1837), 266; Mary Elsie Thalheimer, *Eclectic History of the United States* (Cincinnati: Van Antwerp, Bragg and Co., 1880), 351. Nash, Crabtree, and Dunn also charted Schlesinger and Ravitch's changing stance on the standards. See *History on Trial,* 225–56.

41. Alexander Johnston, *A History of the United States for Schools* (New York: Henry Holt and Co., 1885), iv.

42. The phrasing comes from Benedict Anderson, *Imagined Communities,* 26.

Chapter 2

1. Henry Cleveland, *Alexander H. Stephens in Public and Private: With Letters and Speeches, before, during and since the War* (Philadelphia: National Publishing Company, 1866), 717–29; "Stephens, Alexander Hamilton," in *Dictionary of American Biography,* ed. Dumas Malone (New York: Charles Scribner's Sons, 1959), 9:569–75.

2. "Higginson, Thomas Wentworth," in *Dictionary of American Biography,* ed. Dumas Malone (New York: Charles Scribner's Sons, 1959), 5:16–18; James W. Tuttleton, *Thomas Wentworth Higginson* (Boston: Twain Publishers, 1978), 39.

3. Alexander H. Stephens, *A Compendium of the History of the United States from the Earliest Settlements to 1872* (Columbia, S.C.: E. J. Hale and Son, 1876), 420, 428, 466.

4. Stephens, *History of the United States,* 471, 475–80.

5. Thomas Wentworth Higginson, *Young Folks' History of the United States* (Boston: Lee and Shepard, 1875), 169, 288, 305–6, 319; Tilden J. Edelstein, *Strange Enthusiasm: A Life of Thomas Wentworth Higginson* (New Haven: Yale University Press, 1968), 210, 244.

6. Rush, "Thoughts on the Mode of Education," 19.

7. Paul C. Nagel develops the thesis that nationalist impulses in the nineteenth century pivoted between conservative "stewards," who pledged themselves to maintaining a union as conceived by the Founders, and advocates for the moral and political regeneration of the nation. See his *This Sacred Trust: American Nationality, 1798–1898* (New York: Oxford University Press, 1971).

8. David W. Blight, "'For Something Beyond the Battlefield': Frederick Douglass and the Struggle for the Memory of the Civil War," *Journal of American History* 75 (March 1989): 1156, 1169. For more on the subject, consult Blight's book *Race and Reunion: The Civil War in American Memory* (Cambridge: Belknap Press of Harvard University Press, 2001).

9. "Education at the South," *DeBow's Review* (December 1856): 656; "Our School Books," *DeBow's Review* (April 1860): 438; "Southern School Books," *DeBow's Review* (July 1858): 117. The numbering of volumes for the *Review* is irregular, and therefore I have given only dates of issue.

10. "Southern School Books," *DeBow's Review* (September 1852): 260–61.

11. Willard, *Abridged History of the United States* (1858), 404–5; "School Books by Southern Authors," advertisement, *DeBow's Review* (August 1860). A. S. Barnes pioneered the idea of nationally standardized textbooks. See Hellmut Lehmann-Haupt, *The Book in America: A History of the Making and Selling of Books in the United States* (New York: R. R. Bowker, 1951), 236.

12. John S. Ezell, "A Southern Education for Southrons," *Journal of Southern History* 17 (August 1951): 306–7, 322; John McCardell, *The Idea of a Southern Nation: Southern Nationalists and Southern Nationalism, 1830–1860* (New York: Norton, 1979), 202; David Van Tassel, *Recording America's Past: An Interpretation of the Development of Historical Studies in America, 1607–1884* (Chicago: University of Chicago Press, 1960), 137; Edgar W. Knight, *Public Education in the South* (Boston: Ginn and Co., 1922): 291–92; Avery Craven, *The Growth of Southern Nationalism, 1848–1861* (Baton Rouge: Louisiana State University Press, 1953), 253–56. For a concise summary of White Southerners' objections to these schoolbooks during the antebellum era, see Pierce, *Public Opinion and the Teaching of History,* 136–46.

13. Charles William Dabney, *Universal Education in the South* (Chapel Hill: University of North Carolina Press, 1936), 113; C. Vann Woodward, *Origins of the New South, 1877–1913* (Baton Rouge: Louisiana State University Press, 1951), 61–62. Eric Foner notes that some states did significantly scale back their school systems at some point after the end of Reconstruction. See his *Reconstruction: America's Unfinished Revolution, 1863–1877* (New York: Harper and Row, 1988), 589.

14. Mulford, *The Nation,* 9, 120–27, 145.

15. Mulford, *The Nation,* 348, 362, 397.

16. Sumner, "Are We a Nation?" 13–14, 18, 34.

17. Robert Ellis Thompson, *Political Economy,* 380–82; S. G. F. Spackman, "Beyond the Federal Consensus: A Doctrine of National Power," in *The*

Growth of Federal Power in American History, ed. Rhodri Jeffreys-Jones and Bruce Collins (Edinburgh: Scottish Academic Press, 1983), 56.

18. Alfred H. Kelly, "The Congressional Controversy over School Segregation, 1867–1875," *American Historical Review* 64 (April 1959): 540–47, 559.

19. Quoted in Lloyd A. Hunter, "The Sacred South: Postwar Confederates and the Sacralization of Southern Culture" (Ph.D. diss., Saint Louis University, 1978), 197.

20. "School Histories of the United States," *Southern Review* 3 (January 1868): 155.

21. Stephens, *History of the United States,* 25, 100–102.

22. Stephens, *History of the United States,* 256.

23. Stephens, *History of the United States,* 251.

24. Joseph T. Derry, *History of the United States, for Schools and Academies* (Philadelphia: J. B. Lippincott, 1875), 140.

25. John S. Blackburn and William N. McDonald, *New School History of the United States* (Baltimore: William J. C. Dulany and Co., 1880), 384. The first edition of the book appeared in 1870.

26. Stephens, *History of the United States,* 399.

27. Derry, *History of the United States,* 328 (emphasis added), 317.

28. Every state in the former Confederacy that officially adopted or recommended school histories in the 1870s included the book on their lists, either singly or with other titles. I base claims of popularity on general evidence of use and examination of records of textbook adoption in the state archives of Texas, Alabama, and South Carolina, combined with copies of annual reports by state superintendents of education in these states and in Virginia, Tennessee, Arkansas, Georgia, North Carolina, and Louisiana.

29. George Frederick Holmes, *New School History of the United States* (New York: University Publishing Company, 1884), 4, 33, 83–84, 157, 222.

30. "School Histories of the United States," 154–79; "Southern University Series of Text Books for Schools and Colleges," *Debow's Review* (January 1867): 93–94.

31. C. Vann Woodward, *Origins of the New South,* 321. Woodward's *Strange Career of Jim Crow* (New York: Oxford University Press, 1957) charts the slow development of segregation and disfranchisement from the 1860s through the turn of the century.

32. George Frederick Holmes, *A School History of the United States of America* (New York: University Publishing Company, 1870), 3.

33. Jack Carter Thompson, "Images for Americans in Popular History Surveys, 1820–1912" (Ph.D. diss., University of Michigan, 1976), 30; Lehmann-Haupt, *The Book in America,* 242.

34. G. A. Gates, *A Foe to American Schools* (Minneapolis: Kingdom Publishing Company, 1897), 15, 23. *Publishers' Weekly* covered these changes in the textbook industry as they happened. Good secondary sources include Charles A. Madison, *Book Publishing in America* (New York: McGraw-Hill,

1966), esp. 121–29; and David Sheehan, *This Was Publishing: A Chronicle of the Book Trade in the Gilded Age* (Bloomington: Indiana University Press, 1952), 204–10.

35. The movement for "free textbooks," or those provided at taxpayer expense, advanced slowly over the latter half of the nineteenth and first half of the twentieth centuries, with the South lagging behind the rest of the country. See A. C. Monahan, *Free Textbooks and State Uniformity*, United States Bureau of Education, no. 36 (Washington, D.C.: Government Printing Office, 1915).

36. Gates, *A Foe to American Schools*, 5, 21, 42. Industry leaders maintained that profits in what was an approximately five-million-dollar industry in 1890 remained small. See "Our Supplementary Educational List," *Publishers' Weekly*, December 27, 1879, 880.

37. Gates, *A Foe to American Schools*, 5, 21, 42.

38. Theodore R. Mitchell, *Political Education in the Southern Farmers' Alliance, 1887–1900* (Madison: University of Wisconsin Press, 1987), 128–29.

39. S. M. Finger, *Biennial Report of the Superintendent of Public Instruction of North Carolina for the Scholastic Years 1888 and 1889* (Raleigh: 1890), 25.

40. Ben C. Jones, *The School Book Question* (n.p.: [1890?]), 32, Archive Division, 1989/41–47, Texas State Library, Austin.

41. Michael Apple gives a brief but thorough analysis of the South's embrace of statewide adoption in "Regulating the Text."

42. Jeremiah W. Jenks, "School-Book Legislation," *Political Science Quarterly* 6 (March 1891): 100; W. D. Mayfield, *Twenty-fifth Annual Report of the State Superintendent of Education* (Columbia, S.C.: 1893), 370; "Those Text-Book Adoptions," [Texas] *State Topics*, January 24, 1904, 6–11; Sebron Graham Sneed, *A Discussion of the Questions of State Uniformity and State Adoption of Text-Books* (n.p.: [1890?]), 4, 12, Archive Division, 1989/41–47, Texas State Library.

43. G. R. Glenn, *Thirtieth Annual Report from the Department of Education to the General Assembly of the State of Georgia* (Atlanta: 1902), 17.

44. W. H. Ruffner, *Fourth Annual Report of the Superintendent of Public Instruction* (Richmond, Va.: 1874), 158 (emphasis added).

45. Grand Army of the Republic, *Journal of the Twenty-Second Annual Session of the Grand Encampment* (Minneapolis: 1889), 211. For more on the subject, see Wallace Evan Davies, *Patriotism on Parade: The Story of Veterans and Hereditary Organizations in America, 1783–1900* (Cambridge: Harvard University Press, 1955); and Pierce, *Public Opinion and the Teaching of History*, 164–71.

46. Eric F. Goldman, *John Bach McMaster: American Historian* (Philadelphia: University of Pennsylvania Press, 1943), 82; Grand Army of the Republic, *Journal of the Twenty-Second Annual Session of the Grand Encampment*, 211.

47. William Allen, "Is the 'Eclectic History of the United States' a Proper

History to Use in Our Schools?" *Southern Historical Society Papers* 12 (1884): 235–37.

48. Davies, *Patriotism on Parade,* 238–40; Goldman, *John Bach McMaster,* 83–92; Milton Berman, *John Fiske: The Evolution of a Popularizer* (Cambridge: Harvard University Press, 1961), 201.

49. John William Jones, "Is the 'Eclectic History of the United States,' Written by Miss Thalheimer and Published by Van Antwerp, Bragg and Company, Cincinnati, A Fit Book to Be Used in Our Schools?" *Southern Historical Society Papers* 12 (1884), 286–87; "Denounce the Books—John B. Hood of Confederate Veterans ask [*sic*] Governor Book Contract," *Austin Tribune,* August 31, 1908, 5.

50. Advocates of the Lost Cause promoted the "overwhelming numbers" thesis with great enthusiasm. For more on this argument, and the mythology of the Lost Cause in general, see Rollin G. Osterweis, "Winning the War in the Classroom," in *The Myth of the Lost Cause, 1865–1900* (Hamden, Conn.: Archon Books, 1973), chapter 9; Thomas L. Connelly and Barbara L. Bellows, *God and General Longstreet: The Lost Cause and the Southern Mind* (Baton Rouge: Louisiana State University Press, 1982), 1–39; and Gaines M. Foster, *Ghosts of the Confederacy: Defeat, the Lost Cause, and the Emergence of the New South* (New York: Oxford University Press, 1987).

51. See "Harvest of Heroes: Reconciliation and Vindication," in Charles Wilson Reagan, *Baptized in Blood: The Religion of the Lost Cause* (Athens: University of Georgia Press, 1980).

52. I have generally not considered textbooks unless they deal with the United States as a whole. However, state and regional history also held a prominent place in the curriculum. J. L. M. Curry's *Southern States in the American Union* and Lesslie Hall's *Half Hours in Southern History,* both published by the B. F. Johnson Company of Virginia, led the roster of books devoted to the South.

53. "Jones, John William," in *Dictionary of American Biography,* ed. Dumas Malone (New York: Charles Scribner's Sons, 1959), 5:190–91; "Pendleton, William Nelson," in *National Cyclopedia of American Biography,* ed. Lyman Abbott et al. (New York: James T. White and Co., 1900), 10:240–41.

54. John William Jones, *School History of the United States* (Baltimore: R. H. Woodward Company, 1896), 3; Susan Pendleton Lee, *Lee's Advanced School History of the United States* (Richmond, Va.: B. F. Johnson Company, 1899), preface.

55. Lee, *Lee's Advanced School History of the United States,* 148, 240; Jones, *School History of the United States,* 141.

56. Lee, *Lee's Advanced School History of the United States,* 86.

57. Lee, *Lee's Advanced School History of the United States,* 358.

58. Lee, *Lee's Advanced School History of the United States,* 278.

59. Lee, *Lee's Advanced School History of the United States,* 542. Going further than most advocates of the Lost Cause, Lee also argued that these

same Republicans had begun the war out of envy for the superior civilization of the antebellum South.

60. Lee, *Lee's Advanced School History of the United States,* 546, 550–51.

61. *School History of the United States,* 214, 302–4, 321.

62. George L. Christian, "Official Report of the History Committee of the Grand Camp C.[onfederate] V.[eterans] Department," *Southern Historical Society Papers* 28 (1900): 194–95.

63. Paul S. Buck, *The Road to Reunion, 1865–1900* (Boston: Little, Brown and Co., 1947), 305.

64. Nina Silber discusses the rise and decline of this "climate of national inclusiveness" using evidence from popular culture in "Whitewashed Road to Reunion," in *The Romance of Reunion: Northerners and the South, 1865–1900* (Chapel Hill: University of North Carolina Press, 1993), chap. 5. Foster also notes that White racists used public celebration of symbols of the Lost Cause to legitimate Jim Crow. See his *Ghosts of the Confederacy,* esp. 194–95.

65. For an account of Ginn's decision to publish this Southern-authored textbook as part of a national sales strategy, see Thomas Bonaventure Lawler, *Seventy Years of Textbook Publishing: A History of Ginn and Company, 1867–1937* (Boston: Ginn and Co., 1938), 231–38.

66. Oscar H. Cooper, Harry F. Estill, and Leonard Lemmon, *History of Our Country: A Text-Book for Schools* (Boston: Ginn and Co., 1903), 343.

67. Oscar H. Cooper, Harry F. Estill, and Leonard Lemmon, *History of Our Country* (Boston: Ginn and Co., 1896), 385.

68. James A. McPherson, *The Negro's Civil War: How American Negroes Felt and Acted During the War for the Union* (New York: Pantheon Books, 1965), 174, 26, 332.

69. Cooper, Estill, and Lemmon, *History of Our Country* (1903), 400–401 (emphasis added).

70. Horace E. Scudder, *A History of the United States of America* (Philadelphia: J. H. Butler, 1884), 400.

71. Abraham Lincoln to Michael Hahn, March 13, 1864, in *Lincoln: Selected Speeches and Writings,* ed. Don E. Fehrenbacher (New York: Vintage Books, 1992), 418. For more on the Confederacy's aborted effort to enlist slaves as troops, see Paul D. Escott, *After Secession: Jefferson Davis and the Failure of Confederate Nationalism* (Baton Rouge: Louisiana State University Press, 1978), 239–55.

72. The journal *Confederate Veteran,* the best single source of Lost Cause mythology, is filled with stories of the "faithful negro."

73. Franklin L. Riley, J. A. C. Chandler, and J. G. de Roulhac Hamilton, *Our Republic: A History of the United States for Grammar Grades* (Richmond, Va.: Riley and Chandler, 1910), 414–15; Lawton B. Evans, *Essential Facts of American History* (Boston: Benjamin H. Sanborn Company, 1909), 406.

74. Channing to Brett, July 7, 1897, October 28, 1899, and September 2, 1909, all in Macmillan Company Papers, Author Files, Box 64.

75. For more on the antitrust suit, see Sheehan, *This Was Publishing,* 48.

76. The book was Philip A. Bruce's *School History of the United States* (New York: American Book Company, 1903). See George L. Christian, "Report of the History Committee of the Grand Camp Confederate Veterans of Virginia," *Southern Historical Society Papers* 31 (1903): 361. Herman Hattaway argues that sales agents swarmed over UCV members. See "Clio's Southern Soldiers: The United Confederate Veterans and History," *Louisiana History* 12 (summer 1971): 218–19.

77. "A Review of [Edna] Turpin's Short History of the American People," 13, 18; "Some Historical Errors in [Lawton] Evans's Essential Facts of American History," 18; "Will the Confederate Veteran Stand Such an Error [reviewing *Our Republic*]?" The reviews appeared with a May 17, 1913, letter from the company to the Alabama Text-Book Commission, Governor's Files, SG5078, Alabama Department of Archives and History, Montgomery.

78. Foster, *Ghosts of the Confederacy,* 185.

79. Hattaway, "Clio's Southern Soldiers," 235; A. H. Yeager to Alabama Text-Book Commission, April 23, 1913, Governor's Files, SG5078.

80. Hunter, "The Sacred South," 219.

81. W. T. Pate to George W. Benton, October 14, 1912, American Book Company Records, Box 48, Department of Special Collections, Syracuse University Library, Syracuse, New York.

82. "Virginians Aroused about False History," *Confederate Veteran,* April 1911, 148; "That Detestable Elson Book," *Confederate Veteran,* July 1911, 316. For a summary of the Elson case, see Foster, *Ghosts of the Confederacy,* 188–90.

83. "That Detestable Elson Book," 316.

84. Carleton J. H. Hayes, *The Historical Evolution of Modern Nationalism* (New York: Macmillan, 1931), 164.

85. Nathaniel Wright Stephenson, *An American History* (Boston: Ginn and Co., 1919), 440.

86. Andrew C. McLaughlin, *A History of the American Nation* (New York: D. Appleton and Co., 1919), 430.

87. Higginson, *Young Folks' History of the United States,* 335; David Saville Muzzey, *An American History* (Boston: Ginn and Co., 1911), 486–88.

88. See John David Smith, *An Old Creed for a New South: Proslavery Ideology and Historiography, 1865–1918* (Athens: University of Georgia Press, 1991), esp. chaps. 5 and 6. For more on the AHA generally, consult Novick, *That Noble Dream.*

89. Berman, *John Fiske,* 201–5. James Loewen argues that recent textbooks continue to portray Brown as insane, rather than passionately devoted to the cause of abolition. See Loewen, *Lies My Teacher Told Me* (New York: New Press, 1995), 165–70.

90. A 1903 report by the UCV condemned Ella Hines's *Young People's History of Our Country* (Philadelphia: National Publishing Company, 1902) over treatment of the massacre. See Hattaway, "Clio's Southern Soldiers," 241. For more on the incident itself, see Richard L. Fuchs, *Unerring Fire: The Massacre at Fort Pillow* (Rutherford, N.J.: Fairleigh Dickinson University Press, 1994); and Hondon B. Hargrove, *Black Union Soldiers in the Civil War* (Jefferson, N.C.: McFarland and Co., 1988): 169–76.

Chapter 3

1. Samuel Burchard coined the alliterative phrase at a gathering that included the party's presidential nominee, James G. Blaine. While attacks on Catholics were central to Republican campaigning, such a blatant, public expression of prejudice violated rules of political decorum. Blaine's delay in repudiating the remark cost him dearly in the election. See Mark Wahlgren Summers, *Rum, Romanism and Rebellion: The Making of a President, 1884* (Chapel Hill: University of North Carolina Press, 2000), 281–86.

2. Quoted in Nagel, *This Sacred Trust,* 222.

3. Daniel Dorchester, *Romanism versus the Public School System* (New York: Phillips and Hunt, 1888), 4. Nast's illustration appeared in the September 30, 1871, issue of *Harper's Weekly.*

4. Thomas T. McAvoy, *A History of the Catholic Church in the United States* (Notre Dame: University of Notre Dame Press, 1969), 265.

5. This chapter relies on analysis of thirteen texts created for Catholic schools from the 1870s through the 1920s. Writers and publishers of most of these books officially designated them for parochial institutions or included a note indicating they had passed muster with church censors. A few texts lacked such a designation or the imprimatur of the church, but their content and references to them in contemporary literature make it unmistakable that they were intended for parochial schools. See Sister Mary Celeste [Leger], *American History* (New York: Macmillan, 1926); Franciscan Sisters of the Perpetual Adoration, *A History of the United States for Catholic Schools* (New York: Scott, Foresman and Co., 1914); John Rose Greene Hassard, *An Abridged History of the United States of America, for the Use of Schools* (New York: Catholic Publication Society, 1887); John Rose Greene Hassard, *A History of the United States of America* (New York: Catholic Publication Society, 1885); William H. J. Kennedy and Sister Mary Joseph [Dunn], *America's Story: A History of the United States for the Lower Grades of Catholic Schools* (New York: Benziger Brothers, 1926); William H. J. Kennedy and Sister Mary Joseph, *The United States: A History for the Upper Grades of Catholic Schools* (New York: Benziger Brothers, 1926); Thomas Bonaventure Lawler, *Essentials of American History* (Boston: Ginn and Co., 1918); Charles H. McCarthy, *A History of the United States for Catholic Schools* (New York: American Book Company, 1919); John P. O'Hara, *A History of the United States* (New

York: Macmillan, 1909); *Sadlier's Elementary History of the United States* (New York: William H. Sadlier, 1896); *Sadlier's Excelsior Studies in the History of the United States for Schools* (New York: William H. Sadlier, 1879); *Sadlier's Preparatory History of the United States* (New York: D. and J. Sadlier and Co., 1886); *A School History of the United States* (New York: Benziger Brothers, 1892). The first editions of the Hassard and Sadlier histories appeared in the 1870s.

6. McAvoy, *A History of the Catholic Church in the United States*, 265; *Independent*, quoted in Dorchester, *Romanism versus the Public School System*, 280; Edwin D. Mead, *The Roman Catholic Church and the School Question* (Boston: George H. Ellis, 1888), 39.

7. Lloyd P. Jorgenson, *The State and the Non-public School, 1825–1925* (Columbia: University of Missouri Press, 1987), 132.

8. Franklin, quoted in Robert A. Carlson, *The Quest for Conformity: Americanization through Education* (New York: John Wiley and Sons, 1975), 31.

9. See "The Rise of Know-Nothingism," in Ray Allen Billington, *The Protestant Crusade, 1800–1860: A Study of the Origins of American Nativism* (Gloucester, Mass.: Peter Smith, 1963). For a history of anti-Catholicism in the United States, see John Higham, *Strangers in the Land: Patterns of American Nativism, 1860–1925* (New Brunswick, N.J.: Rutgers University Press, 1955).

10. Rush, "Thoughts on the Mode of Education Proper in a Republic," 10; Billington, *The Protestant Crusade*, 293.

11. Jorgenson, *The State and the Non-public School*, 37, 48. For discussion of the school question I have relied heavily on Jorgenson's book and on David Tyack and Elisabeth Hansot's study *Managers of Virtue: Public School Leadership in America* (New York: Basic Books, 1982).

12. Diane Ravitch analyzes the New York controversy in *The Great School Wars, New York City, 1805–1973: A History of the Public Schools as a Battlefield of Change* (New York: Basic Books, 1974).

13. *American Protestant Vindicator*, October 5, 1841, quoted in Billington, *The Protestant Crusade*, 148; Leslie Woodcock Tentler, *Seasons of Grace: A History of the Catholic Archdiocese of Detroit* (Detroit: Wayne State University Press, 1990), 88–89; Reverend Michael Mueller, *Public School Education* (Boston: P. Donahue, 1872), quoted in Jorgenson, *The State and the Non-public School*, 127–28.

14. Lawrence A. Cremin, *American Education: The Metropolitan Experience, 1876–1890* (New York: Harper and Row, 1988), 128; Jay P. Dolan, *The American Catholic Experience: A History from Colonial Times to the Present* (Garden City, N.Y.: Doubleday, 1985), 256.

15. James S. Clarkson, "General Grant's Des Moines Speech: Circumstances of a Remarkable Utterance," *Century Magazine*, March 1898, 788; Tyack and Hansot, *Managers of Virtue*, 77.

16. *Church Review,* quoted in Jorgenson, *The State and the Non-public School,* 109; Dorchester, *Romanism versus the Public School System,* 183.
17. George Deshon, "A Novel Defense of the Public School," *Catholic World* 50 (February 1890): 678. Nast's illustration appeared in the March 19, 1870, edition of *Harper's Weekly.*
18. Mulford, *The Nation,* 325-30, 346, 372-75.
19. Mulford, *The Nation,* 380 (emphasis added).
20. For examples, see Gellner, *Nations and Nationalism,* esp. the conclusion; and Benedict Anderson, *Imagined Communities,* chaps. 2 and 3.
21. Jorgenson, *The State and the Non-public School,* 150-51. Though Protestant critics exaggerated them, there were real cultural differences between Catholic and public schools. See Dolan, *The American Catholic Experience,* 219.
22. Josiah Strong, *Our Country: Its Possible Future and Present Crisis* (Cambridge: Belknap Press of Harvard University Press, 1963), 79, 90; Dorchester, *Romanism versus the Public School System,* 255.
23. James Aloysius Burns and Bernard J. Kohlbrenner, *A History of Catholic Education in the United States: A Textbook for Normal Schools and Teachers' Colleges* (New York: Benziger Brothers, 1937), 209.
24. Marcius Willson, *History of the United States, for the Use of Schools* (New York: Cales Bartlett, 1846), 80; Marcius Willson, *American History* (New York: Ivison and Phinney, 1857), 150-51.
25. Josiah Leeds, *A History of the United States of America* (Philadelphia: J. B. Lippincott, 1877), 19; Robert Reid Howison, *Student's History of the United States* (Richmond, Va.: Everett Waddey Company, 1892), 101; Joseph W. Southall, *Biennial Report of the Superintendent of Public Instruction* (Richmond, Va.: 1899), xli.
26. Willson, *American History,* 150; Emma Willard, *History of the United States; or, Republic of America* (New York: A. S. Barnes and Co., 1845), 30.
27. Olney, *History of the United States on a New Plan,* 264; Scudder, *A History of the United States of America,* 98.
28. Boorstin, *The Americans,* 364. For more on Bancroft and the development of American historiography, see Van Tassel, *Recording America's Past;* and David Levin, *History as Romantic Art: Bancroft, Prescott, Motley, and Parkman* (Stanford: Stanford University Press, 1959).
29. Ridpath, *History of the United States,* 102; "Ridpath, John Clark," in *Dictionary of American Biography,* ed. Dumas Malone (New York: Charles Scribner's Sons, 1959), 8:599. Unlike many of his peers, however, Ridpath was not a New Englander. He was born on a farm in Indiana in 1840 to parents who had moved from Virginia.
30. Levin, *History as Romantic Art,* 25-38; Willard, *Abridged History of the United States* (1858), 115.
31. Ridpath, *History of the United States,* 178; Muzzey, *An American History,* 333.

32. William H. Mace, *A School History of the United States* (Chicago: Rand McNally, 1904), 133; Mace, *Method in History for Teachers and Students*, 15–16.

33. Robert Ellis Thompson, *Political Economy*, 382; Strong, *Our Country*, 216.

34. Lawler, *Essentials of American History*, 10.

35. Franciscan Sisters, *History of the United States*, 23, 29.

36. Dorchester, *Romanism versus the Public School System*, 243; "The Anti-Catholic Spirit of Certain Writers," *Catholic World* 36 (February 1883): 665. The Catholic writer deftly evaded the arrest of Galileo, that Catholic inventor of the modern telescope who was punished by church officials for promoting the theory that the earth revolved around the sun.

37. S. A. Torrance, "Opinion," May 23, 1921, American Book Company Records, Box 95. John Holland built a fifty-three-foot-long forerunner to the modern submarine for the U.S. Navy, which acquired the vessel in 1900.

38. Franciscan Sisters, *History of the United States*, 62.

39. *Sadlier's Excelsior Studies in the History of the United States*, 100. A similarly graphic account appeared in McCarthy's history, though in this version the "baptismal" water was boiling hot. McCarthy, *History of the United States*, 130.

40. *Sadlier's Excelsior Studies in the History of the United States*, iv; Kennedy and [Dunn], *America's Story*, v.

41. *School History of the United States*, 188; McCarthy, *History of the United States*, iv, 325; *Sadlier's Excelsior Introduction to Geography*, quoted in Mead, *The Roman Catholic Church and the School Question*, 38.

42. Mead, *The Roman Catholic Church and the School Question*, 38.

43. *Sadlier's Excelsior Studies in the History of the United States*, 21; [Leger], *American History*, 110; Franciscan Sisters, *History of the United States*, 22, 53.

44. *Sadlier's Excelsior Studies in the History of the United States*, 121; Franciscan Sisters, *History of the United States*, 85–86; Hassard, *History of the United States*, 80.

45. Hassard, *History of the United States*, 81; Franciscan Sisters, *History of the United States*, 87; *Sadlier's Elementary History of the United States*, 122; *School History of the United States*, 63.

46. Hassard, *History of the United States*, 62–65; *Sadlier's Excelsior Studies in the History of the United States*, 84.

47. *Sadlier's Excelsior Studies in the History of the United States*, 83; Edward Taylor, *The Model History: A Brief Account of the American People, for Schools* (Chicago: Scott, Foresman and Co., 1897), 49.

48. *Sadliers' Preparatory History of the United States*, 90; Hassard, *History of the United States*, 113; Hassard, *Abridged History of the United States*, 35; *School History of the United States*, 80.

49. Willard, *Abridged History of the United States*, 132 (1858); John

Andrew Doyle, *History of the United States* (New York: Henry Holt and Co., 1876), 137.

50. Hassard, *History of the United States,* 66.

51. Bancroft, quoted in Levin, *History as Romantic Art,* 28; John Gilmary Shea, "Puritanism in New England," *American Catholic Quarterly Review* 9 (January 1884): 81; John Gilmary Shea, *The First Book of History Combined with Geography and Chronology, for Younger Classes* (New York: D. and J. Sadlier and Co., 1867), 213.

52. Lawler, *Essentials of American History,* 146–47; Franciscan Sisters, *History of the United States,* 179; [Leger], *American History,* 184.

53. *Sadlier's Excelsior Studies in the History of the United States,* 207; Lawler, *Essentials of American History,* 206; Kennedy and [Dunn], *The United States,* 256. Kosciusko, Pulaski, and de Kalb also appeared in some textbooks for public schools before 1920, but they were never specifically identified as Catholics. François Vigo is actually Joseph Maria Francesco Vigo, who aided George Rogers Clark in his campaigns against the British in the Old Northwest.

54. Franciscan Sisters, *History of the United States,* 240.

55. Franciscan Sisters, *History of the United States,* 254; O'Hara, *History of the United States,* 133, 190.

56. Franciscan Sisters, *History of the United States,* 239.

57. [Leger], *American History,* 422–25; *School History of the United States,* 246; Franciscan Sisters, *History of the United States,* 454.

58. [Leger], *American History,* 422; Franciscan Sisters, *History of the United States,* 452.

59. Hassard, *History of the United States,* 377; Lawler, *Essentials of American History,* 613; *School History of the United States,* 182.

60. Franciscan Sisters, *History of the United States,* 3.

61. Hassard, *History of the United States,* vi–vii.

62. Most historians limit discussion of the Americanist controversy to the 1880s and 1890s. The central questions in the debate can clearly be traced back to the 1850s, however, as Philip Gleason has shown. I examine the issue in this broader context. See "'Americanism' in American Catholic Discourse," in Philip Gleason, *Speaking of Diversity: Language and Ethnicity in Twentieth-Century America* (Baltimore: Johns Hopkins University Press, 1992).

63. Orestes A. Brownson, "Catholic Schools and Education," *Brownson's Quarterly Review* 3 (January 1862): 66–85, reprinted in *Catholic Education: A Book of Readings,* ed. Walter B. Kolesnick and Edward J. Power (New York: McGraw-Hill, 1965), 11.

64. R. Laurence Moore, *Religious Outsiders and the Making of Americans* (New York: Oxford University Press, 1986), 53–58.

65. Jorgenson, *The State and the Non-public School,* 146–58.

66. Cremin, *American Education,* 131; Dolan, *The American Catholic Experience,* 184.

67. For more on Catholic schools and assimilation, see the Rev. T. Edward Shields, "Catholic Education: The Basis of True Americanization," *Catholic Educational Review* 19 (January 1921): 3–19.

68. Buffalo *Volksfreund,* February 17, 1890, quoted in James Hennesey, *American Catholics: A History of the Roman Catholic Community in the United States* (New York: Oxford University Press), 195.

69. Franciscan Sisters, *History of the United States,* 342–43, 353–54; O'Hara, *History of the United States,* 272; *School History of the United States,* 177.

70. William Livengood to Louis E. Cadieux, December 19, 1912, American Book Company Records, Box 14.

71. Rev. John A. Waldron to American Book Company, December 3, 1915; and unsigned review, October 28, 1916; both in American Book Company Records, Box 48.

72. Louis E. Cadieux to Frank A. Fitzpatrick, December 8, 1917, American Book Company Records, Box 48.

73. Dolan, *The American Catholic Experience,* 273.

74. McCarthy, *History of the United States,* 345.

75. For more on the relationship between Catholicism and pluralism, see "Managing Catholic Success in a Protestant Empire," in Moore, *Religious Outsiders and the Making of Americans.*

76. Franciscan Sisters, *History of the United States,* 347, 542.

77. [Leger], *American History,* 571, 615.

78. McCarthy, *History of the United States,* 307; *Sadlier's Excelsior Studies in the History of the United States,* 372.

79. [Leger], *American History,* 613–15.

80. For more on the Oregon law, see David Tyack, "The Perils of Pluralism: The Background of the Pierce Case," *American Historical Review* 74 (October 1968): 74–98.

81. Sister M. Gabriella to American Book Company, May 10, 1921, American Book Company Records, Box 95.

82. The offending book was William M. Swinton's *Outlines of History,* published by Ivison, Blakeman, Taylor and Co. Edward Larson mentions the case briefly in "Constitutional Challenges to Textbooks," in *Textbooks in American Society: Politics, Policy, and Pedagogy,* ed. Philip G. Altbach et al. (Albany: State University of New York Press, 1991), 72–73.

83. Edward Channing to George Brett, February 15, 1901, Macmillan Company Papers, Author Files, Box 64.

84. Draft of Channing, *A Students' History of the United States,* Macmillan Company Records, Author Files, Box 65.

85. Howard K. Beale, *Are American Teachers Free? An Analysis of Restraints upon the Freedom of Teaching in American Schools* (New York: Charles Scribner's Sons, 1936), 197–98.

86. Lewis Paul Todd et al., *Rise of the American Nation, John Carroll Edition* (New York: Harcourt, Brace and World, 1961).

87. Pius IX, quoted in Morton Keller, *The Art and Politics of Thomas Nast* (New York: Oxford University Press, 1968), 160.

88. [Leger], *American History,* 616–17; Franciscan Sisters, *History of the United States,* 3.

89. Celeste, *American History,* 613; Lawler, *Essentials of American History,* 174, 255; Franciscan Sisters, *History of the United States,* 427, 553.

90. *Sadlier's Excelsior Studies in the History of the United States,* 359, 371.

91. *Sadlier's Excelsior Studies in the History of the United States,* 125; [Leger], *American History,* 116.

Chapter 4

1. McLaughlin, *A History of the American Nation,* 92–93.

2. Edward Eggleston, *New Century History of the United States* (New York: American Book Company, 1903), 16; Muzzey, *An American History,* 72–73.

3. Henry William Elson, *History of the United States of America* (New York: Macmillan, 1906), 559.

4. Wilbur Fisk Gordy, *A History of the United States for Schools* (New York: Charles Scribner's Sons, 1898), 391–92.

5. For this discussion of race I have relied heavily on five studies: Thomas F. Gossett, *Race: The History of an Idea in America* (New York: Oxford University Press, 1997); George M. Fredrickson, *The Black Image in the White Mind: The Debate on Afro-American Character and Destiny, 1817–1914* (New York: Harper and Row, 1971); Reginald Horsman, *Race and Manifest Destiny: The Origins of American Racial Anglo-Saxonism* (Cambridge: Harvard University Press, 1981); John S. Haller Jr., *Outcasts from Evolution: Scientific Attitudes of Racial Inferiority, 1859–1900* (Urbana: University of Illinois Press, 1971); and Ronald Takaki, *Iron Cages: Race and Culture in Nineteenth Century America* (New York: Knopf, 1979). For the origins of racialism and racial categories, I have also consulted Heidi Ardizzone, "Red-Blooded Americans: Mulattoes and the Melting Pot in United States Racialist and Nationalist Discourse, 1890–1930," (Ph.D. diss., University of Michigan, 1997).

6. Charles A. Goodrich, *A History of the United States of America* (1827), 292.

7. J. Hector St. John de Crèvecoeur, *Letters from an American Farmer and Sketches of Eighteenth-Century America,* ed. Albert E. Stone (New York: Penguin Books, 1986), 68.

8. Augusta Blanche Berard, *School History of the United States* (Philadelphia: Cowperthwait and Co., 1856), ix.

9. See "White Nationalism: Free Soil and the Ideal of Racial Homogeneity," in Fredrickson, *The Black Image in the White Mind.*

10. For more on race in nineteenth-century readers, spellers, geographies, histories, and texts on arithmetic, see Ruth Miller Elson, *Guardians of Tradi-*

tion: American Schoolbooks of the Nineteenth Century (Lincoln: University of Nebraska Press), esp. 65–185.

11. Fredrickson, *The Black Image in the White Mind,* 1–2, 75–80; Gossett, *Race,* 58, 60; Stephen Jay Gould, *The Mismeasure of Man* (New York: Norton, 1996), 97; Quackenbos, *Illustrated School History of the United States,* 12, 21.

12. Haller, *Outcasts from Evolution,* 121–31.

13. John Fiske, "Manifest Destiny," *Harper's New Monthly Magazine,* March 1885, 578, 588; Haller, *Outcasts from Evolution,* 162.

14. Robert Rydell claims that fairs helped to move scientific racism to a popular level. His argument that events like the Centennial Exposition in Philadelphia in 1876 offered Americans "an opportunity to reaffirm their collective national identity in an updated synthesis of progress and white supremacy" has influenced my analysis of race in textbooks. See Rydell, *All the World's a Fair: Visions of Empire at American International Expositions, 1876–1916* (Chicago: University of Chicago Press, 1984), 2–8.

15. Taylor, *The Model History,* 287.

16. Henry E. Chambers, *A Higher History of the United States for Schools and Academies* (New Orleans: F. F. Hansell and Brothers, 1889), 82.

17. For one example, see Goldman, *John Bach McMaster,* 92.

18. Reuben Gold Thwaites and Calvin Noyes Kendall, *A History of the United States for Schools* (Boston: Houghton Mifflin, 1912), 26; McLaughlin, *A History of the American Nation,* 92; Muzzey, *An American History,* 593; Joel Dorman Steele, *A Brief History of the United States* (New York: A. S. Barnes and Co., 1885), 75; Josiah H. Shinn, *History of the American People* (New York: American Book Company, 1893), 117; Mace, *A School History of the United States,* 98; Roscoe Lewis Ashley, *American History for Use in Secondary Schools* (New York: Macmillan, 1923), 333; Charles Kendall Adams and William P. Trent, *A History of the United States* (Boston: Allyn and Bacon, 1903), 192; Lee, *Lee's Advanced School History of the United States,* 119.

19. James Alton James and Albert Hart Sanford, *American History* (New York: Charles Scribner's Sons, 1909), 35, 129, 132; David Montgomery, *The Leading Facts of American History* (Boston: Ginn and Co., 1891), 2; Ashley, *American History for Use in Secondary Schools,* 218; Henry William Elson, *History of the United States of America,* xxix; McLaughlin, *A History of the American Nation,* 124.

20. Channing, *A Students' History of the United States,* 320–21.

21. Stuart Anderson notes that the imprecision of racial categories allowed speakers to adjust definitions to fit almost any circumstance. See *Race and Rapprochement: Anglo-Saxonism and Anglo-American Relations, 1895–1904* (Rutherford, N.J.: Fairleigh Dickinson University Press, 1981), 18.

22. Madison Grant, *The Passing of the Great Race* (New York: Charles Scribner's Sons, 1918), 81.

23. Ashley, *American History for Use in Secondary Schools,* 564–65.

24. Muzzey, *An American History,* 620–21 (emphasis added).
25. Novick, *That Noble Dream,* 81; Fiske, *A History of the United States for Schools,* 1.
26. Archer Butler Hulbert, *United States History* (Garden City, N.Y.: Doubleday, Page and Co., 1923), 386.
27. Ashley, *American History for Use in Secondary Schools,* 565; Muzzey, *An American History,* 620. For an analysis of historians' views on this subject, see Edward Saveth, *American Historians and European Immigrants, 1875–1925* (New York: Columbia University Press, 1948). The best general work on nativism remains Higham's *Strangers in the Land.*
28. Several publishers did ask Turner to write a history for schools, however. See Ray Allen Billington, *Frederick Jackson Turner: Historian, Scholar, Teacher* (New York: Oxford University Press, 1973), 202–8.
29. Frederick Jackson Turner, *Frontier and Section: Selected Essays of Frederick Jackson Turner,* ed. Ray Allen Billington (Englewood Cliffs.: Prentice-Hall, 1961), 61.
30. Billington, *Frederick Jackson Turner,* 64–66, 108–31; Gossett, *Race,* 87–88.
31. Ashley, *American History for Use in Secondary Schools,* 284; Charles Manfred Thompson, *History of the United States: Political, Industrial, Social* (Chicago: Benjamin H. Sanborn, 1917), 177; Willis Mason West, *History of the American People* (Boston: Allyn and Bacon, 1918), 445; Muzzey, *An American History,* 261.
32. Muzzey, *An American History,* 324–29; McLaughlin, *A History of the American Nation,* 329; Charles Beard and Mary Beard, *History of the United States* (New York: Macmillan, 1921), 434–35. There are a few exceptions to this depiction of the West. For instance, Archer Butler Hulbert tried to divest the cowboy of any specific racial identity: "Oddly enough he was of no particular race or country; his fraternity gathered from all the world, built of all timber; but in him the United States gained a new citizen and the world another voyageur and coureur-de-bois of New France." See Hulbert, *United States History,* 410.
33. Quoted in Raymond L. Kilgour, *Lee and Shepard: Publisher for the People* (Hamden, Conn.: Shoe String Press, 1965), 196.
34. The quoted phrase about Pocahontas's descendants appears in at least a dozen nineteenth-century textbooks. Ruth Miller Elson discusses romantic influences on portrayals of Indians in schoolbooks, and particularly the appearance of the noble savage, in *Guardians of Tradition,* 71–76.
35. Charles A. Goodrich, *A History of the United States of America* (1847), 19; Swinton, *A Condensed School History of the United States,* 21.
36. For an excellent introduction to historiography promoting the belief that the Indians' fate was unavoidable, see Gary B. Nash, "The Concept of Inevitability in the History of European-Indian Relations," in *Inequality in*

Early America, ed. Carla Gardina Pestana and Sharon V. Salinger (Hanover: University Press of New England), 267–91.

37. Samuel G. Goodrich, *A Pictorial History of the United States* (Philadelphia: Sorin and Ball, and Samuel Agnew, 1846), 87. Several other writers paid by Goodrich also prepared schoolbooks under the Peter Parley pseudonym. Parley's real-life counterparts included novelist Nathaniel Hawthorne.

38. Quackenbos, *Illustrated School History of the United States,* 367.

39. Willson, *American History,* 534; Quackenbos, *Illustrated School History of the United States,* 21.

40. Frederick E. Hoxie, *A Final Promise: The Campaign to Assimilate the Indians, 1880–1920* (Lincoln: University of Nebraska Press, 1984), 15–32.

41. "Dorchester, Daniel," in *American National Biography,* ed. John A. Garraty and Mark C. Jones (New York: Oxford University Press, 1999), 6:749–50.

42. John William Jones, *School History of the United States,* 12.

43. Shinn, *History of the American People,* 11; Eggleston, *New Century History of the United States,* 18–19.

44. Hoxie, *A Final Promise,* 16–22; Fiske, *A History of the United States for Schools,* 16.

45. Steele, *A Brief History of the United States,* 12. In an afterthought buried in a footnote, Steele admitted there were some exceptions to this general picture.

46. Henry William Elson, *History of the United States of America,* 37. For a typical critique of that division of labor, see Mace, *A School History of the United States,* 22–25.

47. Samuel Eagle Forman, *A History of the United States* (New York: Century Company, 1910), 28; Albert Bushnell Hart, *School History of the United States* (New York: American Book Company, 1920), 384. To be fair to authors in this study, many also used more positive terms to describe typical Indians, including "fierce," "courageous," "dignified," "reserved," and "generous."

48. Henry William Elson, *History of the United States of America,* 35; Muzzey, *An American History,* 549.

49. Hart, *School History of the United States,* 248.

50. Lee, *Lee's Advanced School History of the United States,* 248.

51. Muzzey, *An American History,* 85–86, 159.

52. Henry William Elson, *History of the United States of America,* 175; West, *History of the American People,* 12.

53. West, *History of the American People,* 5; James and Sanford, *American History,* 25; Channing, *A Students' History of the United States,* 1.

54. Fredrickson, *The Black Image in the White Mind,* 237–39. Owing to increased European immigration, the nationwide percentage of "all persons of negro descent," the census's term, did decline from 1870 to 1900, from 12.7 to 11.6 percent. See U.S. Census Office, *Twelfth Census of the United States, Taken in the Year 1900* (Washington, D.C.: U.S. Census Office, 1901), 1:cxv.

55. For a good introduction to these portrayals of African-Americans in the early twentieth century, see Lawrence D. Reddick, "Racial Attitudes in American History Textbooks of the South," *Journal of Negro History* 19 (July 1934): 225–65.

56. Gordy, *A History of the United States for Schools,* 278; Eggleston, *New Century History of the United States,* 304, 361.

57. Allen C. Thomas, *A History of the United States* (Boston: D. C. Heath, 1899), 152.

58. From a history popular in the South: "Men in Massachusetts preached abolition on every corner. They spread tracts over the country, which were couched in language that stirred the blood. The mails carried these to the negroes, who started an insurrection at Southampton, Va., in which men, women, and children were murdered in their beds." Shinn, *History of the American People,* 294, 120.

59. Evans, *Essential Facts of American History,* 53; Waddy Thompson, *History of the People of the United States* (Atlanta: D. C. Heath, 1930), 20.

60. Beard and Beard, *History of the United States,* 331, 379.

61. Thwaites and Kendall, *A History of the United States for Schools,* 393–94; West, *History of the American People,* 582.

62. James and Sanford, *American History,* 430; Forman, *A History of the United States,* 370.

63. Mace, *A School History of the United States,* 391.

64. Henry William Elson, *History of the United States of America,* 800; Muzzey, *An American History,* 550, 619.

65. Willis Mason West, a history professor at the University of Minnesota, critiqued disfranchisement and Jim Crow most forcefully in his 1918 text. He suggested that the ideal of "separate but equal" access to education, transportation, and other public services was little more than a sham. See *History of the American People,* 599.

66. Beard and Beard, *History of the United States,* 383; Adams and Trent, *A History of the United States,* 538.

67. Adams and Trent, *A History of the United States,* 453–54. George M. Fredrickson explains the position of liberal accommodationists in *The Black Image in the White Mind,* 283–319.

68. Muzzey, *An American History,* 619–20; Bruce, *A School History of the United States,* 340. Virginia adopted Bruce's book for its grammar schools from approximately 1905 to 1910.

69. Adams and Trent, *A History of the United States,* 459; Muzzey, *An American History,* 459. For more on the parallels drawn between African Americans and "primitive" peoples outside the United States, see Silber, *The Romance of Reunion,* 181–82.

70. "Johnson, Edward Austin," in *Dictionary of American Biography: Supplement Three, 1941–45,* ed. Edward T. James et al. (New York: Charles Scribner's Sons, 1973), 390–91.

71. Johnson, *School History of the Negro Race in America*, iii.
72. Johnson, *School History of the Negro Race in America*, iii–iv, 91–92.
73. Johnson, *School History of the Negro Race in America*, 48, 72, 156.
74. Johnson, *School History of the Negro Race in America*, 142–44.
75. Hart, *School History of the United States*, 13, 110, 359; West, *History of the American People*, 571.
76. Montgomery, *The Leading Facts of American History*, 354–55; Thalheimer, *Eclectic History of the United States*, 341; Adams and Trent, *A History of the United States*, 485.
77. Eggleston, *New Century History of the United States*, 376; Beard and Beard, *History of the United States*, 583.
78. Hart, *School History of the United States*, 472; Ashley, *American History for Use in Secondary Schools*, 565.
79. Elson, *History of the United States of America*, 801.
80. Ernest Renan, "What Is a Nation?" trans. Martin Thom, in *Nation and Narration*, ed. Homi K. Bhabha (London: Routledge, 1990), 14, 19.

Chapter 5

1. Darrow and Mann, quoted in Lloyd Wendt and Herman Kogan, *Big Bill of Chicago* (Indianapolis: Bobbs-Merrill, 1953), 289, 299.
2. Rupert Hughes, "Plea for Frankness in Writing of History," *Current History* 27 (February 1928): 625, 627; Arthur M. Schlesinger [Sr.], "Points of View in Historical Writing," *Publishers' Weekly*, January 14, 1928, 148.
3. Precise definitions of the New History vary. I use the term fairly broadly to indicate the shift toward institutional approaches in all fields of history and the simultaneous rise of the ideal of objectivity. For more on the subject, see Novick, *That Noble Dream*, 89–92.
4. For an indication of how much this newer style of history had trickled down to schoolbooks by century's end, see New England History Teachers Association (NEHTA), "Text-Books in American History," *Educational Review* 16 (December 1898): 480–502.
5. James Truslow Adams, "History and the Lower Criticism," *Atlantic Monthly*, September 1923, 316.
6. Milton Fairman, "Developments in Chicago," *Publishers' Weekly*, December 3, 1927, 2035.
7. Stuart Anderson, *Race and Rapprochement*, 12–13, 95–100; "Are the Americans Anglo-Saxons?" *Living Age*, June 4, 1898, 681–83, reprinted from the *Spectator*.
8. Stuart Anderson, *Race and Rapprochement*, 39, 112–29.
9. Edward P. Crapol, *America for Americans: Economic Nationalism and Anglophobia in the Late Nineteenth Century* (Westport, Conn.: Greenwood Press, 1973), 14, 222–25.
10. Goldwyn Smith, "Are Our School Histories Anglophobe?" *North*

American Review, September 1897, 257; John Bach McMaster, "The Social Function of United States History," National Herbart Society for the Scientific Study of Teaching, *Yearbook* (1898), 4:28, quoted in Novick, *That Noble Dream*, 83.

11. Quackenbos, *Illustrated School History of the United States*, 205, 259, 302.

12. Quackenbos, *Illustrated School History of the United States*, 266; Anderson, *A Pictorial School History of the United States*, 110; Ridpath, *History of the United States*, 179, 183; Thalheimer, *Eclectic History of the United States*, 124.

13. Goldwyn Smith, "Are Our School Histories Anglophobe?" 259–60; NEHTA, "Text-Books in American History," 487.

14. Albert Bushnell Hart, "School Books and International Prejudices," *International Conciliation* 38 (January 1911): 4–6.

15. Hart, "School Books and International Prejudices," 7.

16. Adams and Trent, *A History of the United States*, v; Novick, *That Noble Dream*, 83.

17. Hart, "School Books and International Prejudices," 13.

18. See Webster, "On the Education of Youth in America."

19. See chap. 5 in Nagel, *This Sacred Trust;* and chap. 6 in Stuart Anderson, *Race and Rapprochement.*

20. For more on nativism among historians, see Saveth, *American Historians and European Immigrants.* The leading but more general work on the subject remains Higham's *Strangers in the Land.* Stuart Anderson explores the versatility of Anglo-Saxon racial definitions in "The Cult of Anglo-Saxonism," in *Race and Rapprochement.*

21. National Education Association (NEA), *Report of the Committee on Secondary School Studies* (Washington, D.C.: Government Printing Office, 1893), 175; American Historical Association, *The Study of History in Schools: Report to the American Historical Association by the Committee of Seven* (New York: Macmillan, 1900), 13; American Historical Association, *The Study of History in Secondary Schools: Report to the American Historical Association by the Committee of Five* (New York: Macmillan, 1911), 60.

22. Gossett, *Race*, 318; Editorial, *Educational Review* 16 (September 1898): 204.

23. Muzzey, *An American History*, 246, 567; Channing, *A Students' History of the United States*, 320–21; McLaughlin, *A History of the American Nation*, 118, 329; West, *History of the American People*,144; Thomas, *A History of the United States*, 241; Ashley, *American History for Use in Secondary Schools*, 218; Eggleston, *New Century History of the United States*, 141. Textbooks in a variety of subjects, not just history, firmly reclaimed British heritage by century's end. See Ruth Miller Elson, *Guardians of Tradition*, 123.

24. Hart, *School History of the United States*, 126; John Holladay Latané,

Notes to Pages 185–92

History of the United States (Boston: Allyn and Bacon, 1918), 104; Beard and Beard, *History of the United States,* 75.

25. Muzzey, *An American History,* 107.

26. Beard and Beard, *History of the United States,* 84; Charles Manfred Thompson, *History of the United States,* 117–18; Everett Barnes, *American History for Grammar Grades* (Boston: D. C. Heath, 1913), 193.

27. Hart, "School Books and International Prejudices," 12; West, *History of the American People,* 191.

28. "A.O.H. Allied with Germans," *Boston Globe,* January 25, 1907, 3.

29. *Mitteilungen,* July 1914, trans. in United States Congress, Senate, *National German-American Alliance: Hearings before the Subcommittee of the Committee on the Judiciary,* Sixty-fifth Congress, S. 3529 (Washington, D.C.: Government Printing Office, 1918), 670.

30. *Mitteilungen,* July 1914, 18, 619–20.

31. For this discussion I have relied on George T. Blakey, *Historians on the Homefront: American Propagandists for the Great War* (Lexington: University Press of Kentucky, 1970); Stephen Vaughn, *Holding Fast the Inner Lines: Democracy, Nationalism, and the Committee on Public Information* (Chapel Hill: University of North Carolina Press, 1980); and James Mock and Cedric Larson, *Words That Won the War: The Story of the Committee on Public Information, 1917–1919* (New York: Russell and Russell, 1939).

32. Quoted in Blakey, *Historians on the Homefront,* 123.

33. Stuart P. Sherman, *American and Allied Ideals,* War Information Series, no. 12 (Washington, D.C.: Committee on Public Information, 1918), 7.

34. Blakey, *Historians on the Homefront,* 43, 47. John Higham explores the partial merging of nationalist and nativist thought during the war in chaps. 8 and 9 of *Strangers in the Land.*

35. Vaughn, *Holding Fast the Inner Lines,* 98.

36. Robert J. Aley, "The War and Secondary Schools," *Education* 38 (May 1918): 629–32.

37. Charles Altschul, *The American Revolution in Our School Text-Books: An Attempt to Trace the Influence of Early School Education on the Feeling towards England in the United States* (New York: George H. Doran Company, 1917), x. For other examples of educators' calls to revise the story of the Revolution to Britain's benefit, along with suggestions to teachers to emphasize England's cultural contributions to the United States, see Clyde Eagleton, "The Attitude of Our Textbooks toward England," *Educational Review* 56 (December 1918): 424–27; and Robert Schuyler, "History and Public Opinion," *Educational Review* 55 (March 1918): 182–90.

38. William Backus Guitteau, *Our United States: A History* (New York: Silver, Burdett and Co., 1919), 482. While the publisher released this edition after the armistice, its revisions reflected wartime influences.

39. Pierce, *Public Opinion and the Teaching of History,* 246–48.

40. T. Everett Harré, "Shadow Huns and Others," *National Civic Federation Review* 4 (February 15, 1919): 18; Pierce, *Public Opinion and the Teaching of History*, 250; West, *History of the American People*, 243, 703, 713.

41. Blakey, *Historians on the Homefront*, 131.

42. Henry L. Mencken, "Star-Spangled Men," *New Republic*, September 29, 1920, 118–20; Blakey, *Historians on the Homefront*, 130. Blakey shows how historians who worked for the CPI, NBHS, and NSL came to be blamed for much of the most incendiary propaganda the organizations produced.

43. "The Trail of the Jesuit," *New Age*, March 1923, 154–55.

44. Edward F. McSweeney, *America First* (Boston: n.p., 1920), 2, 7, 11. For similar Irish-American attacks on textbooks, see Michael O'Brien, *A Hidden Phase of American History* (New York: Dodd, Mead and Co., 1919); and Joseph T. Griffin, *American History: Must It Be Rewritten to Preserve Our Foreign Friendships?* (Boston: Knights of Columbus Historical Commission, 1922).

45. McSweeney, *America First*, 2.

46. Charles Grant Miller, *Treason to American Tradition: The Spirit of Benedict Arnold Reincarnated in United States History Revised in Text Books* (New York: Patriotic League for the Preservation of American History, 1922), 19, 22, 27; West, *History of the American People*, 636.

47. "Anti-English Teaching," *New York Times*, December 28, 1921, 14; Charles Grant Miller, *The Poisoned Loving-Cup: United States School Histories Falsified through Pro-British Propaganda in the Sweet Name of Amity* (Chicago: National Historical Society, 1928), 155.

48. Miller listed groups who supported his charges in the front matter of *Treason to American Tradition* and in the introduction to his later book, *The Poisoned Loving-Cup*.

49. James M. Graham, *Anglicizing Our School Histories* (Illinois: n.p., 1922), 15; *Illinois State Register,* July 1922; and George W. Benton to Louis B. Lee, October 31, 1922; all in American Book Company Records, Box 82; Brother Bernardine, F.S.C., to Charles H. McCarthy, February 27, 1921, American Book Company Records, Box 95.

50. Pierce, *Public Opinion and the Teaching of History*, 276–77; "A Report on History Textbooks Used in the Public Schools of the City of New York," *School Review* 30 (September 1922): 490–92; "Authors Defend School Histories," *New York Times*, December 3, 1921, 28. For a concise summary and analysis of the New York investigations, see Bethany Andreasen, "Treason or Truth: The New York City Textbook Controversy, 1920–1923," *New York History* 66 (October 1985): 396–419.

51. Pierce, *Public Opinion and the Teaching of History,* 279–80; "School Histories Praised and Blamed," *New York Times,* May 16, 1922, 19; "Sustains Charge against Historians," *New York Times,* June 19, 1922, 16.

52. Andreasen, "Treason or Truth," 403–4; "Textbooks Again under Fire," *Publishers' Weekly,* April 29, 1922, 1218; "History Inquiry Ordered by

Hylan," *New York Times,* December 7, 1921, 36; "Hirshfield to Say if History Is Right," *New York Times,* December 8, 1921, 15; "Hirshfield to Set Our History Right," *New York Times,* December 30, 1921, 20.

53. "Hirshfield Charges School Histories Slur U.S.," *Publishers' Weekly,* June 9, 1923, 1764-65; "Behind the Hirshfield History Investigation," *Publishers' Weekly,* November 24, 1923, 1718; "Topics of the Times," *New York Times,* November 6, 1923, 18; David Hirshfield, *Report on Investigation of Pro-British Text-Books in Use in the Public Schools of the City of New York* (New York: n.p., 1923), 11-14.

54. Miller, *The Poisoned Loving-Cup,* 151-52; Pierce, *Public Opinion and the Teaching of History,* 264, 293-94 (Pierce reprints the text of Wisconsin's law and California's report clearing the textbooks in her appendix); J. Franklin Jameson, "The Meeting of the American Historical Association at Columbus," *American Historical Review* 29 (April 1924): 428; Beale, *Are American Teachers Free?* 262-64; Schlesinger [Sr.], "Points of View in Historical Writing," 147; "Boston Council Bars Book as Pro-British," *Publishers' Weekly,* September 30, 1922, 1209; "Who's to Set Standards?" *Publishers' Weekly,* April 7, 1923, 1141.

55. Mary J. Herrick, *The Chicago Schools: A Social and Political History* (Beverly Hills: Sage Publications, 1971), 166-67; David Hogan, *Class and Reform: School and Society in Chicago, 1880-1930* (Philadelphia: University of Pennsylvania Press, 1985), 211-14; Milton Fairman, "Superintendent McAndrew and Chicago Textbooks on Trial," *Publishers' Weekly,* October 29, 1927, 1628; "Chicago on Trial," *New York Times,* October 1, 1927, 18; Wendt and Kogan, *Big Bill of Chicago,* 267-68; George S. Counts, *School and Society in Chicago* (New York: Harcourt, Brace and Co., 1928), 274-75.

56. The *Chicago Tribune,* quoted in Counts, *School and Society in Chicago,* 266-77.

57. Albert Bushnell Hart, "'Treasonable' Textbooks and True Patriotism," *Current History* 27 (February 1928): 630-31; Fairman, "Superintendent McAndrew and Chicago Textbooks on Trial," 1627-29; William Hale Thompson, "Shall We Shatter the Nation's Idols in School Histories?" *Current History* 27 (February 1928): 623; "Patriotism in Chicago," *Publishers' Weekly,* October 29, 1927, 1630-31; "Library Directors Rebuke Thompson," *Publishers' Weekly,* November 5, 1927, 1718; "Thompson Starts Hunt in Libraries," *New York Times,* October 21, 1927, 18; "Four 'British' Books Seized in Chicago," *New York Times,* October 27, 1927, 1; "Denounce Politics in McAndrew Trial," *New York Times,* November 4, 1927, 23; "'Big Billism' again Sets Chicago Agog," *New York Times,* November 6, 1927, sect. 10, p. 1.

58. Lawrence Martin, "Higher Education in Chicago," *Nation,* November 16, 1927, 539.

59. Pierce, *Public Opinion and the Teaching of History,* 278; "Censorship of Text-Books," *School and Society* 18 (July 7, 1923): 19.

60. Muzzey, *An American History*, 621–22; James and Sanford, *American History*, 519; Beard and Beard, *History of the United States*, 411; Hulbert, *United States History*, 531.

61. Miller, *The Poisoned Loving-Cup*, 71.

62. Reuben Post Halleck, *History of Our Country for Higher Grades* (New York: American Book Company, 1923), 6.

63. Miller, *The Poisoned Loving-Cup*, 63.

64. A few textbooks for Catholic schools, however, did mention the Revolutionary contributions of one Italian, Joseph Maria Francesco (a.k.a. François) Vigo.

65. Hart, "'Treasonable' Textbooks and True Patriotism," 631.

66. Pierce, *Public Opinion and the Teaching of History*, 209; Miller, *Treason to American Tradition*, 16, 18; Miller, *The Poisoned Loving-Cu*p, vii, 27; McSweeney, *America First*, 8; Graham, *Anglicizing Our School Histories*, 15.

67. Miller, *Treason to American Tradition*, 46 (emphasis added).

68. Thwaites and Kendall, *A History of the United States for Grammar Schools*, 132.

69. Hart, "'Treasonable' Textbooks and True Patriotism," 632; Albert Bushnell Hart, "Is the Puritan Race Dying Out?" *Munsey's Magazine*, May 1911, 255.

70. West, *History of the American People*, 144.

71. "Hirshfield Finds Heroes for History," *New York Times*, February 4, 1922, 22; Hirshfield, *Report on Investigation of Pro-British Textbooks*, 8–9.

72. William Hale Thompson, "Shall We Shatter the Nation's Idols in Histories?" 624–25; "Mayor Thompson Offers a Prize," *Publishers' Weekly*, November 12, 1927, 1806; "Memorial and Recommendations of the Grand Council Fire of American Indians," quoted in Jeanette Henry, *Textbooks and the American Indian* (San Francisco: Indian Historian Press, 1970), 2.

73. Michael Kammen, *Mystic Chords of Memory: The Transformation of Tradition in American Culture* (New York: Knopf, 1991), 258–59.

74. Miller, *The Poisoned Loving-Cup*, 10; "Hirshfield to Say if History Is Right," 15; "School Histories Praised and Blamed," *New York Times*, May 16, 1922, 19.

75. Beale, *Are American Teachers Free?* 314; Adams, "History and the Lower Criticism"; Harold Underwood Faulkner, "Perverted American History," *Harper's Monthly Magazine*, February 1926, 346; Harry E. Barnes, "The Drool Method in American History," *American Mercury*, January 1924, 31.

76. Jameson, "The Meeting of the American Historical Association at Columbus," 428.

77. William Livengood to J. C. Dockrill, August 4, 1921, American Book Company Records, Box 95.

78. Hirshfield, *Report on Investigation of Pro-British Text-Books*, 10; "What About Our History Textbooks?" *Publishers' Weekly*, July 1, 1922, 17;

Beale, *Are American Teachers Free?* 279. Beale summarizes many of these revisions on pages 279–319.

79. "Chicago Buys a Hundred Per Cent Textbook," *Publishers' Weekly,* December 17, 1927, 2164; "K. of C. to Spend $500,000 on New History of U.S.," *Chicago Examiner,* May 29, 1921, 3.

80. Charles F. Horne, *The Story of Our American People,* 2 vols. (Washington, D.C.: United States History Publishing Company, 1926); Faulkner, "Perverted American History," 345.

81. Charles F. Horne, *The Divided Colonies,* vol. 1, *Story of Our American People,* 8; Charles F. Horne, *The United States,* vol. 2, *Story of Our American People,* 463–66. For a contemporary critique of the portrayal of Chinese and Chinese-Americans in these books, see Timothy Tingfang Lew, "China in American School Text-Books," supplement to the *Chinese Social and Political Science Review* 7 (July 1923): 1–150.

82. For instance, see Miller, *The Poisoned Loving-Cup,* 8–9.

83. Beale, *Are American Teachers Free?* 200–202.

84. Miller, *Treason to American Tradition,* 6, 46; William Hale Thompson, "Shall We Shatter the Nation's Idols in School Histories?" 625. I base the claim of ghostwriting on similar passages that appeared in Miller's earlier pamphlet, *Treason to American Tradition.*

85. Beale, *Are American Teachers Free?* 281, 301, 317; Upton Sinclair, *The Goslings* (Pasadena: n.p., 1924), 307.

Chapter 6

1. These figures are an approximation based on several sources. See "Propaganda Purge," *Time,* July 10, 1939, 42; "Prof. H. O. Rugg on Carpet in Row over 'Radical' Texts," *Newsweek,* December 4, 1939, 47–48; Ruth Byrns, "Professor Harold Rugg: How an Educator Becomes an Issue," *Commonweal,* October 31, 1941, 42–45; "Rugg Critics Lose Ground," *Publishers' Weekly,* October 12, 1940, 1942.

2. Elmer A. Winters, "Man and His Changing Society: The Textbooks of Harold Rugg," *History of Education Quarterly* 7 (winter 1967): 510.

3. Robert Iversen, *The Communists and the Schools* (New York: Harcourt, Brace and Co., 1959), 248, 342.

4. Benedict Anderson, *Imagined Communities,* 7.

5. Jack Nelson and Gene Roberts Jr., *The Censors and the Schools* (Boston: Little, Brown and Co., 1963), 39.

6. *Lincoln: Selected Speeches and Writings,* 234.

7. Curti, *The Roots of American Loyalty,* 193–94.

8. Horatio Alger Jr., *Ragged Dick; or, Street Life in New York with the Boot Blacks* (New York: Signet Books, 1990), 1–2.

9. Edward Bellamy, *Looking Backward* (New York: New American Library, 1960), 51, 53.

10. For an example, see Rabbi Solomon Schindler, "What Is Nationalism?" *New England Magazine,* September 1892, 53–61. Schindler argued that activist central states would assume increasing responsibility for social welfare, pointing to his native Germany as a model.

11. Curti, *The Roots of American Loyalty,* 174, 194, 233–34; Nagel, *This Sacred Trust,* 273, 274.

12. Taylor, *The Model History,* 286.

13. McMaster, *A School History of the United States,* 187, 375.

14. FitzGerald, *America Revised,* 106.

15. Elizabeth Sadler, "One Book's Influence," *New England Quarterly* 17 (December 1944): 530–55; Erich Fromm, foreword to Bellamy, *Looking Backward,* v, vi. For more on the influence of Bellamy's ideas, see "Edward Bellamy and the Nationalist Movement," in John Hope Franklin, *Race and History: Selected Essays* (Baton Rouge: Louisiana State University Press, 1989).

16. Franklin Delano Roosevelt, *Nothing to Fear: The Selected Addresses of Franklin Delano Roosevelt, 1932–1945,* ed. B. D. Zevin (Cambridge, Mass.: Riverside Press, 1946), 91.

17. "Rugg, Harold [Ordway]," in *The National Cyclopaedia of American Biography* (New York: James T. White and Co., 1946), G:543; Peter F. Carbone Jr., *The Social and Educational Thought of Harold Rugg* (Durham: Duke University Press), 8, 18–20.

18. Winters, "Man and His Changing Society," 495–96, 501–3.

19. Harold Rugg, *That Men May Understand: An American in the Long Armistice* (New York: Doubleday, Doran and Co., 1941), 172–76.

20. Lawrence A. Cremin, David A. Shannon, and Mary Evelyn Townsend, *A History of Teachers College, Columbia University* (New York: Columbia University Press, 1954), 110; Carbone, *The Social and Educational Thought of Harold Rugg,* 140–41.

21. Rugg, *That Men May Understand,* 208, 223; Winters, "Man and His Changing Society," 510.

22. Harold Rugg, *America's March toward Democracy: A History of American Life, Political and Social* (Boston: Ginn and Co., 1937), 3–4, 14; Harold Rugg, *The Conquest of America: A History of American Civilization, Economic and Social* (Boston: Ginn and Co., 1937), 8.

23. Rugg, *The Conquest of America,* 210, 214.

24. Rugg, *America's March toward Democracy,* 69.

25. West, *History of the American People,* 243.

26. Rugg, *America's March toward Democracy,* 106–10, 113, 136–37.

27. Rugg, *The Conquest of America,* 451–56; Rugg, *America's March toward Democracy,* 352, 422.

28. Rugg, *America's March toward Democracy,* 430; Harold Rugg, *Our Country and Our People: An Introduction to American Civilization* (Boston: Ginn and Co., 1938), 552.

29. Carbone, *The Social and Educational Thought of Harold Rugg*, 39–42. For more on educational radicalism that flourished in a "minor key" during the 1920s and 1930s, see Lawrence A. Cremin, *The Transformation of the Schools* (New York: Knopf, 1961), esp. 224–36.

30. Iverson, *The Communists and the Schools*, 64–65; Cremin, *The Transformation of the Schools*, 233. Rugg briefly edited the journal in the late 1930s under its new name, *Frontiers of Democracy*. For a critical look at the reconstructionists, see Ravitch, *Left Back*, 218–24

31. Rugg, *An Introduction to Problems of American Culture*, 96–103; FitzGerald, *America Revised*, 108.

32. Rugg, *An Introduction to Problems of American Culture*, 197, 597–98.

33. Rugg, *The Conquest of America*, 502–4.

34. Rugg, *That Men May Understand*, 212.

35. To see how this argument applies to more contemporary history, particularly the teaching of the American war in Vietnam, see "Down the Memory Hole: The Disappearance of the Recent Past," in Loewen, *Lies My Teacher Told Me*.

36. Rugg, *The Conquest of America*, 511–14, 522, 530.

37. Nelson and Roberts, *The Censors and the Schools*, 31–34; Bruce Raup, *Education and Organized Interests in America* (New York: G. P. Putnam's Sons, 1936), 17–21; Beale, *Are American Teachers Free?* 555–71.

38. Carbone, *The Social and Educational Thought of Harold Rugg*, 170.

39. Rugg, *That Men May Understand*, 123, 165–66; "Histories of U.S. Held Provincial," *New York Times*, November 12, 1941, 25; "Prof. H. O. Rugg in Row over 'Radical' Texts," 47; "Iowa School Bars Rugg's Books," *New York Times*, June 20, 1940, 25; "The Crusade against Rugg," *New Republic*, March 10, 1941, 327.

40. Rugg, *That Men May Understand*, 20.

41. "Propaganda Purge," *Time*, July 10, 1939, 42; "Advertising Groups Pursuing Professor Rugg's Books," *Publishers' Weekly*, September 28, 1940, 1322–23.

42. "Textbook Digests for N.A.M. Finished," *New York Times*, January 2, 1941, 21; "Un-American Tone Seen in Textbooks on Social Studies," *New York Times*, February 22, 1941, 1, 6; "Rugg Texts Receive Favorable Report in Philadelphia," *Publishers' Weekly*, April 12, 1941, 1548.

43. "Legion Attacks Rugg's Books," *New York Times*, May 3, 1941, 21; "The Crusade against Rugg," 327; Iversen, *The Communists and the Schools*, 176.

44. Oliver Carlson and Ernest Sutherland Bates, *Hearst: Lord of San Simeon* (New York: Viking, 1936), 302–3.

45. Quoted in Carbone, *The Social and Educational Thought of Harold Rugg*, 28.

46. Guardians of American Education, *Undermining Our Republic: Facts*

about Anti-American School Books and the Nationwide Scheme of Radical Educators (New York: n.p., 1941), 17; O. K Armstrong, "Treason in the Textbooks," *American Legion Magazine,* September 1940, 8.

47. "Un-American Tone Seen in Textbooks on Social Sciences," 1 Guardians of American Education, *Undermining Our Republic,* 27; "Asks Ban on Rugg Books," *New York Times,* October 13, 1940, 47.

48. Ravitch, *Left Back,* 236.

49. Guardians of American Education, *Undermining Our Republic,* 13–15.

50. Guardians of American Education, *Undermining Our Republic,* 36.

51. Armstrong, "Treason in the Textbooks," 8–9, 51, 70; Harold Rugg *Teachers Guide and Key for Our Country and Our People* (Boston: Ginn and Co., 1937), 38. The illustration provides a good example of what Lawrence A Cremin has called the "caricature of the radical pedagogue using the schools to subvert the American way of life." See Cremin, *The Transformation of the Schools,* 233.

52. George Sokolsky, "Is Your Child Being Taught to Loaf?" *Liberty,* May 4, 1940, 42.

53. Rugg, *The Conquest of America,* 355; John Dewey, "Nationalizing Education," in National Education Association, *Addresses and Proceedings of the Fifty-fourth Annual Meeting* (Washington, D.C.: n.p. 1916), 183–89.

54. Rugg, *That Men May Understand,* 51; "Rugg Textbooks Receive Favorable Report in Philadelphia," 1548.

55. Carbone, *The Social and Educational Thought of Harold Rugg,* 28.

56. George H. Sabine et al., *The Text Books of Harold Rugg: An Analysis* (New York: American Committee for Democracy and Intellectual Freedom 1942), 26–27.

57. "Rugg Textbooks Restored in Englewood," *Publishers' Weekly,* January 25, 1941, 434; Rugg, *That Men May Understand,* 34; "Ridgefield Backs Rugg Books," *New York Times,* February 12, 1941, 15; "The Present Status on the Textbook Controversy," *School and Society* 53 (April 12, 1941): 465 "Advertising Groups Pursuing Professor Rugg's Books," 1322; Frederic G Melcher, "Rugg Serves Freedom of Education," *Publishers' Weekly,* April 12 1941, 1533; "Book Burnings," *Time,* September 9, 1940, 65.

58. Bertie C. Forbes, "Does This Smell of Sovietism?" *Forbes,* February 1 1940, 10.

59. Rugg, *America's March toward Democracy,* 352; Harold Rugg, *The Teacher of Teachers: Frontiers of Theory and Practice in Teacher Education* (New York: Harper and Brothers, 1952), 75–76, 166. Peter F. Carbone Jr. also suggests Rugg's books grew less relevant during and after World War II and cites Rugg's views on the mixed economy. See *The Social and Educational Thought of Harold Rugg,* 28–33, 65, 67.

60. Novick, *That Noble Dream,* 332–48; 380–96. For representative examples of consensus work, see Hans Kohn, *American Nationalism: An Interpretive Essay* (New York: Macmillan, 1957); Arthur M. Schlesinger Jr., *The Vital*

Center: The Politics of Freedom (Boston: Houghton Mifflin); Daniel J. Boorstin, *The Genius of American Politics* (Chicago: University of Chicago Press, 1953).

61. David Caute, *The Great Fear: The Anticommunist Purge under Truman and Eisenhower* (New York: Simon and Schuster, 1978), 425.

62. Iversen, *The Communists and the Schools*, 257, 268.

63. Nelson and Roberts, *The Censors and the Schools*, 20. For more on the Alabama law, see "Complex Problems Posed by Alabama Textbook Law," *Publishers' Weekly*, February 13, 1954, 938–39; "Publishers Engage Counsel to Fight Ala. Textbook Law," *Publishers' Weekly*, April 10, 1954, 1677; "Twenty-five Textbook Publishers File Suit in Alabama," *Publishers' Weekly*, April 17, 1954, 1822–24.

64. *Report of the State Textbook Committee to the State Commissioner of Education on Books Offered for Adoption* (1961), 10, Texas State Library, Archive Division, Austin; House Textbook Investigating Committee of the Fifty-seventh Legislature, *Report to Speaker Byron Tunnell and Members of the Texas House of Representatives of the Fifty-eighth Legislature* (1962), 48, Texas State Library, Archive Division; Nelson and Roberts, *The Censors and the Schools*, 5–6, 120–23.

65. John Edward Weems, "Textbooks under Fire," *Publishers Weekly*, October 2, 1961, 23; "Publishers Engage Counsel to Fight Ala. Textbook Law," 1677.

66. *Report of the State Textbook Committee to the State Commissioner of Education on Books Offered for Adoption* (1961), appendix A, 11; Fred M. Hechinger, "The Textbook Problem," *Saturday Review*, April 19, 1952, 15; Richard M. Pearson, "Can Textbooks Be Subversive?" *Phi Delta Kappan* 34 (January 1953): 249.

67. Casner and Gabriel, *The Story of American Democracy*, 482.

68. Henry W. Bragdon and Samuel P. McCutchen, *History of a Free People: Teachers Annotated Edition* (New York: Macmillan, 1958), 64, 99, 154–59, 376–77; Ruth Wood Gavian and William A. Hamm, *The American Story* (Boston: D. C. Heath, 1959), 356.

69. E. Merrill Root, *Brainwashing in the High Schools: An Examination of Eleven American History Textbooks* (New York: Devin-Adair Company, 1958).

70. Gertrude Hartman, *America: Land of Freedom* (Boston: D. C. Heath, 1952), 553, 571, 574 (emphasis added).

71. Everett Augspurger and Richard A. McLemore, *Our Nation's Story* (Chicago: Laidlaw Brothers, 1954), 659.

72. Hartman, *America: Land of Freedom*, vi, 556.

73. Augspurger and McLemore, *Our Nation's Story*, 462 (emphasis added).

74. Paul F. Boller and E. Jean Tilford, *This Is Our Nation* (St. Louis: Webster Publishing, 1961), 639; Lewis Paul Todd and Merle Curti, *Rise of the*

American Nation (New York: Harcourt, Brace and World, 1961), 802; Hartman, *America: Land of Freedom,* vi; Leon H. Canfield and Howard B. Wilder, *The Making of Modern America* (Boston: Houghton Mifflin, 1958), 585.

75. Canfield and Wilder, *The Making of Modern America,* 10–11.

76. I. James Quillen and Edward Krug, *Living in Our America: A History for Young Citizens* (Chicago: Scott, Foresman and Co., 1953), 32.

77. Boller and Tilford, *This Is Our Nation,* 662.

78. Leon H. Canfield et al., *The United States in the Making* (Boston: Houghton Mifflin, 1944), 603; Bragdon and McCutchen, *History of a Free People,* 576; Augspurger and McLemore, *Our Nation's Story,* 200; Boller and Tilford, *This Is Our Nation,* 660; Armstrong, "Treason in the Textbooks," 71.

79. David M. Kennedy, *Freedom from Fear: The American People in Depression and War* (New York: Oxford University Press, 1999), 208–13.

80. Weems, "Textbooks under Fire," 22; Nelson and Roberts, *The Censors and the Schools,* 115–22, 138.

Chapter 7

1. See Jonathan Zimmerman, "Each 'Race' Could Have Its Heroes Sung: Ethnicity and the History Wars in the 1920s," *Journal of American History* 87 (June 200): 92–111.

2. For critiques of authors for papering over ideological differences and producing bland histories, see Albert Alexander, "The Gray Flannel Cover on the American History Textbook," *Social Education* 24 (January 1960): 11–14; and Frederic R. Hartz, "Watered-Down American History," *High School Journal* 46 (February 1963): 175–78. For more on Wall Street's interest in textbook publishers during the 1950s and 1960s, see Jack Allen, "Corporate Expansion and Social Studies Textbooks," *Social Education* 33 (March 1969): 279–86.

3. Detroit's population had already begun to decline by 1960, however, well in advance of the 1967 riots. Between 1950 and 1960, it dropped by approximately 10 percent. See Harry Hansen, ed., *The World Almanac and Book of Facts, 1961* (New York: New York World-Telegram Corporation, 1961), 82.

4. For more on Henry, GOAL, and the city's school politics in the 1960s, see Jeffrey Mirel, *The Rise and Fall of an Urban School System: Detroit, 1907–1981* (Ann Arbor: University of Michigan Press, 1993).

5. "Rev. A. B. Cleage: Center of Controversy," *Michigan Chronicle,* February 3, 1962, 10; "'GOAL' Hits School Board," *Michigan Chronicle,* April 14, 1962, 1, 12; "Brownell Checking Local School Bias," *Michigan Chronicle,* July 7, 1962, 2; "'I'll Go to Jail,' Says Boy's Father," *Michigan Chronicle,* December 1, 1962, 1; "Schools' Postscript Tells History of Negro Struggle," *Detroit News,* May 2, 1963, 1. For a summary of the Detroit case, see Hillell Black, *The American Schoolbook* (New York: William Morrow, 1967), 108–17.

6. Harold H. Eibling, Fred M. King, and James Harlow, *Our United States: A Bulwark of Freedom* (Chicago: Laidlaw Brothers, 1962), 254, 619.

7. Eibling, King, and Harlow, *Our United States,* 294.

8. Eibling, King, and Harlow, *Our United States,* 102, 298, 361, 362, 390, 615, 621 (emphasis added).

9. Eibling, King, and Harlow, *Our United States,* 380–82. Textbook resemblances to Margaret Mitchell's epic novel are not coincidental. Some texts actually recommended *Gone with the Wind* as a useful source for history students. See Canfield and Wilder, *The Making of Modern America,* 333.

10. "Schools in Detroit Reject Negro Plea," *New York Times,* November 24, 1962, 10; " 'I'll Go to Jail,' Says Boy's Father," 1; Sol M. Elkin, "Minorities in Textbooks: The Latest Chapter," *Teachers College Record* 66 (March 1965): 503.

11. "Schools Fire Warning on Textbooks," *Detroit Free Press,* December 19, 1962, 3.; "Schools Urged to Drop Textbooks," *Detroit Free Press,* January 23, 1963, 3; "History Books: Ultimate Victory Predicted," *Michigan Chronicle,* December 8, 1962, 1, 4.

12. "Minutes of the State Board of Education of Alabama, 22 May 1952," SG20903, Alabama Department of Archives and History.

13. Boller and Tilford, *This Is Our Nation,* 662–63.

14. Ralph Volney Harlow, *The United States: From Wilderness to World Power* (New York: Henry Holt and Co., 1953), 216, 217.

15. Quillen and Krug, *Living in Our America,* 339, 342, 361.

16. Casner and Gabriel, *The Story of American Democracy,* 259.

17. Harlow, *The United States,* 386–87; Canfield and Wilder, *The Making of Modern America,* 328; Todd and Curti, *Rise of the American Nation,* 412.

18. Canfield, Wilder et al., *The United States in the Making,* 435; Canfield and Wilder, *The Making of Modern America,* 330.

19. Eibling, King, and Harlow, *Our United States,* 391.

20. Hartman, *America: Land of Freedom,* 426; Harlow, *The United States,* 385; Quillen and Krug, *Living in Our America,* 400.

21. Gavian and Hamm, *The American Story,* 330.

22. Todd and Curti, *Rise of the American Nation,* 393; "Report of the House Textbook Investigating Committee of the Fifty-seventh Legislature (1962)," 48. The illustration of the Klansmen appeared on page 342 of Boller and Tilford's *This Is Our Nation.*

23. Quillen and Krug, *Living in Our America,* 710; Eibling, King, and Harlow, *Our United States,* 506, 606.

24. Boller and Tilford, *This Is Our Nation,* 663, 690; Augspurger and McLemore, *Our Nation's Story,* 416–17, 523.

25. Kenneth L. Stampp et al., *The Negro in American History Textbooks* (Sacramento: California State Department of Education, 1964), 13–15.

26. Quillen and Krug, *Living in Our America,* 217.

27. Nelson and Roberts, *The Censors and the Schools,* 169.

28. "Union Protests Textbooks," *New York Times,* January 31, 1951, 22; "Eight Books Dropped as School Texts," *New York Times,* February 29, 1952, 25; "City Asks Balance of Races in Textbooks," *New York Times,* April 16, 1959, 35; Elkin, "Minorities in Textbooks," 505; "GOAL Drafts Resolution," *Michigan Chronicle,* June 16, 1962, 2.

29. "'Integration' in Textbooks," *New York Times,* April 19, 1959, sect. 4, p. 11; "Legion Plans to Check Mississippi Textbooks," *New York Times,* September 6, 1959, 50; "Mississippi Mud," *Time,* May 16, 1960, 65.

30. Nelson and Roberts, *The Censors and the Schools,* 174; "It's a Bad Textbook," *Detroit News,* December 9, 1962, sect. B, p. 18. The 1961 study *The Treatment of Minorities in Secondary School Textbooks* was written by Lloyd Marcus.

31. Department of Social Studies, Detroit Public Schools, *The Struggle for Freedom and Rights: The Negro in American History* (Detroit: Board of Education, 1963), 14, 16, 19. Laidlaw Brothers chose to incorporate material from this pamphlet into the new edition of *Our United States,* which Detroit subsequently adopted.

32. "Schools' Postscript Tells of Negro Struggle," 1, 17; "Schools Fire Warning on Textbooks," 3.

33. Black, *The American Schoolbook,* 121.

34. *Brown et al. v. Board of Education of Topeka et al.,* from the complete ruling reproduced in Leon Friedman, ed., *Argument: The Oral Argument before the Supreme Court in Brown v. Board of Education of Topeka, 1952–55* (New York: Chelsea House Publishers, 1969), 330.

35. Elkin, "Minorities in Textbooks," 503; New York policy, quoted in U.S. House of Representatives, Committee on Education and Labor, *Books for Schools and the Treatment of Minorities: Hearings before the Ad Hoc Subcommittee on De Facto School Segregation* (Washington, D.C.: Government Printing Office, 1966), 118; Mervyn M. Dymally, "The Struggle for Inclusion of Negro History in Our Text-Books . . . A California Experience," *Negro History Bulletin* 33 (December 1970): 189–90.

36. "Textbooks Assailed on Racial Issue," *San Francisco Chronicle,* February 3, 1965, 13; Lerone Bennett Jr., "Reading, 'Riting, and Racism: Massive Thrust Focuses Attention on the Built-in Biases of the American Educational System," *Ebony,* March 1967, 132, 134.

37. *Social Studies* 55 (February 1964): inside back cover.

38. Nelson and Roberts, *The Censors and the Schools,* 175; "Integrated Texts on the Rise: Opposition in the South," *Library Journal* 90 (May 15, 1965): 41; Bennett, "Reading, 'Riting and Racism," 137.

39. Franklin, *Race and History,* 278–85. For details on the disputed death counts, see *Tulsa Race Riot: A Report by the Oklahoma Commission to Study the Tulsa Race Riot of 1921* (Oklahoma City: 2001). The report is available online.

40. Paul Finkelman, "John Hope Franklin," in *Clio's Favorites: Leading Historians of the United States, 1945–2000,* ed. Robert Allen Rutland (Columbia: University of Missouri Press, 2000), 54–55; Samuel Eliot Morison and Henry Steele Commager, *The Growth of the American Republic* (New York: Oxford University Press, 1950), 521; Franklin, *Race and History,* 287, 304–7.

41. Finkelman, "John Hope Franklin," 55–62; Novick, *That Noble Dream,* 472–73.

42. U.S. House of Representatives, *Books for Schools and the Treatment of Minorities,* 114–15; Harry Gilroy, "Minorities' Story Traced in Series," *New York Times,* January 23, 1965, 23; "Integrating the Texts," *Newsweek,* March 7, 1966, 93.

43. John W. Caughey, John Hope Franklin, and Ernest R. May, *Land of the Free: A History of the United States* (New York: Benziger Brothers, 1966), 102–3, 302, 306–7. While Benziger published the work, a firm called Franklin Publications handled distribution in California.

44. Caughey, Franklin, and May, *Land of the Free,* 304, 306, 365, 368, 424, 569, 614.

45. Caughey, Franklin, and May, *Land of the Free,* 117, 539, 591, 615.

46. Caughey, Franklin, and May, *Land of the Free,* 304, 306, 365, 368, 424, 569, 614.

47. Nicholas J. Karolides, *Banned Books: Literature Suppressed on Political Grounds* (New York: Facts on File, 1998), 297; Caughey, Franklin, and May, *Land of the Free,* 612, 623.

48. "Information Regarding School Enrollment and Estimated Numbers of Copies of Textbooks . . . Required for Distribution," July 1, 1965, State Board of Education, F3752:117, California State Archives, Sacramento.

49. "Rafferty's View on History Text," *San Francisco Chronicle,* August 20, 1966, 2.

50. Benziger Brothers advertisement in *Catholic School Journal* 66 (January 1966): 61.

51. "History Textbook—Rafferty Attack," *San Francisco Chronicle,* May 11, 1966, 1, 12.

52. "Alabama Car Crash Kills Max Rafferty," *Los Angeles Times,* June 14, 1982, sect. 1, p. 20.

53. "Alabama Car Crash Kills Max Rafferty," 20; Zan Thompson, "Max Rafferty's Second-Happiest Day," *Los Angeles Times,* June 17, 1982, sect. 5, p. 2.

54. The book was E. Merrill Root's *Brainwashing in the High Schools,* published in 1958. The theory, however, had been circulating in right-wing circles for several years.

55. Carol Dunlap, *California People* (Salt Lake City: Peregrine Smith Books, 1982), 165.

56. Max Rafferty, *What They Are Doing to Your Children* (New York: New American Library, 1965), 30.

57. William O'Neill, *Readin, Ritin, and Rafferty! A Study of Educational Fundamentalism* (Berkeley: Glendessary Press, 1969), 42–43, 62–65. I have relied heavily on O'Neill's book for my analysis of Rafferty's educational philosophy.

58. Rafferty, *What They Are Doing to Your Children*, 29.

59. Editorial cartoon, *San Francisco Chronicle*, May 13, 1966, 48; "Alabama Car Crash Kills Max Rafferty," 21.

60. Max Rafferty, *Max Rafferty on Education* (New York: Devin-Adair, 1968), 38; Max Rafferty, "Textbook Furor," *San Francisco Chronicle*, May 17, 1966, 40; Max Rafferty to John W. Holmdahl, August 23, 1963, Department of Education, F3752:840, California State Archives.

61. Dymally, "The Struggle for Inclusion of Negro History," 188, 190; "Brown Signs Textbook Bill," *New York Times*, July 8, 1965, 29; Allen J. Matusow, *The Unraveling of America: A History of Liberalism in the 1960s* (New York: Harper and Row, 1986), 362.

62. "Assembly Hassel [*sic*] over a Textbook," *San Francisco Chronicle*, May 17, 1966, 9; Karolides, *Banned Books*, 297.

63. Harry N. Scheiber, "The California Textbook Fight," *Atlantic*, November 1967, 43; *Criticisms of* Land of the Free (Sacramento: July 1966), 164, California State Department of Education, F3752:842, California State Archives. Superintendent of Public Instruction Maxwell Rafferty compiled and published the letters in this collection. Franklin argues that no evidence supports the story of Stevens's mistress and that it was concocted by the novelist Thomas Dixon Jr. See Franklin, *Race and History*, 20.

64. "Rafferty's View on History Text," 2.

65. *Criticisms of* Land of the Free, 179.

66. *Criticisms of* Land of the Free, 48, 130, 142, 161; Karolides, *Banned Books*, 300; Land-of-the-Free Committee, *Critical Appraisal of* Land of the Free (Pasadena: 1966), 1.

67. *Criticisms of* Land of the Free, 172; Land-of-the-Free Committee, *Critical Appraisal of* Land of the Free, 11, 17; "Assembly Hassel over a Textbook," 9.

68. *Criticisms of* Land of the Free, 47, 164, 208D; Karolides, *Banned Books*, 298.

69. *Criticisms of* Land of the Free, 29.

70. *Criticisms of* Land of the Free, 29; Caughey, Franklin, and May, *Land of the Free*, 316, 354.

71. Rafferty, quoted in O'Neill, *Readin, Ritin, and Rafferty!* 62–63.

72. Allan Nevins, Glenn S. Dumke, and Charles G. Sellers, "Report to the State Board of Education on the Eighth-Grade Text in American History" (August 1966), 4, 11, 13, Department of Education, F3752:843, California State Archives.

73. *Criticisms of* Land of the Free, 171, 200–202.

74. *Criticisms of* Land of the Free, 125, 179, 186.

75. *Criticisms of* Land of the Free, 130; "Alabama Car Crash Kills Max Rafferty," 21.

76. D. K. Thomas to Maxwell Rafferty, September 18, 1964, Department of Education, F3754:840, California State Archives; Karolides, *Banned Books,* 299. A group in Columbus, Ohio, did attack the book, however, arguing that it was communist-inspired and taught "guilt and shame" about America's past.

77. Charles V. Hamilton, *Adam Clayton Powell, Jr.: The Political Biography of an American Dilemma* (New York: Atheneum, 1991), 181, 379; "U.S. Textbook Study Is Urged by Powell," *New York Times,* March 7, 1964, 50; "House Hearings Hit Textbooks on Grounds of Racial Bias," *Publishers' Weekly,* September 6, 1966, 39.

78. "Integrated Texts on the Rise," 41; Nicholas C. Poulos, "Textbooks and the Invisible Man," *Educational Forum* 31 (May 1967): 478.

79. U.S. House of Representatives, *Books for Schools and the Treatment of Minorities,* 320–21.

80. A. Kent MacDougall, "Integrated Books," *Wall Street Journal,* March 24, 1965, 1.

81. Matusow, *The Unraveling of America,* 201–3.

82. See Msgr. Edmund J. Goebel, Sister Mary Richardine, and John E. O'Loughlin, *United States History* (Chicago: Laidlaw Brothers, 1966).

83. Murry Nelson, "Merle R. Eppse and the Studies of Blacks in American History Textbooks," *International Journal of Social Education* 3 (winter 1989): 88.

84. "Integrating the Texts," 94.

85. U.S. House of Representatives, *Books for Schools and the Treatment of Minorities,* 586; *Criticisms of* Land of the Free, 208H; Theodore B. Dolmatch, "Color Me Brown—I'm Integrated," *Saturday Review,* September 11, 1965, 73; Elkin, "Minorities in Texts," 505.

86. "I.S. 201 Experiment to Scrutinize Texts," *New York Times,* April 20, 1970, 39.

87. William W. Bragdon, "Dilemmas of a Textbook Writer," *Social Education* 33 (March 1969): 293; "Textbooks: Big Drive for Balance," *Time,* August 19, 1966, 52; William Borders, "Connecticut Passes Bill on Political Testimonials," *New York Times,* June 7, 1967, 39.

88. Quoted on the cover of *Negro History Bulletin* 30 (March 1967).

89. Casner and Gabriel, *The Story of American Democracy,* 536.

90. *Criticisms of* Land of the Free, 210A.

91. Louis R. Harlan, "Tell It Like It Was: Suggestions on Black History," *Social Education* 33 (April 1969): 390–91; Edwin Fenton, "Crispus Attucks Is Not Enough," *Social Education* 33 (April 1969): 399.

92. James P. Shenton, Judith R. Benson, and Robert E. Jakoubek, *These United States* (Boston: Houghton Mifflin, 1981), 88, 200, 368.

93. Stampp et al., *The Negro in American History Textbooks,* 1–2.

94. Shenton, Benson, and Jakoubek, *These United States,* 625.

95. Henry N. Drewry, Thomas H. O'Connor, and Frank Friedel, *America Is* (Columbus: Charles E. Merrill Publishing, 1984), 365; Jack Abramowitz, *American History* (Chicago: Follett Publishing Company, 1971), 379; Gerald Leinwand, *The Pageant of American History* (Boston: Allyn and Bacon, 1775), 287.

96. Abramowitz, *American History,* 375; Herbert J. Bass, George A. Billias, and Emma Jones Lapsansky, *Our American Heritage: Teachers Edition* (Morristown, N.J.: Silver, Burdett, 1979), 381; Shenton, Benson, and Jakoubek, *These United States,* 331 (emphasis added).

97. My analysis on the subject is influenced by James Loewen's arguments about the "invisibility of antiracism" in *Lies My Teacher Told Me.*

98. Abramowitz, *American History,* 540; Jack Allen and John L. Betts, *History U.S.A.: Bicentennial Edition* (New York: American Book Company, 1976), 642, 691.

99. Drewry, O'Connor, and Friedel, *America Is,* 613; Bragdon, "Dilemmas of a Textbook Writer," 297–98.

100. For an excellent example, see James W. Davidson et al., *Nation of Nations: A Narrative History of the American Republic,* vol. 2, *Since 1865* (New York: McGraw-Hill, 1990), 115. The authors tell a story of a White, Southern-born woman who is emotionally paralyzed when she first uses a racially integrated bathroom and shower.

101. Abramowitz, *American History,* 667; Joan DelFattore, *What Johnny Shouldn't Read: Textbook Censorship in America* (New Haven: Yale University Press), 123.

102. James Loewen makes a similar argument about textbook photographs of the Vietnam War, where a downplaying of violence is even stranger. See "Down the Memory Hole: The Disappearance of the Recent Past," in *Lies My Teacher Told Me.*

103. The one exception to the ban on displays of lynching is a reproduction of a *Harper's Weekly* illustration that appeared on page 459 of Henry Graff's *The Free and the Brave* (Chicago: Rand McNally, 1972). A tiny figure in the background of the illustration does hang from the branch of a tree, but the race of the person is not clear. A caption in Gerald Leinwand's *Pageant of American History* explained that firefighters in Birmingham used water hoses against protesters, but the accompanying photograph did not directly show them doing so.

104. James W. Loewen and Charles Sallis, eds., *Mississippi: Conflict and Change* (New York: Pantheon Books, 1974), 178–79, 274, 281.

105. "Teaching Mississippi History," *New York Times,* October 10, 1975, 37; "Mississippi Is Sued on History Books," *New York Times,* November 9, 1975, 27; Wendell Rawls Jr., "Court Bars Rejection of Textbooks for Racial Reasons," *New York Times,* April 5, 1980, 6; Loewen, *Lies My Teacher Told Me,* 6, 160, 274.

106. "State Bars Slave Photo in Textbook," *San Diego Union,* April 10, 1964, 4; Nicholas C. Poulos, "Negro Attitudes toward Textbook Illustrations," *Journal of Negro Education* 38 (spring 1969): 177–81.

107. "Integrated Texts on the Rise," 41.

108. Nathan Hare, "The Teaching of Black History and Culture in the Secondary Schools," *Social Education* 33 (April 1969): 388.

109. "Criteria for Screening Content of New Instructional Materials with Regard to Their Treatment of Cultural Minorities" (Los Angeles City Schools); Michigan Department of Education, *Guidelines for the Selection of Human Relations Content in Textbooks* (Lansing: 1965); both in U.S. House of Representatives, *Books for Schools and the Treatment of Minorities,* 265, 530.

110. Robert F. Madgic et al., *U.S.A.: The American Experience: A Study of Themes and Images in American History* (Menlo Park, Calif.: Addison-Wesley, 1975), 106, 639.

111. "Textbook Policy Arouses Arizona," *New York Times,* July 7, 1973, 17.

112. Delfattore, *What Johnny Shouldn't Read,* 123, 139, 155, 157. DelFattore also argues that different content requirements among the states tend to create fragmented and superficial textbooks. I have adapted my claims, in part, from her work.

113. James Moffett, *Storm in the Mountains: A Case Study of Censorship, Conflict, and Consciousness* (Carbondale: Southern Illinois University Press, 1988), 28.

114. Casner and Gabriel, *The Story of American Democracy,* 328.

115. Bragdon and McCutchen, *History of a Free People,* prologue, xi–xiii.

116. Bragdon, "Dilemmas of a Textbook Writer," 297–98.

117. Abramowitz, *American History,* 32; Caughey, Franklin, and May, *Land of the Free,* 105; Madgic et al., *U.S.A: The American Experience,* 167.

118. *Report of the National Advisory Commission on Civil Disorders* (Washington, D.C.: U.S. Government Printing Office, 1968), 1.

119. Drewry, O'Connor, and Friedel, *America Is,* 2.

120. Caughey, Franklin, and May, *Land of the Free,* 49. Not surprisingly, Native Americans in California had many criticisms of the book. For examples, see Henry, *Textbooks and the American Indian,* 33–35. Their dissatisfaction contributed to the state's decision not to renew *Land of the Free*'s adoption when its original term expired.

121. Graff, *The Free and the Brave,* 3, 63.

122. Graff, *The Free and the Brave,* 559–60.

123. Daniel J. Boorstin and Brooks M. Kelley, *A History of the United States* (Boston: Ginn and Co., 1981), 1, 705.

124. Brent Staples, "Celebrating World War II—and the Whiteness of American History," *New York Times,* December 9, 2001, sect. D, p. 12.

Conclusion

1. William H. McNeill, "The Care and Repair of Public Myth," *Foreign Affairs* 61 (fall 1982): 1.
2. McNeill, "The Care and Repair of Public Myth," 7.
3. Gilbert T. Sewall, "The Triumph of Textbook Trendiness," *Wall Street Journal,* March 1, 1994, 14.
4. Paul Boyer, the lead writer of the new edition, strongly defended the book. See his letter "An Esteemed Textbook Unfairly Caricatured," *Wall Street Journal,* March 11, 1994, 13.
5. Bass, Billias, and Lapsansky, *Our American Heritage,* 460; Madgic et al., *U.S.A.: The American Experience,* 608; Leinwand, *The Pageant of American History,* 230.
6. McNeill, "The Care and Repair of Public Myth," 1.
7. "Senator Byrd Seeks Funds to Promote U.S. History," *Boston Globe,* June 3, 2001, B9; Bruce Craig, "$50 million for History Education," *OAH Newsletter,* February 2001, 9–10.
8. Franklin Publications to California State Board of Education, November 1966, in papers of State Superintendent Maxwell Rafferty, F3752:843, Department of Education, California State Archives.
9. See Edmund Morgan, *American Slavery, American Freedom: The Ordeal of Colonial Virginia* (New York: Norton, 1975).
10. Renan, "What Is a Nation?" 11.

References

Abbott, Edward. *A Paragraph History of the United States.* Boston: Roberts Brothers, 1875.

Abramowitz, Jack. *American History.* Chicago: Follett Publishing Company, 1971.

Adams, Charles Kendall, and William P. Trent. *A History of the United States.* Boston: Allyn and Bacon, 1903.

Allen, Jack, and John L. Betts. *History U.S.A.: Bicentennial Edition.* New York: American Book Company, 1976.

Anderson, John J. *A Pictorial School History of the United States.* New York: Clark and Maynard, 1885.

Anderson, Vivienne, and Laura M. Shufelt. *Your America.* Englewood Cliffs: Prentice-Hall, 1967.

Ashley, Roscoe Lewis. *American History for Use in Secondary Schools.* New York: Macmillan, 1923.

Augspurger, Everett, and Richard A. McLemore. *Our Nation's Story.* Chicago: Laidlaw Brothers, 1954.

Bailey, Thomas A., and David M. Kennedy. *The American Pageant.* Boston: D. C. Heath, 1979.

Barker, Eugence C., Henry Steele Commager, and Walter P. Webb. *The Building of Our Nation.* Evanston, Ill.: Row, Peterson and Co., 1937.

Barnes, Everett. *American History for Grammar Grades.* Boston: D. C. Heath, 1913.

Bass, Herbert J., George A. Billias, and Emma Jones Lapsansky. *Our American Heritage: Teachers Edition.* Morristown, N.J.: Silver, Burdett, 1979.

Beard, Charles, and Mary Beard. *History of the United States.* New York: Macmillan, 1921.

Berard, A[ugusta]. B[lanche]. *School History of the United States.* Philadelphia: Cowperthwait and Co., 1856, 1870.

Blackburn, John S., and William N. McDonald. *New School History of the United States.* Baltimore: William J. C. Dulany and Co., 1880.

——. *Southern School History of the United States.* Baltimore: George Lycett, 1869.

References

Boller, Paul F., and E. Jean Tilford. *This Is Our Nation.* St. Louis: Webster Publishing Company, 1961.

Boorstin, Daniel J., and Brooks Mather Kelley, with Ruth Frankel Boorstin. *A History of the United States.* Boston: Ginn and Co., 1981.

Bragdon, Henry W., and Samuel P. McCutchen. *History of a Free People: Teachers Annotated Edition.* New York: Macmillan, 1958.

Brown, Harriet M., and Joseph F. Guadagnolo. *America Is My Country: The Heritage of a Free People.* Boston: Houghton Mifflin, 1961.

Bruce, Philip A. *School History of the United States.* New York: American Book Company, 1903.

Buggey, L. Joanne. *America! America!* Glenview, Ill.: Scott, Foresman and Co., 1980.

Canfield, Leon H., et al. *The United States in the Making.* Boston: Houghton Mifflin, 1944.

Canfield, Leon H., and Howard B. Wilder. *The Making of Modern America.* Boston: Houghton Mifflin, 1958.

Casner, Mabel B., and Ralph H. Gabriel. *The Story of American Democracy.* Chicago: Harcourt, Brace and Co., 1950.

Caughey, John W., John Hope Franklin, and Ernest R. May. *Land of the Free: A History of the United States.* New York: Benziger Brothers, 1966.

Chambers, Henry E. *A Higher History of the United States for Schools and Academies.* New Orleans: F. F. Hansell and Brother, 1889.

Channing, Edward. *A Students' History of the United States.* New York: Macmillan, 1898.

Cooper, Oscar H., Harry F. Estill, and Leonard Lemmon. *History of Our Country: A Text-Book for Schools.* Boston: Ginn and Co., 1896, 1903.

Current, Richard N., et al. *United States History: Search for Freedom.* Glenview, Ill.: Scott, Foresman and Co., 1974.

Davidson, James W., et al. *Nation of Nations: A Narrative History of the American Republic.* New York: McGraw-Hill, 1990.

Department of Social Studies, Detroit Public Schools. *The Struggle for Freedom and Rights: The Negro in American History.* Detroit: Board of Education, 1963.

Derry, Joseph T. *History of the United States, for Schools and Academies.* Philadelphia: J. B. Lippincott, 1875.

Doyle, John Andrew. *History of the United States.* New York: Henry Holt and Co., 1876.

Drewry, Henry N., Thomas H. O'Connor, and Frank Friedel. *America Is.* Columbus: Charles E. Merrill Publishing, 1984.

Drummond, Donald F., Dorothy M. Fraser, and Frank Alweis. *Five Centuries in America.* New York: American Book Company, 1966.

Eggleston, Edward. *New Century History of the United States.* New York: American Book Company, 1903.

References

Eibling, Harold H., Fred M. King, and James Harlow. *Our United States: A Bulwark of Freedom*. Chicago: Laidlaw Brothers, 1962.

Elson, Henry William. *History of the United States of America*. New York: Macmillan, 1906.

Evans, Lawton B. *Essential Facts of American History*. Boston: Benjamin H. Sanborn Company, 1909.

Field, Lida A. *A Grammar School History of the United States*. New York: American Book Company, 1897.

Fiske, John. *A History of the United States for Schools*. Boston: Houghton Mifflin, 1894.

Forman, Samuel Eagle. *A History of the United States*. New York: Century Company, 1910.

Franciscan Sisters of the Perpetual Adoration. *A History of the United States for Catholic Schools*. New York: Scott, Foresman and Co., 1914.

Frost, John. *A History of the United States: For the Use of Schools and Academies*. Philadelphia: Charles DeSilver, 1856.

Gavian, Ruth Wood, and William A. Hamm. *The American Story*. Boston: D. C. Heath, 1959.

Goodrich, Charles A. *A History of the United States of America, on a Plan Adapted to the Capacity of Youth*. Bellows Falls, Vt.: James I. Cutler, 1827.

———. *A History of the United States of America, on a Plan Adapted to the Capacity of Youth*. Boston: Jenks, Palmer and Co., 1847.

Goodrich, Samuel G. [Peter Parley, pseud.]. *A Pictorial History of the United States*. Philadelphia: Sorin and Ball, and Samuel Agnew, 1846.

Gordy, Wilbur Fisk. *A History of the United States for Schools*. New York: Charles Scribner's Sons, 1898.

Graff, Henry F. *The Free and the Brave*. Chicago: Rand McNally, 1972.

Guitteau, William Backus. *Our United States: A History*. New York: Silver, Burdett and Co., 1919.

Hale, Salma. *History of the United States from Their First Settlement as Colonies, to the Close of the War with Great Britain in 1815*. New York: Collins and Hannay, 1829.

Hall, Robert, Harriet Smither, and Clarence Ousley. *The Student's History of Our Country*. Dallas: Southern Publishing Company, 1912.

Halleck, Reuben Post. *History of Our Country for Higher Grades*. New York: American Book Company, 1923.

Harlow, Ralph Volney. *The United States: From Wilderness to World Power*. New York: Henry Holt and Co., 1953.

Hart, Albert Bushnell. *School History of the United States*. New York: American Book Company, 1920.

Hartman, Gertrude. *America: Land of Freedom*. Boston: D. C. Heath, 1952.

Hassard, John Rose Greene. *An Abridged History of the United States of America, for the Use of Schools*. New York: Catholic Publication Society, 1887.

References

————. *A History of the United States of America.* New York: Catholic Publication Society, 1885.

Higginson, Thomas Wentworth. *Young Folks' History of the United States.* Boston: Lee and Shepard, 1875, 1887.

Holmes, George Frederick. *New School History of the United States.* New York: University Publishing Company, 1884.

————. *A School History of the United States of America.* New York: University Publishing Company, 1870.

Horne, Charles F. *The Story of Our American People.* 2 vols. Washington, D.C.: United States History Publishing Company, 1926.

Howison, Robert Reid. *Student's History of the United States.* Richmond, Va.: Everett Waddey Company, 1892.

Hulbert, Archer Butler. *United States History.* Garden City: Doubleday, Page and Co., 1923.

James, James Alton, and Albert Hart Sanford. *American History.* New York: Charles Scribner's Sons, 1909.

Johnson, Edward Austin. *A School History of the Negro Race in America.* Raleigh: Edwards and Broughton, 1891.

Johnston, Alexander. *A History of the United States for Schools.* New York: Henry Holt and Co., 1885.

Jones, John William. *School History of the United States.* Baltimore: R. H. Woodward Company, 1896.

Kennedy, William H. J., and Sister Mary Joseph [Dunn]. *America's Story: A History of the United States for the Lower Grades of Catholic Schools.* New York: Benziger Brothers, 1926.

————. *The United States: A History for the Upper Grades of Catholic Schools.* New York: Benziger Brothers, 1926.

Latané, John Holladay. *History of the United States.* Boston: Allyn and Bacon, 1918, 1921.

Lawler, Thomas Bonaventure. *Essentials of American History.* Boston: Ginn and Co., 1918.

Lee, Susan Pendleton. *Lee's Advanced School History of the United States.* Richmond, Va.: B. F. Johnson Company, 1899.

Leeds, Josiah. *A History of the United States of America.* Philadelphia: J. B. Lippincott, 1877.

[Leger], Sister Mary Celeste. *American History.* New York: Macmillan, 1926.

Leinwand, Gerald. *The Pageant of American History.* Boston: Allyn and Bacon, 1975.

Link, Arthur S., and David Saville Muzzey. *Our American Republic.* Boston: Ginn and Co., 1963.

Loewen, James W., and Charles Sallis, eds. *Mississippi: Conflict and Change.* New York: Pantheon Books, 1974.

Lossing, Benson J. *A History of the United States for Schools and Libraries.* New York: Mason Brothers, 1859.

References

Mace, William H. *A School History of the United States.* Chicago: Rand McNally, 1904.

Madgic, Robert F., et al. *U.S.A.: The American Experience: A Study of Themes and Images in American History.* Menlo Park, Calif.: Addison-Wesley, 1975.

McCarthy, Charles H. *A History of the United States for Catholic Schools.* New York: American Book Company, 1919.

McLaughlin, Andrew C. *A History of the American Nation.* New York: D. Appleton and Co., 1919.

McMaster, John Bach. *A School History of the United States.* New York: American Book Company, 1897.

Montgomery, David. *The Leading Facts of American History.* Boston: Ginn and Co., 1891.

Moon, Glenn W. *Story of Our Land and People.* New York: Henry Holt and Co., 1949.

Morison, Samuel Eliot, and Henry Steele Commager. *The Growth of the American Republic.* New York: Oxford University Press, 1950.

Muzzey, David Saville. *An American History.* Boston: Ginn and Co., 1911.

O'Hara, John P. *A History of the United States.* New York: Macmillan, 1909.

Olney, Jesse. *History of the United States on a New Plan.* New Haven: Durrie and Peck, 1837.

Quackenbos, George Payn. *Illustrated School History of the United States and the Adjacent Parts of America from the Earliest Discoveries to the Present Time.* New York: D. Appleton and Co., 1868.

Quillen, I. James, and Edward Krug. *Living in Our America: A History for Young Citizens.* Chicago: Scott, Foresman and Co., 1953.

Ridpath, John Clark. *History of the United States, Prepared Especially for Schools.* Cincinnati: Jones Brothers and Co., 1876.

Riley, Franklin L., J. A. C. Chandler, and J. G. de Roulhac Hamilton. *Our Republic: A History of the United States for Grammar Grades.* Richmond, Va.: Riley and Chandler, 1910.

Rugg, Harold. *America's March toward Democracy: A History of American Life, Political and Social.* Boston: Ginn and Co., 1937.

————. *The Conquest of America: A History of American Civilization, Economic and Social.* Boston: Ginn and Co., 1937.

————. *An Introduction to Problems of American Culture.* Boston: Ginn and Co., 1931.

————. *Our Country and Our People: An Introduction to American Civilization.* Boston: Ginn and Co., 1938.

Sadlier's Elementary History of the United States. New York: William H. Sadlier, 1896.

————. *Sadlier's Excelsior Studies in the History of the United States for Schools, by the Author of Sadlier's Elementary History.* New York: William H. Sadlier, 1879.

References

————. *Sadlier's Preparatory History of the United States.* New York: D. and J. Sadlier and Co., 1886.

A School History of the United States. New York: Benziger Brothers, 1892.

Scudder, Horace E. *History of the United States of America.* Philadelphia: J. H. Butler, 1884.

Shea, John Gilmary. *The First Book of History Combined with Geography and Chronology, for Younger Classes.* New York: D. and J. Sadlier and Co., 1867.

Shenton, James P., Judith R. Benson, and Robert E. Jakoubek. *These United States.* Boston: Houghton Mifflin, 1981.

Shinn, Josiah H. *History of the American People.* New York: American Book Company, 1893.

Steele, Joel Dorman. *A Brief History of the United States.* New York: A. S. Barnes and Co., 1885.

Stephens, Alexander H. *A Compendium of the History of the United States from the Earliest Settlements to 1872.* Columbia, S.C.: E. J. Hale and Son, 1876.

Stephenson, Nathaniel Wright. *An American History.* Boston: Ginn and Co., 1919.

Swinton, William M. *A Condensed School History of the United States.* New York: Ivison, Blakeman, Taylor and Co., 1879.

Taylor, Edward. *The Model History: A Brief Account of the American People, for Schools.* Chicago: Scott, Foresman and Co., 1889, 1897.

Thalheimer, Mary Elsie. *Eclectic History of the United States.* Cincinnati: Van Antwerp, Bragg and Co., 1880.

Thomas, Allen C. *A History of the United States.* Boston: D. C. Heath, 1899.

Thompson, Charles Manfred. *History of the United States: Political, Industrial, Social.* Chicago: Benjamin H. Sanborn, 1917.

Thompson, Waddy. *A History of the United States.* Boston: D. C. Heath, 1904.

Thorpe, Francis Newton. *A History of the American People.* Chicago: A. C. McClurg and Co., 1901.

Thwaites, Reuben Gold, and Calvin Noyes Kendall. *A History of the United States for Grammar Schools.* Boston: Houghton Mifflin, 1912.

Todd, Lewis Paul, and Merle Curti. *Rise of the American Nation.* New York: Harcourt, Brace and World, 1961.

Todd, Lewis Paul, et al. *Rise of the American Nation, John Carroll Edition.* New York: Harcourt, Brace and World, 1961.

West, Willis Mason. *History of the American People.* Boston: Allyn and Bacon, 1918.

Willard, Emma. *Abridged History of the United States; or, Republic of America.* New York: A. S. Barnes and Co., 1843, 1858.

————. *History of the United States; or, Republic of America.* New York: A. S. Barnes and Co., 1845.

References

Willson, Marcius. *History of the United States, for the Use of Schools.* New York: Cales Bartlett, 1846.

———. *Juvenile American History for Primary Schools.* New York: Mark H. Newman and Co., 1847.

Index

Abolitionists, 36, 40, 46, 53, 56, 63,
65, 77, 83, 85, 135, 142, 154, 164,
274, 285, 289, 315
influence on antebellum texts, 33,
58, 59
Abramowitz, Jack, 315–16, 324
absolute union, theory of, 30, 35–36,
41
Adams, Charles Kendall, 167–69, 182
Adams, Herbert Baxter, 45
Adams, James Truslow, 213
Adams, John, 64
Addison-Wesley, 320–21
Adoption of textbooks
effects of statewide adoption,
57–58, 83–87, 90–91, 321–22
evolution of, 21, 57–58, 69–71
Advertising Federation of America,
241–42
African-Americans, 6, 11, 14, 20, 22,
24, 57, 142–45, 163–71, 177, 207,
211, 215, 264–328
as abolitionists, 165, 170, 281, 287,
289, 315
in the American Revolution, 56,
164, 170–71, 211, 313, 328
in the Civil War, 20, 53, 55, 80–83,
90, 136, 170, 211, 270–72, 283,
315
and disfranchisement, 79, 86, 88,
167–68, 321, 323

under Jim Crow, 23, 87, 89, 171,
277, 288–99, 321, 323, 326–27
lobbying over texts, 10, 12, 14, 23,
263–69, 271–72, 278–83, 286–87,
304–10, 319–20
in Reconstruction, 56, 77, 81, 83,
90, 140, 164–68, 274–76, 285,
301, 315–18, 324
under slavery, 20, 35, 52–53, 66,
76–77, 136–40, 160, 163, 269–74,
278–81, 285–89, 299–303, 311–15,
319, 323–26, 336–37
Afrocentrism, 6, 9, 15, 20, 21
Agassiz, Louis, 143
Alamo, Battle of, 294, 303
Alaniz, John, 263
Aley, Robert, 191–92
Alger, Horatio, Jr., and myth of, 219,
223, 226, 247, 262, 314
Allyn and Bacon, 214
Al-Qaeda, 333
Altschul, Charles, 192
American Book Company, 68–70,
73, 84–85, 108, 198, 213–14, 316
American Civil Liberties Union, 251,
292
American Committee for Democ-
racy and Intellectual Freedom,
250
American Council of Education,
279

Index

American Federation of Teachers, 244
American Historical Association, 13, 50, 166, 183, 187, 213
"Americanization" of immigrants, 177, 195, 201, 209
  through education, 191–92, 197
American Legion, 14, 194, 256, 280
  in British "conspiracy," 197
  and critique of Harold Rugg, 219–21, 242–46, 251
  and *Story of Our American People*, 215
American Protective Association, 131
American Revolution, 14–15, 21–22, 30–32, 41–45, 63, 73, 78, 96, 116, 118–20, 122, 134, 135, 141, 146, 164, 171, 175, 179–80, 181, 193, 195–99, 201–2, 206–7, 211, 214, 299, 300, 311–13, 322, 328
  in Harold Rugg's texts, 231–32
  and the New History, 182, 184–86, 193, 201, 205
American Textbook Council, 332
American Textbook Publishers Institute, 279
Ancient Order of Hibernians, 186–87, 215
Anderson, John Jacob, 38, 67, 180
Andersonville prison, 73
"Anglo-Saxonism," 23, 144, 174, 177, 194, 217, 265, 334
  influence on texts and teaching, 184–86, 192
  opposition to, 178, 186–89, 194, 195, 204
  origins, 178–84
  during World War I, 89, 191–93
Anglo-Saxons, 89, 93, 113, 146, 148, 153, 157, 175, 177, 210, 214, 232
Anti-Defamation League, 280
Apple, Michael, 22
Appleton, D., and Co., 68
Appleton, William H., 68

Armstrong, O. K., 242–43, 246, 248–49
Arnold, Benedict, 32, 46, 202
Articles of Confederation, 232
Asante, Molefi Kete, 6, 9
Ashley, Roscoe Lewis, 148, 150, 183, 208
Association for the Study of Negro Life and History, 278, 312
Atlanta Compromise, 277
Attucks, Crispus, 4, 56, 135, 311–15
Augspurger, Everett, 257–59

Bagley, William, 188–89
Baldwin, James, 283
Ballif, Serge R., 264
Baltimore, Lord. *See* Calvert, George
Bancroft, George, 1, 33, 103, 118, 154–55
Banneker, Benjamin, 307, 311
Barker, Eugene C., 240
Barnes, A. S., and Co., 59, 68
Barnes, Everett, 185, 199, 207, 213
Barnett, Ross, 280, 294, 305, 317
Barry, John, 14, 120, 186, 207
Beard, Charles, 50, 153, 165, 167, 173, 184, 188, 205, 240, 253
  and *Economic Interpretation of Constitution*, 228–29, 233, 240, 243–44, 253
Beard, Mary, 50, 153, 165, 167, 173, 184, 205, 240
Beauregard, P. G. T., 62
Becker, Carl, 231, 253
Beecher, Lyman, 97, 106, 133
Bell, Daniel, 253
Bellamy, Edward, 223–27, 237
Bennett, Lerone, Jr., 282
Bennett, William, 15
Benton, Elbert, 187
Benton, George W., 198
Benziger Brothers, 133, 287, 290–91
  See also *Land of the Free*

Index

Bible, 27, 68, 77, 143
  readings in school, 96–97, 98, 101, 106
Bible Riots of 1844, 97, 127
Blackburn, John S., 63–66, 74, 81
Black Panthers, 5, 320–21
Black Power movement, 314, 320
Black studies, 310. See also Afrocentrism
Blaine, James G., 98
Bloom, Allan, 7
Boller, Paul F., 277
Boone, Daniel, 32–33
Boorstin, Daniel, 253, 327
Boston Massacre, 14, 56, 211, 300
Bourne, Henry, 187
Boutwell, George, 62
Bragdon, Henry W., 256, 261, 311, 323–24
Brébeuf, Jean de, 112–13
British "conspiracy" in history teaching, 175–78, 194–218, 242, 278, 335
Broca, Paul, 143
Brooks, Van Wyck, 228
Browder, Earl, 236
Brown, Edmund G., 295
Brown, John, 56, 84, 90
Brown, William Wells, 287
Brownell, Samuel, 268, 272
Brownson, Orestes, 124–25, 131
Brown v. Board of Education, 277–78, 281–82, 285, 289, 293, 302
Bruce, Blanche K., 315
Bruce, Philip A., 168
Buchanan, Patrick, 10
Buck, Paul S., 78
Bunche, Ralph, 314
Burr, Aaron, 32–33, 202
Bush, George H. W., 3
Byrd, Robert, 334

Cadieux, Louis, 129
Calhoun, John, 35–36, 60, 316

California Council for the Social Studies, 304
California State Curriculum Commission, 287, 291–92, 295, 297
Calvert, George, 114–15, 118
Calvert, Leonard and Cecil, 115
Canfield, Leon H., 259, 261, 275
Cardinal Principles of Secondary Education, 131
Carmichael, Stokely, 264
Carnegie, Andrew, 226
Carroll, Charles, 120–21
Carroll, John, 121, 134
Carver, George Washington, 277, 300, 311, 329
Casner, Mabel B., 274, 323
Catholics and Catholicism, 34, 92–136, 145, 147–48, 266
  Americanist controversy, 124–27
  and church-state separation, 101, 125–26, 131
  hostility to, 13, 19, 92–107, 115–23, 127–30, 208
  influence over mainstream texts, 15, 19–20, 105, 322
Catholic schools, 15, 92–98, 101–2, 125, 129, 132–33, 146
  and Catholic texts, 15, 21–23, 93–95, 106–24, 127–36, 309
  opposition to, 92–94, 97–99, 125, 131–33, 135
Caughey, John, 2, 287. See also Land of the Free
Celeste, Mary, 95, 122, 131–32, 135
Chandler, J. A. C., 85
Channing, Edward, 21, 26–27, 45, 49, 133–35, 146, 160, 162
Cheney, Dick, 3
Cheney, Lynne, 3, 9, 10–12, 25
Cherokees, and Trail of Tears, 160–61, 167
Chinese and Chinese-Americans, 138, 144, 153, 172–73, 215
Chivington, John, 158

Index

Civil Rights Act of 1875, 62
Civil Rights Act of 1957, 277
Civil Rights Act of 1964, 295, 306, 316–17
Civil rights movement, of 1950s and 1960s, 8, 264, 267–68, 271–72, 277, 279–91, 295, 300, 306, 311, 315–18
Civil War, 15, 18, 36, 38–41, 45–48, 51–52, 93, 136, 141, 165, 170–71, 192, 197, 211, 270–72, 301, 315–18
conflicts over teaching of, 15, 53–57, 63–67, 71–90
Clay, Henry, 36, 38, 65, 336
Cleveland, Grover, 178, 225
Cold War, 257, 259, 265
Collier, John, 300
Columbus, Christopher, 46, 206, 289
in Catholic texts, 107–9, 114, 131
Commager, Henry Steele, 240
Committee of Ten. *See* National Education Association
Committee on Public Information, 188–93, 196
Communism, 195, 240, 298, 335–36
alleged influence in teaching, 219, 221, 236, 243–44, 252, 254–55, 292
Compact theory, of Constitution, 29–31, 34–36, 41, 56, 72, 75
Compromise of 1850, 34–36, 46, 65
Connally, John, 312
Consensus school of historians, 253–54
Constitution, 10, 19, 27, 35, 41–42, 45, 53, 56, 64, 66, 98, 192, 247, 312, 322
convention of 1787, 44, 64, 75–76, 299
economic interpretation of, 228–29, 232–34, 240, 243–44, 253, 256
Fifth Amendment, 254

Reconstruction amendments, 19, 36, 57, 61, 79, 165, 174, 277, 232, 282, 323, 327
Cooper, James Fenimore, 156
Cooper, Oscar H., 79–81, 85, 90, 99
Coughlin, Charles, 239
Council for Basic Education, 11
Council on Interracial Books on Children, 2
Counts, George, 205, 235–36, 244
Crabtree, Charlotte, 3, 10–12
Crèvecoeur, J. Hector St. Jean de, 142–43
Crockett, Davy, 32–33
Cummings, Matthew, 186
Curti, Merle, 134, 275, 332
Custer, George Armstrong, 155

Daley, Richard, 308
Darrow, Clarence, 176
Darwin, Charles, 42, 144, 176
Daughters of Colonial Wars, 242–43
Daughters of the American Revolution, 197–221, 255, 279–80, 321
Davis, Jefferson, 78, 81, 84–85
Dawes Act, 157–58, 160
DeBow, James, 58–60, 63, 67, 69, 86
Declaration of Independence, 5, 30, 120, 123, 174, 192, 195–96
Democratic Party, 60, 67, 138, 193, 201, 290
Depression, Great, 219, 221, 227–28, 230, 235, 238–40, 252, 261
Derry, Joseph T., 63–66, 72–74
DeSmet, Peter, 113
Devlin, Joseph, 199, 202
Dewey, John, 4, 243, 247, 292
Dies, Martin, 242, 250
Dilling, Elizabeth, 240
Dixiecrats, 316
Dixon, Thomas, Jr., 90
Dolan, Jay P., 130
Dorchester, Daniel, 15, 93, 98, 101, 106, 108, 122, 124, 157–58

Index

Doubleday and Co., 286
Douglass, Frederick, 19, 40, 57, 83, 88–89, 136, 174, 281, 287, 311
"Dual editions," as a response to racial integration in texts, 306–9
Du Bois, W. E. B., 90, 171, 289, 300, 315, 319, 335–36
Dunning, William, and Dunning school, 165–67, 274–76, 324
Dymally, Mervyn, 295–96

Edison, Thomas, 226
Eggleston, Edward, 184
Eibling, Harold. See *Our United States*
Eisenhower, Dwight D., 215, 316
Elementary and Secondary Education Act, 306
Eliot, Charles W., 183
Elson, Henry William, 87–88, 139–40, 146, 159, 162, 167, 173–74
Emancipation Proclamation, 38, 88, 271, 277
Emerson, Ralph Waldo, 44–45
Eppse, Merle, 309
Erickson, Leif, 145, 206
Estill, Henry F., 79–81, 85, 90
Ettinger, William, 198

Fair Employment Practices Commission, 273
Falk, Alfred, 241, 245
Farmers' Alliance, 69
Faubus, Orval, 316
Federal Bureau of Education, 62
Federalist Party, 29–30, 44, 216
Federal Trade Commission, 239
Fenton, Edward, 313
Field, Lida, 85
Fillmore, Millard, 96
Fish, Carl R., 188
Fiske, John, 45, 46, 48, 73, 90, 144, 150, 152, 159

FitzGerald, Francis, 2, 3, 5, 11–13, 16, 22, 24
Fitzhugh, Thomas, 316
Follett Publishing Co., 319–20
Forbes, Bertie, 240–41, 251–52
Ford, Guy Stanton, 188, 191
Ford, Henry, 191
Formalism, 4
Forrest, Nathan Bedford, 78, 276
Fort Pillow Massacre, 90
Franciscans, 107, 112
Frank, Waldo, 228
Franklin, Benjamin, 64, 96, 121
Franklin, John Hope, 267, 304–5, 310, 319–20, 326, 330
early life and career, 283–87
See also *Land of the Free*
Freedmen's Bureau, 77, 85
French and Indian War, 208–9
Fugitive Slave Act, 35, 40, 65

Gabler, Mel, 321
Gabler, Norma, 321
Gabriel, Ralph H., 274, 323
Garrison, William Lloyd, 35
Gates, G. A., 69
General Motors, and sit-down strike, 245
George III, 201
George V, 201
German-American Alliance, 129, 186–88, 194, 215
Germans and German-Americans, 14, 96, 120, 124, 126, 129–30, 134, 145–46, 150, 173–74, 194, 201, 204–5, 207, 211, 215, 265
influence over texts, 14, 20, 186–88, 211
prejudice against, 130–31, 189, 191, 193, 205
Gibault, Pierre, 120
Gingrich, Newt, 7, 8, 12, 13
Ginn and Co., 72, 79–80, 84–85, 128, 133, 214, 218, 286–87

Index

Ginn and Co. (*continued*)
  and Harold Rugg, 218–19, 230,
    240, 242, 251
Gluck, Carol, 11
Goodrich, Charles A., 31–32, 39, 45,
    141–42, 155, 294, 337
Goodrich, Samuel G. (Peter Parley),
    58, 155, 176
Graff, Henry F., 317, 326–27
Graham, James, 198
Grand Army of the Republic, 21, 57,
    71–73, 84, 86, 197
Grant, Madison, 147–48, 206
Grant, Ulysses S., 56, 62, 73, 98, 336
Griffith, D. W., 90
Group on Advanced Leadership,
    268, 271, 291
Guardians of American Education,
    242
Guitteau, William Backus, 192–93,
    214

Hale, Nathan, 14, 185
Hale, Salma, 33
Haley, J. Evetts, 263
Hall, Stuart, 20
Halleck, Reuben Post, 206
Haller, Mark, 286
Hamilton, Alexander, 29–30, 44, 216,
    229, 233, 256
Hamilton, J. A. C. de Roulhac, 85
Hammond, James Henry, 316
Hancock, John, 10, 120, 175, 185,
    198
Hansell, F. F., and Brother, 74
Harcourt, Brace and World, 307–8
Harding, Samuel, 188
Hare, Nathan, 320
Harlan, Louis R., 312
Harlow, Ralph Volney, 273–75
Harper and Brothers, 68
Harrington, Michael, 162
Harrison, Benjamin, 157
Hart, Albert Bushnell, 160, 161, 171,

173, 181–82, 184–85, 188, 199,
    201, 207, 209–10
Hart, Merwin K., 242
Hartman, Gertrude, 257–58
Hassard, John Rose Greene, 93–94,
    115–16, 122–23
Hayes, Patrick, 132
Haymarket Riot, 195, 151
Haynes, Lemuel, 313–14
Hearst, William Randolph, 196, 215,
    240, 242
Heath, D. C., 84–85, 187, 213–14
Hemmings, Sally, 337
Henry, Frederick, 264–65, 272
Henry, Patrick, 14, 46, 299, 170
Henry, Richard, 264–65, 268–72,
    278, 280–81
Hicks, Hamilton, 245
Higginson, Thomas Wentworth,
    14–15, 52–53, 55–58, 80, 88–89,
    154, 267
Higham, John, 286
Hirsch, E. D., Jr., 3–5, 8, 17–18
Hirshfield, David, 199–202, 212–13,
    335
Hofstadter, Richard, 1
Holland, John, 108, 131
Holmes, George Frederick, 66–67,
    74
Hoover, Herbert, 238
Hopper, Dennis, 286
Horne, Charles F., 215
Houghton Mifflin, 73, 283, 300, 305,
    313
House Committee on Education and
    Labor, 306–11
House Committee on Un-American
    Activities, 242, 250, 254, 263,
    290
Howard, Ruth, 295
Hughes, John, 125
Hughes, Langston, 314, 335
Huguenots, 195
Hurst, James, 268

Index

Hutchinson, Anne, 116
Hylan, John, 199–201, 211
Hyman, Julius, 211

Immigrants and immigration, 126,
    130, 141, 145, 189, 209, 211, 247,
    322
    from Asia, 8, 131, 144, 172–73, 177
    from northern and western
        Europe, 131, 138, 142, 145–47,
        152–54, 174, 204, 215
    from southern and eastern
        Europe, 18, 131, 138–39, 148–51,
        172, 177, 183, 204–5, 215
    opposition to, 18, 93, 96, 99, 116,
        122, 138–39, 144, 148–51, 172–73,
        177–78, 183, 205–7, 215, 232,
        265, 322
Immigration Restriction League, 150
Indians. See Native Americans
International Ladies Garment
    Workers Union, 256
Ireland, John, 125
Irish and Irish-Americans, 14, 96,
    116, 119, 124–25, 130, 134, 139,
    142, 145–46, 150, 173, 194, 198,
    201, 204, 207, 210, 214, 265
    influence over texts, 14, 16, 21,
        186–87, 197, 215
Irving, Washington, 107
Italians and Italian-Americans, 14,
    120, 124, 147, 201, 205, 210, 215,
    265, 290
    influence over texts, 14, 16, 21,
        186–87, 197, 215
Ivison, Blakeman, Taylor and Co.,
    68

Jackson, Andrew, 45–46, 147, 164
Jackson, Helen Hunt, 157
Jackson, Thomas J. (Stonewall), 78
James, Henry, 183
Japanese and Japanese-Americans,
    138, 144, 172–73, 265

Jefferson, Thomas, 10, 14, 18, 29, 44,
    46–47, 58, 64, 142–43, 147, 160,
    197, 216, 226, 256, 287–88,
    336–37
Jeffries, Leonard, 9
Jesuits, 104, 112–17, 194
Jewish Welfare Board, 211
Jews, 34, 147, 205, 211, 215, 265, 311
    prejudice against, 13, 142, 215, 239
    influence over texts and education,
        211, 280
Johnson, Andrew, 165
Johnson, B. F., Co., 74
Johnson, Eastman, 288
Johnson, Edward Austin, 20–21, 169,
    170–71, 278, 309
Johnson, Lyndon B., 8, 289, 299,
    308, 316, 325
Johnston, Alexander, 45, 50, 152
Jones, Ben C., 69
Jones, John William, 73–78, 121

Kalb, Johann, or Baron de Kalb,
    120
Kastle, Leonard, 272
Kelley, Brooks Mather, 327
Kennedy, John F., 14, 289, 295
Kerner Commission. See National
    Advisory Commission on Civil
    Disorders
Keynes, John Maynard, 228, 252
Kimball, Roger, 217
King, Fred. See Our United States
King, Martin Luther, Jr., 264, 295,
    314–19
Know-Nothing (American) Party,
    96, 99, 127–30
Korean War, 292
Kosciusko, Thaddeus, 120, 205, 207,
    214
Knights of Columbus, 194, 214–15
Krug, Edward, 259–61, 274, 276, 278
Ku Klux Klan, 11, 62, 90, 132, 135,
    208, 276, 288–89, 316, 318, 335

Index

Lafayette, Marquis de, 120, 170
Laidlaw Brothers, 269, 309. See also
    Our United States
Lalement, Gabriel, 110, 112
Land of the Free, 266–67, 287–305,
    306, 311–16, 324, 326, 330,
    335–36
    adoption by California, 287,
        290–91, 297–98
    composition, 287–90
    critiques of, 291–92, 298–303, 305
    defense of, 303–4
Land-of-the-Free Committee, 299
Lange, Dorothea, 221
Lawler, Thomas Bonaventure, 119,
    123, 128, 135
Lawrence, James, 37, 294
Lee, Robert E., 56, 78, 80–81, 88
Lee, Susan Pendleton, 74–78, 121, 161
LeFevere, Peter, 97
Leger, Mary Celeste. *See* Celeste,
    Mary
Lemmon, Leonard, 79–81, 85, 90, 99
Leo, John, 12, 14
Leo XIII, 127
Leuchtenburg, William, 286
Lewis and Clark Expedition, 269
Limbaugh, Rush, 10, 217
Lincoln, Abraham, 18, 21, 36, 41, 53,
    74, 81, 85, 88, 122, 142, 209, 222,
    224, 271
Lincoln School, 229–30
Little Big Horn, Battle of, 155
Livengood, William, 213–14, 128
Locke, John, 197
Lodge, Henry Cabot, 79
Loewen, James, 318–19
Long, Huey, 239
Lost Cause, mythology of, 76–79, 83,
    90, 276
Louis, Joe, 319
L'Ouverture, Toussaint, 135
Lowell, James Russell, 40
Luther, Martin, 100, 103, 114, 118

Lyell, Charles, 42
Lynching, 318–19
Lynd, Robert S., 250–51
Lyons and Carnahan, 255

MacArthur, Douglas, 290
MacDougall, Walter, 11
Mace, William H., 44–46, 105–6, 167
Macmillan Co., 84, 87, 133, 255
Madison, James, 64, 229
Malcolm X, 316, 320
Man and His Changing Society. *See*
    Rugg, Harold
Mandel, Edward, and Mandel Com-
    mittee, 198–99, 204, 213, 217
Mann, Horace, 97
Marshall, John, 160
Marshall, Thurgood, 285, 314
Marx, Karl, 227
Mason, George, 299
Matzeliger, Jan E., 313
May, Ernest R. *See Land of the*
    Free
McAndrew, William, 175, 178, 201–2
McCaffrey, Austin, 279
McCarthy, Charles, 113, 128–33, 198,
    213–14
McCarthy, Joseph, 11, 259, 290, 335
McCoy, Elijah, 313–14
McCutchen, Samuel P., 261
McDonald, William N., 63–66, 74,
    81
McElroy, Robert, 189–90
McGraw-Hill Publishing Co., 242,
    272–73
McGruder, Aaron, 329
McIntosh, Ebenezer, 12, 17–18
McLaughlin, Andrew, 84, 89,
    137–39, 153, 163, 188, 192–93,
    197–98, 207, 212, 216
McLemore, Richard, 257–59
McMaster, John Bach, 45, 47–48,
    128, 160, 179, 183, 226, 260
McNeill, William H., 331–32

Index

McSweeney, Edward, 194–96, 204, 207, 210
Mead, Edwin, 15
Melting pot theory, 135, 147, 150, 196, 209, 214, 334
Mencken, Henry L., 193
Meredith, James, 318
Metacomet. *See* Philip, King
Mexican War, 32, 113, 184
Mexican-Americans, 124, 139, 153, 263, 265
Miller, Charles Grant, 196–99, 202, 204, 206–8, 210, 212, 215–17
Miller, Dorie, 312, 328
Miller, Perry, 253
Miscegenation, 87, 161–62, 298
Montgomery, David H., 72–73, 172, 230
Montgomery bus boycott, 264, 300, 317
Morgan, Edmund, 336–37
Morgan, Lewis Henry, 158
Morison, Samuel Eliot, 285
Mormons, 34
Morton, George, 142
Moseley, Cameron, 307–8
Mulford, Elisha, 41–43, 61, 64, 81, 99–101, 106, 122, 124, 174
Multiculturalism, 1–2, 8–9, 14, 18, 321, 331, 334
critiques of, 1–2, 6–13, 18, 267
Mundelein, George, 132
Muzzey, David Saville, 23, 89, 105, 148–53, 161–62, 167–68, 184–85, 199, 205, 214–17, 220, 226–27, 237, 287, 334
Myrdal, Gunnar, 279

Nash, Gary B., 3, 8, 10–12
Nast, Thomas, 93–94, 99
National Advisory Commission on Civil Disorders, 325
National Association for the Advancement of Colored People (NAACP), 194, 211, 278–79, 285, 307
and dispute over *Our United States,* 271, 281, 291
National Association of Manufacturers, 241–42, 250
National Board for Historical Service, 188, 193, 196
National Center for History in the Schools, 3, 8, 9
National Education Association, 184, 251
Committee of Ten report, 47, 183
National Endowment for the Humanities, 3
National History Standards, 3, 8–14, 24–25, 334–35
critiques of, 10–14
defense of, 11–12
Nationalism
alleged Catholic hostility to, 99–102
liberal vs. humanitarian understandings of, 222–28, 237–39, 246–47, 250–56, 262, 266, 337
organic, 27, 41–44, 61, 100, 124
as an outgrowth of the Civil War, 19–20, 39–45, 56, 61–62, 79, 99–102
in republican and antebellum eras, 18–19, 26–36
National Origins Act, 132–33, 204
National Security League, 93, 188–89, 196
A Nation at Risk, 3, 5
Native Americans, 2, 11, 14, 17, 24, 27, 29, 32, 38, 49, 113, 116–17, 120, 136, 138–39, 142–43, 154–64, 180, 262, 265, 325–26
influence over text reform, 9–10, 14, 211–12
as noble savages, 155–56, 158
plans for assimilation, 157–61

Index

Native Americans *(continued)*
  theory of eventual extinction,
  155–57, 159, 163
Nativism. *See* Immigration, opposition to
Nevins, Allan, 258–59, 298
New Deal, 227–28, 238–39, 244–45,
  255–57, 262, 324
New History, 43–51, 162–63, 176, 212,
  294
  opposition to, 176–77, 194, 294
New York Economic Council, 242
Nordicism, 147–48, 204, 206
Nott, Josiah, 143
Novick, Peter, 13

Objectivity, as goal in writing history, 6, 13, 16, 19, 46, 84, 90, 128,
  177, 181–82, 186, 188, 194, 197,
  212–13, 216–17, 220, 250, 286,
  293, 305, 335
  opposition to, 192, 305
O'Hara, John P., 121, 198
Orono, 120
*Our United States: A Bulwark of
  Freedom,* 269–71, 275, 279–80,
  309–10
  attacked in Detroit, 264–65, 268,
  271–72, 278, 280–82, 329, 332

Page, Thomas Nelson, 274
Palmer, A. Mitchell, and "Palmer
  raids," 197
Papal infallibility, doctrine of, 126
Parkman, Francis, 104–5, 134, 154–55
Parks, Rosa, 264, 300, 311, 316
Parley, Peter. *See* Goodrich, Samuel
  G.
Penn, William, 34, 46
Pérez, Juan, 108–9, 114, 131
Perkins, Bradford, 286
Persons, Gordon, 272–73
Philip, King, 155–56
Phillips, Wendell, 84

Pickens, William, 211
Pierce v. Sisters of the Holy Names,
  132
Pilgrims, 2, 50, 116, 189
Pitt, William, 180
Pius IX, 135
Plessy v. Ferguson, 88
Pocahontas, 153, 161, 337
Polygenesis. *See* Race
Populism and Populist Party, 225
Powell, Adam Clayton, Jr., 306
  and textbook hearings in Congress, 306–11
Powell, John Wesley, 153–54, 158
Prentice-Hall, 279
Prescott, William, 154
Progressive education, 220–21,
  230–31, 235, 238, 243
  critiques of, 4, 243–44, 246–49,
  292–93, 301
Progressives, 148, 225, 323
Protestants and Protestantism, 148,
  151, 177, 204, 208, 210
  influence on nineteenth-century
  teaching, 15, 16, 19–20, 50,
  93–99, 101–7
  Protestant Compromise, 96–97
"Public utility question," and textbooks, 239–40
Pucinski, Roman, 308
Pulaski, Casimir, 120, 205, 207, 214
"Pure" history laws, 201
Puritans, 33–34, 63, 75, 96, 103, 106,
  114, 141, 189, 209–10, 253
  in Catholic texts, 115–19, 122

Quackenbos, George, 36–37, 67, 143,
  156–57, 176, 179–82
Quakers, 34, 116
Québec Act, 118–19
Quillen, I. James, 259–61, 274, 276,
  278

Race, 52, 61, 137–64

Index

polygenesis, 143, 157
"race-suicide" theory, 147–48, 210
racial Darwinism, 143–44, 163
scientific racism, 142–45, 158, 162, 165, 168, 173
Rafferty, Maxwell, 267, 291–97, 305, 320, 328
critiques of *Land of the Free*, 297–303, 305
on progressive education, 292–93
views of history, 293–94, 310
Randolph, A. Philip, 273, 316
Rasles, Sebastien, 117
Ravitch, Diane, 5, 8, 11, 25
Reagan, Ronald, 298, 328
Reconstruction, 13, 23, 39, 48, 53–57, 61–67, 74, 77–81, 83–85, 89, 90, 128, 140, 164–67, 174, 274–76, 285, 337
under Dunning school, 165–67, 274–76, 324
revised in 1960s and 1970s, 286–87, 298, 301, 315–18, 324
Reformation, Protestant, 100, 102–3, 133
Renan, Ernest, 174, 337
Republican decline, fears of, 30, 51
Republican Party (Jeffersonians), 29–30
Republican Party (modern), 18, 169, 201, 239, 255, 290, 293
and Catholics, 92–94, 98–99, 132
in Reconstruction (*see* Reconstruction)
Republic Steel, 257–58
Revere, Paul, 10, 14
Rhodes, James Ford, 165
Ridpath, John, 104, 180
Riley, Franklin, 85–86
Robey, Ralph, 241
Robinson, James Harvey, 192, 218, 228
Rolfe, John, 155, 161, 337

Roosevelt, Franklin Delano, 227–28, 238–39, 245, 262, 273
Roosevelt, Theodore, 147–48
Root, E. Merrill, 256–57
Rosencrans, William, 122
Rudd, A. G., 242, 245
Ruffner, W. H., 70–71
Rugg, Harold, 23, 219–22, 228–54, 256, 258–62, 266, 290, 292, 335
early life, 228–30
critiques of, 240–50
defense of, 250–52
Rush, Benjamin, 30–31, 46, 96
Russell, Charles Edward, 279

Sadlier, W. H., Co., 133
Sacco, Nicola, 290
Sallis, Charles, 318–19
Salmon, Lucy M., 47
Saloman, Haym, 211, 311, 314
Sampson, Deborah, 313–14, 328
Santayana, George, 25
Schlafly, Phyllis, 10
Schlesinger, Arthur M., Sr., 176
Schlesinger, Arthur M., Jr., 1, 5–6, 9, 11, 15–19, 22–23, 134, 253
Scopes, John, and evolution trial, 175–77, 204, 217–18
Scott, Dred, 36, 164, 312
Scott, Foresman and Co., 278–307
Serra, Junipo, 113
Sewall, Gilbert T., 332
Shakespeare, William, 4, 182
Shea, John Gilmary, 118
Sheridan, Philip, 122
Sherman, Stuart P., 189, 210
Shinn, Josiah, 85
Silver, Burdett and Co., 286
Sinclair, Upton, 263
Slavery, 34, 38, 46–47, 52–53, 56, 59–66, 73–76, 80, 83, 86, 88–89, 96, 105, 153, 222, 303
defense of, 75–77, 316

Index

Slavery (*continued*)
  as threat to national unity, 33–35,
    40, 42–45, 51, 92, 100
  See also African-Americans
Smalls, Robert, 315
Smith, Al, 132
Smith, Goldwyn, 180–81
Smith, John, 27, 50, 155, 326
Social reconstructionists, 235–36
Social Security, 228, 252, 255, 256
Sokolsky, George, 242, 246–47
Sons of Liberty, 18, 185
Sons of the American Revolution,
    14, 176, 194, 197
Southern Historical Society, 63, 67,
    72, 75
Southern Literary Company, 60
Soviet Union, 235–36, 240, 259
Spalding, John, 123–25
Spanish-American War, 86, 88,
    168–69, 171, 179, 184
Spencer, Herbert, 143–44, 167
Stalin, Josef, 240, 244, 253, 336
Stampp, Kenneth, 291, 294, 301,
    313
Steele, Joel Dorman, 67
Stephens, Alexander, 15, 19, 52–58,
    63–66, 72, 74, 86, 92, 267
Stephenson, Nathaniel Wright, 85
Steuben, Friedrich von, 14, 186, 205,
    214
Steuben Society. *See* German-Amer-
    ican Alliance
Stevens, Thaddeus, 77, 298–99
Stevenson, Adlai, 290
Stoddard, Lothrop, 147–48, 206
Stoops, Emery, 291, 297, 294, 300,
    310, 320
Stowe, Harriet Beecher, 65, 170, 225
Strong, Josiah, 101, 106–7, 124, 133,
    154
Strothmann, Fred, 190
Stuart, James E. B. (Jeb), 78
Sullivan, John, 21–22

Sumner, Charles, 40, 62, 77, 84, 88,
    89
Swinton, William, 36, 38, 67

Taft-Hartley Act, 257
Taliban, 333
Tecumseh, 156
Telegraphic style, in textbooks, 67,
    72, 75
Tennessee Valley Authority, 245
Tenney Committee, and Jack Ten-
    ney, 254
Terrorism, 331, 334, 338
Teutonic constitutionalism, 167
Teutonic germ theory, 152–53, 192,
    206
Texans for America, 255
Texas State Teachers Association, 70
Thalheimer, Mary Elsie, 67, 72, 180
Thomas, Allen C., 184
Thompson, Robert Ellis, 106
Thompson, Waddy, 85
Thompson, William "Big Bill,"
    175–76, 201–3, 205–17, 335
Thorpe, Francis Newton, 43–45
Thurmond, Strom, 316
Thwaites, Reuben Gold, 166, 208–9
Tocqueville, Alexis de, 7
Todd, Lewis Paul, 134, 275, 332
Toleration Act, 115
Trail of Tears. *See* Cherokees
Trent, William P., 167–69, 182
Truman, Harry, 316
Truth, Sojourner, 287
Tubman, Harriet, 10, 165, 281, 287
Tulsa race riot, 284–85
Turner, Frederick Jackson, and
    "frontier thesis," 1, 151–53,
    228–29
Turner, Nat, 20, 65, 170, 281
Twain, Mark, 16, 303

Underground Railroad, 165, 281
United Civil Rights Council, 304

Index

United Confederate Veterans, 21, 57, 72–73, 78–79, 84–88
United Daughters of the Confederacy, 22, 78, 87
United Steel Workers, 257
University Publishing Company, 67

Van Antwerp, Bragg and Company, 68
Vanderbilt, Cornelius, 234
Van Tyne, Claude H., 188, 192–93, 197–98, 201, 207, 212–16
Vanzetti, Bartolomeo, 290
Vatican, 125, 135
Venezuela Crisis, 178, 180, 192
Vespucci, Amerigo, 326
Veterans of Foreign Wars, 197, 215, 242
Vietnam War, 321
Vigo, François, 120
Virginia and Kentucky Resolutions, 64
Voting Rights Act of 1965, 295, 310

Wagner Act, 256, 257
Walker, David, 287
Walker, Wyatt T., 309
Wallace, George, 294, 317
Ward, C. H., 199, 207
War of 1812, 37, 165, 180, 201, 214
Washington, Booker T., 171, 277, 289, 300, 319
Washington, George, 10, 21, 27, 43, 47–48, 62, 116, 120–21, 170, 180, 182, 201, 205, 209, 211, 243, 278, 299, 336
as model of virtue, 31–32, 42
Watts riot of 1965, 8, 295–96, 304
Webb, Walter P., 240
Webster, Daniel, 38, 41, 42
Webster, Noah, 30–31, 33, 46, 68, 96
Weems, Mason Locke, or "Parson," 31
West, Willis Mason, 171, 172, 184, 186, 193, 197, 199, 207, 210, 232
Wheatley, Phillis, 311
Whig Party, 96
White, Andrew, 115–16
White Citizens Councils, 280, 289
Wilder, Howard B., 259, 261, 275
Willard, Emma, 26–29, 31–36, 39, 42, 44–49, 59, 102–5, 107, 117, 134, 162–63, 176, 180–81, 225, 294, 328, 334, 337
Williams, Roger, 34, 116, 287
Willson, Marcius, 58, 103, 157
Wilson, Woodrow, 11, 47, 86, 183, 225, 258
Witchcraft trials of 1692, 116–17
Woods, Granville T., 313
Woodson, Carter G., 278
Woodward, R. H., Co., 74
World War I, 13, 150, 187, 205, 211
effects on texts and teaching, 191–93
propaganda in, 126, 188–93, 196, 210, 213
World War II, 244, 252, 261, 265, 273, 279, 312, 316, 324, 328, 332, 333

Zenith Books, 286